Women in the Club:
Gender and Policy Making in the Senate

Michele L. Swers

The University of Chicago Press :: Chicago and London

Michele L. Swers is associate professor of American government at Georgetown University. She is the author of *The Difference Women Make*, also published by the University of Chicago Press.

The University of Chicago Press, Chicago 60637
The University of Chicago Press, Ltd., London
© 2013 by The University of Chicago
All rights reserved. Published 2013.
Printed in the United States of America

22 21 20 19 18 17 16 15 14 13   1 2 3 4 5

ISBN-13: 978-0-226-02279-6 (cloth)
ISBN-13: 978-0-226-02282-6 (paper)
ISBN-13: 978-0-226-02296-3 (e-book)

Library of Congress Cataloging-in-Publication Data

Swers, Michele L., author.
   Women in the club : gender and policy making in the Senate /
Michele L. Swers.
      pages cm
   Includes bibliographical references and index.
      ISBN 978-0-226-02279-6 (cloth : alkaline paper) — ISBN 978-0-226-
02282-6 (paperback : alkaline paper) — ISBN 978-0-226-02296-3
(e-book)   1. Women legislators—United States.   2. Women—Political
activity—United States.   3. United States. Congress. Senate.   4. United
States—Politics and government.   I. Title.
   JK1161.S94 2013
   328.73′071082—dc23

                                                        2012036977

Women in the Club

To my husband
Andrew Todd Swers

And my children
Alexander Evan Swers
Lisa Danielle Swers

Contents

Figures and Tables

Figures

Tables

Acknowledgments

I have spent much of my career following the slow progress of women into political office in the United States. I wanted to understand whether electing women influences policy outcomes and what it means to say women bring a distinctive perspective to policy making. My first effort to examine these questions involved a comprehensive study of gender differences in legislating on women's issues in the House of Representatives. *The Difference Women Make: The Policy Impact of Women in Congress* (2002) showed that women are more active advocates for policies related to women, children, and families in comparison with male colleagues. However, the study also showed that gender interacts in complex ways with partisanship, ideology, institutional norms, and the electoral context.

The desire to further explore these questions of when gender matters and when it does not and how legislators utilize gender strategically to advance their policy and political goals led me to write a book on gender and the Senate. Senators have more individual power than House members do, and they can reach into more policy areas, which allowed me to broaden my focus to policy arenas outside of women's issues, including defense policy and judicial nominations. The storied history of the Senate as a club with strong institutional norms could provide fresh

perspective on the integration of women into legislative bodies. The polarization of contemporary politics and the high-profile role played by
senators as party messengers invited further study of the interaction of
party and gender.

Throughout this project I have benefited from the generous support
of many. I thank Georgetown University and the Department of Government for research support through grants and a sabbatical. I am
very grateful to all of my wonderful and dedicated research assistants
over the duration of this project, including Christine Kim, Holly Boux,
Shauna Shames, Carin Robinson, Meg Massey, and Bryce Myers. I particularly thank Christine Kim, who collaborated with me on articles on
judicial nominations. Some of the research on Supreme Court nominations also appears in "Replacing Sandra Day O'Connor: Gender and
the Politics of Supreme Court Nominations," in the *Journal of Women,
Politics, and Policy*. Some of the data and theory on defense policy also
appear in "Policy Leadership Beyond 'Women's' Issues," in *Legislative
Women: Getting Elected, Getting Ahead*.

Many friends and colleagues have shared valuable insights and expertise as I tried to master new policy literatures on defense policy and
judicial nominations. Liz Stanley and Pat Towell gave me crash courses
in military force structure and the geographic distribution of important
bases and defense contracts. My dad, Theodore Probst, a retired captain
in the naval reserve, kept me updated on military personnel and retiree
concerns by sending me the legislative updates from the Association of
the U.S. Navy. Amy Steigerwalt, Nancy Scherer, Lauren Cohen, Sarah
Binder, Steve Rutkus, and Kevin Scott shared their knowledge and data
on the judicial nominations process. Longtime scholars of the Senate
offered invaluable advice and guidance, including Larry Evans, Frances
Lee, Pat Sellers, and Sarah Binder. I am very grateful to women and
politics scholars who inspired me and laid the foundation for my work,
including Clyde Wilcox, Karen O'Connor, Sue Carroll, Debra Dodson,
Cindy Simon Rosenthal, Sue Thomas, Marian Palley, Joyce Gelb, Peggy
Conway, and Beth Reingold.

I am particularly indebted to the many anonymous Senate staffers,
former senators, and interest group leaders who generously shared their
time and insider accounts of how things really work in the Senate. Their
insights reshaped my thinking and illuminated the strategic calculations
senators make every day about how to achieve their policy goals and
secure reelection. I thank Frances Lee, Jennifer Lawless, and anonymous
reviewers for reading chapter drafts and offering advice. I am very grateful to my editors John Tryneski and Rodney Powell at the University of

Chicago Press for their support and encouragement to bring this project to fruition. I also thank Kailee Kremer, Sharon Brinkman, Melinda Kennedy, and Meg Cox for shepherding my manuscript from copy edits to the final book.

This book could not have been written without the love and support of my family. My parents, Theodore and Belle Probst, and in-laws, Ron and Gwen Swers, set the example of hard work and dedication to family and supported me through college, graduate school, and career. I am especially lucky to be surrounded by the love of my sister and brother-in-law and their families, Arlene, Marvin, Joey, and Aaron Birnbaum; and Jeff, Shana, and Isaac Swers; as well as Ralph and Stuart Herman. We miss Shana and Gwen every day, but their spirits live on through their sons and grandchildren. Finally, I dedicate this book to my husband, Andrew Swers, and children, Alex and Lisa Swers. Alex and Lisa have brought more joy to my life than I could have imagined. My husband Andy is my best friend and greatest champion. He made sure I had the latest technology and read the whole manuscript. Thank you for 1,001 pep talks to keep me going as I worked on this book and for always believing in me.

1   Women and the New Senate Club

In the months leading up to the 2012 presidential election, the Republican and Democratic parties were locked in a battle for women's votes. Democrats and President Barack Obama's campaign accused Republicans of waging a "war on women." Republicans and Republican presidential candidate Mitt Romney countered that Democrats were instigating a false gender war and President Obama's policies undermined the interests of women. The women of the Senate played key roles in this quest for the hearts and minds of female voters. Female Democratic senators took to the Senate floor, called press conferences, and appeared on political news shows to shine a spotlight on Republican policies that hurt women including Republican efforts to defund Planned Parenthood and Republican opposition to coverage of contraception in Obama's health reform bill (McCarthy 2012c; Sanger-Katz 2012). The Democratic women also lamented Republican obstruction of the Violence Against Women Act and the Paycheck Fairness Act, a bill to strengthen equal pay legislation (Weisman 2012b; Steinhauer 2012). Patty Murray (D-WA), the head of the Democratic Senate Campaign Committee, launched an advertisement denouncing the Republican war on women and urging voters to elect more women to the Senate (http://www.youtube.com/watch?v=MohCoT_fHlU).

In response, Republicans deployed their own female surrogates to push back on the Democratic message of a war on women. Republican senator Kelly Ayotte (R-NH) became a prominent spokesperson for the Republican Party and the Romney campaign (Schultheis 2012). Utilizing her moral authority as a woman, Ayotte countered that Republican opposition to forcing employers, including Catholic universities and hospitals, to cover contraception was a matter of religious freedom and not women's health (McCormack 2012). Republicans frequently noted that the economy was the top concern of women voters and that more than 92% of the jobs lost on Obama's watch were women's jobs (Associated Press 2012).

Clearly, both Republican and Democratic women utilize the power of their position as senators to influence the public debate over the representation of women's interests and to shape policy that addresses the needs of women and their families. The emergence of women as a significant force in the Senate is a recent phenomenon. Indeed, the United States Senate is among the most powerful legislative institutions in western democracies. At the same time it is in many ways the least representative (Dahl 2003; Lee and Oppenheimer 1999). In both its demographic makeup and its institutional rules the Senate defies ideals of equal representation. For most of its history the Senate has been a white male bastion, and the number of women and minorities in the Senate continues to lag far behind their share of the U.S. population. The institutional structure and rules of the Senate are antimajoritarian. The filibuster gives individuals and small groups of senators the ability to obstruct legislation and the allocation of two seats for each state gives outsized influence to senators representing small state populations (Koger 2010; Wawro and Schickler 2006; Lee and Oppenheimer 1999). In contrast to the House of Representatives, the Founders intended for the Senate to be the less responsive body, cooling the passions of the masses in an effort to reach decisions that reflect the national character and interest (Federalist 63 in Rossiter 1961; Dahl 2003). As a result of this design, the Senate has often been described as both the world's greatest deliberative body and an insular old boys club where powerful white men meet behind closed doors to shape public policy (Dahl 2003).

The modern Senate club is a study in contradictions. Senators are freewheeling policy entrepreneurs whose large staffs, ready media access, and institutional prerogatives, including the ability to offer nongermane amendments, place holds, and threaten filibusters, allow them to become important players on any issue they choose (Evans 1991;

Baker 2001; Sinclair 1989). At the same time, ideological polarization and tight electoral competition between the parties has created a Senate divided into partisan teams. Senators work together to create a party message and policy agenda. They are expected to be loyal to the team or risk a loss of standing and influence with their colleagues (Sinclair 1989, 2006, 2009; Lee 2009, 2008b; Sellers 2010).

The evolution of the Senate into an institution that is both partisan and individualistic coincided with the opening up of the Senate to new groups, particularly women. As late as 1991, women constituted only 2% of the Senate membership. By 2001, 13% of senators were women and the number of women in the Senate was equivalent to the proportion of women serving in the House. In the 112th Congress (2011–12), women make up 17% of the Senate's membership (Center for the American Woman and Politics 2011a, 2011b). While the number of women in the Senate remains relatively small, the power wielded by individuals and the procedural rules protecting participation rights give senators outsized influence and an ability to engage any and all policy areas regardless of committee assignment or majority/minority party status.

By focusing on the Senate, I can examine how gender influences legislative behavior on a wider range of issues from social welfare policy to national security. Moreover, if senators feel strongly about championing gender-related causes, the organization of the Senate gives them the resources and tools to force consideration of these interests, thus magnifying senators' influence beyond their numbers. In this book, I utilize the fact that senators are policy generalists who are involved in a wide variety of issues and wield extensive individual prerogatives to analyze the ways in which gender influences the legislative behavior of senators. I demonstrate that gender is a fundamental identity that affects the way senators look at policy questions, the issues they prioritize, and the perspective they bring to develop solutions. The importance of gender also transcends individual identity, creating opportunities and imposing obstacles in the electoral and governing arena that senators must confront when they design their political strategies and build their legislative reputations.

My research shows that, as they develop their legislative portfolio, female senators take into account long-standing public assumptions and voter stereotypes about women's policy expertise. The strong link between gender and women's interests on various social welfare and women's rights issues enhances the credibility of women in these policy areas. Thus, women are able to leverage their gender to influence policy debates on a range of issues from health care and education to abortion rights and pay equity. These "women's issues" routinely constitute at least one-third of the Senate agenda (see chapter 2). By contrast, deeply held voter perceptions that men are more capable of handling defense policy hinder women's efforts to become leaders on defense issues. To counteract voter stereotypes that portray women as soft on defense, female senators construct policy records to demonstrate toughness and seek out opportunities for position taking through cosponsorship to highlight their support for the military.

Gendered perceptions of issue competencies are mediated by party reputations. I show how party ownership of issues can temper or exacerbate the importance of gender in policy debates. I highlight how these partisan and gendered perceptions of issues alter senators' strategic calculations about which issues to engage and how much political capital to invest in the debate. Thus, the perception of the Republican Party as strong on defense can moderate the negative impact of gender stereotypes for Republican women. The view of Democrats as weak on national security reinforces gender stereotypes that women are soft on defense, making it more important for Democratic women to demonstrate toughness and commitment to our troops. The association of social welfare and women's rights issues with the Democratic Party reinforces incentives for Democratic women to highlight these issues as they develop their legislative portfolios. Indeed, the centrality of these issues to Democratic voters, particularly female Democrats, can only benefit Democratic women senators as they work to achieve their policy goals and secure re-election. By contrast, Republican women do not reap the same level of benefits from pursuing women's issues because these policies are not part of the core principles that make up the Republican Party's message of lower taxes, strong defense, and support for business. At worst, women's rights initiatives can antagonize key elements of the party's base. Proposals promoting reproductive rights will antagonize social conservatives, and business-oriented Republicans will object to employment discrimination initiatives that impose more regulations on corporations and small businesses. Thus, Republican women must exercise more caution as they decide whether to focus on women's issues and which policies to champion.

Furthermore, my research shows that partisan polarization and the resulting demands for party loyalty in the contemporary Senate affect senators' calculations about whether to emphasize policy preferences based on gender. The ideological polarization and intraparty homogeneity that characterizes the contemporary Senate increase pressure on senators to act as members of partisan teams (Lee 2009; Sinclair 2006).

Thus, my analysis indicates that in settings requiring party loyalty, such as judicial confirmation fights over Supreme Court nominees, even the most moderate female Republicans are hesitant to publicly oppose nominees based on their conservative records on women's rights.

Finally, as members of partisan teams in an era of fierce electoral competition for control of the Senate, women are encouraged to utilize their gender in ways that will bolster the party's standing with voters, particularly women voters. Women frequently participate in party messaging activities that highlight their status as women as they advertise the party message. Thus, Democratic women often join together to promote Democratic initiatives on social welfare and women's rights issues. Republican women are often deployed in a defensive capacity to counter Democratic accusations that Republican policies are anti-women. Women senators can leverage these messaging opportunities to raise their media profile, gain power within the party caucus, and advance their own policy initiatives. However, they also run the risk of being pigeonholed in specific policy areas or used as symbols of diversity without influence over the details of policy.

In sum, through careful analysis of senators' policy activity, I demonstrate that gender is a fundamental identity that interacts with traditional influences on legislative behavior like partisanship and ideology to shape legislative priorities. Women senators are more vigorous advocates for inclusion of women's interests in the development of policy, and they devote more attention to how specific policies differentially impact various groups of women. A senator's own ideological views and the political context surrounding an issue impact whether senators pursue policy preferences based on gender. However, beyond personal preferences, senators also develop their legislative portfolio with an eye to public expectations regarding gender roles and party reputations. Thus, the history of women's integration into politics and voter assumptions about women's expertise facilitate women's efforts to stake a legislative claim on social welfare policy while creating additional hurdles for female senators working to demonstrate expertise on defense issues. Party reputations for ownership of issues interact with gendered perceptions of policy expertise, creating opportunities for legislative entrepreneurship and shaping senators' political strategies. However, demands for loyalty to one's partisan team also complicate senators' decisions about when to pursue gender-based policy preferences, particularly for Republican women. Finally, in an era of heightened electoral competition, gender has become a tool of partisan warfare as the parties turn to female senators to reach out to women voters by advertising how the party's agenda will help women or by defending the party against criticism that their policies will hurt women. Female senators must decide whether employing gender to promote party messages will advance or inhibit their political and policy goals.

A Brief History: Evolution from the Old Senate Club to the New Senate Club

Classic treatments of the Senate of the 1930s to the late 1950s including Robert Caro's *Master of the Senate*, William White's *Citadel*, and Donald Matthews' *U.S. Senators and Their World* provide a picture of a U.S. Senate that was inward looking, conservative, resistant to constituent pressures, and almost exclusively made up of white men (White 1956; Matthews 1960; Caro 2002). When future majority leader Lyndon Johnson (D-TX) arrived in the Senate, he saw an institution populated by whales and minnows, senior power brokers and more junior members with limited influence (Rae and Campbell 2001; Caro 2002). Johnson's Senate was governed by norms of apprenticeship, specialization, reciprocity, and courtesy. New senators were expected to serve an apprenticeship where they were seen and not heard, taking the time to learn the rules and norms of the Senate before actively participating in policy making. As specialists, senators focused their efforts on the policy areas within their committee jurisdictions and those initiatives that affected their states. They offered few floor amendments and did most of their work in committee. The norm of reciprocity required senators to do favors for each other and keep their word once a bargain had been struck. In the spirit of reciprocity, senators rarely utilized their institutional prerogatives such as the right to filibuster, making the historic filibusters against civil rights legislation all the more notable. Finally, senators were expected to show each other courtesy. Senators did not engage in personal attacks against each other nor did they engage in self-promotion or any activity that would reflect poorly on the institution of the Senate (Sinclair 1989; Baker 2001; Schickler 2011).

By the election of 1958, the restrictive norms of the old boys club were already falling as the Senate began its transformation into what Barbara Sinclair calls the "individualist partisan Senate" in which party polarization, electoral competition, and the demands of the modern campaign led senators to abandon strict adherence to the institutional norms that enforced collegiality and maintained the exclusive nature of the Senate club (Sinclair 1989, 2006, 2009). The election of liberal Northern Democrats in competitive races and the realignment of the

South toward the Republican Party led to increasing ideological polarization among senators, encouraging them to organize into partisan
teams that utilize the procedural prerogatives held by the majority and
minority party to score political points against the other side in an effort
to win majority control in the next election (Lee 2011, 2009, 2008b;
Sinclair 1989, 2006; Koger 2010).

The political ferment of the 1960s and 1970s rapidly expanded the
policy agenda of government and the size and diversity of the interest
group community. New issues from civil rights to environmental regulation provided senators with opportunities to become policy leaders on a
range of issues. Senators responded by increasing their staffs to enhance
their policy expertise and expanding their number of committee assignments and their participation on the floor to become policy generalists who could influence any issue that caught their attention (Sinclair
1989; Evans 1991; Fenno 1991). A proliferation of new interest groups
representing business groups, trade associations, consumers, women's
rights, and civil rights organizations reinforced senators' efforts at
policy entrepreneurship by working to recruit senators as champions
for the group's causes (Sinclair 1989, 2006; Berry and Wilcox 2009).
The ever-expanding news media, from state and national newspapers to
network and cable news, offered senators opportunities to become national spokespersons on various policy issues. Today the Internet blogosphere and the social media of Facebook and Twitter provide additional
avenues for senators to raise their profiles with constituents and policy
activists (Sinclair 1989, 2006, 2009; Sellers 2002, 2010).

Gender Politics, Women, and the New Senate Club

The emergence of social identity as a political force in the social move-
ments of the 1960s and 1970s coincided with the evolution of the Senate into a more individualist partisan institution. Women's rights groups
benefited from the newfound willingness of individual senators to employ the rules of the Senate in ways that would force consideration of
their individual and/or partisan priorities. Liberal senators like Birch
Bayh (D-IN) and Ted Kennedy (D-MA) took up feminist causes from
the Equal Rights Amendment to gender equity in the workplace (Mansbridge 1986; Gelb and Palley 1996; Conway, Ahern, and Steurnagel
2005). Still the Senate was largely closed to female members. As late
as 1991 there were only two women serving in the Senate, Republican
Nancy Landon Kassebaum (KS) and Democrat Barbara Mikulski (MD)
(Center for the American Woman and Politics 2011a, 2011b).

By 1992, the political climate was ripe for the election of more women to Congress. Women candidates, particularly Democrats, benefited from the Bush-Clinton presidential campaign's focus on the economy and social welfare issues, particularly health care. The end of the Cold War diverted attention from defense and foreign policy concerns that favor male candidates. The media frenzy surrounding Anita Hill's testimony during the Supreme Court confirmation hearings for Clarence Thomas spotlighted women's rights issues, particularly sexual harassment and the underrepresentation of women in Congress. Women benefited from their status as outsiders in a Congress that was beset by ethics scandals and suffered from a dismally low approval rating. As a result, the 1992 "Year of the Woman" election saw four new Democratic women but no Republican women elected to the Senate, the largest contingent of women elected in one cycle (Wilcox 1994; Chaney and Sinclair 1994; Fox 1997). All four of these Democratic women, Barbara Boxer (CA), Dianne Feinstein (CA), Carol Moseley Braun (IL), and Patty Murray (WA), portrayed themselves as champions of women's rights, and each claimed that the spectacle of the all-male Judiciary Committee's handling of the Clarence Thomas hearings contributed to their desire to run for the Senate. One candidate, Patty Murray (D-WA), explicitly utilized her gender as a reason to support her candidacy by adopting the campaign slogan "Just a Mom in Tennis Shoes." Dianne Feinstein (D-CA) sold fundraising merchandise emblazoned with the assertion that "2% is not enough," highlighting the fact that there were only two women in the Senate (Smolowe, McDowell, and Shannon 1992; Schroedel and Snyder 1994).

The advancement of women into the Senate continued at a slow pace in the 1994, 1996, and 1998 elections. In 2000, the election of another four Democratic women, including former first lady and future presidential candidate Hillary Clinton (NY), Maria Cantwell (WA), Jean Carnahan (MO), and Debbie Stabenow (MI), increased the number of women in the Senate from nine to thirteen. Thus, in the 107th Congress (2001–2002), women for the first time held an equivalent proportion of seats, 13% in the House and Senate (Center for the American Woman and Politics 2011b).[1] The Democratic wave elections of 2006 and 2008 brought several new Democratic women into the Senate including Amy Klobuchar (MN), Claire McCaskill (MO), Jeanne Shaheen (NH), and Kay Hagan (NC). Kirsten Gillibrand (NY) was appointed to fill Hillary Clinton's seat after Clinton became Secretary of State in the Obama administration. While Democratic women continue to hold more Senate seats than Republican women, Republican women increased their

Senate representation from three to five in the 108th Congress when Lisa Murkowski (AK) and Elizabeth Dole (NC) joined Kay Bailey Hutchison (TX), Olympia Snowe (ME), and Susan Collins (ME) in the Republican caucus.[2] To date, there have never been more than five Republican women in the Senate (Center for the American Woman and Politics 2011b).[3] Republican women did not make substantial gains in the Tea Party–fueled Republican wave in 2010. Kelly Ayotte (NH) was the only female Republican senator elected in that year. While Republicans are expected to gain Senate seats in the 2012 election, the number of Republican women in the Senate will remain small because Kay Bailey Hutchison (TX) and Olympia Snowe (ME) are retiring and Republican women are likely nominees in few competitive Senate races (Hotline Staff 2012).[4]

The contemporary Senate provides an important opportunity to systematically evaluate the impact of gender on the policy-making decisions of senators across several issue areas and in a context with strong institutional and partisan norms of behavior. The election of increasing numbers of women to the Senate coincided with political turmoil on a range of social welfare and women's rights concerns. The pursuit of comprehensive health insurance reform by Democratic presidents Bill Clinton and Barack Obama instigated fierce Senate battles over policy changes in all aspects of the health care system. Campaigning as a compassionate conservative, Republican George W. Bush sought to put his mark on social welfare policy by promoting legislation to add a prescription drug benefit to Medicare and to overhaul federal education policy through his No Child Left Behind initiative. The Republican takeover of Congress in 1994 and the election of President Bush in 2000 intensified legislative activity on abortion. Efforts to impose abortion-related funding restrictions have snarled debates on annual appropriations bills and threatened to derail President Obama's health reform plan. Congress engaged in an eight-year battle (1995–2003) over legislation to ban partial birth abortion that altered public opinion on the issue and resulted in the first ban of a specific abortion procedure (Ainsworth and Hall 2011). Senators continue to raise the stakes in conflicts over judicial confirmations as these nomination fights have become another front in the war between the social conservative and liberal bases of the two parties (Epstein and Segal 2005; Binder and Maltzman 2009). Finally, the terrorist attacks of September 11, 2001, vaulted defense policy to the forefront of the Senate agenda. Senators compete to offer initiatives that will improve homeland security and strengthen the nation's defenses. The pursuit of wars in Afghanistan and Iraq has forced senators to address questions of war and peace and the human and budgetary costs of these conflicts (Wheeler 2004).

Senators engage these policy debates in a political context that is increasingly polarized and electorally competitive. The ideological agreement that characterizes each party caucus encourages members to eschew compromise and act as loyal members of partisan teams (Lee 2009; Sinclair 2006; Smith 2007). Partisan activity has increased as majority control of the Senate shifted; often with narrow margins determining which party prevailed. Republicans gained the majority in 1994 and lost it in the 107th Congress (2001–2002) when Jim Jeffords' (VT) decision to leave the Republican Party elevated Democrats to the majority. Republicans regained the majority in the 2002 elections but lost control to the Democrats in 2006. Democrats briefly achieved a filibuster-proof majority of sixty senators for parts of the 111th Congress (2008–2009) allowing them to push through comprehensive health reform and a large economic stimulus package, but Republicans dramatically narrowed that majority in the 2010 elections.

In sum, the increased presence of women in the Senate coincided with the emergence of a more polarized political atmosphere and a policy agenda focused on dramatic changes in the social welfare state and the scope of women's rights, particularly on abortion. The 9/11 terrorist attacks expanded that agenda and forced members of Congress to devote more attention to questions of national security. The power of individual senators to insert themselves into policy debates on any issue invites a systematic look at how gender impacts the policy priorities of senators. Are senators simply policy generalists with a set of proposals on all major issues, or do women prioritize the needs of women, children, and families and do they bring this perspective to policy debates beyond social welfare concerns? The institutional rules of the Senate that favor individual action combined with a more polarized political context offer an opportunity to analyze the strategic behavior of senators as they decide whether and how to pursue gender-based policy preferences. The fact that senators advance legislation as individuals and members of partisan teams requires examination of how gender both creates opportunities and imposes barriers on senators' efforts at policy entrepreneurship and their pursuit of power within the institution of the Senate.

Women and Representation Theory

The quality of representation provided by Congress has been a major point of contention since the founding period. Federalists asserted that groups such as merchants and farmers, laborers and landowners, have overlapping interests and that the imperative to stand for re-election would keep legislators faithful to the needs and interests of their constituents (Federalist 35, 55 in Rossiter 1961). Conversely, anti-Federalists maintained that the membership of Congress should be a microcosm of society. They feared that wealthy merchants and landowners would pursue their interests at the expense of the middling classes of farmers, merchants, and laborers. They were highly suspicious of the power and exclusivity of the Senate, and they argued vehemently for expanding the size of the House of Representatives so more of the social classes of men would have an opportunity to attain election to the national legislature (Storing 1981; Dahl 2003).

Today the debate continues with a focus on the underrepresentation of social groups, particularly women and minorities. Advocates for majority/minority districts and proponents of electing more women to office assert that these groups require expanded seats at the policy table in order to achieve equal representation of their interests. Meanwhile, critics and even some supporters assert that to demand increased representation for women and minorities unnecessarily divides citizens based on demographic characteristics and essentializes group members by asserting that all women/minorities share a set of interests and these interests can only be fully represented by members of the group (Mansbridge 1999; Dovi 2002; Phillips 1991, 1995, 1998; Williams 1998).

This dilemma of group representation is often characterized as a question of whether electing more descriptive representatives will lead to better representation of group interests. In her classic work, *The Concept of Representation*, Hanna Pitkin (1967) makes a distinction between descriptive representatives who "stand for" a particular group because they share characteristics such as race and gender and substantive representatives who "act for" the group by providing substantive representation of the group's interests. Contemporary scholars continue to debate whether the election of more descriptive representatives is either a necessary or a sufficient condition for achieving the substantive representation of the interests of women and minorities. Alternatively, descriptive representation may not be strictly necessary or sufficient for ensuring group representation, but it may still be beneficial, providing advantages that enhance the representation of group interests (Mansbridge 1999; Dovi 2002; Phillips 1991, 1995; Swers and Rouse 2011).

Advocates for expanding the representation of women and minorities in Congress generally point to two sets of benefits. One set of arguments relates to the relationship between legislators and their constituents.

According to proponents, the election of more women and minorities to Congress provides role models for members of the underrepresented group, allowing them to see themselves as part of the political process, thereby enhancing their feelings of trust in government. Moreover, the increased presence of women and minorities in government will further a belief in their ability to rule among all members of society (Mansbridge 1999; Phillips 1991, 1995).

Another set of arguments in favor of descriptive representation focuses on the improvement of the quality of deliberation among legislators and on the influence on the content of public policy. First, it is frequently argued that women will bring new issues to the congressional agenda and will provide a different perspective on established debates by delineating how specific policies differentially impact various groups of women. Moreover, because of their shared background, women will be more vigorous advocates for inclusion of women's interests in policy outcomes and colleagues will respond to their perceived expertise and moral authority on issues relating to women's lives (Mansbridge 1999; Dovi 2002; Phillips 1995, 1998). The impact of electing more women on policy outputs and deliberation in the Senate is the focus of this book.

Of course, it is not universally accepted that women have shared interests upon which to base political representation (Sapiro 1981; Diamond and Hartsock 1981). Indeed, women are divided by age, race, class, and ideology, creating different visions for what it means to act in women's interests and disagreement over whether such interests exist (Reingold and Swers 2011; Smooth 2011; Strolovitch 2007). Generally representational claims for the existence of women's interests are based upon research in psychology and sociology and the history of the integration of women into politics. Psychological studies of childhood socialization and personality development including work by Nancy Chodorow and Carol Gilligan maintain that women's gender identity is based on relation and connection to their mothers, while men develop their masculinity based on separation and differentiation from others (Chodorow 1974; Lips 1995). These psychological patterns in combination with women's traditional responsibility for raising children leads to the development of what Carol Gilligan calls a "different voice" in which women take a contextual approach to moral dilemmas emphasizing community, attachment, and relationships, while men focus on individual rights and autonomy (Gilligan 1982).

The case for women's interests also draws on sociological data concerning women's role as primary caregivers raising children and caring for elderly relatives. The desire to meet their caregiving responsibilities also contributes to women's greater economic vulnerability and the re-sulting feminization of poverty. Because many women drop out of the workforce at different points in time to raise their children or take jobs that require fewer hours, women earn less money over their lifetimes, leaving their families more vulnerable to poverty. These problems are exacerbated in minority communities as African Americans and His-panics experience much higher unemployment rates and are employed in lower wage jobs in comparison with the white population (Billitteri 2008; Blau and Kahn 2007; Conway, Ahern, and Steurnagel 2005). Ris-ing divorce rates have also contributed to women's economic vulner-ability. Furthermore, by basing Social Security benefits on work years, the time women spend out of the workforce raising families is devalued, and these women face greater retirement insecurity (Conway, Ahern, and Steurnagel 2005). While women continue to achieve higher levels of education and are entering previously male-dominated fields like law, business, and medicine in larger numbers, there is still a great deal of sex segregation in the workforce. For example, the vast majority of el-ementary school teachers are women, while men dominate the field of computer science (Billitteri 2008; Glazer 2005). Indeed, according to census data, in 2009, 39.7% of women held jobs in female-dominated occupations meaning that women make up at least 75% of workers in those fields, and 43.6% of men worked in male-dominated occupations (Hegewisch et al. 2010). Many jobs that require similar skill levels pay more in those fields dominated by men. For example, among low-skilled workers, truck drivers, a male-dominated occupation, earn more than home health aides, a female-dominated field (Drago and Williams 2010; Hegewisch et al. 2010). These workforce trends all contribute to a per-sistent gender wage gap in which a comparison of median weekly earn-ings indicates that full-time working women earned 82 cents for each dollar made by their male counterparts in 2011 (Institute for Women's Policy Research 2012).[5]

The evolution of women's place in American society has shaped their political participation and political attitudes over time. During the founding period, the division of society into a public sphere focused on economics and politics and a private sphere centered on the home was universally accepted. The designation of the private sphere as women's proper domain formed the basis for women's exclusion from voting and all types of political participation (Kraditor 1981; Flexner and Fitzpat-rick 1996). Thus, the concept of separate spheres made it unnecessary for women to vote, and indeed it was believed that granting women voting rights would corrupt women's morality and lead to marital strife.

Suffragists and political activists from causes ranging from temperance to public sanitation and cleaning up corruption in government sought to justify women's participation in politics by blurring the lines between the public and private sphere. Proponents of "civic motherhood" in the Progressive Era of the late 1800s argued that in order to fulfill their duties as mothers, women needed to vote and participate in politics (Kraditor 1981; Baker 1984; Skocpol 1992). As Rheta Childe Dorr, a journalist and member of the General Federation of Women's Clubs, explained, "Woman's place is in the home . . . But Home is not contained within the four walls of an individual home. Home is the community. The city full of people is the Family. The public school is the real Nursery. And badly do the Home and the Family and the Nursery need their mother" (Dorr 1910, 327).

Activists in the reinvigorated feminist movement of the 1960s and 1970s also worked to incorporate private sphere concerns into the public domain by adopting the mantra that "the personal is political." Framing their demands under universal principles of equality, feminist activists sought to open up greater opportunities for women in education and the workplace and to tear down legal structures that made women subordinate to men. Feminists also advocated for policies addressing women's special needs by promoting child care funding, reproductive rights, and family leave policies (Hartmann 1989; Costain 1992; Gelb and Palley 1996). Increasingly disturbed by the cultural changes taking place, social conservatives mobilized to protect the traditional family, accusing feminists of devaluing motherhood and endangering the welfare of children (Mansbridge 1986; Klatch 1987; Schreiber 2008).

The sociological patterns of women's lives and the history of women's integration into politics influence their political participation as voters and candidates. As candidates, women's late entry into the realm of politics has impeded their progress. The power of the incumbency advantage and the importance of seniority within Congress and the state legislatures have slowed women's election to office and their advancement to positions of power and leadership (Burrell 1994; Swers 2002). Studies of voter attitudes demonstrate that the electorate continues to subscribe to gender stereotypes about male and female leadership traits and issue expertise. Thus, voters associate leadership traits of toughness and strength with men and favor these traits in political leaders over leadership traits associated with women such as compassion and morality (Sapiro 1981–82; Huddy and Terkildsen 1993a; Koch 1999; Dolan 2004). With regard to issues, female candidates are seen as more capable of handling social welfare issues like health care and education, but voters favor male candidates to tackle issues including taxes, defense, and foreign policy (Huddy and Terkildsen 1993b; Sanbonmatsu 2002a; Dolan 2004; Lawless 2004; Fridkin and Kenney 2009). Some scholars argue that these issue-based stereotypes transcend party (Sanbonmatsu and Dolan 2009), while others maintain that party cues overwhelm gender-based stereotypes (Hayes 2011). Focusing on ideology, voters believe women candidates are more liberal than male candidates regardless of their actual ideology, a factor that can hinder Republican women as they compete for the nomination in primaries increasingly dominated by conservative voters (Koch 2000; King and Matland 2003; Sanbomatsu and Dolan 2009). These beliefs about leadership traits and issue competencies can impact women's electoral prospects depending on the electoral environment. Women candidates must actively formulate strategies to address these deeply held views about women's political skills.

Looking at women's voting patterns and their public policy views as a group, women exhibit distinctive attitudes on political issues, which in turn affect their voting behavior. Studies of public opinion demonstrate that in comparison with men, women are more supportive of social welfare spending and they favor a more activist role for government in assisting the poor and guaranteeing a standard of living. Women are more likely to express feelings of insecurity and pessimism about the general economy and their own personal finances (Box-Steffensmeier, De Boef, and Lin 2004; Norrander 1999, 2008). There is also evidence that men are more likely to be pocketbook voters, basing their vote on their personal economic situation, while women are more likely to be sociotropic voters, placing greater weight on societal conditions (Huddy, Cassese, and Lizotte 2008). Beyond social welfare issues, women also hold distinctive attitudes on defense policy as women are less likely to support increases in defense spending or the deployment of troops into battle (Shapiro and Mahajan 1986; Eichenberg 2003; Norrander 1999, 2008). On the domestic front, women are more likely to favor gun control and to oppose capital punishment (Seltzer, Newman, and Leighton 1997; Norrander 1999, 2008). While women's rights issues such as abortion do not drive the gender gap, the abortion issue is more salient for women and women are more likely to hold extreme positions on the issue, favoring or opposing abortion in all circumstances (Norrander 1999, 2008; Kaufmann 2002; Jelen and Wilcox 2005).

Since 1980, these gender differences in public opinion have translated into voting behavior that favors the Democratic Party (Kanthak and Norrander 2004; Kaufmann and Petrocik 1999; Chaney, Alvarez, and Nagler 1998). While the gender gap is not large, according to the

National Election Study, it reached a high of fourteen points in the 1996 Clinton-Dole presidential race. In 2008, Barack Obama enjoyed a more modest edge of seven points among women voters. Still, the gap has become important in recent election cycles. The higher turnout among women voters and the status of women as a potential swing voting group in an era of tight electoral competition means that both parties seek to frame issues and promote policies that will reach out to women voters (Dolan, Deckman, and Swers 2010; Burrell 2005; Swers 2002). As I demonstrate, the competition between the parties to reach women voters creates opportunities for policy leadership and party messaging among women senators. Indeed, women senators act as ambassadors to women voters, promoting how the party's policies help women. This is particularly true for Democratic women as female voters more strongly favor the Democratic Party.

A Theory of the Impact of Gender on Policy Making in the New Senate Club

The primacy of re-election concerns in the minds of legislators is universally accepted as a key feature of representative democracy. As a result, congressional scholars generally discount the importance of identity and assume that the need to stand for re-election guarantees that all legislators will be responsive to the demands of the constituency, adjusting their voting records and policy proposals to fit with constituent opinions (Mayhew 1974; Arnold 1990). Yet the constituency is better viewed as defining the boundaries and setting the outer limits for what policy initiatives are acceptable to a legislator's voters. To understand how a member chooses to fill in the black box requires information about personal background, occupational experience, and policy interests (Burden 2007; Hall 1996).

I assert that a senator's gender encompasses a fundamental identity that will color a legislator's perceptions of the nature of policy questions and will influence a member's position on issues. Shared experiences of gender role socialization, the unique pressures and responsibilities faced by women as primary caregivers, trends in public opinion, and the history of women's integration into politics all suggest that gender will influence senators' policy views and priorities. Whether a legislator chooses to pursue gender-based preferences depends on a number of factors including the nature of the issue and the senator's own ideological views. Beyond a senator's own preferences, public expectations regarding gender roles make it easier for women senators to establish a legislative niche in some areas like social welfare policy and more difficult in others such as national security. These public perceptions of gender interact with party reputations for issue ownership and internal Senate norms of behavior to create opportunities for legislative entrepreneurship and structure female senators' political strategies. The desire of the party caucuses to capitalize on the symbolism of gender in their efforts to attract women voters creates additional incentives and pitfalls for women as they decide when to highlight their gender in pursuit of partisan goals.

The Nature of Issues and the Saliency of Gender to Policy Debates. The importance of gender as a factor in determining whether a senator decides to champion a specific policy will depend on the saliency of gender to the policy debate over the issue. There is a large literature demonstrating that gender exerts the greatest impact on legislative activity in the broadly defined area of women's issues (for example, Thomas 1994; Bratton and Haynie 1999; Reingold 2000; Swers 2002; Dodson 2006; Osborn 2012). Women's issues incorporate social welfare policies that underlie the gender gap in public opinion, such as health care and education, as well as feminist initiatives that emerged from the women's rights movement including reproductive rights and gender equity in the workplace. Based on women's traditional roles as caregivers, voter expectations about policy expertise, and public opinion trends demonstrating that women are more likely to support increases in social welfare spending and government support for the poor, I expect that female senators will be more active proponents of women's issue initiatives in comparison with their male colleagues.

However, within the broad range of women's issue proposals, the salience of gender as a determinant of participation will vary. Thus, the fact that social welfare issues have constituted one of the major fault lines in domestic politics since the New Deal means that these policies underlie competition between the Democratic and Republican parties and that they are highly integrated into the committee system of the Senate chamber (Carmines and Stimson 1989; Lee 2009). Moreover, the increasing cost of social welfare entitlement programs including Medicare, Medicaid, and Social Security as a proportion of the federal budget makes them a prime target for partisan battles over who will protect and who will trim the costs of these fast growing entitlement programs (Lee 2009, 2008a, 2008b; Bradbury, Davidson, and Evans 2008). All of these factors heighten the importance of social welfare issues to legislators, creating incentives for all senators to demonstrate leadership and decreasing the substantive importance of gender as a determinant of which senators are actively involved in debate over social welfare issues.

While I expect gender to remain a significant factor in determining participation in the development of social welfare policy, I anticipate gender will be most salient as a predictor of activism on feminist issues. Women's health, reproductive rights, violence against women, and pay equity are issues that clearly highlight the connection between female senators and the interests of women, making women legislators more sensitive to the importance of these issues. The direct connection between feminist issues and consequences for women as a group makes it more likely that other senators will view women as experts on these issues and turn to them for leadership. In the competition to advance one's policy priorities, the credibility, expertise, and moral authority female senators wield on feminist issues will facilitate their efforts to emerge as policy leaders. Moreover, when there is so much competition for the policy attention of senators, the intensity of commitment to an issue matters. If female senators place more priority on these women's rights policies, they will be more willing to expend political capital and resources championing group interests.

Willingness to engage in vigorous advocacy becomes even more important when an issue is controversial. As Douglas Arnold (1990) points out, representatives are concerned with both credit claiming and blame avoidance: they want to claim credit for popular programs and avoid blame for decisions that will be unpopular with voters. Some feminist issues such as abortion are particularly controversial. While a Democrat's or a Republican's actions on these issues can energize their liberal or conservative bases, respectively, these issues can also unleash the wrath of the opposing interest groups, resulting in negative ads against the senator and potential ammunition for a future challenger. These problems are exacerbated for senators in the middle, such as Democrats who represent socially conservative states. In these cases, the intensity of a senator's commitment born of personal connection to the interests of a group becomes particularly important. Moreover, a senator's willingness to act as a champion of group interests will be further tested when interests are being compromised away and deals are negotiated. Thus, when abortion became a sticking point that threatened to derail President Barack Obama's comprehensive health reform plan, Senate majority leader Harry Reid (D-NV) turned to Barbara Boxer (D-CA) and Patty Murray (D-WA) to negotiate a deal with conservative Democratic holdout Ben Nelson (D-NE). Reid knew that Boxer and Murray's bona fides in the abortion rights community would bring along other pro-choice senators and mollify the interest groups (Alonso-Zaldivar 2009; Kane 2009).

Countering Negative Stereotypes and Bringing a Different Perspective to Policy Debates. While a great deal of the research on women in office focuses on their interest in women's issues, there is very little work that moves beyond women's issues to test the importance of gender on legislating in other policy domains. Thus, we have little evidence to support the common assertion that women bring a different perspective that considers women's interests in deliberations over all policy areas, not just debates over social welfare issues and women's rights. Furthermore, the focus on women's issues demonstrates how shared interests and positive voter stereotypes about women's greater expertise on compassion issues translate into greater activism by women legislators. Yet there are no analyses of how negative stereotypes about women impact their legislative behavior.

How do negative stereotypes influence senators' legislative choices? Analyzing senators' actions on defense policy provides a perfect opportunity to address this question. Studies of voter attitudes indicate that the electorate prefers male candidates to handle defense policy (Lawless 2004; Kenski and Falk 2004; Falk and Kenski 2006). These preferences reflect the long history of war and the military as an exclusively male domain. Furthermore, public opinion analyses demonstrate that women are less supportive than men of increases in military spending and the deployment of troops into conflict, and these differences are an important component of the gender gap in public opinion and the electorate (Shapiro and Mahajan 1986; Eichenberg 2003; Norrander 1999, 2008). Candidate studies show that women running for office try to counter these stereotypes by emphasizing their toughness (Kahn 1996; Dolan 2004). One of the more famous examples of this strategy was Hillary Clinton's 3 A.M. ad in the 2008 Democratic primary to show that in comparison with Barack Obama she was the tougher more experienced candidate that voters can trust when a foreign policy crisis breaks in the middle of the night (Lawrence and Rose 2010; Cillizza 2008).

Beyond the campaign, gender stereotypes about defense policy expertise may affect legislative activity. I expect that partisanship and ideology will drive senators' votes on high-profile issues of troop deployments and war funding. However, gender may influence the content of senators' defense policy proposals. If women do bring a different perspective to policy making that prioritizes the impact of policies on women, children, and families then women may be more likely to advocate proposals improving conditions for military families, expanding military benefits, and addressing issues related to women in the military. Furthermore, negative stereotypes about women's lack of interest and expertise on military issues could have tangible consequences for their policy behavior and legislative success. Women may face a higher hurdle in their efforts to demonstrate competence and gain credibility on defense issues.

Gender and the Political Opportunity Structure of the U.S. Senate. To this point, I have laid out how gender may influence policy preferences. However, policy preferences do not exist in a vacuum. Senators' desire and ability to act on gender-based interests depends on their own ideology and their strategic calculations about the political opportunity structure. These calculations will be affected by institutional norms, party imperatives, and the larger political context.

The most enduring feature of the contemporary Senate is the power that its rules and organization give to individual senators. In comparison with their House counterparts, senators have a much larger staff and a greater number of committee assignments. Each senator serves on at least three committees, and all are guaranteed one prestige assignment: Appropriations, Finance, Foreign Relations, or Armed Services. Majority party freshmen senators often receive a subcommittee leadership post (Sinclair 1989, 2009; Evans 1991). These enhanced staff and committee resources facilitate senators' efforts to emerge as leaders on favored issues. The six-year term gives senators more time to develop their policy agendas and allows senators to stray from strict adherence to constituent preferences in order to pursue their vision of good public policy (Erikson, MacKuen, and Stimson 2002). Thus, studies demonstrate that senators' voting behavior changes over the electoral cycle, adhering more closely to constituent views in the last two years of a term in anticipation of their re-election campaign (Levitt 1996; Thomas 1985).

Senators are also opinion leaders as national and local media outlets are more likely to turn to senators than individual House members for comments on all types of policy issues (Schiller 2000; Baker 2001; Sellers 2002, 2010). This higher media profile makes it easier for senators to command public attention for their policy proposals. Commenting on the value of a Senate seat for policy leadership on national issues, a staffer for a Democratic senator noted that when his boss served in the House, "he was known for his work on Merchant Marine and Fisheries because those were the industries in the district. As a senator he still works on those issues but he was able to make a name for himself on health care and now that is his signature issue."[6] The greater media attention and expectations for leadership on national issues also makes the Senate a breeding ground for presidential hopefuls including the 2008 Democratic frontrunners Barack Obama (D-IL) and Hillary Clinton (D-NY) and Republican nominee John McCain (R-AZ).

These organizational features of the Senate that encourage policy entrepreneurship by individual senators are reinforced by permissive procedural rules that favor the rights of the minority. The fact that senators are allowed to offer nongermane amendments on the floor means that a senator who feels strongly about an issue can offer an amendment on the subject to any bill that comes to the floor regardless of its relevance to the legislation being considered. The Senate's reliance on unanimous consent agreements to conduct legislative business means that each senator must give his or her consent to move legislation to the floor for debate and to apply limits on the time for debate and the type of amendments that can be offered. Finally, the ability of senators to place holds on legislation and nominations and to threaten filibusters increases their ability to force consideration of their policy priorities (Bell 2011; Koger 2010; Smith 1989, 2010; Evans and Lipinski 2005; Binder and Smith 1997). In sum, the procedural rules protecting individual and minority rights reduce the control of the majority party over the agenda and the exclusive power of committees in favor of creating opportunities for individual senators to press their issue priorities. Thus, if senators feel strongly about gender-based preferences, the organization of the Senate gives them the resources to pursue gender-related interests and the rules of the Senate give them the tools to force consideration of those preferences.

At the same time, other aspects of Senate organization and electoral incentives caution against a distinctive impact of gender on senators' policy behavior. The fact that one hundred senators need to cover the same policy ground as 435 members of the House of Representatives encourages senators to be policy generalists with a finger in every pot rather than specialists developing expertise in a limited set of issues. This desire to participate in as wide a range of issues as possible is reinforced by the facts that senators are representing an entire state and states have a more heterogeneous range of needs and interests in comparison with an individual House district (Lee and Oppenheimer 1999; Schiller 2000; Baker 2001). The need to build a statewide electoral coalition increases the pressure to have a proposal on every issue that might interest constituents, potentially reducing the importance of gender in senators' policy choices as all senators will want to point to proposals that address women's interests.

Furthermore, to achieve action on their policy priorities, senators must build coalitions that can win a majority and potentially a supermajority of sixty votes if cloture is required to approve passage of an initiative. As senators work to establish a legislative niche and build support for a policy, there are norms that must be observed and pitfalls to be avoided. First there are questions of policy turf. Senators serve six-year terms that are staggered, meaning only one-third of senators are up for re-election in any given election cycle. Thus, there are likely to be more senior members who already have established records on an issue who must be consulted and brought on board to support a proposal. While committees do not have the stringent gatekeeping power to kill proposals in the Senate that they enjoy in the House, committees are still the major sources of legislation on issues under their jurisdiction (Evans 1991; Hall 1996; Woon 2009). Senators will have greater success if they are a member of the committee or if they get the support of committee leaders for their policy initiatives.

As relatively new members of the Senate club, women who were elected in the 1990s and early 2000s have only recently gained the seniority necessary to become committee leaders. Thus, a Democratic staffer noted, "over time the women senators have been disadvantaged by seniority rules in the Senate. Lazy, dying, dead people have been chairs because it is all on seniority, but now they [the women] are getting seniority." Indeed, in the 112th Congress, five women chair policy committees, including Dianne Feinstein (D-CA), chair of the Select Committee on Intelligence; Barbara Boxer (D-CA), chair of the Environment and Public Works Committee; Debbie Stabenow (D-MI), chair of Agriculture, Nutrition, and Forestry; Patty Murray (D-WA), chair of Veterans' Affairs; and Mary Landrieu (D-LA), chair of Small Business and Entrepreneurship. Murray also heads the Democratic Senatorial Campaign Committee, and she was tapped by majority leader Harry Reid (NV) to cochair the bicameral committee, dubbed the "Supercommittee," that ultimately failed to come to a deal to reduce the budget deficit. Most of the Republican women also hold committee leadership posts. Four of the five Republican women are ranking members on policy committees, including Kay Bailey Hutchison (R-TX), ranking member on Commerce, Science, and Transportation; Susan Collins (R-ME), ranking member on Homeland Security and Governmental Affairs; Lisa Murkowski (R-AK), ranking member on Energy and Natural Resources; and Olympia Snowe (R-ME), ranking member on Small Business and Entrepreneurship. Yet Senate women have not achieved enough seniority to chair one of the prestigious "Super A" committees: Appropriations, Finance, Armed Services, or Foreign Relations.[7] Most of the leaders on these committees were elected in the 1970s. The success of women in gaining committee leadership positions reflects the broad distribution of power in the Senate as senators' multiple committee assignments and the smaller size of the body allow senators to advance to leadership positions more quickly than House members. However, the most senior female senator, Barbara Mikulski (D-MD), is also the most senior Democratic senator who does not hold a committee chair.[8]

Beyond their committee position, a senator's policy agenda is shaped with an eye to the legislative portfolio of his or her same-state colleague. Schiller (2000, 2002) finds that the two senators in a state, whether they are from the same or opposing parties, draw electoral support from different geographic areas and groups of voters. Same-state senators are to varying degrees in competition with each other as they work to build distinctive policy records. Therefore, each senator is constrained to a certain extent by the established legislative record and committee choices of his or her same-state colleague. If one senator in the state has built a reputation as a leader on a particular policy such as health care, the affected interest groups within the state will gravitate toward that member for leadership and the state media will look to that senator for comments. The other senator's dominance of the issue will require a more costly investment of time and resources by the same-state counterpart to gain the attention necessary to emerge as a leader on the issue. Moreover, a senator's efforts to develop a legislative profile on the issue could alienate his or her same-state colleague. Thus, the division of labor between senators representing the same state could affect the relevance of gender to a senator's policy profile. Interestingly, in the 112th Congress, two female senators represent California, Maine, New Hampshire, and Washington.[9]

Party Polarization and the Division of the Senate into Partisan Teams. Increasing ideological polarization and the division of the Senate into partisan teams is an enduring feature of the Senate that shapes legislators' policy priorities and political strategies. Studies of ideology and partisanship indicate that over time party members have become increasingly homogeneous in their ideological outlook, with Democrats becoming more liberal and Republicans more conservative (Poole and Rosenthal 1997, 2007; McCarty, Poole, and Rosenthal 1997, 2006). As a result of this homogeneity, the ideological viewpoints of the parties are also increasingly distant from one another (Smith 2007; Theirault 2008; Aldrich and Rhode 2000). At the individual level, the ideological views of female legislators, as measured by their DW-NOMINATE scores, have largely followed the trends of their male counterparts.[10] Like their male colleagues, Democratic women in the House and Senate have become more liberal over time. However, the conservatism of Republican women has lagged behind their male colleagues. In the House, Republican women were consistently more liberal than Republican men through the 104th Congress (1994–1996). With the election of more conservative Republican women from the South and West, the ideological viewpoints of Republican men and women converged by the 108th and 109th Congresses (2003–2006) (Frederick 2009, 2010; Pearson 2010; Palmer and Simon 2008; Elder 2008; Evans 2005). Yet in the Senate, Republican women remain more liberal than their male counterparts (Frederick 2010, 2011). These differences are largely driven by the small number of women within the Republican caucus. Moderate Republicans Olympia Snowe and Susan Collins of Maine anchor the liberal end of the Republican caucus. Still, in the 108th Congress (2003–2004), the DW-NOMINATE score of the most conservative female Republican, Elizabeth Dole (R-NC), was at the median of the Republican caucus, and the scores of Lisa Murkowski (R-AK) and Kay Bailey Hutchison (R-TX) were, respectively, in the first and second lowest quartiles of Republican senators and less conservative than their male Republican same-state colleagues. It remains to be seen whether the slowly increasing population of conservative Republican women in the House, state legislatures, and governor's mansions will seek election to the Senate and move the ideological profile of Republican women further right.

The internal homogeneity and increasing polarization between the two parties has created a Senate divided into partisan teams fighting over national policy and competing for majority control of the Senate (Lee 2011, 2009, 2008b; Sinclair 2006, 2009; Smith 2007; Theirault 2008). In response to their ideological agreement and increasingly volatile elections that saw the Senate flip control between Democrats and Republicans multiple times since 1980, senators have given more power to their party leadership to invoke party discipline and to craft policy messages that will resonate with voters (Lee 2011, 2010, 2009, 2008b; Pearson 2008; Sinclair 2006, 2009; Smith 2007). Over time, both Democrats and Republicans have given party leaders more control over committee assignments and subjected chairs to approval by the party caucus. Both the Democratic and Republican party caucuses have significantly augmented the budgets of their leadership arms, including the policy committees and party conference chairs. These entities sponsor weekly lunches to discuss policy and plan party strategy. They distribute party talking points and policy briefs on issues and organize press conferences and floor speeches to sell the party message (Lee 2011, 2010, 2009; Smith 2007; Pearson 2008; Sellers 2002, 2010).

The increased power wielded by party leaders and the team mentality of party caucuses have real consequences for senators' ability to act independently and pursue policy positions that are based on their view of women's interests. When Arlen Specter (R-PA) suggested that President Bush should not select a Supreme Court nominee who would overturn *Roe v. Wade*, there was an immediate backlash in which conservative senators spurred on by socially conservative interest groups tried to deny Specter the chairmanship of the Judiciary Committee. Specter was only able to keep the chairmanship after he made certain promises to push through President Bush's conservative appellate nominees and his Supreme Court picks (Perine 2004). However, Republicans utilized the scuffle to achieve passage, by one vote, of a plan to give Republican leader Bill Frist (R-TN) control of half the vacancies on prestige committees rather than awarding these seats on the basis of seniority (Pearson 2008). Responding to this effort to enhance party discipline and reign in independence, moderate Republican Senator Olympia Snowe (ME) publicly complained, "I think it's a punitive measure by any interpretation" (Ota 2004).

The overwhelming importance of party loyalty and the desire to be a part of the partisan team will constrain senators' choices about how and when to pursue gender-based policy preferences even in contexts where gender is highly salient. This is particularly true for Republican senators because the women's rights agenda often conflicts with the principles of the party's socially conservative base. By analyzing senators' actions and votes in the highly polarized judicial confirmation process over President Bush's Supreme Court, I show how Republican senators with liberal preferences on women's issues like abortion and pay equity strategically approach the confirmation process, keeping a low profile and reiterating their commitment to women's rights in their public statements, while sublimating their preferences on cloture and confirmation votes that demand party loyalty.

Gender, Issue Ownership, and Party Messaging. The ability to pursue gender-based preferences and the value of women's issues as vehicles for achieving policy success or advancement within one's caucus is markedly different for Republican and Democratic women. Since the early 1970s, women's issues, from health care and education to women's rights concerns like reproductive choice and workplace equity, are increasingly associated with the Democratic Party (Wolbrecht 2000; Sanbonmatsu 2002b; Evans 2005). Winter (2010) finds that voters increasingly associate feminine traits such as compassion with the Democratic Party, while associating masculine traits of strength with the Republican Party. The responsiveness of Democratic voters to policies that enhance the social safety net and the alignment of feminist interest groups with the Democratic Party mean that Democratic senators will want to pursue these issues and their colleagues will be open to these concerns based on their shared ideological liberalism and a desire to attract Democratic voters and mobilize activists.

By contrast, when a Republican woman advocates women's issues like education and health care, she is pursuing policy initiatives that do not advance core Republican principles of fiscal conservatism, lower taxes, probusiness growth, and anti–burdensome regulation. At worst, if she advocates for explicitly feminist concerns like enhancement of family planning services or pay equity, she is antagonizing socially conservative base voters and activists and in turn alienating her natural allies, other members of the Republican caucus. These fellow Republican senators will now be less willing to work with her and help her achieve her numerous other policy priorities, a significant problem in an institution that relies on personal relationships and deal making to advance one's legislation.

The advantages Democratic women enjoy in their pursuit of women's issues are reinforced by perceptions of issue ownership among voters and party messaging strategies. When parties develop a history of attention and innovation on an issue, voters will view the party as more competent on the issue and will be more likely to trust messages that come from the party that owns the issue (Petrocik 1996; Petrocik, Benoit, and Hansen 2003). Studies of issue ownership demonstrate that voters prefer Democrats to handle issues like health care, education, Social Security, and the environment, while they trust Republicans more on defense, foreign policy, and taxes (Petrocik 1996; Petrocik, Benoit, and Hansen 2003; Sides 2006; Sellers 2010). The size of the party advantage is not static as the parties compete to demonstrate effectiveness and undermine confidence in the other side's ability to handle an issue. Indeed, the job of the party caucus and leadership is to create a message that will enhance the party brand in the mind of voters (Pope and Woon 2009; Cox and McCubbins 1993, 2005). Therefore, party leaders design their messaging strategies with an eye to emphasizing issues owned by the party. Leaders work to frame other issues in ways that are favorable to the party and invoke themes that enhance the reputation of the party (Sellers 2002, 2010). The fact that the public positively associates numerous women's issues with the Democratic Party means that Democratic women will be offered and will be able to create more opportunities to advertise their own and party proposals on these issues in press conferences and on the floor. Interviews with Senate staff demonstrate that Democratic women participate in party messaging as individuals and that these women also organize themselves as a group to leverage their gender to call public attention to Democratic causes. Through these efforts to sell the party message to the public, their individual profiles are raised with voters and interest groups and their standing is enhanced within the party caucus.

The advantages Democratic women gain from patterns of issue ownership and party messaging are enhanced by the close electoral competition for party control of Congress and the presidency. When party competition is tight, both sides look to capitalize on advantages with groups of voters. Since 1980, women have favored Democratic candidates, and Democrats design their campaign messages to capitalize on this gender gap. Indeed, Schaffner (2005) demonstrates that Democratic Senate candidates prime gender issues even more when there has been a gender gap that helped the Democratic candidate in previous statewide races. Thus, Democratic Senate candidates in states with gender gaps in previous races ran more ads featuring women's issues including health, education, and child care. Women voters responded to these messages by voting in larger numbers for the Democratic Senate candidate. Efforts by the Democratic Party to attract more women voters provide additional opportunities for female Democratic senators to advertise party messages and raise their profiles with voters. Moreover, female senators may be able to translate these favors that they do for the party into additional opportunities for consideration of their policy initiatives and advancement within the leadership ranks of their party caucus.

Concerns over the gender gap also create opportunities for Republican women. Republicans are eager to court groups of women voters who favor the Republican Party, particularly white, suburban, married women (Norrander 2008). The effort to reach these voters creates opportunities for individual Republican women to serve as spokespersons for Republican issues. Moreover, Republicans want to counter Democratic criticisms that the Republican Party lacks diversity and that Republican policies are anti-women. These more defensive goals mean that Republicans will turn to women to speak for the party and offer high-profile bills and amendments in cases where the party is trying to counter Democratic accusations that Republican policies will hurt women. For example, Susan Collins (R-ME), along with Bill Frist (R-TN), a heart surgeon, were appointed as the Republican floor managers when the Senate debated the Patients' Bill of Rights in the 106th Congress (1999–2000), in order to take advantage of the symbolism of gender and the credibility of having a doctor countering Democratic arguments (Sinclair 2001). Similarly, according to staffers, in the 111th Congress (2009–2010), Republicans recruited Kay Bailey Hutchison (R-TX), who was not a member of the committee of jurisdiction, to offer a Republican alternative to the Democrats' Lilly Ledbetter Fair Pay Act to diffuse the argument that Republicans were against equal pay for women. When the Senate considered Obama's health reform initiative, Lisa Murkowski (R-AK) offered a competing amendment on preventive care to demonstrate that Republicans were more committed than Democrats to preserving women's access to mammograms (Herszenhorn and Pear 2009).

The desire to demonstrate that Republicans are an increasingly diverse party has also helped individual Republican women in their bids for leadership within the caucus. At different points in time, Kay Bailey Hutchison (R-TX), Elizabeth Dole (R-NC), and Lisa Murkowski (R-AK) all held leadership positions within the Republican caucus. Hutchison achieved the most influence rising from vice chair of the Senate Republican Conference to chair of the Republican Policy Committee in the 110th Congress (2007–2008). Of course, Republican women can only advance in the caucus leadership if their ideological views are compatible with the majority of the caucus (Center for the American Woman and Politics 2009; Rosenthal 2008). Thus, Lisa Murkowski (R-AK) was pushed out of leadership by more conservative colleagues when she lost the Republican primary in Alaska, and she did not regain her leadership post when she was reelected as a write-in candidate. Moreover, Maine Republicans Olympia Snowe and Susan Collins have ideological profiles and voting records that are too moderate for the Republican caucus to vote them into leadership.

The Parties and Critical Mass. The numerical presence of women within their party caucuses also will impact the ability of women to leverage gender to influence the party's agenda and advance their own policy goals. Studying the presence of minority groups in corporations, Rosabeth Moss Kanter (1977) found that when there are few women in an organization they are treated as token representatives of the group and they feel pressure to conform and downplay gender differences. By contrast, when women reach a critical mass (approximately 15%), they will feel more comfortable championing group interests and demanding a seat at the table. In comparison with Republican women, Democratic women constitute a larger proportion of the Democratic caucus. Given their larger numbers and the greater openness of the Democratic Party agenda to women's issues, Democratic women are likely more able to capitalize on their numbers to gain influence over the party's policy agenda and increase their power within the institution. Indeed, staffers noted that Democratic women frequently work together as a group to push particular policy priorities, develop party messages, and engage in electoral campaigning. By contrast because of their small numbers and disparate ideologies as well as a party culture that is less open to claims based on gender, Republican women cannot easily translate their gender into policy influence. Instead individual Republican women gain prominence on a case-by-case basis.

In sum, the Senate provides an important opportunity for examining the impact of gender on policy activity. The heightened profile of senators and the procedural rules protecting their rights to participate in any and all policy areas allows us to evaluate the influence of gender in a wide range of policies, from social welfare to national security. The institutional norms guiding relations between senators and the emergence of the Senate as a more polarized institution divided into partisan teams encourages analysis of how institutional rules and party imperatives channel the role of gender in senators' legislative decisions.

Gender constitutes both an aspect of identity coloring senators' perception of issues and a strategic resource opening opportunities for women to leverage their credibility as women and mothers into avenues for policy entrepreneurship. Because of the Democratic Party's association with social welfare and women's rights issues and the greater presence of women within the Democratic caucus, gender is more of an asset for Democratic women as they develop their legislative reputation and craft public positions to connect with Democratic voters. Within the institution of the Senate, female senators can leverage their gender to promote party messages that demonstrate their partisan team's commitment to policies that are popular with female voters or they can provide a shield of credibility to a party's efforts to deflect criticism of its proposals as hurting women. Still gender also serves as a constraint, erecting barriers that women must navigate in their efforts to become important players on defense policy. The small number of women in the

Senate means that they face increased pressure to speak for women and to represent the party with women voters in the media. Women senators must balance the party's desire to capitalize on the symbolism of gender against their own policy goals and the impact on their reputation with colleagues and voters.

Looking Ahead

To understand the influence of gender on senators' legislative behavior, I utilize a combination of quantitative and qualitative techniques. Using regression analysis, I analyze gender differences in senators' legislative activity, including the bills they sponsor and cosponsor, the amendments they offer on the floor, and their voting records on a variety of women's issue and defense policy initiatives in the 107th and 108th Congresses (2001–2004). I also examined the role of gender and women's rights concerns in the key battles over President Bush's Supreme Court nominees John Roberts and Samuel Alito in the 109th Congress (2005–2006). I supplement this data analysis with evidence from interviews with staffers to Democratic and Republican senators. Between 2004 and 2011, I interviewed fifty Senate staffers associated with forty-four senators including nineteen Republicans and twenty-five Democrats. I also interviewed one Republican and two Democratic senators. The staffers interviewed included chiefs of staff, legislative directors, legislative assistants with special responsibility for particular issues such as defense policy or health care, and campaign managers. In addition to staff, I also interviewed liberal and conservative interest group leaders who took an active role in the confirmation battles over President Bush's nominees to the Supreme Court.[11] All interviews were anonymous. The interviews shed light on the strategic calculations of senators concerning the policies they choose to champion and how those calculations are affected by the views of their state constituency, their electoral interests, their committee positions, and their relationships with other senators and the party caucus. Through the interviews, I also explore the ways in which gender is perceived as an asset and an obstacle to senators' achievement of their policy goals. I examine the partisan implications of gender including the ways in which the parties and individual female senators seek to utilize gender to advance the party message and their own positions within the caucus.

In chapters 2 and 3, I examine whether female senators are more committed to pursuing policies related to women, children, and families than are their male partisan colleagues. Analyzing bill sponsorship and cosponsorship in chapter 2, I demonstrate that because senators build legislative records as policy generalists rather than specializing in one or two areas, all senators have proposals on women's issues as part of their policy agenda. Still, gender does influence the content of senators' policy initiatives because women are more active sponsors and cosponsors of women's issue legislation under certain circumstances. Gender differences are most evident in senators' advocacy of feminist legislation that focuses on issues of women's rights. Women have enhanced credibility with their colleagues and the electorate on these issues because of the clear connection to consequences for women as a group. The analysis of senators' participation in the development and debate over the Partial Birth Abortion Act and the Lilly Ledbetter Fair Pay Act in chapter 3 highlight the gender dynamics of policy debate on women's rights. I illuminate the strategies utilized by the parties to shape these debates in a way that enhances the party's reputation with women voters and voters more generally. The analysis also details Republican efforts to counter Democratic messages that portray their policies as damaging to women's interests.

In chapter 4, I analyze the impact of gender identity in a policy context where gender issues are highly salient and there is intense pressure to stick together as a party team. The fight to replace Supreme Court Justice Sandra Day O'Connor brought gender-related concerns from the scope of women's rights to expanding diversity on the federal bench to the forefront of the debate. Yet the politics of judicial nominations have become increasingly contentious as senators' votes on a president's nominees are almost completely determined by their ideological views and party affiliations (Epstein and Segal 2005; Epstein et al. 2006; Primo, Binder, and Maltzman 2008). In this tightly constrained atmosphere, imperatives of party loyalty generally trump issues of gender identity as determinants of senators' votes on nominees. Yet Republican women do consider women's rights concerns in their public explanations of their votes. Similarly, while ideology generally guides the votes of Democratic senators on nominations, in comparison with Democratic men, Democratic women are more likely to discuss women's rights issues in their explanations of their votes and to point to women's rights concerns outside of abortion including pay equity, sexual harassment, family leave, and a desire to see more women on the court.

In chapter 5, I move beyond women's issues to examine the impact of gender on senators' defense policy proposals. While the politics of women's issues favor the Democratic Party and women legislators, voters generally prefer Republicans to handle defense policy. Moreover, studies of voter stereotypes indicate that voters trust male candidates on issues of defense and foreign policy, compounding problems of issue ownership for Democratic women and creating conflict between the party and gender cues for Republican women. The partisan and gendered context of defense policy making has real consequences for the content of women's defense policy agendas and the strategies women employ in their efforts to be seen as credible authorities on defense issues.

In contrast to studies of public opinion showing that women are less likely to support increases in defense spending and deployment of troops, gender had no independent impact on senators' votes on the resolution authorizing war in Iraq. Moreover, an analysis of amending activity on Congress's major policy statement on defense policy, the annual defense authorization bills in the 107th and 108th Congresses (2001–2004), shows that all senators are more active proponents of "soft defense initiatives," which are designed to expand benefits for military personnel and veterans, rather than "hard defense proposals," which deal with weapons and war. Still, women are more likely than their male partisan colleagues to cosponsor the soft defense proposals that expand benefits for the military. Staffers for female senators believe that gender stereotypes create an additional hurdle for women, particularly Democratic women, as they seek to establish their reputation on national security. As a result women, especially Democratic women, look for more opportunities to highlight their defense credentials by, for example, increasing their cosponsorship of national security initiatives as a means of position taking with voters and stakeholder groups in the state.

Finally chapter 6 summarizes the findings of this study and looks toward the future of women's representation in the Senate. In this concluding chapter, I discuss the implications of examining the Senate as a gendered and partisan institution. By paying careful attention to the interaction of gender with the unique institutional and partisan features of the Senate, we can deepen our understanding of how the expansion of the representation of women and other minority groups in Congress will impact the policy agenda and the political culture of our representative institutions.

2 A Stronger Voice for Women, Children, and Families? Gender Identity and Policy Making on Women's Issues

In September 2009, the Finance Committee was locked in a contentious markup of President Obama's health care plan. Republican Senator John Kyl (AZ) offered an amendment to eliminate the requirement that all health plans must offer a defined minimum package of benefits. Kyl argued that requiring insurers to offer a specific set of health benefits would raise costs and premiums. In response, Senator Debbie Stabenow (D-MI) asserted that these standards are needed because many insurance policies do not cover basic services like maternity care. To highlight the unnecessary costs of a minimum benefits package, Kyl retorted, "I don't need maternity care." Stabenow shot back, "Your mom probably did" (Pear and Herszenhorn 2009; Slajda 2009). The video of this exchange went viral on YouTube (http://www.youtube .com/watch?v=3Jj6pqajvB8).

Senator Stabenow's presence on the Finance Committee and her vigorous defense of women's health care needs support assertions that women bring a different perspective to policy debates that considers the impact of public policies on women and that female legislators are more likely to advocate for the inclusion of women's interests in legislation. In this chapter, I explore whether women senators are more active advocates of women's issue legislation by examining senators' sponsorship and cosponsorship activity in the 107th and 108th Congresses (2001–2004) on issues related to women, children, and families. These issues constitute fully one-third of the policy agendas of senators in each Congress. I draw on evidence from interviews conducted from 2004 to 2011 to illuminate the strategic calculations driving senators' decisions to pursue particular women's issue initiatives.

Legislative Entrepreneurs for Women's Interests

Senate offices are individual legislative enterprises in which the senator, with the help of a large staff, fashions policy proposals and seeks to insert himself/herself into policy debates. Senators are what Wawro (2000) calls legislative entrepreneurs, utilizing their resources of time and staff to gather information on issues as they work to identify opportunities for legislating and to build coalitions for their priorities. In comparison with House members, senators are often described as generalists involved in a wider range of debates and looking to have a finger in every pot in order to meet the needs of heterogeneous statewide constituencies and develop a national profile (Baker 2001; Sinclair 1989, 2009). Confirming the reputation of senators as generalists, a Republican staffer explained that a great deal

> of what senators do is reactive. You can't be big picture because the country is coming at you with their concerns. You can reserve 10% of your time for priority setting and execution. If 2/3 of what is in your memo [of legislative goals] gets done the senator had a great year. Most of the time they get distracted because the President comes down with his State of the Union and priorities. Your committee goes in a different direction. You have a war and the country is not listening to your priorities.

Still senators come into office with their own policy interests and campaign promises. The need to focus their policy agendas and develop a set of issues with which they are identified is reinforced by electoral concerns. According to a senior Republican staffer, a senator needs a record to run on, "you can't just have votes and pork. I tell freshmen staffers to think from six years back. I keep a notebook to keep specific results for specific areas and counties of [the state]. When we go to the Women's

Economic Forum in [the state], we want to be able to say this is the five
or six things he has done like on SBA [Small Business Administration]
and health care, not just I support and vote for tax cuts."

Thus, senators look to develop a set of issues with which they want
to be identified,and they compete to establish reputations as leaders on
those issues. At the beginning of each legislative session, most Senate
offices engage in strategic planning in which the legislative assistants
under the direction of the legislative director and the chief of staff draft
memos identifying issues within their portfolio that they believe the senator should pursue. The staff and the senator then engage in a process
of winnowing designed to identify the issues on which the senator can
have the most impact. The description of one Democratic chief of staff
typifies the process:

> You start the year in January. [The senator's] office is organized
> in clusters. Finance has a senior legislative person and a junior
> LA [legislative assistant] that deals with Social Security, tax re-
> form, budget deficit. We have an environmental cluster, a foreign
> policy cluster; domestic issues deals with Medicare, senior citi-
> zens. In January the senior LAs meet with the legislative director
> to start planning their memos. They go over ideas and delegate
> research assignments to find out if anyone introduced a bill on
> x, y, or z in the last Congress. They analyze the bill and deter-
> mine how our idea differs and if there is enough of a distinction
> to pursue the issue or we will just be replicating. Issues from the
> year before that were not complete will roll over. Rollover issues
> may be dropped because they looked promising last year but a
> change in the committee makeup or the preferences of the new
> chair make it a dead issue. They come up with a list of legisla-
> tive items, and the chief of staff looks at it. The chief of staff has
> the political antenna up to identify issues on the list that could
> cause heartburn with constituents or remember in the campaign
> the senator made a commitment to do something on free trade
> that the legislative staff overlooked. The chief of staff tries to
> marry the good public policy from the staff with the political
> calculations. The legislative staff develop their list and put the
> issues into three tiers. They meet with the senator, and he will
> ask questions: if they think it can pass, how do we pay for it,
> is their opposition in the committee? The senator may move
> something from tier 1 to 2. It is very collaborative.

Through this process of winnowing and testing ideas against the senator's policy interests, campaign promises, and the political environment inside and outside of the Senate, senators develop their policy goals. Thus, senators work to establish themselves as players on a defined set of issues. It is an open question whether female senators will be more likely to include women's issues in their cluster of policy priorities.

Developing a Policy Agenda through Bill Sponsorship and Cosponsorship. Sponsorship and cosponsorship of bills and amendments are tools that senators use to stake their claim to policy areas and establish themselves as experts who need to be consulted. The decision to sponsor a bill is an important indicator of the issues a senator wants to be associated with and the reputation he or she wants to cultivate with colleagues (Schiller 1995). The bills senators initiate vary in their complexity and the level of attention that senators devote to them. However, studies of legislative activity note that bill sponsorship and cosponsorship serve legislators' electoral interests and further their public policy goals (Schiller 1995, 2000; Woon 2009; Koger 2003; Harward and Moffett 2010). In the electoral arena, sponsorship and cosponsorship offer opportunities for position taking and credit claiming with constituents (Mayhew 1974; Arnold 1990). Senators like to have a bill to point to to show that they are taking action to meet constituent needs. Cosponsoring widens the net by allowing senators to indicate support for policies by signing on as a cosponsor. Through their sponsorship and cosponsorship activity, members can appeal to voters, interest groups, and donors. Moreover, senators can inoculate themselves against criticism over troublesome votes by showing they have sponsored or cosponsored a better alternative (Schiller 1995, 2000; Koger 2003; Woon 2009; Harward and Moffett 2010).

Sponsorship and cosponsorship of legislation also allow members to more clearly delineate their policy views by initiating and supporting legislation that is closer to their policy preferences (Koger 2003; Woon 2009; Harward and Moffett 2010). Moreover, legislators who are active sponsors and cosponsors are more likely to attain power within the institution, moving more quickly into committee and party leadership posts (Wawro 2000). Social network analyses of legislative activity indicate that more prolific sponsors and cosponsors are more socially connected within the institution, having the ability to persuade more members to sign on to their proposals (Fowler 2006a, 2006b). In addition to defining one's own vision of good public policy, cosponsorship serves as a legislative signal whereby bill sponsors seek out cosponsors in an effort to signal other legislators and party leaders about the content of their bills and the level of support for their initiatives as they compete for attention on the Senate agenda (Krehbiel 1995; Kessler and Krehbiel 1996; Wilson and Young 1997). Wilson and Young (1997) note that bills with more cosponsors are more likely to be acted on by committees, although the number of cosponsors had no impact on which legislation made it to the House floor. Furthermore, senators also pursue cosponsors with an eye to maximizing the potential for media coverage of their proposal, which in turn will improve the odds that party leaders will schedule the bill for a vote or incorporate it into other legislation. High-quality cosponsors include party or committee leaders, relevant committee members, legislators with prior entrepreneurial effort in a policy area, or members with a personal connection to the bill content based on race, gender, region, or career background (Koger 2003).

Research on the factors that influence senators' sponsorship and cosponsorship activity highlights the importance of committee position and constituent demand. Senators devote more attention to the issues within the jurisdiction of their committees, and this is reflected in their sponsorship activity (Evans 1991; Woon 2009). Thus, senators who serve on committees with jurisdiction over education will be more likely to offer bills to improve various aspects of education policy. In addition to having a seat on a relevant committee, seniority and holding a leadership position on a committee also affect sponsorship behavior. In comparison with first-term legislators, committee leaders and more senior members have more resources in the form of experience with issues, more staff, and an established legislative record to enhance their ability to sponsor legislation (Evans 1991; Schiller 1995, 2000; Hall 1996; Woon 2009). However, freshmen are more likely to cosponsor legislation as a cheaper method of staking out issue positions (Koger 2003; Harward and Moffett 2010; Rocca and Sanchez 2008). Constituent need is another important guide to sponsorship and cosponsorship activity. The importance of an industry to the state and other indicators of constituent need for benefits encourage senators to increase their activity on specific issues (Woon 2009; Balla and Nemacheck 2000; Koger 2003; Harward and Moffett 2010). Finally, ideology plays a role in senators' cosponsorship decisions. More liberal members cosponsor more legislation, a fact that likely reflects their preference for more active government (Koger 2003; Harward and Moffett 2010; Rocca and Sanchez 2008).

Legislative Entrepreneurship and Social Identity. Scholars who have examined the impact of social identity on legislative activity in Congress and state legislatures find that race and gender do influence the policy priorities of legislators. Research on minority legislators indicates that African Americans and Latinos are more committed to advocating for minority interests including civil rights, poverty, criminal justice, and immigration (Fenno 2003; Haynie 2001; Bratton, Haynie, and Reingold 2006; Bratton 2006). Minority legislators are more likely to sponsor and cosponsor legislation with racial content such as civil rights bills (Canon 1999; Haynie 2001; Bratton and Haynie 1999; Bratton, Haynie, and Reingold 2006). They participate more actively in committee hearings dealing with minority interests including enforcement of fair housing laws or racial profiling (Minta 2009, 2011; Gamble 2007).

Similarly, there is a vast literature on women and representation demonstrating that women in the House of Representatives and state legislatures are more vigorous advocates for women's interests. The greatest differences are found in analyses of bill sponsorship and cosponsorship as these agenda-setting activities allow members to bring new issues and ideas to the legislative process (Kingdon 2005; Baumgartner and Jones 1993). Studies of women in Congress and the state legislatures demonstrate that women are more active sponsors and cosponsors of women's issue legislation on subjects ranging from social welfare concerns to women's rights (Osborn 2012; MacDonald and O'Brien 2011; Gerrity, Osborn, and Mendez 2007; Dodson 2006; Swers 2002, 2005; Wolbrecht 2002, 2000; Reingold 2000; Bratton and Haynie 1999; Thomas 1994; Saint-Germain 1989). These results hold even after accounting for party affiliation, constituency characteristics, and institutional position, including committee assignments and membership in the majority or minority party. Furthermore, women bring a unique perspective to committee deliberations and floor debate on issues because women are more likely to advocate for women's interests in committee, speak about women's issues on the floor, and invoke their authority as women and mothers in committee and floor debate (Rosenthal 1998; Shogan 2001; Cramer Walsh 2002; Levy, Tien, and Aved 2002; Norton 1995, 1999, 2002; Swers 2002; Dodson 2006; Pearson and Dancey 2010, 2011). Female legislators are also more likely to view women as a distinct element of their constituency and to feel a responsibility to represent the interests of women as a group (Rosenthal 1998; Reingold 1992, 2000; Carroll 2002; Dodson 2006). The increasing presence of women in Congress and state legislatures has also influenced the behavior of men: male legislators have increased their attention to women's issues as more women have entered the legislature (Wolbrecht 2002).

While the influence of gender identity on legislative behavior is well documented, the existence of these differences and the magnitude of the effects are mediated by the partisanship and ideology of the legislator, the position of women within the institution, and the contemporary political context. For example, in an analysis of legislative activity on women's issues in the 103rd and 104th Congresses, Swers (2002) found that both Republican and Democratic women were more likely to push proposals on social welfare issues when they were in the majority party and had access to the legislative agenda of the House. However, when Republicans gained the majority in the Republican Revolution that elected the 104th Congress, moderate Republican women reduced their activism on feminist issues. These women recognized that the political context of fiscal and social conservatism that ushered in the Republican majority would not support these issues. Therefore, they were better off pursuing other priorities that would not anger the social conservative base that helped the party win the majority and in turn alienate fellow Republican colleagues whose support they would need to achieve action on their policy initiatives (Swers 2002; see also Dodson 2006; and on state legislatures Osborn 2012; Reingold 2000).

Since the 1990s, the parties have continued to move apart on feminist issues such as abortion, and the overall ideological polarization between the parties in the House and Senate has steadily increased (Poole and Rosenthal 1997, 2007; Lee 2009). Thus, it is possible that in a Congress of more homogeneously conservative Republicans and liberal Democrats squaring off as members of partisan teams, the impact of gender on support for various types of women's issue legislation will be reduced or eliminated. Beyond ideology, women in the House of the 1990s were highly constrained by the policy jurisdiction of their committees and their relatively low seniority (Swers 2002; Dodson 2006). While seniority and committee position are important features of the Senate, senators have more committee assignments than House members, and procedural rights guaranteeing floor participation give senators more freedom to pursue policy priorities outside of their committee jurisdictions. The greater staff resources at their command and rules protecting the participation rights of individuals facilitate their efforts to make a mark on legislation regardless of their level of seniority. Thus, it is essential to examine how the unique institutional structure of the Senate and the more polarized political atmosphere of the contemporary Congress affect the desire of legislators to pursue policy preferences based on gender. In this chapter I analyze whether the impact of gender is overwhelmed by the fact that senators are policy generalists on partisan teams who must respond to the needs of a statewide constituency.

Alternatively, the importance of gender may be magnified in the Senate because of the power given to individuals. As a result, female senators can utilize their broad influence over policy to ensure consideration of the needs of women, children, and families.

A Theory of Legislative Entrepreneurship on Women's Issues in the Senate

On the basis of the theoretical arguments about the impact of gender on policy making in the Senate that I laid out in chapter 1, I expect that women will be more active proponents of women's issue legislation. Women's issue bills are defined as "bills that are particularly salient to women because they seek to achieve equality for women; they address women's special needs, such as women's health concerns or child care issues; or they confront issues with which women have traditionally been concerned in their role as caregivers, such as education, health care, or the protection of children" (Swers 2002).

The personal experiences of female senators as women and for some as mothers may make them more sensitive to the needs of women and more focused on examining how policies will impact the patterns of women's lives (Sapiro 1981; Phillips 1991, 1995, 1998; Mansbridge 1999; Dovi 2002). Moreover, candidate studies indicate that voters prefer female candidates to handle compassion issues including welfare, education, and health care (Huddy and Terkildsen 1993a, 1993b; Dolan 2004; Fridkin and Kenney 2009). Public opinion research demonstrating that social welfare issues such as health care and education are important drivers of the gender gap in voting behavior should heighten the interest of female legislators in these issues, particularly among Democrats as women voters are increasingly trending toward the Democratic Party (Kaufmann and Petrocik 1999; Box-Steffensmeier, De Boef, and Lin 2004; Norrander 2008). The perceived policy preferences of their electorate and voter stereotypes relating to gender and policy expertise shape senators' strategic calculations about what policies to champion. Thus, Democratic women should be particularly likely to engage in policy entrepreneurship on women's issues. Indeed, one staffer for a female Democrat asserted that even more than Democratic men, "most [Democratic] women get elected with a gender gap so their contract is weighted toward giving back to women. Democratic women on the campaign trail will talk more about choices and will move to more aggressively target women and the women's vote. There are certain white men that Democrats will never get. You need to know who your base is and how to feed them and who is gettable with votes and how to appeal to them."

Gender and Issue Saliency. The importance of gender as an influence on legislative behavior will vary with the saliency of gender to the policy debate. The more directly an issue can be connected to consequences for women as a group, the more likely it is that gender identity will spur female senators to activism. Issues such as Social Security and Medicare expose cleavages on social welfare policy that have defined differences between the Republican and Democratic parties since the New Deal (Carmines and Stimson 1989; Sundquist 1983; Lee 2008a, 2008b, 2009). The centrality of these issues on the congressional agenda encourages all senators to develop proposals on these issues and may reduce the importance of gender as a determinant of senators' engagement in these policy debates. By contrast, feminist initiatives such as bills concerning women's health, reproductive rights, pay equity, and child care subsidies have clear consequences for women as a group and directly invoke concerns about women's rights. Because of this connection women will be able to draw on their moral authority as women and/or mothers to build a coalition of support for these policies and to gain media attention and publicity for their initiatives. Moreover, other coalition leaders including bill sponsors, interest groups, and party leaders will be more likely to recruit women as sponsors and cosponsors of these initiatives to capitalize on their perceived credibility and expertise.

Gender differences arising from women's greater connection to feminist initiatives will be augmented by electoral incentives that steer senators away from engaging controversial issues. As Arnold (1990) notes, senators are often more concerned with avoiding blame for bad outcomes than claiming credit for policy innovations. Feminist issues, particularly abortion, are extremely contentious. Pro-choice groups are part of the core of the liberal base of Democratic activists, and pro-life forces are a key element of the social conservative base that supports the Republican Party. Both sides vigilantly monitor senators' actions on abortion and will pour activists and advertising into a state whenever senators take positions on the abortion issue. The potential for an overwhelming wave of negative publicity and the creation of campaign fodder for a future opponent means that most senators should limit themselves to voting on abortion issues that reach the Senate floor and should not want to push their own policy initiatives on abortion. Only senators in safe seats with very liberal or conservative constituencies and/or those with a personal connection to the issue based on shared gender identity should actively engage abortion politics. Abortion politics are routinely embroiled in high-stakes battles over the federal budget as legislative riders on appropriations bills, and they often snarl end game negotiations on omnibus legislation. Thus, President Obama's health plan was almost torpedoed by a policy rider concerning whether insurance policies in the new state exchanges could cover abortions because many of the people purchasing these plans would be receiving federal subsidies to buy insurance (MacGillis 2009; Brown and O'Connor 2009). Politically charged negotiations like these require the vigorous advocacy of senators with a personal commitment to the issue.

Gender, Women's Issues, and the Political Opportunity Structure of the Senate. The political opportunity structure of the Senate facilitates women's efforts to pursue policy preferences based on gender in several important ways. The multiple committee assignments and large staff controlled by senators give them the tools to incorporate a range of women's issues as part of their policy agendas if they choose (Sinclair 1989; Evans 1991; Baker 2001). The six-year term provides a longer time frame to develop a legislative record and the opportunity to engage national issues (Baker 2001; Levitt 1996; Thomas 1985). Moreover, procedural rules of the Senate protecting a senator's right to participate make it easier for senators to press their individual agendas and provide senators with intense preferences with the means to force consideration of their priorities by offering nongermane amendments, placing holds, and threatening filibusters (Sinclair 1989, 2002, 2009; Binder and Smith 1997; Evans and Lipinski 2005; Wawro and Schickler 2006; Smith 2010; Koger 2010; Bell 2011). As one Republican staffer explained, "In the Senate your legislative priorities start with the committees but you are not as constrained because there is no germaneness rule and no Rules committee . . . There is more daylight to run in. In the House if you want to get involved on the issue of refugees there is going to be someone there who has been working on it for years. In the Senate there is less opportunity for specializing and more opportunity for freelancing." Similarly, a staffer for a Republican woman maintained,

> In the House she was a minority in the minority as a woman and a moderate. She could introduce a lot of bills to try to get attention to issues but unless you were on the committee you needed to put together a big coalition to have influence. The Senate was very freeing for her. You can go down on the floor and talk for more than a minute about issues . . . Now she can't

> say anything in less than thirty minutes. In the Senate you can talk about what you want and introduce an amendment regardless of the topic on the floor. She has the freedom to legislate and to make a difference.

The desire to become a player on national issues is reinforced by senators' higher media profile in which media outlets are much more likely to turn to senators rather than House members as opinion leaders on a range of national issues (Baker 2001; Schiller 2000; Sellers 2010). As a Democratic staffer whose boss previously served in the House explained,

> When you move from the House to the Senate you have a broader constituency, you take on the issues of the state and are more of a national spokesperson representing the nation as a whole. He became a health expert after the Medicare Commission. Chairing the Agriculture Committee and cochairing the Medicare Commission got him on the talk shows, and he is invited to speak at a lot of health care events. In 1995 he was not a national figure. Now 10% of Americans probably know who he is. That is a lot for a senator.

At the same time, other institutional features of the Senate will limit the importance of gender as a guide to which senators engage with women's issues. The pressure to be generalists with a proposal on every issue may reduce the significance of gender as a predictor of advocacy for women's issues. Furthermore, while the Senate is no longer a club populated by whales and minnows in which junior members serve an apprenticeship and wait their turn to participate, there are still enduring norms of behavior (Rae and Campbell 2001; Caro 2002). The development of personal relationships is still very important for building coalitions, and senators compete with each other to establish themselves as the experts who must be consulted when policies are being developed on specific issues.

As senators work to define their legislative niche they must be cognizant of the legislative records of other senators who have carved out reputations and records of accomplishment on specific issues. The topography of policy turf is reinforced by the Senate's reliance on seniority to determine access to committee seats and leadership positions and the deference that is given to these committee leaders to initiate policy development on issues. A Democratic staffer explained, "There is a change from the LBJ era where the back row does not speak. Now they engage but are mindful of the pecking order. When you're a freshman you don't want to crystallize a bad opinion about you, there is no harm to being conservative. When you are on solid ground you can shine. In six years you need to make sure you have a record for constituents."

As relatively new members of the Senate club, women are beginning to acquire the party leadership positions and committee chairmanships associated with power in the Senate. Women elected in the 1990s and early 2000s hold committee leadership posts on important policy committees. A few women such as Patty Murray (D-WA), chair of the Democratic Senate Campaign Committee, and Kay Bailey Hutchison (R-TX), former head of the Republican Policy Committee and vice chair of the Republican caucus, achieved party leadership posts. However, many of the women are still junior members who must navigate the established reputations and legislative records of senior colleagues as they work to define a policy niche. Explaining the challenge of making a mark even when the senator has a personal interest in the issue, one Democratic staffer asserted, "Senator [—] and Senator [—] have been there forever. There are issues they think they own. You cannot presume to think you are entitled to an issue; you have to make your way up the ladder. If she wants to do something on child care and this is [—]'s issue, you get in the conference committee with seniority, and he will take it from her and make it his own, or she can try to bring him in on it." Similarly a Democratic staffer maintained, "Senator [—] thinks he owns VAWA [Violence Against Women Act] so even though [female senator] worked on it since law school, she cannot get into it here. They will put the big foot on you. If you ignore them then you are throwing a firecracker into the Senate. The chair of Judiciary is going to defer to [Senator] and take his bill and his suggestions for witnesses." Conflicts over policy turf are so widespread that the party leadership often has to step in to mediate. A Democratic leadership staffer explained, "[I]f you have seniority and have been attached to an issue for a long time, a newer person should respect the senior person's niche. The leadership has to help negotiate whose name is first on an amendment, who gets how much time at a press conference when there will only be three speakers and there are five people who have an absolute right to speak."

In addition to the committee and subcommittee leaders and more senior colleagues who are the gatekeepers for policy innovation on specific issues, a senator must also pay attention to the legislative agenda of their same-state colleague. As Schiller (2000, 2002) points out, same-state colleagues compete to develop a unique electoral coalition and to bring benefits home to the state. As a result they generally seek out different committee assignments and work to develop a distinctive legislative record. If one senator establishes a reputation as a leader on an issue such as defense policy, the media will naturally turn to that senator for expertise, and the state colleague will have to work even harder to get attention on that issue. Thus, staffers maintained that they paid close attention to the policy priorities of their state colleague. One Democratic staffer explained, "There is a presumption that you have dibs on the issues that are in your committee jurisdiction. If we introduce a bill that will go to his committee then we will let him know and know the rationale, that a constituent asked us to or it was a campaign issue." Schiller (2000) found that the problems born of a shared state constituency were aggravated for members of the same party. These senators felt more of an imperative to distinguish themselves on issues because their voting records were similar. Gender adds another dimension to the political calculus. Staffers contend that having two women of the same party in the delegation makes it more difficult for these same-state partisans to distinguish themselves from one another with voters, while staffers for senators in all-male same-party delegations expressed no gender-based concerns when discussing their relationships with the same-state colleague.

Gender and Party Messaging on Women's Issues. Finally, in planning their policy agendas, senators act both as individuals and as members of partisan teams. To improve their own electoral fortunes, senators will work to raise the party's standing with the public by offering proposals that will be popular with the party's voters and participating in party messaging activities (Cox and McCubbins 2005; Sellers 2010). Studies of issue ownership demonstrate that the Democratic Party owns many of the issues that fall under the rubric of women's issues, meaning the public trusts Democrats more than Republicans to handle policies related to issues like health care and education (Petrocik 1996; Petrocik, Benoit, and Hansen 2003; Sides 2006; Sellers 2010). Moreover, women's rights issues such as reproductive rights and pay equity have become increasingly associated with the Democratic Party, and feminist groups now make up a key element of the Democratic electoral base that provides the activists and enthusiasm to publicize Democratic proposals and get out the vote in elections (Wolbrecht 2000; Sanbonmatsu 2002b). The close electoral competition of recent years means that Democrats will want to highlight initiatives that attract women voters and mobilize their base. Because women's rights proposals mobilize Democratic activists and social welfare initiatives are a key component of the gender gap in which female voters increasingly favor the Democratic Party, all Democratic senators, male and female, should be more active proponents of women's issues than Republicans.

The alignment of women's issues with Democratic policy and electoral goals means that Democratic women who decide to focus on women's issues will find a receptive audience for their policy proposals on women's issues within the Democratic caucus. Furthermore, the moral authority female senators wield on women's issues increases their value as spokespersons for the party's messages on these issues (Sellers 2002, 2010). By participating in party message events such as press conferences, floor debate, and television interviews, women can help their party caucus and raise their own profile with the media, constituents, and fellow Democratic senators.

For Republican women, the decision to promote policies related to women's issues is not as uniformly beneficial. Women's issues generally do not incorporate core Republican principles of reduced government spending, lower taxes, elimination of regulations on business, and strong defense. Therefore, in comparison with the Democratic legislative agenda, women's issues do not occupy a central place on the Republican Party's policy platform and will not provide as many opportunities for credit claiming and advancing one's policy goals. Additionally, if a Republican woman takes a stand on feminist issues by promoting increased spending on family planning or supporting policies to address employment discrimination, she risks alienating social conservative activists who are a core element of the Republican activist base. Such a stand could create electoral risks at home, including a potentially more conservative primary challenger, and will alienate fellow Republican senate colleagues whose support is needed for advancement of the senator's policy initiatives.

Since women's issues are not a primary component of the Republican policy agenda, there is a narrower window for Republican women to utilize their gender to promote party messages and advance their own media profile and position within the caucus. Like Democrats, Republicans are cognizant of the gender gap in voting and the increased support of women voters for the Democratic Party. Republicans work to identify policies that target women voters who support Republicans, particularly white, suburban, married women (Norrander 2008). They also want to counter Democratic efforts to portray Republican policies as anti-women and the Republican Party as a white male bastion. These more defensive goals provide Republican women with a more limited set of opportunities to raise their own senatorial profile by presenting a more diverse face for the party in media appearances and messaging events, demonstrating how Republican proposals help women, and defending the party against Democratic attacks that Republican policies will hurt women.

In sum, I expect Republican and Democratic women will be more active proponents of women's issue legislation than their male partisan colleagues. However, the existence and magnitude of these gender differences will vary with the saliency of gender to the policy debate on issues. Moreover, Democratic women will be the most active proponents of women's issue initiatives because these proposals are more associated with the Democratic Party, while Republican women may experience conflict between their gender-based preferences and the policy positions of the party. Important features of the political opportunity structure of the Senate, ranging from permissive procedural rights to force consideration of one's priorities to the need to be generalists with a policy agenda that appeals to a heterogeneous state electorate, will both facilitate and inhibit the emergence of gender differences in policy activity. Finally women's desire to pursue women's issue legislation will be enhanced by party messaging strategies that seek to capitalize on female senators' moral authority as women to sell party initiatives and defend the party's reputation with women voters. Because of voters' greater association of women's issues with the Democratic Party, these messaging opportunities will be more plentiful for Democratic women.

Advocacy for Women's Interests in the Senate: Trends in Sponsorship and Cosponsorship of Women's Issue Legislation

To examine the influence of gender on the decision of senators to promote women's issue initiatives, I analyze the sponsorship and cosponsorship records of senators on a range of women's issues. I developed a database of women's issue legislation, by reading the bill summaries of all bills excluding resolutions sponsored by senators in the 107th and 108th Congresses.[1] As previously stated, women's issue bills are defined as bills that are particularly salient to women because they seek to achieve equality for women; they address women's special needs, such as women's health concerns or child care issues; or they confront issues with which women have traditionally been concerned in their role as caregivers, such as education, health care, or the protection of children (Swers 2002).

Across the two Congresses, senators offered a large number of proposals on women's issues, with ninety-four senators sponsoring 991 women's issue bills in the 107th Congress and ninety-eight senators offering 969 women's issue initiatives in the 108th Congress. Bills related to women's issues constituted a large part of senators' agendas as 30% of the stand-alone bills (excluding resolutions) offered in each Congress concerned women's issues.[2] Indeed, on average, senators sponsored thirty-two stand-alone bills in the 107th Congress, and they sponsored a mean of ten women's issue bills. Similarly, in the 108th Congress senators authored a mean of thirty bills and offered on average ten women's issue initiatives. These proposals span the range of the ideological spectrum, including bills that expand various social welfare benefits and those that seek to restrict eligibility for specific programs or expand the role of the private sector in the provision of social services. The fact that senators were universally active in offering initiatives on women's issues confirms the notion that senators are generalists who want to have proposals on any issue that interests constituents, raises their national profile, serves their re-election goals, or taps their vision of good public policy. By contrast, in an earlier study of legislative activity on women's issues in the House of Representatives, I found that only about 50% of representatives sponsored a women's issue bill (Swers 2002).

Dividing the women's issue bills by subject area in figures 2.1 and 2.2, it is clear that social welfare issues dominate the agendas of senators. Government spending on social welfare programs such as health care and education has constituted a key fault line between the Republican and Democratic parties since the New Deal (Carmines and Stimson 1989; Burnham 1970; Lee 2009; Bradbury, Davidson, and Evans 2008). The perennial importance of social welfare concerns to voters encourages senators to develop legislative proposals on these issues. Moreover, when issues become presidential priorities, it increases the saliency of these policies with the media and the public and heightens the competition among the parties to develop policy initiatives in response to the president's agenda (Lee 2008a, 2009). Thus, President Bush's focus on development of the No Child Left Behind education law in the 107th Congress and his campaign to create a prescription drug benefit within Medicare in the 108th Congress further sparked the interest of senators in these issues.

Among the women's issue bills, health care issues attracted by far the most legislative attention. Senators offered 503 health-related bills in the 107th Congress and proposed 515 health bills in the 108th Congress. Medicare and Medicaid are linchpins of the American social safety net, and these programs constitute an increasing portion of entitlement

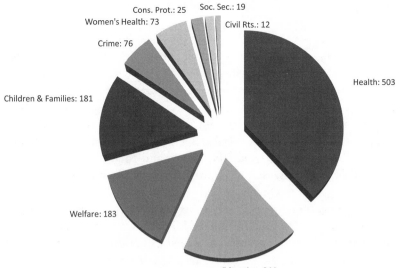

FIGURE 2.1 Women's Issue Bill Sponsorship, 107th Congress

Note: Ninety-four senators sponsored 991 women's issue bills in the 107th Congress. Some bills fall into multiple categories. For example, a bill addressing the kidnapping of children would be included in the crime category and children and families. However, targeted bills on women's health issues like breast cancer are only in the women's health category and are not included in the general health category.

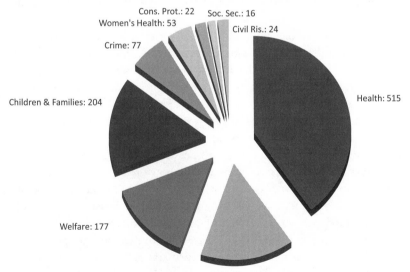

FIGURE 2.2 Women's Issue Bill Sponsorship, 108th Congress

Note: Ninety-eight senators sponsored 969 women's issue bills in the 108th Congress. Some bills fall into multiple categories. For example, a bill addressing the kidnapping of children would be included in the crime category and children and families. However, targeted bills on women's health issues like breast cancer are only in the women's health category and are not included in the general health category.

spending. Senators sought to expand benefits, change funding formulas, and protect particular elements of their constituencies such as rural hospitals or long-term care services. Senators also used their bills to influence the debate on the expansion of Medicare to include prescription drug coverage, a program that ultimately passed in the 108th Congress. Health insurance reform was another prominent area of contention as Congress had spent several years sparring over a Patients' Bill of Rights. Senators also offered various bills to expand funding for medical research on specific diseases, to improve veterans' health care programs, and, in the wake of 9/11, to combat bioterrorism.

Beyond health care, issues related to education, children and families (non-education), and welfare received the most attention as the number of proposals on these subjects ranged from 177 welfare bills in the 108th Congress to 244 education bills in the 107th Congress. President Bush's focus on education and the major reforms embodied in the No Child Left Behind Act made education policy a popular focus of senators' attention. Efforts to reauthorize welfare reform spurred many senators to offer reform proposals as well as bills related to housing, food stamps, and other benefits for the poor. Bills in the children and families category incorporate a range of initiatives from child tax credits to legislation focused on children's health, child support collection, and protection of children against crime.

Approximately one-third of members offered bills related to women's health and bills concerning crime issues. Women's health bills included efforts to expand health coverage and services for pregnant women and mothers; funding for research on diseases that predominantly affect women, such as breast cancer and osteoporosis; expansion of coverage for preventive services related to women's health, such as mammograms and pap smears; and bills related to abortion and contraception. Among the 126 women's health bills offered across the two congresses, there were twenty-two bills sponsored by Republican men that sought to restrict abortion or impose bans on human cloning and stem cell research. Crime legislation focused on such issues as domestic violence, rape, protection of children, and punishment of crimes against women and children. Finally, less than 20% of members proposed bills related to Social Security, consumer protection (largely on issues related to children and health care), and civil rights/economic equality. The civil rights/economic equality bills dealt with issues such as employment discrimination, equal pay, and expansion of benefits to domestic partners.

Gender, Party, and the Dynamics of Women's Issue Bill Sponsorship

Examining women's issue bill sponsorship by gender and party in table 2.1, reveals some interesting patterns. Democrats are more active sponsors of women's issue legislation across both congresses. Support for an expanded social safety net is one of the core tenets uniting Democratic legislators and activists. The Democratic Party's association with issues like health care and education in the minds of voters means that Democrats have an additional incentive to capitalize on this issue ownership by offering more proposals on these issues to enhance the party's standing with the electorate (Petrocik 1996; Petrocik, Benoit, and Hansen 2003; Sides 2006; Sellers 2010). Staffers easily identified Democratic senators as national leaders whose names are synonymous with certain social welfare and women's rights policies and who must be consulted in any serious discussion on these topics. For example, staffers highlighted Democrats Ted Kennedy (MA), Hillary Clinton (NY), John Rockefeller (WV), Tom Harkin (IA), and Ron Wyden (OR) as leaders on health care. Chris Dodd (CT) was often cited for his work on child care and family leave, and Barbara Boxer (CA) and Patty Murray (WA) are leaders on women's health, particularly reproductive rights.

Fewer Republicans were mentioned as leaders on social welfare issues, and many of these senators have occupational backgrounds in these fields or were senior members with committee leadership positions on these issues. Thus, medical doctors Bill Frist (TN) and Tom Coburn (OK) were often mentioned as leaders on health care. Judd Gregg (NH) helped negotiate the No Child Left Behind Education law as ranking member of the Health, Education, Labor, and Pensions (HELP) Committee, and long-serving senator Orin Hatch (UT) helped craft the State Children's Health Insurance Program (SCHIP), a health insurance program for low-income children. Indeed, comparing the mean numbers of women's issue bills sponsored by senators we see that across both congresses, Democrats sponsor almost twice as many women's issue bills as Republican men. The relatively weaker interest of Republicans in social welfare legislation and women's issues more broadly was confirmed by one Republican staffer who noted that

> women's issues are not Republican issues. Republicans do not want to work on these issues. The HELP Committee is not a sexy committee for Republicans. It is unheard of that within eight years you can move up to the chairmanship of a commit-

tee the way that Enzi [Mike Enzi (R-WY)] did on HELP. For Republicans, Banking, Finance, and Appropriations where you can shovel tons of money back to your state, especially when we were in a time of surplus, are the committees to be on.

Another staffer to a Republican senator who left the committee echoed this sentiment declaring, "Going on HELP was a mistake. It is a constituency committee with the wrong constituents, education and labor."

Focusing more specifically on gender, among Democrats, on average, men and women sponsored an equivalent number of women's issue bills in the 107th Congress, when Democrats controlled the majority for most of that Congress. However, as minority party members in the 108th Congress, female Democrats sponsored more women's issue bills than male Democrats, sponsoring a mean of 14.7 bills, in comparison

Table 2.1 107th and 108th Congresses: Women's Issue Bill Sponsorship by Gender and Party

	Mean	Standard Deviation	Median	Minimum	Maximum
		107th Congress			
Democrats (n = 51)	13.1	9.5	12	0	38
Republicans (n = 49)	6.6	6.9	5	0	29
Democratic Men (n = 41)	12.9	9.6	12	0	38 Rockefeller (WV)
Democratic Women (n = 10)	12	9.2	13.8	5	35 Feinstein (CA)
Republican Men (n = 46)	5.5	5.3	4	0	24 Frist (TN)
Republican Women (n = 3)	23.7	7.6	27	15	29 Collins (ME)
		108th Congress			
Democrats (n = 49)	11.3	7.9	10	0	37
Republicans (n = 51)	7.9	7.1	5	0	28
Democratic Men (n = 40)	10.5	8.3	8	0	37 Bingaman (NM)
Democratic Women (n = 9)	14.7	4.6	14	10	22 Clinton (NY)
Republican Men (n = 46)	7.3	6.6	5	0	28 DeWine (OH)
Republican Women (n = 5)	13.2	10.5	13	1	28 Snowe (ME)

with an average of 10.5 bills among Democratic men. Turning to gender differences among Republicans, Republican women defy expectations about partisan activity on women's issues. While Republican men sponsor the smallest number of women's issue bills across the two congresses, on average Republican women sponsor more women's issue bills than Democratic men, and Republican women sponsored the largest number of women's issue bills in the 107th Congress.

It is difficult to generalize about the behavior of Republican women because so few serve in the Senate, three in the 107th Congress and five in the 108th Congress. As of this writing, the number of Republican women in the 112th Congress remains at five. Moreover, two of the Republican women, Susan Collins (ME) and Olympia Snowe (ME), are among the most moderate Republican senators. However, sorting senators by their DW-NOMINATE scores as an indicator of ideology, the Republican senators closest to Snowe and Collins are Lincoln Chafee (RI) and Arlen Specter (PA).[3] Across the two congresses, Collins and Snowe sponsored more women's issue bills than Chafee and Specter. Thus, Collins sponsored twenty-nine (107th) and eighteen (108th) women's issue bills, and Snowe sponsored twenty-seven (107th) and twenty-eight (108th) women's issue bills, while Specter sponsored ten (107th) and eleven (108th) women's issue bills and Chafee sponsored four (107th and 108th) women's issue bills. These numbers suggest that gender does have an impact on the priorities of these moderate Republicans beyond their more liberal ideology.

Gender, Issue Saliency, and Legislating on Feminist Issues. To examine whether gender differences in legislative behavior increase when policies have a direct connection to women as a group and/or issues of women's rights are more central features of the policy environment, table 2.2 displays the number of feminist bills that senators sponsored in the 107th and 108th Congresses. Among the over nine hundred women's issue bills sponsored in each Congress, approximately 10% of these bills can be characterized as feminist legislation because they focus their benefits directly on women as a group or they seek to achieve role equity or role change for women (Gelb and Palley 1996). As Gelb and Palley explain in their book *Women and Public Policies: Reassessing Gender Politics*, "role equity issues are those policies that extend rights now enjoyed by other groups (men, minorities) to women. Role change issues appear to produce change in the dependent female role of wife, mother, and homemaker, holding out the potential of greater sexual freedom and independence in a variety of contexts" (Gelb and Palley 1996, 6). Forty

Table 2.2 107th and 108th Congresses: Feminist Bill Sponsorship by Gender and Party

	Mean	Standard Deviation	Median	Minimum	Maximum
		107th Congress			
Democrats (*n* = 51)	1.7	2.2	1	0	8
Republicans (*n* = 49)	.5	1.6	0	0	2
Democratic Men (*n* = 41)	1.6	2.4	0	0	8 Wellstone (MN)
Democratic Women (*n* = 10)	1.9	1.4	2	0	5 Boxer (CA)
Republican Men (*n* = 46)	.2	.5	0	0	2 Specter (PA), Chafee (RI)
Republican Women (*n* = 3)	4.7	5.5	2	1	11 Snowe (ME)
		108th Congress			
Democrats (*n* = 49)	1.4	1.7	1	0	6
Republicans (*n* = 51)	.8	2.1	0	0	14
Democratic Men (*n* = 40)	.98	1.5	0	0	5 Daschle (SD)
Democratic Women (*n* = 9)	3.1	1.8	3	0	6 Boxer (CA)
Republican Men (*n* = 46)	.52	.98	0	0	4 Hatch (UT)
Republican Women (*n* = 5)	3.6	5.9	1	0	14 Snowe (ME)

senators sponsored 109 feminist bills in the 107th Congress, and forty-one senators sponsored 110 feminist bills in the 108th Congress.

Feminist proposals cover a wide range of issues including child care, family leave, domestic violence, employment discrimination, equal pay, abortion, health and welfare services for specific groups of women (e.g., pregnant, low-income), and expansion of coverage for and research on diseases that particularly impact women such as breast and cervical cancer and osteoporosis. As expected, the vast majority of these bills are sponsored by Democrats. Democratic senators sponsored eighty-six (79%) of the 109 feminist bills offered in the 107th Congress and sixty-eight (62%) of the 110 feminist bills sponsored in the 108th Congress. Across the two congresses, moderate Republican Olympia Snowe (ME) was the most active sponsor of feminist legislation, sponsoring eleven feminist bills in the 107th Congress and fourteen feminist initiatives in the 108th Congress. Snowe's proposals focused on an array of issues including women's health proposals regarding insurance coverage of contraceptives and preventive care for breast cancer and osteoporosis, support for women-owned businesses, and child support collection. Snowe's advocacy for these feminist causes has helped her win the support of Maine's female Democratic voters and build a winning electoral coalition.

Assumptions about majority party status and agenda control lead us to expect that senators will increase their sponsorship activity when they are in the majority and offer fewer bills when they are in the minority and no longer driving the legislative agenda. This pattern holds true for Democrat men and Republican men and women. However, the activism of Democratic women on feminist issues intensified when they were in the minority trying to protect feminist causes from the Republican Party's more socially conservative agenda. Thus, when Democrats controlled the majority in the 107th Congress, male and female Democrats sponsored a similar number of feminist bills, with Democrat men sponsoring a mean of 1.6 feminist proposals and Democratic women initiating an average of 1.9 feminist bills. Since women constitute a smaller proportion of the Democratic caucus, this translated into sixty-seven feminist bills sponsored by Democratic men and nineteen feminist bills sponsored by Democratic women. Of these bills, nine (13%) of the feminist proposals offered by Democratic men saw some legislative action ranging from committee hearings to passage into law, while only one of the bills (5%) sponsored by a Democratic woman moved beyond committee referral.

By contrast, as minority party members in the 108th Congress, Democratic women increased their activism on feminist causes while Democratic men reduced their attention to these issues. Thus, Democratic women sponsored a mean of 3.1 feminist bills, yielding a total of twenty-eight feminist initiatives sponsored by Democratic women compared with a mean of .98 bills for Democratic men, resulting in forty feminist proposals. Four (14%) of the feminist bills sponsored by Democratic women saw legislative action in comparison with only one (3%) of the feminist initiatives offered by Democratic men.

The feminist bills sponsored by senators cover a diverse range of feminist issues. However, some interesting patterns emerge across party and gender. Legislation concerning violence against women and children, such as bills on sexual assault and domestic violence, made up the largest proportion of the feminist bills offered by Democratic men in both congresses and by Republican men when they were in the majority in the 108th Congress. Twenty-eight percent of the sixty-seven feminist bills Democratic men offered in the 107th Congress and 35% of the forty feminist bills they proposed in the 108th Congress concerned policies related to violence against women. Similarly, 46% of the twenty-four feminist initiatives authored by Republican men in the 108th Congress focused on issues of violence against women.

The proposals offered by Democratic and Republican men were a mix of bills providing health and welfare–related services to victims of violence and bills focused on criminal procedure and punishment, such as DNA evidence, rape kits, and sex offender registries. The bills of Democratic men leaned more toward initiatives offering services to victims, while Republican men were more likely to focus their proposals on questions of criminal justice. The large number of bills offered on issues of violence against women represents a striking evolution of these issues on the national agenda as problems such as domestic violence and date rape that used to be considered private matters have become more accepted targets of public policy (Weldon 2002; Meier and Nicholson-Crotty 2006). Democratic male senators were also particularly active sponsors of child care legislation such as grants for child care centers, increased funding for child care for low-income women, and expansions of tax credits for child and dependent care. Almost 20% of the feminist bills they offered in each Congress dealt with child care.

Like their male colleagues, female senators sponsored a wide range of feminist bills. Among Democratic and Republican women, the greatest area of focus concerned women's health issues including expansion of coverage and research on specific diseases such as breast and cervical cancer and the more controversial issues of abortion and contraception. Thus, almost 50% of the feminist bills sponsored by Democratic women in each Congress focused on these women's health issues. Interestingly, Democratic women offered more bills concerning access to family planning services, emergency contraception, and abortion during the Republican controlled 108th Congress. Twenty-five percent of the twenty-four feminist proposals by Democratic women in the 108th Congress concerned issues related to abortion and contraception, compared with only 11% of the nineteen feminist bills these women sponsored in the 107th Congress. It appears Democratic women were trying to protect reproductive rights against a newly invigorated socially conservative majority that wanted to cut funding for family planning services and was pressing forward with new restrictions on abortion, most prominently the Partial Birth Abortion Act. Democratic women focused most of their reproductive rights bills on contraception in an effort to move public attention away from partial birth abortion to the family planning services that are more broadly supported by the public (Wilcox and Carr 2009).

Ideas of stronger personal commitment and enhanced moral authority figured prominently in staffers' explanations of senators' bill sponsorship activities on feminist issues. When asked about women's issues and gender differences in legislating, staffers most frequently pointed to women's health concerns. According to staff, women frequently collaborate across party lines to promote legislation expanding research on diseases such as breast cancer and osteoporosis because they have a special understanding of and interest in women's health needs. Abortion was frequently cited as an issue where women, particularly Democratic women, are especially active. Staffers claimed that the women care more about this issue and that increased commitment makes them more likely to take a stand or lead the fight on an issue that many politicians would prefer to avoid because it is so polarizing and controversial. Moreover, some staffers asserted that male senators are more likely to defer to the women on this issue and look to them for guidance because they believe that as women they have more at stake and more moral authority on the issue. Thus, the direct association of gender with issues related to women's health and reproductive rights makes it easier for women to claim ownership of these issues.

In contrast to the feminist bills that were sponsored by all groups of senators and encompassed a wide range of issues, only a small minority of socially conservative male Republican senators sponsored anti-feminist legislation. Eight Republican men offered fourteen anti-feminist bills in the 107th Congress, and seven Republican men proposed eleven anti-feminist initiatives in the 108th Congress. Anti-feminist legislation seeks to inhibit role change as a threat to the traditional family (Gelb and Palley 1996). The vast majority of these bills, twenty-two of the twenty-five proposals across the two congresses, sought to add restrictions on abortion. Senators also offered bills to curtail affirmative action and restrict access to family and medical leave. Senators pursuing anti-feminist legislation achieved their greatest success in the 108th Congress, when the Partial Birth Abortion Act and the Unborn Victims of Violence Act, which increased penalties for criminals who harm an unborn child, both passed into law. As priorities of the Republican caucus, these two proposals were cosponsored by almost the entire Republican caucus.

The trends in senators' sponsorship activity support the notion that senators are generalists seeking to have a finger in every pot rather than specialists concentrating in a narrow area of policy. While almost all senators offer women's issue bills, Republican women are much more active sponsors of women's issue legislation than are Republican men. In comparison with Democratic men, Democratic women increased their sponsorship activity as minority party members in the 108th Congress. This increased activism may reflect Democratic women's enhanced desire to protect their favored social welfare programs and feminist causes against the more socially and fiscally conservative efforts of the new Republican majority.

Gender and Cosponsorship: Taking Positions and
Signaling Support for Women's Issues

In addition to sponsoring their own legislation, senators can promote their support for women's issues by cosponsoring women's issue initiatives. Through cosponsorship senators can advertise their support for women's interests to voters, donors, and interest group supporters. By cosponsoring legislation, senators also signal their policy preferences on these social welfare and women's rights issues to other senators. The gender differences in cosponsorship activity in tables 2.3 and 2.4 are quite striking. It is clear that Democratic women are the most active cosponsors of women's issue bills across both congresses. Thus, Democratic women use their cosponsorship activity to reinforce their commitment to these issues with voters and to signal other legislators about the saliency of women's issues to their own legislative agendas. By contrast, the cosponsorship activity of Republican women changed markedly between the two congresses. In the 107th Congress, the cosponsorship behavior of Republican women is similar to that of Democratic men, with Republican women cosponsoring on average as many or more bills than Democratic men across issues. By the 108th Congress, with Republican women serving in the majority and more conservative women elected, the cosponsorship activity of Republican women moved closer to their fellow partisans, falling between Democratic men and Republican men in most policy areas.

Focusing on specific policies, the greatest gender differences in cosponsorship occur on the general health bills. In comparison with Democratic men, Democratic women cosponsored on average twenty more health bills in the 107th Congress (62.7 vs. 42.4) and twenty-eight more health bills in the 108th Congress (71.8 vs. 43.4). Similarly, on average, Republican women cosponsored more health care legislation than Republican men across both congresses, and they cosponsored more health bills than Democratic men in the 107th Congress. Republican

Table 2.3 107th and 108th Congresses: Women's Issue Bill Cosponsorship by Gender and Party

	Mean	Standard Deviation	Median	Minimum	Maximum
		107th Congress			
Democrats (n = 51)	86.4	38.3	80	13	176
Republicans (n = 49)	39.9	26.5	34	6	136
Democratic Men (n = 41)	80.1	35.9	75	13	160 Johnson (SD)
Democratic Women (n = 10)	112.4	38.4	104.5	75	176 Landrieu (LA)
Republican Men (n = 46)	36.4	21.4	33	6	98 Hutchinson (AR)
Republican Women (n = 3)	92.3	46.8	98	43	136 Collins (ME)
		108th Congress			
Democrats (n = 49)	87.7	44.6	78	7	176
Republicans (n = 51)	38.7	20.7	38	10	112
Democratic Men (n = 40)	79	42	73	7	168 Kennedy (MA)
Democratic Women (n = 9)	126.3	35.8	115	70	176 Murray (WA)
Republican Men (n = 46)	36.5	18	35	10	85 Smith (OR)
Republican Women (n = 5)	58.2	34.3	51	22	112 Collins (ME)

women cosponsored a mean of thirty-five more health bills than Republican men in the 107th Congress (54.3 vs. 19.4) and sixteen more health bills than their male partisans in the 108th Congress (34.6 vs. 18.8). The gender differences in cosponsorship of health bills are striking when one considers that health care was the dominant focus of women's issue legislation across the two congresses, with over five hundred bills introduced on the subject in each congressional session. Health care is a central focus of partisan strife over the role of government and the dimensions of the social safety net in the United States. Moreover, such dramatic gender differences do not emerge in cosponsorship activity in other women's issue areas that attracted significant legislative attention. Thus, gender differences in cosponsorship of education bills are small, particularly in the 107th Congress, when the Senate considered the No Child Left Behind Act.[4]

In addition to general health bills, cosponsorship activity on women's

Table 2.4 107th and 108th Congresses: Feminist Bill Cosponsorship by Gender and Party

	Mean	Standard Deviation	Median	Minimum	Maximum
		107th Congress			
Democrats (n = 51)	15.7	9.4	14	0	41
Republicans (n = 49)	3.5	5	2	0	25
Democratic Men (n = 41)	13.6	8.1	13	0	35 Corzine (NJ)
Democratic Women (n = 10)	24.1	9.8	22.5	10	41 Murray (WA)
Republican Men (n = 46)	2.7	2.8	2	0	11 DeWine (OH)
Republican Women (n = 3)	17	11.4	22	4	25 Collins (ME)
		108th Congress			
Democrats (n = 49)	17.5	11.5	15	1	52
Republicans (n = 51)	3.7	3.6	3	0	18
Democratic Men (n = 40)	14.8	9.7	12.5	1	38 Corzine (NJ)
Democratic Women (n = 9)	29.4	11.6	32	14	52 Murray (WA)
Republican Men (n = 46)	3	2.6	2	0	11 Specter (PA)
Republican Women (n = 5)	10	5.8	7	4	18 Collins (ME)

health bills reveals several interesting trends. While members sponsored relatively few women's health bills (seventy-three in the 107th Congress and fifty-three in the 108th Congress) in comparison with other issues like general health, education, and welfare, there are substantial gender differences in support for these bills. Democratic women cosponsored an average of eight more women's health bills than Democratic men in the 107th Congress (14.2 vs. 6.1) and seven more women's health bills than their male partisan colleagues in the 108th Congress (12 vs. 4.6). Among Republicans, women's health bills are the one issue area where Republican men on average cosponsored more legislation in the 108th Congress than Democratic men and Republican women (a mean of 5.6 bills cosponsored by Republican men compared with 4.8 by Republican women and 4.6 by Democratic men). This disparity is due to the Republican Party's focus on antiabortion legislation in the 108th Congress. Legislation banning partial birth abortion and protecting unborn victims of violence by increasing penalties for criminals who harm an unborn child while perpetrating a crime were high priorities for social conservatives. Almost the entire Republican caucus cosponsored one or both of these bills, and both were passed into law.

Looking at cosponsorship of feminist legislation in table 2.4, women of both parties cosponsored more feminist legislation than their male partisan colleagues did. Democratic women cosponsored the most feminist bills across the two congresses, a mean of twenty-four bills in the 107th Congress and a mean of twenty-nine bills in the 108th Congress. Differences in cosponsorship activity among male and female Democrats are larger when Democrats were in the minority, with Democratic women cosponsoring an average of ten more feminist bills than Democratic men in the 107th Congress and fourteen more bills than Democratic men in the 108th Congress. In support for feminist legislation, Republican women are more similar to Democratic men than their male Republican colleagues, cosponsoring slightly more feminist bills than Democratic men in the 107th Congress and slightly fewer bills than Democratic men in the 108th Congress. Meanwhile, Republican men are the most prolific cosponsors of anti-feminist legislation as thirty of the forty-six Republican men cosponsored an anti-feminist bill in the 107th Congress. With the Partial Birth Abortion Act and Unborn Victims of Violence Act as party priorities in the 108th Congress, only five moderate Republican senators, Ted Stevens (R-AK), Olympia Snowe (R-ME), Susan Collins (R-ME), Arlen Specter (R-PA), and Lincoln Chafee (R-RI), did not cosponsor an anti-feminist bill.

Overall, the empirical data on senators' sponsorship and cosponsorship activities on women's issues paints a picture of Democratic activism. Democratic men and women are more prolific sponsors of women's issue legislation than are Republican men. The small contingent of Republican women behave more like Democrats in their sponsorship of women's issue and feminist bills. On average, Democratic men and women sponsored an equivalent amount of women's issue and feminist legislation when the party controlled the legislative agenda in the 107th Congress. However, as minority party members in the 108th Congress, Democratic women sponsored slightly more women's issue and feminist bills than their male colleagues sponsored. It is possible that Democratic men realized these issues were not a priority in a Republican-controlled Congress and moved on to other policy areas. Alternatively, Democratic women may have increased their activism in response to an increasingly conservative Republican agenda on social issues ranging from general health care to abortion. Indeed, in the

108th Congress there was an increase in the number of feminist proposals sponsored by Democratic women that focused on abortion and contraception, reflecting the efforts of Democratic women to counter conservative Republican proposals to restrict reproductive rights. Gender differences are even more pronounced in senators' cosponsorship activity as across both congresses, Democratic and Republican women are much more active cosponsors of women's issue and feminist legislation than are their male colleagues. Democratic women were the most active cosponsors of these initiatives across both congresses.

Explaining Women Senators' Greater Activism on Women's Issues

The patterns of sponsorship and cosponsorship activity demonstrate that female senators are more likely to include women's issues in their legislative agenda. Interviews with Senate staff suggest that women's greater activism on these issues stems from a variety of factors including personal commitment and connection to the issues, the desire of coalition leaders to capitalize on women's perceived expertise, and party messaging strategies that utilize women senators to reach out to women voters and enhance the party reputation on these issues.

Personal Commitment and Connection to Women's Interests. A connection to a group's concerns based on personal experience and a desire to give voice to the group's interests underlie calls for expanded representation of women and minorities in government (Phillips 1991; Mansbridge 1999). Staffers generally agree that commitment to issues and willingness to engage in vigorous advocacy often stems from having personal experience with an issue. As one Democratic staffer put it, "you are passionate and eloquent about what you know well. You start at tier II without personal experience, a vested personal interest, and an understanding beyond constituency interest." Given the importance of personal experience as a catalyst for senators' legislative interests and an important tie in the representational relationship, a Democratic leadership staffer explained that "the women have a more innate sense of women's issues and how issues affect women because they deal with them in their own lives and families." Echoing this sentiment another Democratic staffer said, "Personal interests and experience from their own lives affect[] what they legislate. They [the women senators] recognize the pressures women face and share that point of view. They champion issues concerning women and kids. Hutchison [R-TX] and Landrieu [D-LA] adopted children, and they are leaders on those issues.

They are not altruistic in choosing to do these issues; it is based on their life experience."

This gendered life experience can make women legislators more sensitive to the problems faced by female constituents and more willing to take up those causes and expend political capital advocating for a legislative solution. Thus, a Democratic staffer noted that Blanche Lincoln (D-AR), often in cooperation with fellow committee member Olympia Snowe (R-ME), has spent years leveraging her Finance Committee seat to expand the child tax credit and the child and dependent care credit and to make these credits refundable for low-income families.

> Arkansas has a high poverty rate and this issue is personal for her. . . . I remember one exchange in the Finance Committee markup when she and Santorum [R-PA] were in a debate about the need for refundability of the child tax credit. She was saying about how she just went shopping for her kids for back to school and she had to get jeans for her kids and new tires on her car and washing powder and low-income families with kids have these same expenses with less money.

Similarly another Democratic staffer said, "Lincoln is not an oratorical genius or a celebrity but on the floor speaking about this issue she was the face and the voice of these parents and children who needed the tax code to be more decent to poor families."

Personal commitment to an issue drives senators to vigorous advocacy and increases their willingness to make their support for legislation contingent on the inclusion of women's interests in legislation. Thus, Olympia Snowe (R-ME), a moderate Republican and often a swing vote on high-profile policy initiatives, has utilized her status as a pivotal voter to extract concessions for women's interests. As one Republican staffer explained,

> Snowe's issues are based on her history. Breast cancer research funding and availability of mammograms are important to her. Her mom died of breast cancer when she was six or seven. She got into genetic nondiscrimination in insurance coverage because there was a woman in Maine, Bonnie, who had a large number of female relations with breast cancer and she had daughters, and she wanted to be tested and have her daughters tested, but she knew if her insurance company found out she would not be able to afford insurance. Snowe said she would not vote for

> managed care legislation unless they put in a provision on ge-
> netic nondiscrimination and Frist [R-TN] and Nickles [R-OK]
> [the Republican majority whip] helped her. . . . When they were
> doing the Bush tax cut, she was a pivotal vote and she wanted
> the child care tax credit. Bill Thomas [R-CA] [the Republican
> House Ways and Means Chair] would call and come into the
> office screaming because he did not want to include it. Grassley
> [R-IA] [the Finance Committee chair] and Breaux [D-LA] were
> the conferees and on her side so that helped. [President] Bush
> had to call Thomas and tell him to take it.

Another argument for increasing women's representation in government is that women bring a different perspective to legislative deliberations in which they think more about the consequences of policies for
women and children (Phillips 1991; Mansbridge 1999). Thus, Senator
Lisa Murkowski (R-AK) maintains that she brings a unique perspective
to the evolving debate on education reform:

> When I came to Congress, NCLB [No Child Left Behind Educa-
> tion Act] had just passed. I looked at it as a former head of the
> PTA in my son's school. This is where I got my political start, on
> the PTA. I got on HELP to focus on NCLB and not just look at
> the law and think about meeting standards of adequate yearly
> progress. I was the only mother of kids in a Title I school on the
> committee. My kids were in a Title I school and I had been in
> the school and met with the teachers and the principals. It is not
> just dispassionate standards of adequate yearly progress. I can
> show passion and understanding because it impacted my family
> and kids . . . Women are living a different reality and offering
> that perspective. (Murkowski 2010).

Another Democratic staffer suggested that a common perspective
as women and mothers leads the female senators to work together to
advocate for the needs of children and families.

> The big thing is they bring a woman's perspective to the table,
> and most of them bring a mom's perspective too. The women
> have worked together for environmental standards for children's
> health such as asbestos in schools and arsenic in water because
> the women will worry about the vulnerable populations, kids,
> and what the impact on their health will be from exposure lev-

els that are OK for a 240-pound man [that] are not OK for a 40-pound child . . . They speak on women's health issues with more authority. They work together on preschool education and after-school programs, child-related issues.

Finally, some staffers believed that the female senators felt an additional responsibility to consider the interests of women and children because the Senate remains a male-dominated institution. Thus a Democratic staffer for a female senator said,

> [S]he feels a responsibility to be a voice on women's issues, to bring a women's perspective to issues and that this is critical to her role in a Senate that is overwhelmingly male. [For example,] issues of military wives have often gone unnoticed by the Defense Department. The wives are often the single providers for the kids. She had been a single mom at one point, and it strikes a chord in her and she will amplify the issue and get others to lobby Congress on it.

Building Coalitions and Capitalizing on Women's Moral Authority. The personal commitment a female senator might feel toward women's issues is reinforced by the desire of coalition leaders to recruit female senators as supporters of their women's issue legislation and to capitalize on their moral authority as women to increase media attention for a policy proposal. According to a Democratic staffer,

> [S]enators do what they can to make themselves noticeable and get the press to write about them more. You sell yourself to sell the product and sell the product to sell yourself. When you have a women's issue you want to highlight women; it is marketing. You put a hold to get attention to an issue, make a bipartisan coalition to make something look unstoppable, find a victim who can make your case. These are all strategies to move things forward.

One of the first and most common steps senators take to build a coalition to support a policy initiative is to recruit cosponsors for their legislation. Numerous Republican and Democratic staffers claimed that female senators were often recruited to cosponsor women's issue legislation because the sponsor believed that female senators were natural supporters who could therefore secure votes that would bolster the sponsor's efforts to claim widespread support for his or her policy idea. Thus a Democratic staffer said,

> [W]hen you want to build a coalition on a specific issue you will identify the members that might be responsive. You start with who cares about an issue and who is on the committee that deals with it when you look for cosponsors and allies. She also always looks for a Republican to make it bipartisan. When people seek her out as a cosponsor it is usually because they want her because of her position on Appropriations. If it is a women's issue they will seek her out because they want a female cosponsor.

In addition to signaling the depth of support in the Senate for a policy proposal, coalition leaders recruit cosponsors with an eye to framing an issue and gaining media coverage. A Republican staffer said, "[W]ho you choose as cosponsors depends on how you want the issue perceived. You choose women if you want it perceived as a women's issue." Thus, when a proposal directly addresses the status of women in society, the bill's sponsor will recruit a female senator in order to capitalize on her moral authority as a woman and gain attention for the legislation. Describing his boss's efforts to build a coalition for a bill on women's rights in the Muslim world, another Republican staffer recounted,

> [W]e did seek to work with Boxer [D-CA] on women's rights in the Islamic world because this is a bill of import to women so it makes sense from a domestic and an international perspective to have a woman as a leader on the bill. Boxer and [—] had been working on women's rights and the Taliban since 1997–98 and no one was paying attention. For that bill you want an outspoken liberal who is female so we can show we have American unanimity in our stand on human dignity and rights so it needs to be a liberal female Democrat and not a Republican woman.

Emphasizing the importance of cosponsorship as a mechanism to frame issues and attract the attention of colleagues and the media, a Democratic staffer argued,

> [T]he coalition you assemble makes a statement about the content of the bill and its chance at passage. The coalition is designed to gain media attention. [For example], Clinton [D-NY]

was interested in girls' education issues as first lady and she had interactions with New York advocates of single sex education. Hutchison [R-TX] and she found out they had the interest in common. By doing the amendment together they could make the statement that single-sex education is not harmful to girls.

Beyond the desire of individual coalition leaders to recruit women as cosponsors for specific women's issue initiatives, the female senators themselves will occasionally work together as a group to leverage their numbers to affect policy on a defined set of issues that clearly address women and are not party or presidential priorities. In these cases, one female senator will want to get all the other women senators to sign on as cosponsors to draw media attention to the bill and make a statement to their fellow male senators that the women are lined up behind this issue and think it is important. For example, to emphasize their concern for the protection of women in Afghanistan and Iraq, Kay Bailey Hutchison (R-TX) and Barbara Mikulski (D-MD) offered bills to provide health and education services to women and to promote women's participation in the new governments. All of the women senators cosponsored these bills, and the Hutchison bill was signed into law.[5] Describing the range of issues that women collaborate on, a Democratic staffer noted,

> The women have pushed making women a part of the government in Afghanistan. This gets controversial because people say you don't want to rock the Muslim world too soon by forcing them to put women in . . . When the senators are talking about health care and medical coverage of Viagra by insurance the women will talk about contraception. When they are discussing NIH [National Institutes of Health] funding for cancer research, the women will form a coalition for breast cancer money. They speak on women's health issues with more authority.

Citing women's health issues as an area of bipartisan collaboration among the women, a Republican staffer recounted, "[W]hen the FEHBP [Federal Employee Health Benefits Plan] decided to cover Viagra but not contraception the women got together on that. Kay Bailey Hutchison [R-TX] offered an amendment on the floor with all the women cosponsoring it." Finally, commenting on the propensity of women to work together on specific issues, a Democratic staffer stated, "The Republican and Democratic women send cosponsored letters to the Appropriations Chair asking him to fully fund the WIC [Women Infants and Children] program, heating oil subsidies for the poor, Title I education funding. A lot of individuals believe in these things, but the women work together and support things as a group, a bipartisan group and not just as individuals." Thus, on a narrow band of issues the women senators leverage their gender in a cross-party coalition to achieve progress for women.

The desire of bill sponsors to enlist the support of women as they build a coalition for their policy proposals provides opportunities for women to take a leadership role on issues, heighten their media profile, and gain credibility with constituents who care about the issues. To illustrate this point, a male Republican senator partnered with a Democratic woman to pass an amendment that would overturn a Department of Defense policy requiring women to wear an *abaya* when they went off base in Saudi Arabia. The Republican senator asserted that he was "looking for a Democratic sponsor and I was thrilled to get a Democratic woman" on the bill. While the amendment passed unanimously, the bill was controversial because the Department of Defense argued that the bill tied its hands on personnel issues. Therefore, they had to work the amendment with news conferences and press releases and contacting other senators to get their support. Describing the benefits that the Democratic woman achieved from this partnership, the female senator's staffer maintained, "The bill raised her profile with veterans groups in the state, [the state] has a lot of veterans . . . and she likes working with conservatives because it makes her look more moderate."

Selling the Party Message on Women's Issues. Beyond personal commitment and the strategies of coalition leaders, female senators' greater activism on women's issues may also reflect party messaging efforts that capitalize on women's association with policy areas including health care, education, and women's rights to sell the party's message to the public and attract voters in the next election. Polarization in Congress and among the electorate means that a senator's fate is increasingly tied to the reputation of the party. As the party contingents have become more ideologically homogeneous, senators view themselves as members of partisan teams with a vested interest in the success of their party (Smith 2007; Lee 2009). In his study of party messaging, Sellers (2010) finds that party leaders work to raise the party's standing with voters by emphasizing issues and messages that tap positive voter opinion about the party. Thus, in their messaging strategies party leaders prefer to talk about issues that are owned by the party such as health care and education for Democrats and defense policy and lower taxes for Republicans. When the country is focused on the opposition party's issues, a party leader will try to frame the message in terms favorable to the party. For example, discussing health care, Republicans emphasize costs and choice, while Democrats speak about benefits and expanded coverage (Sellers 2010). Senators who actively participate in party messaging activities raise their own profile with the media and colleagues on national issues, and they may be rewarded with opportunities to advance bills on the floor, secure additional appropriations projects for the state, or take on party leadership roles.

Democratic Women and Party Messaging. Republican and Democratic staffers universally agreed that the association of many women's issues with the Democratic Party makes it easier for Democratic women to champion these causes and that Democratic women reap more political rewards from taking on women's issues. A Democratic leadership staffer asserted, "Democratic women do more stuff on women's issues because there is less of an internal problem for them with the party. Snowe [R-ME] and Collins [R-ME] try to do women's issues, but they are moderates so they are not trusted by Republicans. The Democratic leadership is proud that we have more women than the Republicans, and we want them out in front on things." Indeed several Democratic staffers, especially those who work for female members, believe that Democratic women are pivotal to reaching out to Democratic voters, particularly women voters, and they can expand the Democratic voter base. Thus, one staffer for a female Democrat said, "There are some opportunities and issues where women can be the most effective messengers and marketers of a legislative change. It was this way with [the Senator] and her work on spousal impoverishment from long-term health costs. This reaches the sandwich generation of women who are concerned about health care and unfairness. People will listen to her because she is a woman and they say she understands what it is like to be the daughter, mother, wife." Another staffer for a Democratic woman said, "[The Senator] believes that they [female senators] should use being a woman to get more attention. Women's faces talking about issues can break into the swing vote. Democrats are losing a share of the women's vote, and there are a lot of women who are not voting that if you could get them to vote they would vote Democrat."

There are generally three paths that lead Democratic women to promote party messages. First, the party can come to them as individuals with a specific policy expertise and ask them to speak on the floor and in press conferences about an issue. According to one Democratic staffer, "For the party, the goal is to have a list of people with specialized interest and knowledge on an issue that they can call to speak on the floor and that can pull things out of their head if an amendment comes to the floor that was not expected. On women's issues like abortion, child care, health issues related to women's health, education somewhat women will be on the top of those lists." In addition to seeking out individual women, the party sometimes asks Democratic women to work together as a group to promote the party message, believing that a coordinated message by all Democratic women will draw media attention and highlight the importance of an issue to women voters. Generally, the leader will approach Barbara Mikulski (D-MD) and ask her to coordinate floor speeches in the morning hour or a press conference. As the longest serving female member, Mikulski is referred to as the "Dean of the Democratic women," and she is particularly committed to advancing the role of women in the party and government more generally.

In addition to these party coordinated events, the Democratic women themselves will initiate party messaging opportunities seeking to leverage their gender to gain more influence over the party message or to take a larger leadership role in party strategy. A Democratic staffer said, "The Democratic women get together for the specific purpose of working on issues. Mikulski as Dean of the Women calls the meetings and suggests they work together on issues in common. Then the chiefs of staffs have to plan it. . . . [In other cases], some woman senator sees a void and says we can get a bigger bang for our buck if we all work together on this." These coordinated messaging events generally emphasize a woman's perspective, often the perspective of a mother trying to take care of her family, on a party priority. Thus a Democratic staffer said, "They did a big push on Social Security privatization and how it would affect women. How women would be impacted by the Bush prescription drug law. These are caucus priorities where they put the women's point of view and push it." Referring to the campaign against President Bush's efforts to privatize Social Security, another Democratic staffer said, "[T]he women were the in-house experts on fighting Social Security privatization and how bad this would be for women. Talking about the fact that women live longer and women's history in the workforce."

Beyond promoting a woman's viewpoint on the party priorities, the Democratic women try to utilize their numbers to impact what issues the party promotes and the direction of the party message. Thus, during election season the Democratic women put out their own agenda for the campaign. In 2006 and 2008 they called it the "Checklist for Change" to reference the checklists that women keep to coordinate their families.

According to a Democratic staffer, the women "wanted a leadership role in determining the Democratic agenda, and the women realize they have more power when they join together so they do it on a few occasions to increase the impact." Creating the checklist provides a platform for each individual senator to promote and gain media attention for one of their policy priorities. Thus a staffer said, "[E]ach [senator] picks an issue to manifest and market. They gather their best strategist, the chief of staff, communications director, and legislative director, and they all announce it on the same day." Although the checklist and the press conferences and floor speeches surrounding it are steeped in the language of gender, referring to "the family checkbook" and women's commitment to "focus on not only the macro issues but the 'macaroni-and-cheese' issues that confront America's families," the issues that senators promote are not necessarily women's issues. Thus, in 2008 Barbara Mikulski (D-MD) and Blanche Lincoln (D-AR) promoted the women's issues of equal pay and health care, respectively. However, Dianne Feinstein (D-CA) focused on the Bush administration's terrorism policies and restoring American credibility in the world, and Claire McCaskill (D-MO) took up the cause of fiscal accountability and strengthened federal oversight of government spending (United States Senate Democrats 2008). They promoted these issues in a venue devoted to women and with language to explain why they are important to women. The coordinated effort raised the media profile of these women senators by giving them a venue to highlight their favored issues. They gained further media attention with speaking slots at the 2008 Democratic convention to promote the checklist for change.

Republican Women and Party Messaging. While there is ample evidence that Democratic women play a prominent role in the messaging activities of the Democratic Party on women's issues and more generally, Republican staffers maintained that Republican women generally do not mobilize as women to promote party messages. Instead, individual Republican women are deployed in a more defensive capacity to explain why Republican policies do not hurt women and to reach out to women voters who support the Republican Party. Moreover, the small number of Republican women and their divergent ideological views mean that the women do not coordinate their activities to promote a women's perspective on issues in the way that Democratic women do. However, concerns about the party's image as a white male bastion have helped individual women advance within the party leadership.

Commenting on the role of Republican women in party messaging on women's issues, one Republican staffer explained, "Republican women can't leverage their gender into power as easily [as Democratic women] because women's issues are not Republican issues. The only women's issue Republicans work on is abortion. Republicans don't embrace women's issues and women [senators] don't want abortion to be their public face." However, this staffer maintained that "Republicans do want a spokesperson to put a good public face on an issue and deflect the criticism of Republicans as anti-women."

Noting the reticence of Republican women to serve as party spokespersons on women's issues, a Republican leadership staffer lamented that leadership "has a very difficult time getting the Republican women to do anything on women's issues." For example, in an effort to pressure Democrats to confirm some of President Bush's conservative female and minority nominees to the lower federal courts, the Republican leadership wanted Republican women to participate in events to drive home the message that Democrats were discriminating against qualified female and minority Republican nominees. However, the Republican leadership staffer complained, "the Republican women in the Senate were MIA when it came to trying to push judges. Elizabeth Dole only went to one event. We tried to have a women's event about opposing Kuhl, Brown, and Owen [three female appellate court nominees], and we had to bring women over from the House. The Republican women House members walked to the Senate steps for a press conference." A Democratic staffer was less charitable, claiming that "Republicans know they are at a deficit on women's issues so they send their Republican women out there to show they are good on women's issues, and they encourage them to do more on women's issues, but at the same time the positions of these women on those issues is not the position of the party so it is a catch-22."

Owing to their small numbers and their varying ideological stances, staffers maintain that Republican women do not work together as a group to promote women's issues or other issues. Thus, a Republican staffer said, "Democrats use women to do public messaging. [For example,] they coordinate to do colloquies on health care. Republicans do not use women in a coordinated effort." Instead Republicans will seek out individual women to defend the Republican position on issues and to push back on the Democratic narrative that Republican policies are anti-women. Serving as conference vice chair in the 107th to 109th Congresses, Kay Bailey Hutchison (R-TX) has played a prominent role in the Republican message team. A Republican staffer maintained, "Republicans wanted Kay Bailey Hutchison [R-TX] as vice chair because they want a woman to help respond to Democratic attacks." Describing Hutchison's role, a Republican leadership staffer said, "[T]here always has to be a staffer from the leadership on the floor at all times so that when Democrats come to make an attack the Republican leaders can counter it. Hutchison makes the speeches and lines up other people to make speeches." Other staffers pointed to Elizabeth Dole (R-NC) and occasionally Lisa Murkowski (R-AK) as female senators who have been asked by the party to defend the Republican position on women's issues including abortion, health care, and equal pay. Beyond the defensive role of countering Democratic efforts to stigmatize Republican policies as harming women, another former Republican senator maintained that Hutchison also paid attention to how Republican positions would be perceived by women voters, and she pushed this viewpoint in the caucus. "Kay Bailey Hutchison [R-TX] used her charm very effectively to deliver party messages. She was always very low key and explaining this is why we need to do something and very soothing. She would say you don't want to do that guys or you will lose the women's vote."

While Republican women do not campaign together for presidential and Senate candidates in the way that Democratic women do, Republican women work as individuals campaigning for specific candidates and speaking to groups of women voters. Republican staffers pointed to Kay Bailey Hutchison (R-TX) as a particularly effective spokesperson for the party and one who is able to reach women voters. Another Republican staffer pointed to Elizabeth Dole (R-NC) as having a prominent campaign role but a limited policy profile on women's issues. "Dole is a major spokesperson for Republicans to women's groups. She is there for optics and it is symbolic. When Bush was running [for re-election] they pushed her to the front to appeal to women and she spoke to a lot of 'Women for Republicans' groups. You can take her to the backwoods of nowhere and she will draw a crowd. She energizes the women's vote, but she does not carry the water on those issues."

Gender, Legislative Reputations, and Institutional Power. While women can and do utilize their gender to advance their policy priorities on women's issues, gain a seat at the decision-making table, and spread the party message to voters, the association of women with social welfare and women's rights issues can also create constraints. Although staffers believe that as a group, women are more committed to these issues, some staffers felt that the strong association of women with these policies can create expectations that constrain the ability of some female senators to define their own legislative agendas. In some cases, women feel compelled to devote time to these issues by colleagues or outside groups. Others worry about their press coverage and the resulting impact on their reputation. According to one Democratic staffer to a female senator,

> She is criticized because she does not do enough women's issues so we were always looking for women's issues for her and pushing her to do them. Women are inspected and examined by the media for what they do on soft issues. She has a tech background and does energy issues. We wanted to do something humanizing for her and something with kids, but even when she does the soft she does abstract technical things, like her interest in education and the No Child Left Behind Act was for distance learning. Somehow if a woman is not pictured surrounded by children there is something wrong with her.

Commenting on the power of issue framing in the media, a Republican staffer stated simply, "[I]f something becomes portrayed as supporting a women's issue in the press, she does not want to be perceived as not supporting women and she will support it."

The pressure from colleagues to marshal their gender to build a coalition for a bill can also have negative effects if it takes away time and resources from women senators' efforts to advance other policy priorities or if female senators feel compelled to support policies they do not believe in to demonstrate solidarity with colleagues. For example, a Republican staffer complained, "Landrieu [D-LA] had a sense of the Senate resolution to increase aid for the Iraqi women and children and to emphasize their welfare. She wanted all the women senators to sign on to it. I thought the bill was fluffy and not good policy but not harmful. [My senator] agreed, but she said she had to sign on to it." Similarly a Republican staffer said,

> The interest groups come to Collins [R-ME] and Snowe [R-ME] and other moderate Republican women anytime a bill has a woman or child in it. Human rights, AIDS groups . . . There is a higher expectation that women will be interested in these issues and work harder on them. Boxer [D-CA], Murray [D-WA], Landrieu [D-LA] live and breathe the women's issues, and Hutchison [R-TX] to some extent, especially on Iraqi women. [The Senator] will support women's issues, but she is not motivated to do it on her own because there are so many opportunities

always coming to her. [For example], Santorum [R-PA] [the Republican Conference Chair in the 108th Congress] wanted her to partner with him on a bill concerning the Iraq transitional constitution. He wanted her to lead on women's rights. Santorum had a press conference, and she did not want to do it. She was tired and overscheduled and had fifteen other things to do that day. She asked me if she really had to do it and I told her she did because it was a favor to leadership; so she did it, but grudgingly. She was not really volunteering for it; the opportunity came to her. In the press they want to see her championing women's rights. These groups and women's issues always come to us. Like for blacks it is hard to have to speak for all blacks. There is a sense of a burden to have to speak for all women, but [the women] will also use [gender] to their advantage. They also want to be seen as just a senator and not a woman senator.

The desire to send a message of diversity in public arenas also led some staffers to complain that the opportunities given to women are sometimes more optical and symbolic than substantive. Thus, one Democratic staffer opined,

The women are very sought after for press conferences. You never want the TV to pan all white males. Any public forum, they want as many women senators as they can. Anything to change the old white men dynamic. It benefits women because they would not be included otherwise if they did not need them publicly. [After the Enron meltdown when the Senate was working on corporate tax reform] there were so many press conferences on banking, I had to struggle to make sure Stabenow [D-MI] [the only Democratic woman on the Banking Committee in the 107th Congress] could attend. They want to make sure it looks like the decisions are not being made by all men, but the women are still there to advertise more than they are at the decision-making table.

In addition to fearing that they will be valued more as symbols of diversity rather than for the substance of their work, staffers for both Republican and Democratic women wanted to make sure that their senator was not perceived as being too focused on women's issues. These staffers maintained that women senators need to maintain a careful balance. If they do too many women's issues they will not be taken seriously in

the male-dominated Senate because these issues are not the power issues. A Democratic staffer explained,

> All women in some combination work with one another on one
> to five issues. It is a catch-22 because you don't want people to
> think of women differently, you want them to think she could
> be president or majority leader. It is a balancing act; you do
> not want to overstress your differences because it risks being
> perceived as the weaker sex at a time when national security is
> front burner. Women are not looking to label things as women's
> issues. You need to limit the number of women moments they
> have if you want to be qualified for a man's job.

Similarly, a Republican staffer asserted that to become president, Hillary Clinton needed to downplay her involvement in women's issues and
raise her profile on national security, saying, "Democratic women are
more focused on traditional women's issues than Republican women,
but Hillary Clinton is not. She is about homeland security and defense
because everyone knows she is an expert on children, education, and
health. She wants to establish her credentials on the others for her national ambition."

Still their status as women and a minority within the Senate and their
own parties has helped women gain leadership positions within their
caucuses. While Republicans reject the idea of identity politics, they
want to combat the image of the party as a white male bastion. Concern for diversifying the public face of the party has helped several Republican women in their bids for leadership positions. Thus, Kay Bailey
Hutchison (R-TX) served as conference vice chair in the 107th to 109th
(2001–2006) Congresses, and she advanced to Policy Committee chair
in the 110th Congress (2007–2008). Elizabeth Dole (R-NC) was elected
National Republican Senate Campaign Committee chair in the 109th
Congress (2005–2006), and Lisa Murkowski (R-AK) became conference vice chair in the 111th Congress (2009—2010) (Center for the
American Woman and Politics 2009). She lost this position after her
defeat in the 2010 Republican primary. Murkowski went on to win re-
election as an independent write-in candidate. Although she continues
to caucus with the Republicans, she is no longer on the leadership track
because her ideological profile is not compatible with the increasingly
conservative Republican caucus and leadership. The desire to show diverse faces at the leadership table creates some conflict within the caucus
with some members asserting that women are being advanced because

they are women rather than on merit. Indeed one Republican staffer complained, "[T]he parties are concerned about showing diversity and being gender conscious. This sometimes leads to women being advanced over others because they are women and want to show a woman's face at the table. Kay Bailey Hutchison is a case in point. There are a lot of men who would have done a better job in leadership than her, and the same with electing Dole to head the NRSC [National Republican Senate Campaign Committee]." While this characterization of women in leadership was not widespread, there is a conflict between Republican Party values and the desire to spotlight more diverse faces to expand the party's electoral coalition. This conflict can create resentment among some members.

Like Republicans, Democrats also want to project an image of diversity among their leadership. While Republicans reject direct appeals to gender, Democratic women will point to gender as a reason for expanding seats at the leadership table. The position of conference secretary is viewed as reserved for women (Rosenthal 2008). However, staffers maintain that this post wields little power; rather it gives women a seat at the table and provides the senator serving in the position with more staff. At the committee level, a former Democratic senator maintained that when Tom Daschle (D-SD) was Democratic leader, Barbara Mikulski extracted a promise from him to make sure women senators had a seat on every major committee in the Senate. Individual Democratic women have used gender in their arguments to secure better committee seats. Thus a Democratic staffer noted, "[Female senator] used the fact that she was a woman to get on Finance. She said there are no Democratic women on this committee, and there has not been a woman on it for decades. The committee deals with health, social security, taking care of elderly parents. These are all things that women deal with, and you need a woman on the committee." Thus, both Democratic and Republican women with ideological profiles that are compatible with the majority of the caucus have capitalized on their gender to gain a seat at the leadership table. However, these seats do not reach the highest levels of decision making within the parties.

In sum, Senate staff believe that Republican and Democratic women are more committed to pursuing social welfare and feminist legislation. A commitment to women's issues derived from personal experience is at the foundation of these gender differences. Because of their gendered life experience, women are more likely to begin with a predisposition to pay attention to the social welfare and feminist concerns that constitute women's issues. Other legislators, political activists, and interest group leaders who want to further their policy agendas recognize this predisposition. These political actors recruit women to cosponsor their bills, speak about their proposals on the floor, and sell their initiatives in press conferences. These coalition-building activities incorporate differing degrees of policy influence and messaging.

Because of the alignment of women's issues with the Democratic Party, staffers felt that Democratic women were particularly likely to champion causes related to women's issues. As the parties continue to polarize and target segments of women voters in an era of tight electoral competition, Democratic women will increasingly be called upon to sell the party message on women's issues, and Republicans will look to their female senators to counter Democratic attacks. Moreover, Democratic women utilize their greater numbers within the Democratic caucus to elevate their standing and gain attention for their policy priorities. Asserting themselves as a critical mass, Democratic women work as a group to shape party priorities and messaging strategies and to gain seats at the policy-making table. Republican women have not achieved similar levels of influence within their party because they represent a smaller proportion of the caucus and their disparate ideologies limit cooperation. Since women's issues are not central to the core message of the party and caucus members are not as responsive to claims based on diversity, there are fewer opportunities for Republican women to leverage their gender into positions of power and increased attention to their issue priorities. Finally, women in both parties are concerned about maintaining a balanced portfolio so they are not perceived solely as women senators working on women's issues.

Testing the Influence of Gender on Senators' Sponsorship and Cosponsorship Activity

The patterns of senators' sponsorship and cosponsorship activity and the observations of Senate staff support the contention that women are more active advocates for women's interests. Both Republican and Democratic women bring a perspective to legislating that considers the impact of policy on women, children, and families. Democratic women are particularly engaged on these issues because of the alignment of the gender-related policy preferences of Democratic women with the policy goals and reputation of the Democratic Party on social welfare and feminist issues. To fully examine the impact of gender on senator's policy choices, I utilize negative binomial regression analysis to test whether gender remains a significant influence on senators' policy activities once we account for other important predictors of legislative behavior. These influences include partisanship, ideology, constituency interests, and the senators' institutional resources such as his or her committee seat and leadership positions held.

The negative binomial models in tables 2.5 and 2.6 are event count models that allow one to estimate the number of bills a member with a given set of characteristics will sponsor in a set period of time.[6] The dependent variable is a count of the number of women's issue (table 2.5)

Table 2.5 107th and 108th Negative Binomial Models of Women's Issue Bill Sponsorship (Standard Errors in Parentheses)

Independent Variables	107th	108th
Republican Women	.613*	.004
	(.301)	(.297)
Democratic Women	.221	.242+
	(.174)	(.138)
Republican Men	.195	−.134
	(.289)	(.269)
Ideology	−.712*	−.354
	(.324)	(.352)
First-Term Senator	−.054	−.224
	(.186)	(.199)
Retiring Senator	−1.01**	−.092
	(.388)	(.189)
State Vote for Bush	.002	.012
	(.01)	(.008)
African American Population	−.02*	−.019*
	(.01)	(.008)
Hispanic Population	.002	−.007
	(.009)	(.007)
Median Household Income	.035	.209
	(.156)	(.134)
Urban Population	.001	−.001
	(.006)	(.005)
Elderly Population	.097*	.076*
	(.041)	(.035)
Southern State	.424*	.311*
	(.215)	(.188)
Up for Reelection	.135	−.023
	(.104)	(.092)
HELP	.288*	.411***
	(.118)	(.105)
Finance	−.02	−.051
	(.14)	(.115)
Judiciary	.155	−.022
	(.125)	(.112)
Veterans' Affairs	−.195	.089
	(.153)	(.116)
Special Aging	.074	−.04
	(.123)	(.104)

(*continued*)

Table 2.5 (*continued*)

Independent Variables	107th	108th
Appropriations Labor, Health and Human Services, and	.143	.124
Education Subcommittee	(.158)	(.114)
Women's Issue Committee Chair	−.203	.098
	(.218)	(.218)
Women's Issue Committee Ranking Member	.213	−.158
	(.264)	(.162)
Women's Issue Subcommittee Chair	.446*	.334[+]
	(.203)	(.198)
Women's Issue Subcommittee Ranking Member	.163	.189
	(.2)	(.158)
Same-State Senator's Women's Issue Bills	−.009	−.01
	(.007)	(.006)
Total Bills Sponsored	.03***	.03***
	(.004)	(.003)
Constant	−.544	−.997
	(1.37)	(1.12)
Dispersion Parameter	.067	.013
	(.029)	(.018)
Log Likelihood	−261.48	−249.57
Log Likelihood Ratio χ^2	143.17	149.78
Pseudo-R^2	.215	.231
N	100	100

[+]$p \le .1$.
*$p \le .05$.
**$p \le .01$.
***$p \le .001$.

and feminist (table 2.6) bills a senator sponsored in the 107th and 108th Congresses. The regression models in tables 2.7 and 2.8 analyze the impact of gender on cosponsorship of women's issue and feminist bills. Because so few senators sponsor anti-feminist bills and sponsorship and cosponsorship activity on anti-feminist issues is dominated by Republican men, there is not enough variation in the dependent variable to warrant further regression analysis.

The independent variables employed in the regression analyses in this chapter and throughout the book draw on the vast congressional literature concerning the factors that motivate legislators' policy decisions. Since party affiliation is one of the most reliable guides to how members of Congress approach issues (Rhode 1991; Cox and McCubbins 1993, 2005; Lee 2009), I created variables for Republican men and women and Democratic men and women. Dividing men and women by party allows me to address the possibility that gender differences in legislative behavior actually stem from the fact that most women are Democrats and public opinion favors Democrats to handle many of the issues incorporated in the concept of women's issues (Petrocik 1996;

Table 2.6 107th and 108th Negative Binomial Models of Feminist Bill Sponsorship (Standard Errors in Parentheses)

Independent Variables	107th	108th
Republican Women	2.05**	2.77***
	(.732)	(.812)
Democratic Women	.571+	1.4***
	(.314)	(.324)
Republican Men	−.605	1.35+
	(.743)	(.8)
Ideology	−1.78**	−1.93*
	(.692)	(.971)
African American Population	−.037*	−.033+
	(.018)	(.017)
Median Household Income	.937*	−.351
	(.466)	(.451)
Urban Population	−.02	−.006
	(.012)	(.012)
Proportion with a Bachelor's Degree	−.102	.044
	(.063)	(.063)
HELP	1.15***	.686*
	(.301)	(.292)
Finance	.708+	.458
	(.388)	(.371)
Judiciary	.693*	1.08***
	(.281)	(.31)
Veterans' Affairs	−.714+	−2.03***
	(.379)	(.617)
Special Aging	−.778*	−.456
	(.37)	(.344)
Appropriations Labor, Health and Human Services, and Education Subcommittee	.035	.725+
	(.441)	(.392)
Women's Issue Committee Chair	−1.02*	−.745
	(.427)	(.673)
Women's Issue Committee Ranking Member	.396	−.903+
	(.787)	(.505)
Women's Issue Subcommittee Chair	.455	−1.8*
	(.397)	(..856)
Women's Issue Subcommittee Ranking Member	−.247	.972*
	(.651)	(.423)
Same-State Senator's Feminist Bills	−.166*	−.084
	(.076)	(.065)
Total Bills Sponsored	.016*	.013
	(.007)	(.008)
Constant	−1.04	−.725
	(.1)	(1.16)
Dispersion Parameter	0	0
	(0)	(0)
Log Likelihood	−95.86	−101.59
Log Likelihood Ratio χ^2	85.1	79.04
Pseudo-R^2	.307	.28
N	100	100

+$p \leq .1$.
*$p \leq .05$.
**$p \leq .01$.
***$p \leq .001$.

Table 2.7 107th and 108th Negative Binomial Models of Women's Issue Bill Cosponsorship (Standard Errors in Parentheses)

Independent Variables	107th	108th
Republican Women	.247[+]	.521***
	(.127)	(.147)
Democratic Women	.189**	.066
	(.067)	(.081)
Republican Men	.065	.38**
	(.105)	(.141)
Ideology	−.243*	−.658***
	(.123)	(.195)
First-Term Senator	−.028	−.029
	(.065)	(.085)
Retiring Senator	−.323*	−.056
	(.129)	(.11)
State Vote for Bush	−.009*	−.003
	(.004)	(.005)
African American Population	−.001	.002
	(.004)	(.004)
Hispanic Population	−.003	−.001
	(.003)	(.004)
Median Household Income	.134	−.082
	(.078)	(.094)
Urban Population	.0003	.004
	(.003)	(.003)
Elderly Population	.027[+]	.014
	(.016)	(.019)
Southern State	.174*	.126
	(.083)	(.1)
Small State	.119*	.05
	(.054)	(.062)
Proportion with a Bachelor's Degree	−.021*	−.00008
	(.009)	(.01)
Up for Reelection	−.017	.016
	(.043)	(.054)
HELP	.131**	.088
	(.051)	(.062)
Finance	.024	.019
	(.054)	(.059)
Judiciary	−.074	−.149*
	(.052)	(.065)
Veterans' Affairs	.092	.135*
	(.056)	(.065)
Special Aging	−.025	.055
	(.051)	(.056)
Appropriations Labor, Health and Human Services, and Education Subcommittee	.002	−.031
	(.065)	(.069)
Women's Issue Committee Chair	.065	.072
	(.09)	(.138)
Women's Issue Committee Ranking Member	.002	−.026
	(.115)	(.098)
Women's Issue Subcommittee Chair	.057	.015
	(.083)	(.111)
Women's Issue Subcommittee Ranking Member	.046	.002
	(.088)	(.09)

Independent Variables	107th	108th
Same-State Senator's Women's Issue Bills	−.006*	−.006[+]
	(.003)	(.003)
Total Bills Cosponsored	.007***	.007***
	(.0004)	(.0004)
Constant	2.81***	2.63***
	(.58)	(.629)
Dispersion Parameter	.012	.021
	(.005)	(.006)
Log Likelihood	−370.83	−377.64
Log Likelihood Ratio χ^2	255.49	240.79
Pseudo-R^2	.256	.242
N	100	100

[+]$p \leq .1.$
*$p \leq .05.$
**$p \leq .01.$
***$p \leq .001.$

Table 2.8 107th and 108th Negative Binomial Models of Feminist Bill Cosponsorship (Standard Errors in Parentheses)

Independent Variables	107th	108th
Republican Women	.83***	.46[+]
	(.249)	(.249)
Democratic Women	.481***	.168
	(.112)	(.115)
Republican Men	−.21	−.033
	(.224)	(.259)
Ideology	−.853***	−1.49***
	(.241)	(.335)
First-Term Senator	−.147	−.117
	(.118)	(.144)
Retiring Senator	−.307	−.174
	(.37)	(.214)
State Vote for Bush	−.018*	−.019*
	(.008)	(.008)
African American Population	.003	−.003
	(.007)	(.006)
Hispanic Population	−.007	−.001
	(.006)	(.006)
Median Household Income	.468**	.084
	(.15)	(.158)
Urban Population	.002	−.004
	(.005)	(.005)
Elderly Population	−.005	−.082*
	(.033)	(.032)
Southern State	.194	.439*
	(.172)	(.184)
Small State	.258*	.067
	(.117)	(.114)
Proportion with a Bachelor's Degree	−.056**	−.013
	(.021)	(.02)

(continued)

Table 2.8 *(continued)*

Independent Variables	107th	108th
Up for Reelection	−.064	.028
	(.085)	(.093)
HELP	.265**	−.087
	(.099)	(.11)
Finance	.173	.044
	(.113)	(.109)
Judiciary	.088	−.158
	(.102)	(.104)
Veterans' Affairs	.252*	.07
	(.111)	(.114)
Special Aging	−.138	−.142
	(.113)	(.103)
Appropriations Labor, Health and Human Services, and	.029	.156
Education Subcommittee	(.127)	(.11)
Women's Issue Committee Chair	.212	.731**
	(.159)	(.271)
Women's Issue Committee Ranking Member	.32	−.133
	(.272)	(.152)
Women's Issue Subcommittee Chair	−.131	.598*
	(.147)	(.258)
Women's Issue Subcommittee Ranking Member	−.224	.209
	(.228)	(.138)
Same-State Senator's Feminist Bills	.009	.041*
	(.02)	(.019)
Total Bills Cosponsored	.007***	.006***
	(.001)	(.001)
Constant	.834	2.95**
	(1.15)	(1.05)
Dispersion Parameter	0	0
	(0)	(0)
Log Likelihood	−221.39	−225.45
Log Likelihood Ratio χ^2	220.9	227.3
Pseudo-R^2	.333	.335
N	100	100

$^+p \leq .1.$
$^*p \leq .05.$
$^{**}p \leq .01.$
$^{***}p \leq .001.$

Petrocik, Benoit, and Hansen 2003; Sides 2006; Sellers 2002, 2010). Moreover, by examining the interplay between gender and party, I can test whether certain assumptions about party and/or gender are magnified for particular groups. For example, does the Democratic Party's perceived issue ownership of policy areas such as health care and education combined with gender stereotypes related to women's greater interest in these issues lead Democratic women to focus more on women's issue legislation than other groups of legislators? Since one expects Democrats to be the most supportive of women's issue initiatives, the models include the dummy variables for Democratic women and Republican men and women. Democratic men are the "out category" and therefore the comparison category. Thus, a positive and significant coefficient for Democratic women would indicate that being a Democratic woman exerts an important influence on the decision to sponsor/cosponsor a women's issue bill and that Democratic women are even more likely to sponsor/cosponsor these bills than are Democratic men.

Ideology is another increasingly important influence on senators' policy activity. Poole and Rosenthal find that 80% of roll-call voting decisions can be predicted with a single liberal-conservative dimension (Poole and Rosenthal 1997, 2007). I utilize Poole and Rosenthal's DW-NOMINATE scores as an indicator of senators' ideology.[7] The scores range from -1, indicating most liberal, to $+1$, indicating most conservative. Therefore, an expected negative relationship between ideology and support for women's issue bills would indicate that more liberal members promote women's issue initiatives. While party and ideology are highly correlated, these scores allow me to capture intraparty differences in policy priorities among liberal and conservative Democrats and moderate and conservative Republicans.[8]

The needs of the constituency rank foremost in the minds of senators (Fenno 1978; Mayhew 1974; Baker 2001; Sinclair 1989). I account for constituency characteristics that may affect a state's demand for various women's issue bills by incorporating census data measuring key characteristics of each state, including median household income, the percentage of the population living in urban areas, the African American population, the Hispanic population, the state's elderly population (over sixty-five), and the proportion of state residents with a bachelor's degree. I also include a variable measuring whether the senator represents a southern state. A variable for small states (states with three or fewer congressional districts) draws on the insights of Lee and Oppenheimer (1999), who find that small-state senators have qualitatively different relationships with their constituents than large-state senators including an expectation that they will be more available to constituents and devote more attention to constituent service. I account for constituent ideology by including the state vote for President Bush in the 2000 election. Finally, a measure indicating whether the senator is up for re-election captures the political imperatives of senators who might increase their activism on women's issues that are salient to voters in an election year such as health care and education. As one staffer noted, things are different when "a senator is in cycle." The senator looks to highlight aspects of his or her record that will appeal to voters, and the party will give the senator more latitude to serve his or her constituency, sometimes even giving the senator a high-profile bill or amendment to offer that will be popular with voters and attract positive media coverage.

Finally, a legislator's position within the institution affects his or her calculation concerning the best allocation of scarce legislative resources to meet his or her policy and re-election goals. I include variables measuring senators' institutional position that impact their ability and desire to offer women's issue legislation, including whether senators are retiring, whether they are in the first two years of their term, and senators' committee positions. In an institution that values seniority, freshmen legislators generally sponsor fewer bills than more senior members because they are still learning the norms of the Senate and developing their legislative expertise (Schiller 2000, 1995). These senators are often more active cosponsors because cosponsorship offers a less costly opportunity to express policy preferences for members who lack legislative experience and the leadership positions in committees that facilitate policy influence (Koger 2003). Conversely, retiring members may be more active than other senators as they seek to establish their legacy before leaving the Senate. Alternatively, these senators may reduce their legislative activism in anticipation of moving on to the next phase of their careers.

While the expansive floor rights granted to individuals reduce the gatekeeping power of Senate committees, senators' entrepreneurial role in initiating and drafting legislation is still very important and influences bill sponsorship (Evans 1991; Hall 1996; Deering and Smith 1997). Staffers indicated that a senator's committee assignments are a primary driver of his or her legislative agenda. Using information on bill referral and jurisdiction (King 1997), I include measures that capture membership on the following committees: Health, Education, Labor, and Pensions (HELP); Finance; Judiciary; Special Committee on Aging; Veterans' Affairs; and the Appropriations Committee's Subcommittee on Labor, Health and Human Services, and Education.[9]

Among committee members, the chairmen and ranking members wield the most power over legislation that is considered by the committee. These senators have more experience with the issues under their jurisdiction and have expanded staff to help formulate legislation. Moreover, chairs decide what hearings will be held and which bills will be moved through the committee. They play an outsized role in shaping the policy details of the final bill (Evans 1991; Hall 1996). Ranking members lead the committee's minority party contingent. Since the minority party has expanded rights in the Senate in comparison with the more majoritarian House, the ranking member often plays a key role in negotiations over the content of legislation (Evans 1991; Hall 1996; Baker 2001). Given the importance of committee leaders, I include variables for women's issue committee chair and women's issue committee ranking member that account for the chairs and ranking members of the above committees.

Variables for women's issue subcommittee chair and women's issue subcommittee ranking member account for senators with leadership positions on the subcommittees of the HELP Committee and the chairs and ranking members of the Finance Committee's subcommittees on Health and Social Security.[10] Because senators hold multiple committee assignments, the chair and ranking members of the committee and subcommittees are often the major or even the only players involved in the development of particular legislation. Additionally, in the Senate, bill markups are frequently held only at the full committee level because senators do not have time to hold multiple markups on bills and a member of the full committee can be expected to offer amendments in the committee markup regardless of whether he or she is on the relevant subcommittee (Evans 1991; Baker 2001; Sinclair 1989). Therefore, I do not include separate variables for subcommittee membership.[11]

Finally, I include a variable that captures the number of women's issue/feminist bills offered by a senator's state colleague. This variable accounts for the strategic calculations senators make about how to navigate the policy reputation and legislative expertise of their same-state colleague (Schiller 2000, 2002). Variables measuring the total number of bills a senator sponsors and cosponsors address the fact that the more bills a member sponsors/cosponsors, the higher the probability that one of those bills will concern a women's issue.

The Role of Gender as a Predictor of Women's Issue and Feminist Bill Sponsorship

The regression results in tables 2.5 and 2.6 demonstrate that even after accounting for the major influences on senators' sponsorship activity, gender does impact senators' policy decisions. Looking at the regression models of women's issue bill sponsorship in table 2.5, the three gender-party variables show that in comparison with Democratic men, Democratic women were significantly more likely to sponsor women's issue bills in the 108th Congress and Republican women were more active sponsors of women's issue initiatives in the 107th Congress. The decline in activism among Republican women in the 108th Congress likely reflects the election of two new female senators, Elizabeth Dole (R-NC) and Lisa Murkowski (R-AK). The election of Dole and Murkowski increased the conservatism of Republican women and, as freshmen, these women were still mastering the norms of the Senate and thus sponsored fewer bills than the average Republican senator. Among Democrats, gender-related concerns may have propelled Democratic women to greater activism in the 108th Congress. Thus, Democratic women felt a greater desire to protect women's rights when they were threatened by the legislative agenda of a socially conservative Republican majority and president, and this enhanced concern is reflected in their legislative agendas.

In addition to gender, ideology is an important predictor of which senators sponsor women's issue legislation. As one would expect, the negative coefficients on ideology indicate that more liberal senators offer more women's issue legislation. With regard to constituency factors, the dominance of health care bills among senators' women's issue proposals helps explain the consistent importance of the state's elderly population across the two congresses. More surprising are the facts that a high African American population is negatively related to sponsorship of women's issue bills and that representation of a southern state is a positive predictor of women's issue bill sponsorship. However, the high correlation among constituency variables and between the constituency and ideology variables means these statistics must be interpreted with caution.[12] Finally, despite the fact that senators are more free to offer proposals and insert themselves into floor debate on any issue area, committee position and the expertise that senators develop within committees is still an important predictor of what bills members offer. Members of the HELP Committee were consistently more active sponsors of women's issue legislation across the two congresses, and the chairs of subcommittees with jurisdiction over more women's issue legislation offered more bills on these issues.

To gain a better understanding of the influence of gender on senators' sponsorship behavior, I calculated predicted probabilities to assess how many women's issue bills the models predict a senator with a given set of characteristics, such as gender, party affiliation, and ideology, would sponsor.[13] Predicted probabilities do not deal with actual members. Instead they allow one to create hypothetical members and to assign them specific characteristics such as a liberal ideology or a seat on the HELP Committee. These probabilities allow us to estimate what legislative advocacy on women's issues would look like with, for example, more liberal Democratic women or more moderate Republican women. As figure 2.3 demonstrates, Democratic women are predicted to sponsor

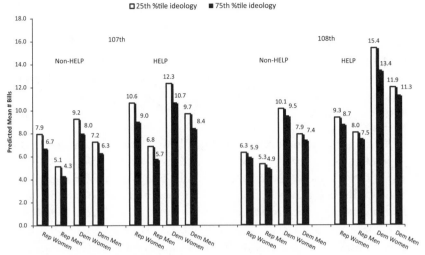

FIGURE 2.3 107th and 108th Congresses: Women's Issue Bill Sponsorship

Note: DW-NOMINATE ideology scores are set at the 25th and 75th percentiles within each party to capture most liberal and conservative senators in each party caucus. HELP Committee membership is varied from 0 to 1, indicating a seat on the committee. All other dichotomous variables are set at the mode of 0, and continuous variables are set at their means.

on average two more women's issue bills than Democratic men across the two congresses and Republican women to sponsor an average of three more women's issue bills than Republican men in the 107th Congress and one more bill than Republican men in the 108th Congress. Thus, in the 108th Congress, liberal Democratic women would sponsor a mean of 10.1 bills and liberal Democratic men would sponsor a mean of 7.9 women's issue bills. If these Democrats held a position with more institutional power over women's issues such as a seat on the HELP Committee, the liberal Democratic women would sponsor a mean of 15.4 women's issue bills, while the liberal Democratic man would sponsor a mean of 11.9 women's issue bills. These are meaningful differences when one considers that the average senator sponsored a mean of ten women's issues bills across the two congresses.

Turning to feminist legislation, the regression models in table 2.6 show that liberal senators are the most active sponsors of feminist bills across both congresses. Once one accounts for liberal ideology, Democratic and Republican women are more likely to sponsor feminist bills than the comparison category of Democratic men across both congresses. It may at first appear surprising that Republican men are more likely to sponsor feminist legislation than Democratic men in the 108th

Congress. However, after accounting for the significant impact of liberal ideology, the gender-party coefficients are now measuring the activities of party moderates, thus moderate Republican men are more likely to sponsor feminist bills in the 108th Congress than are conservative Democratic men. If the regression models are run without the ideology scores, the coefficients for Republican and Democratic women remain positive and significant, while the coefficient for Republican men is negative and insignificant.

Among the constituency variables, only the state's African American population is a consistently negative and significant predictor of feminist bill sponsorship, perhaps reflecting the criticism that feminism has historically been a largely white movement. Committee position plays a strong role in which members sponsor feminist legislation. Members of the HELP and Judiciary committees are consistently active sponsors of feminist legislation across both congresses, reflecting the HELP Committee's jurisdiction over a wide range of women's issues and the jurisdiction of the Judiciary Committee over abortion rights and legislation concerning violence against women as well as the liberal reputations of the Democratic contingent on both of these committees. By contrast, the Special Committee on Aging and the Veterans' Affairs Committee are consistently negative predictors of feminist bill sponsorship as the jurisdictions of these committees incorporate more social welfare legislation.

The impact of holding leadership positions on these committees is less clear. Full committee chairs are consistently less likely to offer feminist bills across both congresses. However, leadership at the subcommittee level is only a significant predictor of feminist bill sponsorship in the 108th Congress, with Democratic ranking members significantly more likely to offer feminist legislation and Republican subcommittee chairs significantly less likely to offer these bills. Finally, consistent with the idea that same-state senators work to develop distinctively different legislative profiles from one another, the number of feminist bills offered by a senator's same-state colleague has a negative impact on the likelihood that a senator will sponsor a feminist bill. This negative relationship is statistically significant in the 107th Congress.

Looking at the predicted probabilities in figure 2.4, in the 107th Congress, gender differences in sponsorship increase as one moves across the partisan spectrum. Thus, the average liberal Democratic woman would sponsor about 0.7 more feminist bills than a liberal Democratic man (1.6 vs. 0.9 bills). If the liberal Democratic woman serves in an institutional position associated with activism on feminist issues such as on

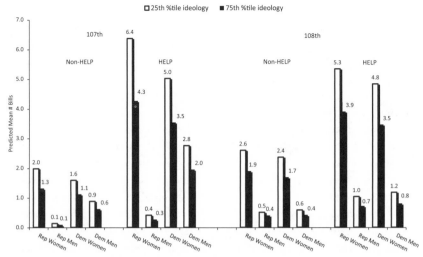

FIGURE 2.4 107th and 108th Congresses: Feminist Issue Bill Sponsorship

Note: DW-NOMINATE ideology scores are set at the 25th and 75th percentiles within each party to capture most liberal and conservative senators in each party caucus. HELP Committee membership is varied from 0 to 1, indicating a seat on the committee. All other dichotomous variables are set at the mode of 0, and continuous variables are set at their means.

the HELP Committee, she would sponsor approximately two more bills than her liberal Democratic male colleagues on the committee (5 vs. 2.8 bills). By contrast, a moderate Republican woman is predicted to sponsor on average two more feminist bills than a moderate Republican man (2 vs. 0.1). If these moderate Republicans served on the HELP Committee, the female Republican is predicted to sponsor six more feminist bills than a Republican man (6.4 vs. 0.4). These differences are more notable when one considers that on average senators sponsor only 1.1 feminist bills across the two congresses.

In the 108th Congress, as Democratic men reduced their sponsorship of feminist legislation when they moved into the minority party and Republican men increased their attention to these issues, gender differences in feminist bill sponsorship among partisans grew more similar. Thus, Democratic and Republican women are predicted to sponsor approximately two more feminist bills than their male partisan colleagues. If these senators are given seats on the HELP Committee, female Democrats and Republicans are predicted to sponsor on average four more feminist bills than are their male partisan colleagues.

Overall, the analysis of bill sponsorship shows that senators are generalists, with most senators offering proposals on a range of women's issues. Yet gender differences still emerge in senators' sponsorship activity, with Democratic and Republican women more likely to sponsor women's issue bills than their male colleagues when they were in the minority. Gender differences are magnified on the feminist issues that can be directly connected to consequences for women as a group. Republican and Democratic female senators were more active proponents of feminist legislation across both congresses.

Looking at cosponsorship activity, the regression models in tables 2.7 and 2.8 indicate that the distinctive influence of gender on senators' cosponsorship decisions persists even after accounting for the other important influences on legislative decision making. Across both congresses, liberals are the most active cosponsors of women's issue legislation. After accounting for liberal ideology, as majority party members in the 107th Congress, Democratic women were more active cosponsors of women's issue bills than were conservative Democratic men. Republican women cosponsored more women's issue legislation than conservative Democratic men did across both congresses, while majority party Republican men cosponsored more women's issue legislation than conservative Democratic men in the 108th Congress. Predicted probabilities in figure 2.5 demonstrate that on average, a Democratic woman is predicted

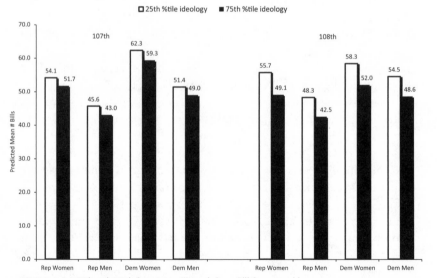

FIGURE 2.5 107th and 108th Congresses: Women's Issue Bill Cosponsorship

Note: DW-NOMINATE ideology scores are set at the 25th and 75th percentiles within each party to capture most liberal and conservative senators in each party caucus. All dichotomous variables are set at the mode of 0, and continuous variables are set at their means.

to cosponsor about ten more women's issues bills than an ideologically similar Democratic man in the 107th Congress and about three more women's issue bills than a Democratic man serving in the 108th Congress. Thus, in the 107th Congress, a liberal Democratic woman is predicted to cosponsor a mean of 62.3 women's issue bills in comparison with a mean of 51.4 women's issue bills cosponsored by a liberal male Democrat. Similarly the models predict that across the two congresses, a moderate Republican woman would cosponsor approximately eight more women's issue bills than a moderate Republican man (54.1 vs. 45.6 in the 107th Congress and 55.7 vs. 48.3 in the 108th Congress).

Beyond gender and ideology, constituency interests, including a more Democratic voting population (as indicated by a lower state vote for President Bush in 2000), a higher elderly population, lower levels of college-educated residents, and representation of a southern state or a small state had an important influence on senators' cosponsorship decisions in the 107th Congress but very little impact on cosponsorship behavior in the 108th Congress. In contrast to bill sponsorship where committee position has an important impact on the bills senators choose to sponsor, committee assignments and committee leadership positions are not significant predictors of the number of women's issue bills that senators cosponsor. Interestingly, the legislative agenda of a senator's same-state counterpart does influence his or her cosponsorship decisions. Senators cosponsor fewer women's issue bills if their same-state colleague is a more active sponsor of women's issue legislation. Thus, senators' desire to create a legislative profile that is unique from their same-state colleague extends to their cosponsorship activity.

Gender is an important predictor of which senators cosponsor feminist bills. As one would expect, liberals cosponsor the most feminist legislation and Republican women and Democratic women are significantly more likely to cosponsor feminist legislation than conservative Democratic men. The impact of Democratic women was strongest when they served in the majority in the 107th Congress. As minority party members in the 108th Congress, the coefficient for Democratic women is significant at the 0.1 level in a one-tailed test. The predicted probabilities in figure 2.6 show that in the 107th Congress, liberal Democratic women would cosponsor approximately six more feminist bills than liberal Democratic men would (14.6 vs. 9.1) and about two more feminist bills than would their liberal male partisans in the 108th Congress (16.3 vs. 13.7). Similarly, moderate Republican women are predicted to cosponsor on average six more feminist bills than are moderate Republican men (9.3 vs. 3.2) in the 107th Congress and two more feminist

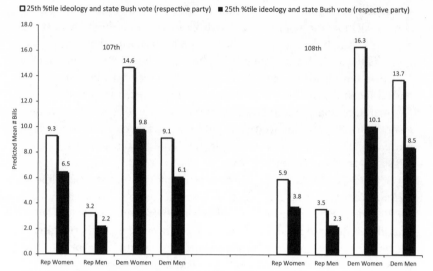

FIGURE 2.6 107th and 108th Congresses: Feminist Issue Bill Cosponsorship

Note: DW-NOMINATE ideology scores and state vote for President Bush are set at the 25th and 75th percentiles within each party to capture most liberal and conservative senators in each party caucus. All dichotomous variables are set at the mode of o, and continuous variables are set at their means.

bills than are their moderate male colleagues in the 108th Congress (5.9 vs. 3.5).

Constituency interests do influence a senator's decision to cosponsor feminist legislation. Senators from liberal states as indicated by a lower state vote for President Bush are more likely to cosponsor feminist legislation. Other constituency variables had a significant influence on cosponsorship activity in one of the two congresses. With regard to institutional position, committee membership was an important determinant of cosponsorship activity in the 107th Congress, with membership on the HELP and Veterans' Affairs committees both being positive predictors of cosponsorship of feminist bills. Holding a leadership position had a positive impact on cosponsorship in the 108th Congress, as the Republican committee and subcommittee chairs were more likely to cosponsor feminist legislation.

In sum, gender does have a consistent and distinctive influence on the policy agendas of both Republican and Democratic women. Women senators are more active advocates for women's issue legislation, including these issues among their package of legislative priorities more frequently than their male partisan colleagues do. Women are also more likely to cosponsor women's issue legislation, thus signaling their greater interest in these issues to colleagues and declaring their commitment to these policies to constituents, activists, and coalition leaders. The intensity of these gender differences increases in the analysis of legislative activity on feminist issues, demonstrating that the saliency of gender to the policy debate does influence senators' choices. Women are particularly active on those issues that have a direct connection to consequences for women as a group.

Legislating Women's Issues in the House and Senate

The analysis of gender differences in legislating on women's issues in the Senate reinforces my findings about gender differences in the House of Representatives (Swers 2002) and provides important insights into the differing institutional dynamics of the House and Senate. In comparison with their House counterparts, senators are clearly generalists who want to have proposals on all issues that interest a statewide constituency and raise their national profile. Thus, only about 50% of House members proposed women's issue legislation in the 103d and 104th Congresses since House members derive much of their influence through the policy areas under the jurisdiction of their committees and their efforts to serve the district. By contrast, almost all senators serving in the 107th and 108th Congresses offered a women's issue bill.

The issue breakdown of women's issue legislation also reflects the Senate's generalist reputation. Senators focused the vast majority of their initiatives on the social welfare concerns that constitute the core issues dividing Republicans and Democrats since the New Deal and that are particularly important to a statewide electorate. Only about 10% of senators' bills addressed more targeted feminist concerns, such as reproductive rights or employment discrimination. By contrast, 43% of the bills offered in the Democratic-controlled House in the 103d Congress and 31% of the legislation proposed in the Republican-controlled 104th Congress addressed feminist issues. Thus, House members are more likely to develop specialized expertise. Furthermore, in comparison with senators, more House members represent uniformly liberal districts that contain higher proportions of constituents that are responsive to feminist proposals.

Reflecting their reputations as individual policy entrepreneurs in comparison with House members, personal ideology plays a more important role in senators' legislative activity on women's issues, while their policy choices are less driven by institutional position. Across both the

107th and 108th Congresses, liberal senators are more likely to sponsor and cosponsor women's issue and feminist bills. However, in the House, ideology had no impact on which senators sponsored women's issue or social welfare bills and ideology was only an important predictor of feminist bill sponsorship in the 104th Congress. For House members, ideology only impacted cosponsorship behavior. Research demonstrates that cosponsorship is an important tool for signaling legislators about the ideological content of bills (Koger 2003; Harward and Moffett 2010). In the House, cosponsorship was also an important tool for freshman members with limited political resources to stake out positions, while seniority had no impact on senators' cosponsorship activity. Finally, House members were more influenced by their status as members of the majority or minority party. In the House, only majority party members have real influence over the content and direction of the policy agenda. In the Senate, the minority has more tools to force the majority to consider its priorities on the floor. Thus, in the House, Democratic and Republican women increased their activity on social welfare policy when their party held the majority and they could influence the policy agenda. Majority status had no similar influence on the women's issue agendas of female senators.[14]

Despite important differences in the institutional dynamics of the House and Senate, gender differences in legislative activity are remarkably consistent across the two institutions. Democrats are generally more active on women's issues than Republicans are, reflecting the Democratic Party's reputation as more committed to social welfare and women's rights concerns. In both the House and Senate, the greatest gender differences are found in sponsorship and cosponsorship activity on feminist issues. These bills represent the legislation that is most easily connected to consequences for women as a group in the minds of voters and policy entrepreneurs including other legislators and interest group leaders. Republican and Democratic women are more active cosponsors of women's issue legislation since cosponsorship provides more opportunities for legislators to highlight issues that are important to them. Bill sponsors and interest groups allies actively recruit women as cosponsors either because they view them as strong supporters of women's issues or because they want to capitalize on their moral authority to gain attention for the legislation. Finally, gender was a more consistent predictor of women's issue bill sponsorship in the House than in the Senate. However, while the statistical significance varied in the Senate (Republican women were significantly more likely to sponsor women's issue bills in the 107th Congress and Democratic women were significantly more active on these bills in the 108th Congress), the coefficient was always in the expected positive direction.[15]

Conclusion

In the modern Senate, senators are both policy generalists and members of partisan teams. Still, a close examination of senators' legislative activities on women's issues clearly demonstrates that both Democratic and Republican women are more likely to include proposals on women's issues in their set of legislative priorities. Gender differences in legislative behavior are even more pronounced on feminist issues that tap questions of women's rights and are most easily connected to consequences for women as a group.

The call for increasing women's representation in government rests on the assumption that female senators will be more aggressive advocates for women's interests and will bring a woman's perspective to deliberations on public policy. It is clear from discussions with Senate staff that Democratic and Republican women are perceived as having a special commitment to social welfare and women's rights issues based on their greater connection to and understanding of the patterns of women's lives. Thus, a significant amount of gender differences stems from the personal experiences senators draw on and utilize to identify with the problems of constituents. This perceived connection to women's interests is a valuable asset in an institution where credibility and expertise are important tools for establishing a legislative niche and claiming ownership of issues. Furthermore, coalition leaders, from bill sponsors to interest group and party leaders, recognize this connection. These policy entrepreneurs seek to capitalize on female senators' moral authority as women to gain media attention for their proposals and build legislative support for their initiatives. When women respond to the requests of policy entrepreneurs, they are able to gain a platform for pushing their policy priorities on women's issues. They also participate in coalition-building efforts to move these policies forward. Occasionally, the participation of women can be more superficial, providing window dressing at press conferences for someone else's agenda. Still, expanding the number of women in the Senate, particularly Democratic and moderate Republican women, would likely lead to more opportunities for coalition building around women's issues.

Senators operate in a highly partisan political context. As a result, Democratic and Republican women do not reap the same level of benefits from working on women's issues. The centrality of women's issues to the agenda of the Democratic Party means that Democratic women have the most to gain from working on women's issues. The Democratic caucus is more likely to prioritize these issues, and Democratic women can raise their own policy and media profile by advocating for these issues and advertising the party message on a range of women's issue initiatives. The increasing importance of the gender gap in a competitive electoral environment increases the value of Democratic women as spokespersons who can turn out the women's vote. As the Senate becomes increasingly partisan and polarized, party leaders will want to highlight party contrasts on social welfare issues like health care and education that favor the Democratic Party. To mobilize women's groups and other elements of the liberal Democratic base, Democrats will want to advertise party positions on women's health, particularly abortion and contraception. These political goals will provide more opportunities for Democratic women senators to promote their initiatives on these issues and raise their media profiles by advertising party positions.

By contrast, women's issues do not hold a pivotal place on the Republican policy agenda, making them a less powerful tool for Republican women seeking to advance their policy priorities and their position in the Republican caucus. Moreover, the increasing attention to feminist issues can alienate the social conservative base of the party and put the more moderate Republican women in an uncomfortable position. As a result, women's issues provide a narrower set of opportunities for Republican women. Republican women act individually to advance their own women's issue priorities, and they are recruited by policy entrepreneurs. In the ideological competition between the two parties, Republican leaders turn to individual women to serve in a more defensive capacity, countering Democratic efforts to portray the Republican Party's policies as harmful to women's interests and reaching out to women voters who will support Republican candidates. Finally, the Senate remains a male-dominated institution. Both Democratic and Republican women are concerned about striking the right balance in their policy portfolios, fearing that too much activism on women's issues will harm their reputations as power players within the Senate.

3

Playing Offense and Defense on Women's Rights

On April 23, 2008, the Senate fell three votes short of the sixty votes needed to invoke cloture on the Lilly Ledbetter Fair Pay Act, a bill designed to reverse a controversial Supreme Court decision and make it easier for women to file pay discrimination lawsuits. After the vote, an incensed Barbara Mikulski (D-MD) took to the Senate floor to denounce the vote. Quoting Abigail Adams's famous letter imploring her husband John Adams not to forget the ladies when drafting the Constitution, Mikulski declared,

> Do not forget the ladies because we will foment a revolution of our own. I was here in 1992 when we didn't get it on Anita Hill. I am here in 2008 when we didn't get it in pay equity. In 1992, we had a revolution that went on. We got six new women in the Senate. There are now 16 of us. The majority of us voted for this bill. I am telling you we are ready for an "Abigail Adams" effort here. If they don't want to put us in the lawbooks so we can have fairness in the checkbooks, we will do a revolution. What do I mean by that? We will take it out to the voting booths. We will go on the Internet. We are going to go on TV, on the blogs. And we are going to tell

everybody about this ignominious vote that occurred. When we tell it, we are going to say: Call to arms women of America, put your lipstick on, square your shoulders, suit up, we have a hell of a fight coming, but, boy, we are ready. The revolution starts tonight. (Congressional Record, April 23, 2008, S3298)

After failing in 2008, ultimately the Lilly Ledbetter Fair Pay Act became the first major piece of legislation signed by newly inaugurated Democratic president Barack Obama. All seventeen women in the Senate voted for the final bill. Among Republicans, only Arlen Specter (R-PA) and the four Republican women, Olympia Snowe (R-ME), Susan Collins (R-ME), Kay Bailey Hutchison (R-TX), and Lisa Murkowski (R-AK), supported the legislation. On the surface, the Ledbetter Fair Pay Act is a prime example of female senators' commitment to women's rights and aggressive advocacy for women's interests. However, the story is more complicated. While all of the Republican women voted for the final legislation in 2009, three of the five Republican women serving in 2008 voted against invoking cloture on the bill. When the final version of the bill was debated in 2009, all but one of the Republican women who supported the legislation also voted in favor of a Republican substitute amendment sponsored by Kay Bailey Hutchison (R-TX) that would have significantly limited the scope of the legislation.[1]

In this chapter, I explore how the heavily male-dominated Senate deals with policy debates that explicitly concern women's rights. I examine the development of the Lilly Ledbetter Fair Pay Act, and I explore senators' actions on the most frequently debated and highly controversial women's issue, abortion. I focus particularly on the eight-year fight to pass the Partial Birth Abortion Act. My analysis demonstrates that women senators do not share one monolithic point of view on these issues. Instead their views are shaped by personal life experiences, constituent opinion, and strategic political calculations. However, women senators are more likely to prioritize issues of women's rights and expend the political capital of time and resources required to advocate for their position on these issues. Rather than simply voting on the final form of a bill, female senators are actively engaged in the development of women's rights legislation, offering amendments and speaking out on the floor. Male senators recognize the greater interest and credibility of female senators on these issues.

Beyond their own individual interest in women's rights, female senators are cognizant of their roles as members of partisan teams. Therefore, Democratic women work together to highlight the Democratic Party's commitment to women's rights and to press the party's advantage on these issues with voters. Republican women try not to draw attention to themselves when they disagree with the party on legislation related to women's rights. Party and committee leaders recruit individual Republican women to rebut Democratic criticisms that Republican Party initiatives are harmful to women.

Lilly Ledbetter and Equal Pay

Lilly Ledbetter spent nineteen years working for the Goodyear Tire and Rubber Co. in Alabama. Just before she retired in 1998, she received an anonymous note showing that as the lone female supervisor, she was being paid substantially less than her lowest paid male counterpart. Ledbetter sued, and the case went all the way to the Supreme Court. In their 2007 decision, the justices agreed that Ledbetter was a victim of gender discrimination. However, writing his first major decision since replacing Sandra Day O'Connor on the Supreme Court, justice Samuel Alito maintained that Ledbetter could not sue because she had not filed the claim within the time frame required by Title VII of the Civil Rights Act. This time limit held regardless of whether the plaintiff knew about the discrimination within the 180-day period. Outraged by the court's decision Justice Ruth Bader Ginsberg, then the lone woman on the court, called on Congress to correct the court's mistake (Barnes 2007a, 2007c).

The Ledbetter case immediately galvanized Democrats and their supporters. Women's groups, civil rights organizations, labor unions, and trial lawyers all called for Congress to act. Democrats believed the issue would help them with women and swing voters in the upcoming 2008 presidential and congressional elections (Kellman 2008). Lilly Ledbetter herself became a tireless crusader for the cause, testifying before Congress, starring in a series of YouTube videos about her experience, and traveling the country to tell her story (Barnes 2007c). She also played a prominent role in Democratic electoral politics. Ledbetter frequently campaigned for Barack Obama after he won the Democratic presidential nomination, helping him heal the rifts with Hillary Clinton supporters and reach out to women voters across the country. She also spoke at the Democratic National Convention. When he won the election, Obama invited Ledbetter to travel with him on the train to Washington, D.C., and danced with her at the inaugural ball (Langel 2008; Stolberg 2009).

Both legislatively and politically, the drive for the Lilly Ledbetter

Fair Pay Act was a clear victory for Democrats. According to staffers, because of the unanimity of support within the Democratic Party and a universal belief that they were on the right side of public opinion, Democratic women were able to aggressively pursue the legislation, working to shape the public debate on the issue and pushing the bill through the Senate. As one male Democratic senator explained, "The party believes in it [the Lilly Ledbetter Fair Pay Act]. With no women in the caucus we would have taken up the issue, but the women were more aggressive on it. They were more outraged by the Ledbetter decision and more aggressive in pushing hard for something to get done on it. It is natural for Boxer [D-CA] and Stabenow [D-MI] to care about discrimination and unfairness, they were probably treated that way themselves over the years." Thus, the personal connection the Democratic female senators felt with the issue of employment discrimination made them prioritize the legislation and devote the time and political capital necessary to move it from a political issue to legislative action.

From the beginning, Democratic women played key roles in drafting the legislation and building public support for the bill. According to Democratic staff, after the Ledbetter decision came down at the end of May 2007, Hillary Clinton (D-NY) and Barack Obama (D-IL), both leading Democratic presidential candidates and members of the Health, Education, Labor, and Pensions (HELP) Committee, began circulating drafts of legislation. One Democratic staffer noted, "There was maybe a sliver of difference between the two bills. Kennedy [the chair of the HELP Committee] went with the Clinton bill because it was simpler. The competing bills were seen [by other senators] as an early testing ground of whom other senators will choose to support in the presidential primary. Eventually Obama dissolved his bill, and all the senators went on the Clinton-Kennedy bill."[2] Moreover, Clinton had a history of leadership on the issue; she was the lead Senate sponsor of the Paycheck Fairness Act. The House version of this broader pay discrimination bill passed that chamber in both the 110th and 111th Congresses. As chair of the committee with jurisdiction over the issue, Ted Kennedy (D-MA) was the lead sponsor of the Ledbetter Fair Pay bill. The fourteen original cosponsors included three Democratic presidential candidates, Hillary Clinton (D-NY), Barack Obama (D-IL), and Chris Dodd (D-CT); two Republicans, Arlen Specter (R-PA) and Olympia Snowe (R-ME); and seven women, Hillary Clinton (R-NY), Olympia Snowe (R-ME), Barbara Boxer (D-CA), Barbara Mikulski (D-MD), Patty Murray (D-WA), Claire McCaskill (D-MO), and Debbie Stabenow (D-MI). Ultimately forty-five senators including almost the entire Democratic caucus cosponsored the legislation in the 110th Congress. When the bill passed in the 111th Congress, fifty-three of the fifty-nine Democrats cosponsored the bill.

To sell the bill and frame the public debate on the issue, Democratic women actively participated in press conferences and floor debate on the legislation. Senate Democrats decided to bring the bill to the floor on Equal Pay Day, April 22, 2008, a day that marks, on average, how far into the next year a woman has to work for her salary to catch up to what a man earned in the previous year (Montgomery 2008a). Barbara Mikulski (D-MD), a senior Democrat on the HELP Committee who is widely regarded as Dean of the Democratic women, organized the Democratic women to speak on the bill. A Democratic staffer explained, "Mikulski organized the women. She got them all to go down to the floor at the same time and to wear red. Kennedy asked Mikulski to lead these efforts to get the women, and she organized as many as would participate." After Democrats failed to get cloture on the bill, the women kept the issue alive for the elections, holding a rally in July 2008 with Lilly Ledbetter and the Democratic women of the House and Senate including Speaker Nancy Pelosi (D-CA) and Senator Hillary Clinton (D-NY), who had recently conceded the Democratic presidential nomination to Barack Obama (U.S. Senate Democratic Steering and Outreach Committee 2008).

When the 111th Congress convened in January 2009 with Democrats controlling the presidency and Congress, the Fair Pay Act was at the top of the Senate agenda. With Senator Kennedy (D-MA) gravely ill with brain cancer, Senator Mikulski (D-MD) became the lead sponsor of the bill. She shepherded the bill to passage by helping to negotiate the amendments that would be considered, leading press conferences to get out the Democratic message about the bill, and serving as the bill manager during floor debate where she argued passionately for the bill's passage and rebutted Republican amendments to weaken the bill. While Mikulski was the most active Senate proponent of the bill, across the two congresses, eleven of the thirteen Democratic women serving in either or both the 110th and 111th Congresses spoke during one of the floor debates held on the legislation.[3] Democrats kept the public focus on women and women's rights by staging a celebratory signing ceremony in which the first pen was given to Barbara Mikulski (D-MD) and the last to Lilly Ledbetter. President Obama spoke of his grandmother's trials working in a bank and his hope for his daughters, and First Lady Michelle Obama gave her first public policy address since the election (Stolberg 2009).

Clearly, for Democratic women, the debate over the Lilly Ledbetter Fair Pay Act allowed them to pursue public policy changes they supported, raise their media profile, and burnish the party's image as a champion of women's rights. For Republican women, decisions about whether and how extensively to involve themselves in the legislation were more complicated. First, business groups, a key element of the Republican base, vigorously opposed the legislation. Led by the Chamber of Commerce, business organizations feared that eliminating the 180-day statute of limitations would result in unlimited lawsuits leaving companies open to liability years after the alleged discrimination occurred. They also opposed other elements of the legislation such as a provision that would give other affected parties such as the spouse and not just the employee legal standing to file a lawsuit (Barnes 2007b; Johnson 2007; Langel 2009a). The Chamber of Commerce, the National Association of Manufacturers, and other business groups vigorously lobbied against the bill (Langel 2009a). The Chamber of Commerce scored the cloture vote in the 110th Congress and the final vote on the legislation in the 111th Congress (U.S. Chamber of Commerce 2008, 2009). Thus, a vote in favor of the equal pay bill would jeopardize a senator's ability to tout his or her 100% support score from the Chamber of Commerce as a symbol of conservative bona fides for the next election.

Republican women who might be inclined to support the Fair Pay Act faced a difficult choice. If they supported the bill, they invited the wrath of allies in the business community and risked alienating fellow Republicans. If they opposed the bill, Democrats would portray them as women who opposed women's rights and the media would echo that sentiment in their reporting on the votes. Indeed after the failed cloture vote in 2008, the *Washington Post* reported that Kay Bailey Hutchison (R-TX) was among those who were "clearly uncomfortable with the vote" and quoted Hutchison as saying, "I'm sure [the vote] will be spun as anti-equal pay, [but] there's definitely something I could have voted for" (Montgomery 2008b). Women's groups reinforced the message of a vote against the bill as a vote against women. Thus, EMILY's List, a group that supports Democratic pro-choice women, promised to highlight the vote in Elizabeth's Dole's (R-NC) re-election campaign to show "how Liddy Dole has lost touch with women voters" (Palmer 2008). A Democratic staffer summed up the dilemma of the Republican women, noting, "Women's groups were pressuring them and the Democratic message machine was pressuring them. Republican women felt pressure because Democrats were framing how the issue is viewed by the public as equal pay. Women are judged on a different standard on this issue. Voters expect a different result from women."

Moreover, Republicans who wanted to support the equal pay legislation had to contend with the fact that Democrats were clearly using the bill as a campaign issue against Republicans and their presidential candidate, Senator John McCain (R-AZ), in the 2008 elections. Democrats brought the legislation to the floor on Equal Pay Day. They did not send the bill through the committee process where Republicans could have offered amendments, and they filed for cloture with no plans to allow amendments on the floor. During floor consideration, Democrats held the debate open and delayed the vote so that their presidential candidates, Hillary Clinton (D-NY) and Barack Obama (D-IL), could return from the campaign trail to make speeches on the issue and contrast their support for women's rights with the absence and opposition to the legislation of presumptive Republican nominee John McCain (R-AZ) (Hulse 2008; Kellman 2008; Montgomery 2008b). Ultimately, procedural votes, particularly cloture votes, are party loyalty votes. Only six Republicans voted to invoke cloture on the Lilly Ledbetter Fair Pay Act in the 110th Congress. These Republicans included Arlen Specter (PA), Olympia Snowe (ME), Susan Collins (ME), and three Republican men who faced uphill battles for re-election including Gordon Smith (OR), John Sununu (NH), and Norm Coleman (MN). The other three Republican women, Lisa Murkowski (AK), Elizabeth Dole (NC), and Kay Bailey Hutchison (R-TX), all voted against cloture.

While Republicans opposed the bill, they did not like being portrayed as anti-women and favoring pay discrimination. As HELP ranking member Mike Enzi (R-WY) put it in the 2009 final floor debate, he was upset that anyone who spoke against the bill was accused of opposing equal pay or portrayed as "a sexist Neanderthal" (Hunt 2009). To fight back, Republicans needed an alternative that business groups could support. They needed to market their alternative in a way that would show that Republicans are for women's rights. Therefore, the party needed a Republican woman to serve as lead sponsor and spokesperson for their bill, and they turned to Kay Bailey Hutchison (R-TX) to offer the alternative legislation. A Republican staffer confirmed the party's strategy explaining,

> Republicans do want a spokesperson to put a good public face on an issue and deflect the criticism of Republicans as anti-women. Enzi [(R-WY), the ranking member on HELP] was writing the Ledbetter alternative but Republican leaders knew they did not

want a middle-aged white guy, that won't help make their case. We needed to find a woman we can get to agree to be the leader on the Republican alternative. We went to Murkowski [who was on the HELP committee] first, but she knows she will have a race [in 2010], and she did not want to be the public voice on this.[4] She does not want to be out there in a public forum on a controversial issue. We thought about Collins. Hutchison is in leadership. She agreed, and it would help her in her governor's race. [Hutchison was planning to challenge Republican Governor Rick Perry (TX) in the primary and needed to demonstrate her strong conservative principles for primary voters]. Enzi's staff helped Hutchison's staff draft the amendment. She told the leaders that at the end of the day, if the alternative fails she will vote for the Democratic bill because she and the other women do not want to be viewed as against women in the workplace.

Similarly, a former male Democratic senator asserted, Hutchison was "acting as a foil for the caucus and being a good soldier. The parties do this a lot where they have a companion amendment that really guts the bill. Republicans needed a woman to do it, and she was being a good soldier. In Texas she is not going to pay a price for this even among women . . . The bill put Republicans on the defensive, but it is not a huge national issue that they will pay a price for." Hutchison actively advocated for the Republican alternative on the floor. The amendment, which was supported by the Chamber of Commerce, would reinstate the six-month clock for filing a complaint after the woman knew or should have known about the discriminatory action. Thus, a woman would need to affirmatively prove that she did not know about the pay disparity before she filed the lawsuit (Langel 2009a, 2009b). On the floor, Hutchison sought to blunt Democratic criticism of the alternative by noting, "I have certainly been a person who has known discrimination. I want everyone who believes they have a cause of action to have that right. I have also been a business owner. I know how important it is that our businesses know what their potential liabilities are" (Congressional Record, January 15, 2009, S588–589).

Among Republicans, Olympia Snowe (R-ME) was the most consistently supportive of the legislation. She was the only Republican to cosponsor the Democratic bill across the two congresses. Arlen Specter (R-PA) had cosponsored the bill when it was first introduced in the 110th Congress, but facing a conservative primary challenger in his bid for re-election in 2010, when the bill came up again in the 111th

Congress, Specter was not a cosponsor. Moreover, during floor consideration, he offered two amendments designed to limit the scope of the legislation. Snowe was also the only Republican to speak in favor of the bill on the floor both times it was debated, emphasizing her long history of activism on the issue dating back to the Reagan years and her work in the House of Representatives (Congressional Record, April 24, 2008, S3395–3396; Congressional Record, January 22, 2009 S769). She was the only Republican who voted against the Republican alternative bill embodied in the Hutchison amendment. She did not appear at the Democratic Party press conferences promoting the legislation. However, she and Susan Collins (R-ME) accepted invitations to President Obama's signing ceremony (Stolberg 2009).

While Snowe strongly supported the bill and often served as the lone Republican advocate, the other women tread more carefully as they balanced their interest in women's rights and their desire to remain loyal to the Republican caucus. Thus, Susan Collins (R-ME) did not cosponsor the legislation and never spoke in favor of the bill on the floor. Collins, Lisa Murkowski (R-AK), and Kay Bailey Hutchison (R-TX) all voted for both the Republican alternative and the final legislation.[5] Murkowski spoke in favor of the Hutchison alternative on the floor and touted her cosponsorship of the measure (Congressional Record, January 21, 2009, S698–S699). After the Hutchison amendment failed, Murkowski gave another floor speech expressing her disappointment that the alternative failed and announcing her intention to support the final bill (Congressional Record, January 22, 2009, S767–S768). After serving as the lead sponsor and floor manager for the Republican alternative, Kay Bailey Hutchison (R-TX) then voted in favor of the Democratic bill.

In sum, the struggle to enact the Lilly Ledbetter Fair Pay Act demonstrates that as a result of shared gender experiences, women are more motivated to engage issues of women's rights. These personal interests are reinforced by beliefs of fellow members and the media that female senators are more connected to issues that concern the status of women in society. For Democratic women the alignment of women's rights with the policy goals of the party provides even more incentive for Democratic women to actively pursue policy change. Thus, Democratic women heavily promoted the Lilly Ledbetter Fair Pay Act, helping to make it a positive issue for Democrats to advertise in congressional campaigns and the presidential race. For Republican women, the Ledbetter bill set up a conflict between female senators' individual desire to support women's rights and long-standing Republican concerns about the impact of this type of legislation on business. At the same time the

Republican leadership wanted to capitalize on the gender identity of individual Republican women, asking them to take the lead in arguing the Republican viewpoint in order to demonstrate that Republicans do not condone discrimination and the Republican position on the bill was not anti-women. As a result, each individual Republican woman engaged in strategic positioning on how publicly to participate in the debate and how to utilize her votes on the bill and the amendments to demonstrate support for women's rights and support for the party.

Abortion Politics

By far the most hotly debated women's rights issue in Congress is abortion. Pro-choice groups and activists are an important force in the Democratic Party, and pro-life organizations and social conservatives represent key elements of the base of the Republican Party. In his study of abortion and the parties, Greg Adams (1997) notes that the evolution of abortion into an issue that largely divides on party lines was driven by elites, including members of Congress and interest group activists. Voters responded to the increasingly distinct party reputations on the issue and began to realign their party affiliations (see also Sanbonmatsu 2002b; Wolbrecht 2000). However, public opinion scholars maintain that the mass public is more ambivalent than elites on abortion and their views have largely remained stable over time. For example, analyses of General Social Survey data since 1972 indicate that 80%–90% of the public supports abortion in traumatic cases including rape, endangerment of the woman's health, or risk of birth defects in the infant. However, public support drops to 40%–50% in more elective cases, including if the family cannot afford the child or if a married or unmarried woman does not want a child (Ainsworth and Hall 2011; Fiorina with Abrams and Pope 2005; Cook, Jelen, and Wilcox 1992).

The ambivalence of the public combined with the intensity of the activists encourages members of Congress to adopt a legislative strategy that Ainsworth and Hall (2011) characterize as strategic incrementalism in which legislators pursue smaller goals that can be framed in a way to attract majority public support. Thus, pro-life activists have largely abandoned serious pursuit of a Human Life Amendment to reverse the *Roe v. Wade* decision in favor of more incremental strategies that restrict access to abortion services. Pro-choice forces emphasize expanded access to contraception and preventive services as a way of reducing unwanted pregnancies. Ainsworth and Hall (2011) note that these incremental proposals are designed to achieve gradual shifts in public policy.

The pursuit of an incremental strategy also means that abortion-related initiatives are constantly on the congressional agenda. These proposals touch a broad range of public policies. For example, the Hyde amendment was initially passed to restrict access to abortion services by prohibiting federal funding for abortion through the Medicaid program. Since the passage of the Hyde amendment, Congress routinely considers a wide range of bills aimed at prohibiting federal funding of abortion including proposals to deny funding for global family planning organizations that also perform abortions, initiatives related to coverage of abortion services in the Federal Employee Health Benefits Plan, and legislation to allow women to utilize their private money to pay for abortions on military bases (O'Connor 1996; Rose 2006; Ainsworth and Hall 2011). Beyond the ubiquity of abortion-related legislation on the congressional agenda, conflicts over abortion often imperil the fate of major legislation. Most recently, President Obama's landmark health insurance reform legislation was almost derailed by a dispute with a coalition of pro-life Democrats over how to ensure that insurance plans on the state exchanges that offer coverage for abortions do not receive any of the federal money used to subsidize the premiums of low-income Americans (MacGillis 2009; Herszenhorn and Calmes 2009). Similarly, in 2011, Congress barely avoided a government shutdown when abortion was inserted into the overriding debate between Republicans and Democrats over how much government spending needed to be cut to demonstrate commitment to deficit reduction. Republicans pressed for a proposal to strip Planned Parenthood of its federal funding for family planning services because it also provides abortions with nonfederal dollars. The provision was among the last conflicts resolved before the budget bill to fund all of the government's services for the rest of the fiscal year could be passed (Bolton 2011a; Kane, Rucker, and Fahrenthold 2011).

The prominence of abortion on the Congressional agenda means that all senators are forced to continuously cast votes on the issue regardless of their desire to engage the subject. It also means that those senators who choose to prioritize abortion disputes must devote significant political capital and a sizeable portion of their legislative portfolio to the issue because abortion-related proposals are guaranteed to reach the agenda and these debates will repeat year after year. As one liberal Democratic staffer put it, "Congress is constantly debating the irrationality of women on abortion." Abortion debates require a particularly intense commitment because of the passion of the activists and the propensity of these disputes to trigger high-profile confrontations that can imperil the fate of larger must-pass legislation from Appropriations bills to major policy initiatives. Moreover, the cultural conflicts embodied in abortion politics and the high stakes attached to many of these debates mean there will be intense media coverage of senators who take an active role in these debates and abortion will become one of the definitive aspects of the senator's public profile. Thus, a Republican staffer to a male senator who is a leading advocate of pro-life legislation complained, "By being so outspoken on life issues [—] and others who do it get pigeonholed by the media and by colleagues as the abortion guy. They don't think he is the guy with the law degree or he is a trade expert or he has expertise and did hearings on reorganization of the executive branch. He gets marginalized. Rick Santorum [R-PA] suffers from that too, and he is going to lose [his 2006 re-election bid] because of it." Reaffirming the sensitivity of the issue and the impact on a senator's reputation, another Republican staffer said, "[—] did not do either gay marriage or abortion. He is more careful about his long-term role and does not want to be the icon on social issues."

Senators who engage abortion policy can achieve important benefits including advancing personal policy priorities and ideological beliefs, attracting base voter and activist support and donations, and gaining media coverage. However, they must weigh these benefits against the costs of mobilizing opposition forces, devoting scarce time and resources to the issue, and attracting media attention that cements a public reputation tied to abortion politics. This cost-benefit calculation is intensified for women senators because of the direct connection of reproductive rights to the status of women in American society. Beyond any enhanced personal commitment that women may feel for the issue, the parties and interest groups seek to capitalize on women's moral authority and credibility as part of their efforts to frame particular proposals and sway public opinion.

The decision of women to actively participate in abortion-related controversies and to serve as party spokespersons on the issue depends on the intensity of their personal views and how well those views match with the opinions of their constituency and the majority position in the party. Thus, Barbara Boxer (D-CA), a liberal Democrat from a solidly Democratic state, can easily champion pro-choice positions, while Mary Landrieu (D-LA), a conservative Democrat representing an increasingly red state with a large population of Catholic voters, must exercise more caution as she decides what position to take and how actively to engage the issue. To date, most Republican women who have served in the Senate espouse a more liberal position on the issue than the rest of their caucus, setting up a conflict between their personal ideology and the views of their constituency against the dominant position of the Republican caucus. Even some of the more conservative women such as Kay Bailey Hutchison (R-TX) have taken more moderate positions on the issue than other ideologically similar colleagues. Other conservative women such as Elizabeth Dole (R-NC) who share a commitment to the pro-life cause have not wanted to take a leadership role on the issue, fearing that it will dominate their agenda and alienate more moderate voters. In recent years, only first-term senator Kelly Ayotte (R-NH) has taken a prominent role in abortion politics, defending the Republican position against requiring contraceptive coverage in the health care bill as an intrusion on religious freedom (Ayotte 2012a, 2012b).

Women Senators and Abortion Politics. In their landmark work on issue evolution in American politics, Carmines and Stimson (1989) divide policies into easy and hard issues. Abortion constitutes a classic easy issue because voters readily understand the subject regardless of their level of political knowledge. Moreover, voters react to abortion instinctively and emotionally and have firm opinions on the topic (Sanbonmatsu 2002b; Alvarez and Brehm 1995). Senators recognize the saliency of the issue for their voters, and they work to balance their personal views on the subject with constituent opinion. Moreover, the senator's political ideology and religious beliefs, constituent views, and the position of the party all impact how actively a senator engages specific policy debates over abortion.

Senate staffers generally agreed that women senators are more liberal on abortion rights than similarly situated male colleagues. Thus, a Democratic staffer asserted simply, "[W]omen are more pro-choice because they believe that women are more competent. [For example,] Durbin [D-IL] is ambivalent about choice, but he understands the political realities of where his constituents are. It is not as intuitive as having a belief about it." Highlighting the depth of belief, another Democratic staffer noted, Dianne Feinstein (D-CA) "has personal memories of an era before *Roe* that the new generation does not." Another Democratic staffer believed that the public recognizes that women have a more vested interest in the subject and expects women to be more liberal on the issue. According to this staffer, "Women are less afraid of these issues [abortion, family planning]. They have the same constituency problem, but the constituency will forgive a woman for being more liberal on women's issues because they think women have more of a right to speak their mind on it."

While women are generally perceived as more pro-choice, there is a great deal of variation among women senators in their personal comfort level with the issue and the constituency pressures they face. Liberal Democratic senators with pro-choice constituencies such as Barbara Boxer (D-CA), Dianne Feinstein (D-CA), Hillary Clinton (D-NY), Kirsten Gillibrand (D-NY), and Patty Murray (D-WA) are the strongest and most vocal supporters of abortion rights. Many staffers identified Barbara Boxer (D-CA) as the leading pro-choice advocate in the Senate. Thus, one conservative Democratic staffer said, "Boxer is the linchpin on abortion. NARAL [National Abortion Rights Action League] sees her as most sympathetic to their cause, and she is used to pressur[ing] people." Another Democratic staffer said, "Boxer likes to talk about abortion. California is a strongly pro-choice state, and abortion is her number one contrast issue [with Republican electoral opponents]. She gets a lot of media coverage in California because she talks about women's lives and what is at stake, and we can't let the right wing take away our rights."

Other female senators who are known as pro-choice advocates express more ambivalence about abortion and are more circumspect about taking a leadership role on the issue. This is particularly true for some of the Catholic senators, who, like their male colleagues, experience conflict among their political position, their own personal religious views, and pressure from the Church. For example, a Republican staffer said, "Collins is a Catholic, and she takes a lot of crap from the Church for her pro-choice position. She tries not to be in your face about it." Another Republican staffer agreed noting, "Snowe is very committed to pro-choice issues. Collins does not want to be out in front on abortion issues. She is Catholic and wants it both ways on abortion. She will never take the lead on abortion or gay marriage; she hates those social issues." Other staffers maintained that Catholic female senators such as Mary Landrieu (D-LA) and Barbara Mikulski (D-MD) will take more time to study an issue and will require staffers to get their personal approval before signing on to letters or proposals dealing with abortion. One Democratic staffer explained, "Mikulski is Catholic. She is pro-choice and will always vote pro-choice. She does not like to talk about the issue. Anything that came into the office on reproductive rights had to be discussed with her. If there was a letter you had to go over it with her before she would sign on to it. Clinton [D-NY] and Murray [D-WA] would sign a letter in a second. Mikulski you had to show it to her and talk to her."

Female Democrats with conservative constituencies including Mary Landrieu (D-LA) and Blanche Lincoln (D-AR) also confront a more complicated environment in which their personal views are more liberal than that of their male Democratic counterparts and their constituency. For example, one Democratic staffer explained, "Lincoln [D-AR] is pro-choice. Pryor [D-AR] would not want a label but he is pro-life. Abortion is a big issue in Arkansas; they all go to church. Abortion and taxes are the biggest issues in the state." Similarly, another Democratic staffer said,

> Arkansas voters are very pro-life. There are 40% of voters in Arkansas that Lincoln will never reach because of abortion and her gay marriage vote. Lincoln is religious, but she is also a believer in women's rights, and her husband is an OBGYN. [She voted for the partial birth abortion ban] because of the barrage of constituent input. She thinks there is no such thing as a partial birth abortion. There are maybe twenty cases per year, but Arkansans who were calling in think hundreds are done every day, and the staff told her that if she votes against it ads will be run against her. This was a political and not an intellectual vote for her. She just votes on abortion issues like Partial Birth and Unborn Victims of Violence. She is not a lawyer and not comfortable in that arena, so she lets the committee people handle it. The longer you are in office the more you can take an intellectually honest vote. Dale Bumpers [former Arkansas Democratic senator 1975–1998] was a liberal voter, but he had been there a very long time and took the attitude that he was going to educate the constituents and could be a statesman. People in their first and second terms like Pryor and Lincoln cannot make intellectually honest votes. They have to pay attention to their constituents.[6]

Interestingly, during the debate over the partial birth abortion ban, Lincoln and Landrieu's male state colleagues, senators Mark Pryor (D-AR) and John Breaux (D-LA), were among the five male Democrats who opposed an amendment endorsing *Roe v. Wade* as an appropriate decision that should not be overturned. Meanwhile, both Blanche Lincoln (D-AR) and Mary Landrieu (D-LA) voted to reaffirm *Roe.*

Like Blanche Lincoln (D-AR), Mary Landrieu's (D-LA) qualified support for abortion rights has caused trouble for her with the Louisiana electorate and complicates her efforts to delineate positions that she is personally comfortable with and reflect the views of her constituency. A Democratic staffer maintained, "Landrieu votes pro-choice in a Catholic state. She is in between pro-life and pro-choice and has upset the Church. The Archbishop of New Orleans called for her defeat. Breaux does not agonize over votes. He supports pro-life and won't analyze every part of the vote. Mary analyzes, she sees shades of gray."

While Lincoln was described as limiting herself to voting on the issue and avoiding any other engagement of social issues, Landrieu has taken a more active role in abortion politics, working to flesh out the shades of gray by promoting policies that focus on child welfare. These proposals are meant to shift attention away from the controversial issue of abortion and deliver the message that Republicans are too focused on abortion and need to support policies to take care of vulnerable populations of children. For example, when legislation banning partial birth abortion was debated for a third time in the 106th Congress, Landrieu offered an amendment expressing the sense of the Senate that the government should fully fund the economic, education, and medical requirements of families who have children with special needs. In the 108th Congress, when Congress was debating the Unborn Victims of Violence Act, more commonly known as Laci and Conner's Law after a seven months pregnant woman and her unborn son who were brutally murdered by the woman's husband, Landrieu tried to draw attention to the need for adoption funding. Adoption is a particularly important cause for Landrieu because she has two adopted children and she is among the most active members of Congress on the issue (Mikulski et al. 2001). A Democratic staffer recounted, "On the Laci and Conner's Law, Mary wanted adoption funding, and she got into an embarrassing fight with Petersen's father-in-law, telling him, if you care about kids you will support adoption funding. Breaux simplifies, Mary complicates."

In addition to these cases where Landrieu has worked to show herself as committed to children, Landrieu has taken some more overtly pro-life positions. Most notably, she became the lead and only Democratic cosponsor on a bill to ban human cloning that became part of the long fight over the ethics of stem cell research. The bill was sponsored by one of the most prominent pro-life senators, Sam Brownback (R-KS).[7] Some staffers characterized Landrieu's decision to cosponsor the bill as an effort to inoculate herself against pro-life criticism in her upcoming 2002 battle for re-election. The Louisiana press did cover her activism on the legislation and her vote to ban partial birth abortion as evidence of her efforts to reach out to pro-life voters (Alpert 2002a, 2002b; B. Walsh 2002). Others felt her participation reflected her sincere belief and opposition to federal funding of stem cell research. Thus, a Republican staffer recounted, "Landrieu got it in her heart, and she offered to be the lead Democratic cosponsor on the bill. This means she worked the Democratic side of the aisle to get support and cosponsors and to keep opposition from becoming Democratic orthodoxy or a Democratic leadership position. She fought to protect their [bill supporters] prerogatives." Landrieu remained the only Democratic cosponsor when the legislation was reintroduced in the 108th, 109th, and 110th Congresses.

In addition to the difficulty of reconciling their personal views with the imperative of representing their constituency, Landrieu and Lincoln also have to navigate the more liberal demands of Democratic campaign donors. Thus, both Landrieu and Lincoln lost their EMILY's List funding after they voted in favor of the partial birth abortion ban. According to one Democratic staffer,

> Lincoln and Landrieu lost their EMILY's List support on that vote. They came into the office, Ellen Malcolm [head of EMILY's List] and their people and said that Mary and Blanche misled them and had said they [Lincoln and Landrieu] would be with them [EMILY's List]. We tried to tell them that if you are not for Lincoln and Landrieu that you will get some crazy nut that says women who are raped won't get pregnant because they have a protective little shield. But they withdrew all their support from her and wrote a letter to their donors telling them that they are no longer supporting them [Lincoln and Landrieu] and they should urge others not to either. Landrieu and Lincoln were pissed off that the group was so all or nothing, but that is politics. That is a lot of money to walk away from but she had to do it because of the constituency.

Indeed, the *Times-Picayune* reported that EMILY's List was the largest single donor to Landrieu's 1996 campaign, donating $375,000 to her race (B. Walsh 2002). As Democrats in conservative southern states, Landrieu and Lincoln always confront highly competitive and expensive elections, underscoring the importance of large donors. Indeed, after surviving a strong primary challenge from a more liberal Democrat, Blanche Lincoln (D-AR) was defeated in the 2010 Republican wave election.

Fighting the Battles

Clearly, female senators, while characterized as generally more pro-choice, are not uniform in their views as some senators are more internally conflicted on the issue than others. Moreover, the female senators represent vastly different constituencies. The ideologically liberal California voters represented by Barbara Boxer (D-CA) and Dianne Feinstein (D-CA) reward a strongly pro-choice advocate, while the more socially conservative constituents of Mary Landrieu (D-LA) and Blanche Lincoln (D-AR) are firmly pro-life. Still, because of the intensity of their commitment to reproductive rights and the strong public connection of the issue to the role of women in American society, female senators are routinely at the center of congressional debates over abortion and contraception. Staffers pointed to numerous cases where female senators, particularly Democratic senators, took a lead role offering amendments, pushing legislation, and aggressively advocating for their position. Many of the abortion battles in Congress are fought over riders to must-pass Appropriations bills. Senate staff noted that women are often the lead proponents of pro-choice amendments to these spending bills. Thus, one staffer recounted, "Murray and Boxer do the abortion amendments on the defense bill. [Pro-choice male Democrat] does not because if you don't need to take the heat as a Catholic . . . He does things quietly in committee on women's rights; women fight the fight on this." Similarly, another staffer said, "Murray has the annual amendment on overseas abortion. It is always women in the debate. Mikulski always does the amendment for the Treasury-Postal Appropriations bill requiring the Federal Health Benefits Plan to cover abortion." Other staffers identified Olympia Snowe (R-ME) as a senator who was particularly committed to abortion rights and often serves as the lead and many times only Republican cosponsor of pro-choice proposals.

In addition to offering amendments on the floor, women will use other senatorial prerogatives to press their position on reproductive rights. Thus, a staffer recounted that among the many liberal Democratic members of the HELP Committee, it was Hillary Clinton (D-NY) and Patty Murray (D-WA) who placed holds on two different Food and Drug Administration (FDA) nominees in a three-year period in order to force the Bush administration and the FDA to issue a decision on whether Plan B, a form of emergency contraception, would be approved for over-the-counter use (Schuler 2005a, 2005b; Crowley 2006).[8] "It was Clinton and Murray on holding the FDA nominee because they have a comfort level and commitment on Plan B that you get from women. [Among HELP Committee members] Murray and Clinton were the bosses who were the most worked up about it, and they are the most comfortable in dealing with it."

For Democratic women, their personal commitment to reproductive rights is reinforced by the party's desire to capitalize on their moral authority to deliver the message that the Democratic Party supports women's rights. Thus, a Democratic leadership staffer explained that the party will have women offer the abortion-related amendments because "women voters are a big electoral voting block, and having women as spokespersons is more compelling to draw the contrast than if you had Sheldon Whitehouse [D-RI] going up against [Jim] Bunning [R-KY] and [Tom] Coburn [R-OK]." Speaking about the Unborn Victims of Violence Act, a Republican initiative that created a separate offense for those who kill an unborn child at any stage of development in the process of committing a federal crime, another Democratic staffer maintained that leadership asked Dianne Feinstein (D-CA), the lone Democratic woman on the Judiciary Committee, to take the lead and offer the Democratic alternative to the bill.

> Leadership wanted Feinstein to take the lead in offering the Democratic alternative because they wanted a woman and someone who could hold her own on the floor and would do her homework and be a good debater against Santorum [(R-PA) Republican conference chair and leading pro-life advocate]. Daschle [(D-SD) the Democratic leader] asked her to be the lead rather than Leahy [(D-VT) Judiciary Ranking Member] doing it. Feinstein is not a cheerleader on abortion. She has her ethics concerns. Feinstein wants to prevent conservative legislation from rolling back time on women. She does not want male legislators rather than doctors to dictate a woman's decisions about her body. She sees it as a slippery slope. She also does not want this to be her only role.

Explaining why Hillary Clinton (D-NY) and Patty Murray (D-WA) took up the cause of getting the FDA to approve Plan B for use without a prescription, a Democratic staffer asserted, "They have more credibility to talk about the issue as women, and they will create more discomfort with colleagues and the administration as they try to defend their position." Similarly, another Democratic staffer said, "It is a win-win for them because they believe in it and they are playing to the women constituency, showing women voters that Democrats care about women's issues and Republicans are hurting them. It is best to have a woman delivering that message."

Finally, the Democratic women also work together as a group to deliver the message that Democrats are fighting for women's reproductive rights. Thus, when funding for Planned Parenthood became part of the 2011 budget battle, Democratic women joined together to denounce Republicans for waging a war on women's health (Sarlin 2011). Nine Democratic women held a press conference decrying what Maria Cantwell (D-WA) characterized as Republicans' decision to "wage a war on women's health, and we [the Senate Democratic women] are the last line of defense." Kay Hagan (D-NC) asked Republicans to "stop playing political Russian Roulette with women's health services" (Gillibrand 2011). The women also organized themselves to give a series of speeches on the Senate floor highlighting the important preventive services offered by Planned Parenthood in their states and accusing Republicans of wanting to take away pap smears and mammograms from low-income women (Congressional Record, April 13, 2011 S2422–S2426, S2441). Thus, Kirsten Gillibrand (D-NY) declared,

> American women, make no mistake about it, this is an attack on you. It is an attack on every preventive health service, every safety net, everything you care about, whether it is early childhood education, Pap smears, mammograms or prenatal care when you are pregnant. That is what their [Republican] efforts are all about, and you should just know you have women of the Senate, who will stand by you. We have drawn this line in the sand, and we will not allow them to cross it. We are your voice in Washington, we are your voice in Congress, and we will protect you and the basic safety nets and equality you should expect out of the US Government." (Congressional Record, April 13, 2011 S2426)

Thus, Democratic women capitalize on their moral authority as women to individually and collectively champion reproductive rights and to denounce Republicans as harming women's health. For most, but not all, of the Democratic women, their individual position on the issue is in line with the majority position of the caucus, and their activism on the issue fires up the Democratic activist and donor base.

For Republican women, navigating the politics of abortion is much more complicated. The individual Republican women hold a wider range of views on the issue than do Democratic women, making it unlikely that they would join together to express a particular view on abortion in the way that Democratic women do. Thus, Olympia Snowe (R-ME) and Susan Collins (R-ME) are firmly pro-choice, while Kelly Ayotte (R-NH) and former senator Elizabeth Dole (R-NC) are strongly pro-life. Kay Bailey Hutchison (R-TX) and Lisa Murkowski (R-AK) have largely pro-life voting records, but both have taken some more liberal positions on reproductive rights. For example, Lisa Murkowski (R-AK) generally supports pro-life initiatives, but she was one of five Republican senators voting against the Republican proposal to eliminate federal funding for Planned Parenthood as part of the agreement on the 2011 federal budget (Kliff 2011a; Bolton 2011b). Kay Bailey Hutchison (R-TX) routinely votes in favor of proposals restricting federal funding and placing constraints on access to abortion, but she also supports *Roe v. Wade* as the law of the land (Ratcliffe 2010). She and Lisa Murkowski (R-AK) voted for a Democratic amendment to reaffirm congressional support for the decision that was attached to the legislation banning partial birth abortion in the 108th Congress.

Since social conservatives are a key component of the Republican Party's base, advocacy of pro-choice policies or position taking that is not uniformly pro-life can activate powerful opposition forces that will run ads and organize votes against a candidate. When moderate senators cast pro-choice votes, they worry that conservative activists will recruit pro-life candidates to challenge them in the next Republican primary. Thus, Scott Brown (R-MA) and Olympia Snowe's (R-ME) votes against the proposal to eliminate federal funding for family planning services provided ammunition for conservative activists hoping to recruit primary challengers to unseat the senators in their 2012 re-election bids (Bolton 2011b). Arlen Specter (R-PA) and Lincoln Chafee (R-RI) both faced strong conservative primary challenges in their races in 2006 and 2010.[9] Fear of losing the Republican primary led Specter to change his party affiliation to Democrat in 2009. He then lost the Democratic primary.

While they fear conservative primary challenges, in the general election, moderate Republicans utilize their pro-choice stance to attract Democratic voters to their electoral coalition. Moderate Republicans value the endorsements of pro-choice groups like NARAL and Planned Parenthood to demonstrate their commitment to women's rights to voters. At the same time, these Republicans have an uneasy relationship with the pro-choice groups because these organizations are largely associated with the Democratic Party. Thus, a Republican staffer complained, "The money and the endorsements from the pro-choice groups go mostly to the Democrats. You are never pro-choice enough if you are a Republican. They will treat a Boxer [D-CA] differently than Snowe [R-ME] doing the same thing."

Party leaders recognize that moderate Republican senators hail from more liberal constituencies whose general election voters are more pro-choice. They are less inclined to forgive pro-choice votes by senators like Kay Bailey Hutchison (R-TX) who represent solidly conservative states. A Republican staffer explained, "A conservative Republican could not get elected in Maine. It does not mean they [the leadership] are never mad if she defects. It would be harder for Kay Bailey Hutchison [R-TX] to defect on women's issues and other issues because she is from Texas with conservative constituents so she has no constituency excuse. The leaders will be less understanding." Indeed, Hutchison has endured significant criticism for her support of the *Roe v. Wade* decision. Incensed by Hutchison's support for *Roe*, in 1996, delegates to the Texas state party convention tried to block her from being seated as a delegate at the Republican National Convention. Pro-life groups organized against Hutchison in her 2010 primary race to become governor of Texas (Ratcliffe 2010).

Since Republican female senators generally hold more liberal views on abortion than the majority of the Republican caucus, these senators do not publicly advocate for pro-life legislation. However, they try not to cross the party leadership by publicly condemning Republican proposals in the way that Democratic women come together to denounce these initiatives. For example, referring to the debate over partial birth abortion, a Democratic staffer said, "Neither Snowe nor Collins will vote for PBA [the Partial Birth Abortion Act], but they won't make a big speech against it either. They are not going to get leadership positions, but they don't want to get kicked further to the curb." Similarly, Republican women including Lisa Murkowski (R-AK), Susan Collins (R-ME), and Olympia Snowe (R-ME) were among the five Republican senators voting against the proposal to eliminate funding for Planned Parenthood (Bolton 2011b).[10] However, while Democratic women organized press conferences and floor colloquies to condemn the Republican plan as jeopardizing women's health, Republican women largely stayed silent. Indeed, press coverage in the run-up to the budget vote portrayed moderate Republicans including Susan Collins (R-ME), Olympia Snowe (R-ME), and Scott Brown (R-MA) as making general statements of support for family planning funding, while trying not to specifically comment on the Republican budget proposal (Kliff 2011b; Marcos 2011).

Even Republican women who are strongly pro-life avoid taking a high-profile role on the issue because they do not want to become the public face of abortion politics. Thus, to respond to Democratic charges that Republicans were waging a war on women's health, the party had to turn to female Republicans in the House. Republicans organized a press conference with fifteen of the House Republican women to divert attention from the Planned Parenthood rider and deliver the message that Democratic refusal to cut spending was "economic child abuse" (Cogan 2011). Clearly, for Republican women the politics of abortion is fraught with complications. They must tread carefully as they try to reconcile their individual views with a strongly pro-life caucus and activist base. Pro-choice Republican women seek to maintain voting records supporting reproductive rights, while avoiding alienating their pro-life colleagues. Pro-life Republican women vote their preferences, while resisting efforts to elevate their public role by becoming party spokespersons.

"Partial Birth" Abortion

The eight-year battle (1995–2003) to enact a ban on "partial birth" abortions represents a landmark struggle in the contemporary politics of abortion. Focusing on the Senate's role in this debate illustrates the gender and partisan dynamics of policy making on reproductive rights. Women, particularly Democratic women and moderate Republican women, were heavily involved in developing and negotiating alternative amendments to the bill and publicly lobbying for their views. Overall, the issue and public opinion strongly favored the pro-life position, and the bill was a high priority of the Republican Party (Sellers 2010; Freedman 2003). In this unfavorable political environment, the depth of women's commitment to reproductive rights became particularly important as a motivating factor for participation. Moreover, the credibility women senators wielded as surrogates for the interests of women in society reinforced their position as opinion leaders within the Democratic caucus. By contrast, Republican men were the prime movers of the Partial Birth Abortion Act. Republican women did not carry the party message on the issue. While only Olympia Snowe (R-ME) and Susan Collins (R-ME) voted against the ban, examination of the votes on the bill and the numerous amendments debated demonstrates that to varying degrees, four of the five Republican women supported positions that were contrary to the majority of the caucus.

The partial birth abortion ban represents the first federal statute to restrict an abortion procedure since the Supreme Court legalized abortion in *Roe v. Wade*. The law makes it a federal crime punishable by fines and up to two years in prison for a doctor to perform the intact dilation and extraction (D&X) procedure unless a pregnant woman's life is endangered. Husbands and the parents of minors under eighteen can sue doctors for damages in civil court (Dlouhy 2003c). Congress debated the legislation five times in an eight-year period before it finally passed in 2003. President Clinton vetoed the bill twice, in the 104th (1995–96) and 105th (1997–98) Congresses, because the legislation only included an exception for the life and not the health of the mother. Both times the House overrode the veto. Abortion rights supporters looked to the Senate as the last bulwark in their efforts to thwart the legislation. The Senate upheld Clinton's veto by the narrowest of margins, nine votes in the 104th Congress and three votes in the 105th Congress (Idelson and Palmer 1995; Palmer 1996; Carey 1998b). In the 106th Congress (1999–2000), the House and Senate passed versions of the bill, but it never reached the president's desk because the Supreme Court declared a similar Nebraska law banning partial birth abortion unconstitutional. In the 5-4 *Stenberg v. Carhart* (2000) decision authored by Sandra Day O'Connor, the court declared that the law constituted an undue burden on a woman's access to abortion because the legislation did not include an exception for the health of the mother and because the definition of the procedure was too broad and could be interpreted to ban not just the D&X procedure but also D&E (dilation and evacuation) procedures commonly used in second trimester abortions (Palmer 2000a; 2000b). The House passed a revised version of the legislation in the 107th Congress (2001–2003), but Democrats kept the issue off of the Senate agenda after they took over the majority in May 2001. Finally, in the 108th Congress (2003–2004), with Republican president George W. Bush in the White House and the House and Senate firmly in Republican control, Congress was poised to pass the Partial Birth Abortion Act. By 2003, thirty-one states had passed partial birth abortion bans. To address the Supreme Court's ruling, the Republican authors of the bill refined the definition of the procedure. Rather than create an exception for the health of the mother, which ban supporters believed would weaken the bill, the sponsors included congressional findings maintaining that the procedure is never necessary to protect the health of the mother (Dlouhy 2003a, 2003b; Gutmacher Institute 2011). The legislation passed into law in 2003, and opponents immediately went to court. In 2007, by a 5-4 majority in *Gonzales v. Carhart*, a newly constituted Supreme Court, in which the more strongly conservative Samuel Alito replaced Sandra Day O'Connor, reversed the *Stenberg v. Carhart* ruling and upheld the partial birth abortion ban (Perine 2007).

Throughout the long debate over partial birth abortion, the issue clearly favored Republicans. From the beginning a majority of the public supported a late-term abortion ban. Thus, Gallup reported that 57% of the public supported a partial birth abortion ban in 1996. By November 2003, 68% of Americans favored a ban with much of the growth in support coming from self-described pro-choice Americans (Freedman 2003). Indeed, the pro-life community dominated the public framing of the issue, coining the term "partial birth" rather than utilizing the medical definition of the procedure, dilation and extraction. The public responded to floor speeches and political ads using the language of infanticide and graphic descriptions of the procedure that showed full-term fetuses being pulled out of the birth canal and having scissors stuck in their skulls (Greenblatt 1998; Carey 2000; Hulse 2003a, 2003b; Stolberg 2003a). As a result, the debate shifted away from a woman's right to choose toward what rights belong to the fetus, and some pollsters reported that the conflict over partial birth abortion decreased overall public support for abortion rights (Carey 1998a; Greenblatt 1998; Freedman 2003).

Recognizing their advantage, Republicans made partial birth abortion a prominent campaign issue. The votes to override the two Clinton vetoes were scheduled as close as possible to the 1996 and 1998 elections. Republicans hoped their presidential candidate Senator Bob Dole (R-KS) could use the issue against President Clinton in the 1996 election (Palmer 1996). In an effort to mobilize base voters in a midterm election year, the 1998 veto override vote was timed to the annual Washington, D.C., meeting of the Christian Coalition (Seeyle 1998). After the 2000 Supreme Court decision overturning the ban, partial birth abortion became one of the symbols of an activist judiciary employed by Republican presidential candidate George W. Bush. Al Gore warned that the next president could use his Supreme Court appointees to overturn *Roe* (Alvarez 2000; Greenburg 2007). When the ban passed the Senate in 2003, the Democratic presidential candidates, John Kerry (D-MA), John Edwards (D-NC), and Joe Biden (D-DE), all missed the vote (Fagan 2003).

At an individual level, Democratic senators were very nervous about the partial birth abortion debate. Many pro-choice senators were troubled by the graphic descriptions of the procedure. A Democratic staffer recounted, "Leahy [D-VT] and Kerry [D-MA] and even Kennedy

[D-MA] who would be fine politically to oppose the ban were personally uncomfortable with the procedure and the description." Liberal Democratic icon Patrick Moynihan (D-NY) declared the procedure was infanticide, and several pro-choice senators became early votes in favor of the ban including Patrick Leahy (D-VT), Joe Biden (D-DE), and Arlen Specter (R-PA) (Sullivan 2003; Carey 1997). The Catholic Church and organizations such as the U.S. Conference of Catholic Bishops actively lobbied for the ban, putting pressure on Catholic senators who were struggling with their own personal religious beliefs and wanted to avoid a confrontation with the Church (Sullivan 2003).

Democratic senators also feared the electoral consequences of opposing the ban. The issue split Democratic Catholic voters and could have alienated pro-choice liberal Democratic women (Sellers 2010). While public opinion was clearly in favor of a ban, the pro-choice and women's rights organizations that constitute the base of the Democratic Party viewed the legislation as a direct threat to *Roe v. Wade* and women's reproductive rights (Idelson and Palmer 1996; Sullivan 2003). Pro-life groups and Republican opponents ran numerous ads against pro-choice Democrats on the issue. For example, Democratic senators watched in horror as Tom Harkin (D-IA) saw a fifteen-point lead disappear in the last weeks of his 1996 re-election bid when his Republican opponent focused on Harkin's partial birth abortion vote (Boshart 1996b; Lynch 1996; Sullivan 2003). The Republican candidate's assault included an ad with a retired Catholic priest denouncing the Catholic Harkin's position on partial birth abortion (Boshart 1996a). Similarly, in 1996, Mary Landrieu (D-LA), who was running her first Senate race, encountered a wave of criticism for her position that she would have voted to uphold President Clinton's veto on the grounds that the legislation needed an exception for the health of the mother. Indeed, the retired Archbishop of New Orleans called for her defeat, claiming it would be a sin for Catholics to vote for her (Grace 1996a, 1996b; Alpert 1996). In 1998, Wisconsin Democrats Russ Feingold and Herb Kohl faced a recall campaign over the issue (Carney 1998). That same year, Tom Daschle (D-SD) drew strong public criticism from church leaders in South Dakota as he sought to create an alternative to the Republican bill (Carey 1997; Sullivan 2003; Bottum 2003). Before the final vote on the bill in 2003, the American Life League launched a campaign to target twelve pro-choice Catholic senators and to pressure the Church to renounce them (Cohen 2002).

With public opinion strongly against them and many senators uncomfortable with the gruesome descriptions of the procedure and horrific pictures used by Republicans in debates showing babies partially delivered and brutally butchered, Democrats had difficulty crafting a response to the Republican bill. In his study of party messaging on the partial birth abortion ban, Sellers (2010) found that Republican senators believed the issue solidified and energized their electoral base, particularly conservatives and pro-life activists. Therefore, Republican senators were much more active in promoting their party's message on the issue than were Democratic senators. By contrast, Democrats could not even get their members to use the medical term for the procedure, dilation and extraction rather than partial birth abortion. As a result, the participation of rank-and-file Republican senators in party messaging activities, such as press conferences and floor speeches, on the issue far outstripped their Democratic counterparts. Republicans received more news coverage on the issue, and the increased news coverage strengthened the advantage Republicans already had on the issue (Sellers 2010).

In a case like partial birth abortion, when the opposition party clearly owns the issue and the electoral consequences for one's party are uniformly negative, senators must feel a more intense commitment to the issue to propel them to actively engage the debate rather than simply voting on the measure. Senate staffers noted that Democratic women and the two moderate Republican women, Olympia Snowe (R-ME) and Susan Collins (R-ME), were pivotal players in Democratic efforts to craft alternative legislation that would pass constitutional muster and satisfy both the conservative and liberal wings of the Democratic caucus. This does not mean that the women all agreed on one position. The major point of contention concerned the drafting of a health exception. The more liberal Democratic women supported a broad health exception that included both physical and mental health, while the conservative Democratic women and the Republican women wanted a more narrowly drawn health exception that focused on serious physical health concerns. While the women had differing views, they were among the most active legislators in the development of alternative legislation.

Democrats realized early in the debate that partial birth abortion was not a good issue for them. Following President Clinton's first veto of the legislation in 1996, constituents confronted senators about the ban. Worried about spending years debating a procedure with such a gruesome description, Democratic senators urged their party leader, Tom Daschle (D-SD), to develop alternative legislation. President Clinton also spoke to him about heading off a protracted fight on the issue. Daschle himself was up for re-election in 1998 in the conservative state of South Dakota. Responding to the pleas of colleagues and to counter the ads that pro-life groups were already running in his state, Daschle decided to develop an alternative bill (Sullivan 2003; Sellers 2010).

When parties develop alternative bills, they are seeking to inoculate themselves against criticism on an issue and to develop public policy that is more in line with their ideological views. As one Democratic staffer explained, "[P]arty leaders will offer a side-by-side [alternative amendment] to give cover to their members. Then the senator can say I wanted this version but when it lost I voted for the final bill. You want to give your party members cover on any tough vote." In the case of the partial birth abortion ban, Daschle wanted to develop legislation that would attract both moderate and liberal Democrats by protecting the right to a safe legal abortion previability and banning postviability abortions except in cases when it was necessary to protect the mother's life and health. To do this, Daschle walked a fine line because he needed to assuage the fears of abortion rights groups and ensure they did not actively oppose the bill, otherwise liberal senators would not support it. At the same time he did not want the endorsement of NARAL and other abortion rights groups because this would make it impossible to attract conservative support (Sullivan 2003; Seeyle 1997).

From the beginning, female senators felt compelled to protect the rights of women, and they were among the most actively engaged senators in negotiating the language of Daschle's alternative amendment. According to a Democratic staffer,

> [W]hen the women found out what he [Daschle] was planning, they did not want him to go forward with it, but they wanted to make sure he gets it. . . . Daschle wanted women involved in the drafting of the partial birth abortion alternative because he was very conscious about being a man proposing restrictions on abortion. The women wanted to be involved because it was very emotional and personal for them. There was crying in the meetings. It is impossible to overstate how personal it was for the women and how mad some of them get over the issue.

Beyond personal commitment to the issue, female senators believed they had to get involved in drafting the legislation because they needed to represent the interests of women in an institution that is predominantly male. Thus, one Democratic staffer asserted, the "women were furious about men showing diagrams of not anatomically correct women on the Senate floor. They feel that women are degraded on the Senate floor over and over. But we never have to talk about men . . . You are in a very imbalanced gender environment when debating abortion." Similarly, another Democratic staffer recounted,

> [T]he women talked about feeling humiliated by the debate over the ban, humiliated at ban supporters putting up big pictures of uteruses with no head but the lower half of the torso. They asked why it is ok to throw up women's body parts. I remember one meeting where Carol Moseley Braun [D-IL] said she was tired of seeing Santorum [R-PA] with a big picture of a vagina on the floor. How would they like it if she threw up a big picture of a penis? That got all the women laughing, and Daschle turned bright red and was very conscious of being the only man in the room.[11]

While a majority of the female senators were actively involved in the crafting of the language of the alternative amendment, this does not mean they shared one point of view. The major point of contention concerned how broadly to define the health exception. The most liberal senators preferred a broad health exception that included both physical and mental health. More conservative senators wanted to limit the health exception to physical health. Supporters of limiting the exception to physical health also disagreed on how strictly to define physical health circumstances. According to one Democratic leadership staffer,

> Two Republican women and two Democratic women were most interested in getting a more conservative compromise on language than what Daschle offered. They were scared of the health exception. If the women get scared, all the men get scared. They take their cues from them. In 1997 a couple of women did us [strongly pro-choice Democrats] in. There was an internal debate about whether to add the term "physical health" instead of just "health" to distinguish it from mental health. Most of the women did not want to do it, but a few did and the men look to the women for leadership on this. The Democratic bill was actually tougher because it would have been a prohibition across all procedures [not just the D&X procedure] postviability but with a health exception. Hutchison [R-TX] was there for some of the meetings. Collins [R-ME], Landrieu [D-LA], Lieber-

man [D-CT] (he is usually very pro-choice so this was noticed),
and others were getting nervous. Landrieu [D-LA] and Durbin
[D-IL] wanted a two-doctor certification.

Without a mental health exception, NARAL threatened to score a
vote for the Daschle alternative as an anti-choice vote. Daschle and his
staff consulted widely on the amendment, meeting with groups of female senators, liberal pro-choice senators, and Catholic senators. They
also met with individual Republican pro-choice senators. The staff
drafted and redrafted the language to define physical health strictly
enough to attract the support of moderate Democrats. Ultimately they
settled on "grievous" physical health, which won over senators Mary
Landrieu (D-LA), Kent Conrad (D-ND), and Byron Dorgan (D-ND)
(Sullivan 2003). Republican senator Olympia Snowe (ME) became
the lead cosponsor of the Daschle amendment, and the seven cosponsors were largely female (Olympia Snowe [R-ME], Barbara Mikulski
[D-MD], Patty Murray [D-WA], Mary Landrieu [D-LA], and Susan
Collins [R-ME]) and Catholic (Barbara Mikulski [D-MD], Patty Murray [D-WA], Mary Landrieu [D-LA], Susan Collins [R-ME], and Ted
Kennedy [D-MA]). Joe Lieberman (D-CT), the Senate's only Orthodox
Jew, also cosponsored the amendment. Senators Landrieu (D-LA) and
Collins (R-ME) were particularly active in lobbying for support for the
bill. Since Democratic whip Harry Reid (D-NV) is a Mormon and pro-
life, Collins (R-ME) and Landrieu (D-LA) worked the phones as the
unofficial whips for the legislation (Sullivan 2003).

While the limited physical health exception won over the support of
moderate senators, the compromise alienated the more liberal Democrats who were strongly pro-choice. A liberal Democratic staffer asserted, "Feinstein and Boxer thought this [the health language] was
constitutionally suspect and withdrew their support." Spurred on by
pro-choice groups, Dianne Feinstein (D-CA), Barbara Boxer (D-CA),
and Carol Moseley Braun (D-IL) cosponsored their own amendment
that banned postviability abortions except in cases to protect the life or
health of the mother. The decision to offer another amendment split the
votes of Democrats and ensured that the Daschle alternative would fail.
According to one Democratic staffer,

> The Feinstein amendment came up at the last minute. They said
> they would not do anything. Daschle did not want it because it
> would give pro-choicers an out to oppose the Daschle amend-
> ment. Choice groups pressed for Feinstein and Boxer to do an

amendment. Daschle tried to get Boxer on board or at least neu-
tralize her. She agreed not to oppose the Daschle amendment
[on the floor] and then broke her promise, which is even worse
when you break your promise to the leader, but maybe she was
more concerned about her standing with NARAL, although
they need her.

Ultimately, Boxer did attack Daschle's amendment by passing around
a letter from Harvard law professor Lawrence Tribe that pronounced
that the Daschle amendment would be declared unconstitutional. The
letter swayed several liberal senators (Sullivan 2003). Both the Daschle
and the Feinstein amendments went down to defeat, with the Daschle
alternative attracting only thirty-six votes and the Feinstein amendment
receiving twenty-eight votes.

With the presence of two alternative amendments in addition to the
ban, several senators voted for multiple alternatives. These multiple
votes provided senators with political cover to tell their pro-life constituents that they favored a ban and their pro-choice constituents that
they tried to improve the bill. Thus, almost half of the Democratic senators serving in the 105th Congress, twenty-two of forty-five, voted for
both the Daschle and the Feinstein alternatives. Six Democratic senators, including Democratic leader Tom Daschle (D-SD), voted for the
Daschle amendment before voting to support the Republican bill, while
seven conservative male Democrats supported the ban and did not vote
for either of the alternative amendments.[12] According to Democratic
staffers, because Daschle ultimately voted for the ban and because of
his high-profile position as the Democratic leader, he dropped his efforts
to create a compromise bill. Senator Richard Durbin (D-IL), a Catholic
Democrat who was trying to move into the party leadership, took up
the cause, introducing a new compromise bill that included the same
language as the Daschle alternative but also required two doctors to certify that the procedure was necessary. Female senators remained at the
core of the cosponsors of the Durbin amendment as five women, senators Olympia Snowe (R-ME), Susan Collins (R-ME), Barbara Mikulski
(D-MD), Mary Landrieu (D-LA), and Blanche Lincoln (D-AR), were
among the thirteen cosponsors of the amendment in the 106th Congress
and the ten cosponsors of the amendment in the 108th Congress.[13] In
both the 106th and 108th Congresses, Republicans successfully used a
procedural motion to table the Durbin alternative to prevent a direct
up or down vote on the substance of the amendment. Feinstein did not
offer her alternative amendment in the 106th Congress. In the 108th

Congress, the Feinstein amendment cosponsored by Debbie Stabenow (D-MI) and Democratic presidential hopeful John Edwards (D-NC) again failed, garnering only thirty-five votes.

In addition to offering alternative proposals, when an issue favors the opposition, members and party leaders try to link the policy debate to issues that favor their party in order to reduce the party's disadvantages by changing the focus of the debate (Sellers 2010). In the eight-year battle over partial birth abortion, Democratic women were at the forefront of efforts to refocus the debate on women's rights and social welfare issues that favor the Democratic Party. Women sponsored or became prime movers of amendments focused on contraception, the constitutionality of *Roe v. Wade*, violence against women, and the expansion of the social safety net for children and pregnant women. For example, in the 106th Congress, Mary Landrieu (D-LA) tried to turn the focus to Republican neglect of child welfare by offering an amendment expressing "the sense of Congress that the federal government should fully support the economic, educational, and medical requirements of families with special needs children."[14] During the final debate on the issue in the 108th Congress, ban proponents were particularly worried about potential Republican defections on an amendment by Patty Murray (D-WA) that would make abortions less necessary by expanding access to contraception and extending health insurance to low-income pregnant women. The Murray amendment required health insurance plans that cover prescription drugs to also cover contraceptives. The proposal would establish an education campaign about emergency contraception and require hospitals that receive federal funding to provide emergency contraception to sexual assault victims. Finally, Murray's amendment would allow states to extend SCHIP (State Children's Health Insurance Program) to low-income pregnant women (Rovner 2003a, 2003b). Fearing they did not have the votes to defeat the Murray amendment on an up or down vote, Republicans successfully avoided a vote on the substance of the proposal and defeated the amendment with a procedural vote on a budget point of order (Rovner 2003b; Dlouhy 2003a).

Democrats gained the greatest political traction with an amendment sponsored by Tom Harkin (D-IA) and championed by Harkin and Barbara Boxer (D-CA) in both the 1999 and 2003 debates that expressed the sense of the Senate that *Roe v. Wade* is the law of the land and that the decision was appropriate and should not be overturned. While partial birth abortion was clearly unpopular with the American people, a majority of the public supports the *Roe v. Wade* decision (Freedman

2003; Ainsworth and Hall 2011). Since both the pro-choice and pro-life forces viewed the partial birth abortion ban as a direct attack on *Roe v. Wade* and the constitutional right to an abortion, Harkin and Boxer sought to put Congress on record as endorsing the decision (Foerstel 1999; Dlouhy 2003a, 2003c). With the battle over the amendment occurring just before the 2000 and 2004 presidential elections, Democrats utilized the amendment and the slim margin by which it passed, 51-47 in the 106th Congress (1999) and 52-46 in the 108th Congress (2003), to highlight the fragility of a woman's right to choose and to fire up their electoral base. Thus, in anticipation of the 2000 presidential election, Barbara Boxer (D-CA) promised to use the vote as a campaign issue in each of the states with Republican senators who opposed the amendment. Democratic presidential candidate Al Gore called the vote a wake-up call and vowed to always defend a woman's right to choose (Foerstel 1999). In the 108th Congress, aspiring Democratic presidential candidates John Kerry (D-MA) and John Edwards (D-NC) cosponsored the Harkin amendment along with Barbara Boxer (D-CA) and Maria Cantwell (D-WA). Highlighting the political stakes for Democratic presidential hopefuls, a Democratic staffer said, "As a Democratic senator in a conservative state, Edwards [D-NC] needed to look more conservative. He cosponsored the *Roe* amendment on the Partial Birth Abortion Act to build his national reputation with the Democratic primary constituency." Clearly, the amendment to reaffirm *Roe v. Wade* directly targeted the Democratic base in an effort to mobilize demoralized activists by reminding them that only Democrats are committed to protecting a woman's right to choose.

The amendment's passage also delayed passage of the partial birth abortion ban by forcing the bill to go to conference. Barbara Boxer (D-CA), who managed the floor debate for the Democrats, delayed the bill's passage for months by first forcing Republicans to agree to an eight-hour debate on the routine motion to disagree that would allow a bill to go to conference. Since the amendment affirming *Roe v. Wade* was the only difference between the House- and Senate-passed bills, Boxer and Harkin tried to find a way to keep the *Roe* language in the bill and thus force President Bush to sign a bill that bans partial birth abortion but also states that *Roe v. Wade* should not be overturned (Pierce 2003; Rovner 2003c; Stolberg 2003a). While their procedural machinations ultimately failed, Boxer and Harkin continued to stall the bill's passage by insisting on more debate on the final conference report (Dlouhy 2003c).

Clearly, Democratic women played a pivotal role in the long fight to enact a ban on partial birth abortion. Democratic women exercised policy leadership by participating actively in the development of alternative legislation. While Democratic women did not universally agree on how broadly to define a health exception, the moral authority they wielded as representatives of women's interests made them opinion leaders for the rest of the caucus. Furthermore, several Democratic women offered key amendments designed to focus the debate on women's rights issues that were more favorable to the Democratic Party.

By contrast, Republican women were not at the forefront of efforts to ban partial birth abortion. Republican Robert Smith (R-NH) sponsored the first Senate bill on the issue in the 104th Congress. By the 105th Congress, Rick Santorum (R-PA) emerged as the foremost Senate champion of the bill. With the election of Republican George W. Bush as president, passage of the bill was assured, and Santorum, who was now conference chair and firmly in control of party messaging, worked with majority leader Bill Frist (R-TN) to make the bill a top priority of the Republican caucus (Cochran 2003). The centrality of the bill to the Republican caucus meant that by actively participating in the development of the Daschle and later Durbin alternatives, the moderate Republican women Olympia Snowe (R-ME) and Susan Collins (R-ME) were directly challenging a Republican caucus priority. Their activism was particularly egregious to Republican base activists who viewed the Democratic alternatives as sham legislation that would not ban the use of the D&X procedure in the second trimester (previability) and created a health exception so broad it would be meaningless (Seeyle 1997; Dlouhy 2003a). The other moderate Republicans, Lincoln Chafee (R-RI) and Jim Jeffords (R-VT), opposed the final bill and supported the even more liberal Feinstein alternative. However, staff reported that while consulted to solicit their support, these senators did not actively participate in the development of alternative legislation in the way that Snowe and Collins did. Moderate Republican Arlen Specter (R-PA) originally opposed the ban but reversed his position early on, voting to override President Clinton's first veto of the legislation in the 104th Congress. Specter also voted against the Daschle and Feinstein alternatives to the legislation. However, he supported the Durbin alternative that required two doctors to certify the necessity of the procedure (Mondics 2003).[15]

Even the more conservative women, Kay Bailey Hutchison (R-TX) and in the 108th Congress, Lisa Murkowski (R-AK) and Elizabeth Dole (R-NC), did not take active roles in promoting the ban. Looking at participation in floor debate during the final battle over the legislation in the 108th Congress, Democratic women led the party's efforts. Strongly pro-choice Barbara Boxer (D-CA) managed the floor debate, and all nine of the Democratic women spoke on the issue. Meanwhile, only 33% (thirteen) of Democratic men spoke on the floor, and five of these men were members of the Judiciary Committee. By contrast, all of the Republicans speaking in favor of the ban were men. Pressing the party's advantage on the issue, 46% (twenty-one) of the men in the Republican caucus gave a floor speech promoting the legislation.[16] Yet none of the three conservative Republican women came down to the floor to promote the ban and defend the party against the attacks of Democratic women who claimed that Republicans were endangering the health of women who faced difficult medical decisions often in tragic circumstances where the baby could not survive (Schonhardt-Bailey 2008). Only the moderate Republican women Olympia Snowe (R-ME) and Susan Collins (R-ME) spoke on the floor, and these women were promoting the Durbin alternative and not advocating for the Republican ban. The fact that there were no Republican women prominently pushing the ban became an issue when President Bush signed the ban surrounded by the ten white male House and Senate members who were the leading advocates of the legislation. The picture of President Bush flanked by ten white men signing legislation on women's reproductive rights was immediately circulated on the Internet, and women's groups like NARAL and NOW used it as a symbol to raise money and galvanize members to action (Stolberg 2003b).

Republican and Democratic staffers maintain that the conservative Republican women do not play a more active role in abortion politics because they are more liberal on women's rights issues than their conservative Republican male colleagues are. Moreover, even when they agree with the party's position, they do not want to be the public face for abortion, fearing it will take over their legislative agenda or that they will lose the support of more moderate female voters who are part of their electoral coalition. Indeed all three conservative women, Kay Bailey Hutchison (R-TX), Lisa Murkowski (R-AK), and Elizabeth Dole (R-NC), supported the Republican legislation banning partial birth abortion. However, only Elizabeth Dole (R-NC) stood with the Republican caucus on all of the critical amendment votes. Kay Bailey Hutchison (R-TX) and Lisa Murkowski (R-AK) were among the Republicans who voted for the Harkin amendment endorsing *Roe v. Wade* as an appropriate decision that should not be reversed. However, Hutchison had voted against this same amendment when it was first considered in the 106th Congress. Also in the 106th Congress, Hutchison was one of twelve Republicans who supported the Landrieu amendment concerning the welfare of special needs children. Moreover, Kay Bailey Hutchison (R-TX) was one of only seven Republican senators who did not cosponsor the legislation. Hutchison's decision not to cosponsor the ban is particularly notable because the bill was a Republican Party priority attracting the cosponsorship of almost the entire Republican caucus in the 105th, 106th, and 108th Congresses.[17] In sum, the conservative women did favor the ban, voting with the party on the legislation. However, the decision of Hutchison not to cosponsor the legislation and the votes by Hutchison and Murkowski reaffirming *Roe v. Wade* indicate that even some of the more conservative women hold more liberal views on abortion than the rest of the Republican caucus. The ambivalence of these women on the issue and their concern over the impact of abortion politics on their public reputation and ability to pursue other priorities means that they try to minimize their involvement in debates over abortion rather than leading the charge as the face of the party in the way that Democratic women do.

Conclusion

The struggle to define women's rights places female senators at the center of the legislative debate. Women senators feel a personal connection and commitment to advocate for women's interests when policy debates clearly impact the place of women in American society. This commitment is reinforced by the fact that there are so few women serving in Congress. Therefore, female lawmakers feel compelled to represent the views of women in a male-dominated institution. Male senators seek to recruit women to lend legitimacy to their efforts to craft public policy regarding women's rights. Thus, Democratic leader Tom Daschle (D-SD) sought out the pro-choice Democratic and Republican women to participate in the drafting of an alternative to the Republican ban on partial birth abortion. Republicans recruited Kay Bailey Hutchison (R-TX) to help craft and sell a Republican substitute for the Lilly Ledbetter Fair Pay Act.

The politics of women's rights is also deeply partisan. The public associates the Democratic Party with policies such as equal pay and the protection of reproductive rights. Women's groups and reproductive rights organizations constitute core elements of the Democratic base. Therefore, Democrats look for opportunities to portray themselves as championing women's rights and to denounce Republican policy proposals as hurting women. Democratic women play key roles in these efforts by designing policy initiatives and selling the party message. For

Republican women, the politics of women's rights is fraught with complications. Republican women hold a range of views on women's rights issues, but they are often more sympathetic to women's rights causes than are their male colleagues. Yet issues of equal pay and abortion rights are strongly associated with the Democratic Party, and policy proposals that threaten the traditional family or potentially undermine business are strongly opposed by the social conservative and business establishment bases of the Republican Party. Taking positions that defy the Republican base can alienate party leadership and other caucus members and may complicate a senator's electoral chances. Yet Republican women do not want to be portrayed as opposing women's rights in the media. As a result, Republican women generally try to maintain a low profile on women's rights issues, avoiding criticism of their party even when they vote against the party position.

At the same time, Republican Party leaders want to capitalize on the credibility Republican female senators wield as women by encouraging them to defend the party against Democratic attacks that Republicans are anti-women. Individual Republican women do take on this task when their policy views and/or electoral goals align with the party, as Kay Bailey Hutchison (R-TX) did in defending Republicans against Democratic attacks that they condone pay discrimination in the fight over the Lilly Ledbetter Fair Pay Act. Yet Republican women often shy away from this role either because their policy views on women's rights do not align with the views of the party or because they fear that becoming the Republican face on issues like abortion will take over their legislative agenda or alienate moderate and independent voters in their electoral coalition.

4

Replacing Sandra Day O'Connor: Gender and the Politics of Supreme Court Nominations

In the fall of 1991, the Senate's handling of the Clarence Thomas Supreme Court confirmation hearings galvanized the women's movement and spurred many women to run for Congress. Women's groups denounced the Senate as insensitive to the interests of women and highlighted the fact that there were no women on the Judiciary Committee and only two women in the Senate when it considered the allegations of sexual harassment made by Anita Hill. The confirmation battle created turmoil inside the institution of the Senate and threatened the electoral fortunes of key members. Within the Senate, to repair the damage created by the all-male committee's conduct of the hearings, members promoted bills to address the problem of sexual harassment and senators Barbara Mikulski (D-MD) and Al Gore (D-TN) began a series of evening seminars for senators on "gender dynamics" to improve the Senate's ability to deal with gender-related issues (Palley and Palley 1992; Cushman 1992).

In the electoral arena, women candidates across the country utilized the hearings as a rallying cry for raising money and attracting votes. Senators who played key roles in the confirmation fight were targeted for defeat (Burrell 1994; Wilcox 1994). Thus Arlen Specter (R-PA), a Judiciary Committee member who helped lead efforts to undermine Anita Hill and her testimony, narrowly survived his race against Democrat Lynn Yeakal (Palley and Palley 1992). Carol Moseley Braun capitalized on Alan Dixon's (D-IL) vote in favor of Thomas's confirmation to defeat Dixon in the Democratic primary and become the first and still only African American woman to serve in the Senate.[1] Democrats, particularly southern Democrats who relied on strong turn-out from African Americans, feared alienating two key voting groups, African Americans and women, since polls demonstrated that the hear-ings strengthened support for Thomas among African Americans and fueled opposition among white women (Frankovic and Gelb 1992; Overby et al. 1992; Palley and Palley 1992; Caldeira and Smith 1996).

The furor over Thomas's confirmation hearings contributed to the characterization of the 1992 elections as the "Year of the Woman" (Bur-rell 1994; Wilcox 1994). Eager to meet demands for more diversity and transparency in the Senate's deliberation on judicial nominees, Dem-ocrats appointed Dianne Feinstein (D-CA) and Carol Moseley Braun (D-IL) to the Judiciary Committee, the committee responsible for the initial screening of all nominees to the federal courts.

These events raise the expectation that women will bring a distinc-tive viewpoint to the Senate's deliberation of nominations to the fed-eral courts. Indeed, the politics of judicial nominations are permeated by gender concerns from the status of *Roe v. Wade* to the symbolism of nominating women and minorities to the bench. At the same time, senators are tightly constrained by expectations to remain loyal to one's political party and president, reducing the importance of factors beyond partisanship and ideology (Epstein and Segal 2005; Epstein et al. 2006; Binder and Maltzman 2009). Moreover, institutional traditions make defeat of the president's nominees more difficult than killing legislation because a bill's opponents must only block the proposal from getting on the agenda. Nominees are expected to come to the floor for a vote and require a public and sustained campaign to convince other senators to risk the necessary political capital to defeat them (Krutz, Fleisher, and Bond 1998).

The confirmation battles over George W. Bush's Supreme Court nominees, John Roberts, Harriet Miers, and Samuel Alito, present the first opportunity to assess the impact of gender on nomination politics. The struggle to replace Sandra Day O'Connor, the first female justice and a swing vote on women's rights, elevated the attention paid to gen-der concerns. Moreover, for the first time, women had a significant pres-ence in the Senate during a contentious confirmation fight, while only two women served in the Senate when Clarence Thomas was confirmed.

Only six female senators deliberated on the nominations of Ruth Bader Ginsburg and Stephen Breyer, and both justices were confirmed by almost unanimous votes. Thus, the long battle to replace Sandra Day O'Connor allows us to examine the impact of gender on a senator's decision making in a case in which women's rights issues were highly salient and institutional and partisan pressures loom large.

In this chapter, I examine whether and how gender influenced senators' support for the nominations of John Roberts and Samuel Alito to the Supreme Court. Drawing on media coverage of the confirmation process, I highlight the information senators had on John Roberts and Samuel Alito's records on women's rights. I analyze senators' confirmation votes and the explanations they offered for their votes on the floor and in press releases to determine whether female senators are more likely to prioritize women's rights concerns. To gain an insider's account of senators' political calculations and the efforts to influence their votes, I supplement the interviews with Senate staffers with interviews with representatives of major liberal and conservative interest groups that work to influence nomination politics. These include five activist leaders from three liberal groups and three interest group leaders from three conservative organizations.

Despite the substantive and symbolic importance of gender in nomination politics, I demonstrate that institutional and partisan constraints dominate senators' voting decisions. Republicans uniformly supported their president's nominees. However, among opposition party senators, gender did play a role in the voting decisions of moderate and conservative Democrats. Moreover, gender does influence senators' explanations of their votes in floor debate. Women, particularly Democratic women, were more likely to refer to women's issues when explaining their vote, providing evidence that female senators prioritize women as a constituency and bring a different perspective to policy deliberations.

The Gender Dimensions of Nomination Politics

The politics of Supreme Court nominations is infused with gender considerations. The importance of the federal courts in determining the scope of civil rights claims under the Constitution gives the courts a pivotal role in defining the parameters of women's rights. (Mansbridge 1986; Mezey 2003). Among Supreme Court decisions, the status of *Roe v. Wade* is a primary motivator for liberal and conservative political activists. While presidents and senators deny that they utilize a "litmus test" in their evaluation of nominees, a nominee's perceived position on

Roe is heavily scrutinized and is a determinative force for senators on both sides of the aisle. Given the prominent role played by Democratic and moderate Republican women in legislative debates on abortion (see chapter 3), one might expect female senators to more carefully examine a nominee's position on reproductive rights and other issues of gender equality.

The politics of descriptive representation is also an important focus of judicial nominations. The media, interest groups, and political elites carefully monitor the influence of diversity on a president's judicial appointments. Thus, the conservative African American Clarence Thomas was nominated to replace Thurgood Marshall, the first African American on the Supreme Court and litigator of the landmark *Brown v. Board of Education* civil rights case. The nomination of Sandra Day O'Connor allowed President Ronald Reagan to fulfill a campaign pledge to appoint the first woman to the Supreme Court (Goldman 1997). President George W. Bush faced tremendous pressure to nominate a woman to replace Sandra Day O'Connor when she retired.

After Justice O'Connor retired, Justice Ginsburg frequently complained about the need for another woman on the court to provide a women's viewpoint on a range of issues. She criticized her male colleagues for their lack of understanding of women's interests and perspective on cases dealing with pregnancy discrimination, equal pay, and partial birth abortion (Biskupic 2009; Liptak 2009). For example, in the partial birth abortion case *Gonzales v. Carhart*, Ginsburg denounced the majority for using language that reflected "ancient notions about women's place in the family and under the Constitution—ideas that have long since been discredited" (quoted in Barnes 2007a). In her dissent in the Ledbetter employment discrimination case, Ginsburg asserted, "[T]he court does not comprehend, or is indifferent to, the insidious way in which women can be victims of pay discrimination." Moreover, Ginsburg maintained that even after discovering the discrimination, women may hesitate to take their case to federal court because "An employee like Ledbetter, trying to succeed in a male dominated workplace, in a job filled only by men before she was hired, understandably may be anxious to avoid making waves" (quoted in Barnes 2007a).

When President Obama began his search for a nominee to replace Justice Souter, it was widely reported that women dominated his short list. The relevance of diversity quickly became a focus of controversy as Obama emphasized that "empathy," meaning an understanding of varied life experiences based on race, class, gender, and/or sexual orientation, would be an important criterion as he weighed the choice of a nominee (Goldman, Slotnick, and Schiavoni 2011). By selecting Judge Sonia Sotomayor, Obama elevated the first Hispanic to the Supreme Court, and the media focused on the importance of the choice to Hispanic voters and women (Allen and Martin 2009; Martin 2009; Smith and Kraushaar 2009). Republicans seized on Obama's empathy litmus test, and they criticized Sotomayor as a judge who allowed her Latina identity to unduly influence her jurisprudence. Critics focused on speeches in which Sotomayor maintained "personal experiences affect the facts that judges choose to see . . . I accept there will be some [differences] based on my gender and my Latina heritage" (quoted in Bolton 2009). She was heavily criticized for a remark in which she refuted Justice O'Connor's past assertion that a wise old man and a wise old woman would reach the same conclusion, instead suggesting that "a wise Latina woman with the richness of her experiences would more often than not reach a better conclusion than a white male who hasn't lived that life" (quoted in Barnes 2009; Bolton 2009). When President Obama nominated Elena Kagan, commentators took note that for the first time there would be three women on the Supreme Court, practically a critical mass (Marcus 2010).

At the appeals and district court levels, presidents, parties, and senators compete to take credit for increasing diversity and appointing the first member of a particular group to the court (Goldman 1997; Scherer 2005). Since women and minorities are a core constituency of the Democratic Party, Democratic presidents emphasize diversity in their appointments more than Republicans (Epstein and Segal 2005; Bratton and Spill 2001). However, in comparison with his Republican predecessors, President George W. Bush gave more attention to diversity. He particularly focused on appointing Hispanic judges as part of his effort to attract Hispanics to the Republican Party (Goldman, Schiavoni, and Slotnick 2009; Diascro and Solberg 2009). President Obama has been particularly aggressive in his efforts to diversify the federal bench. In the first two years of his term, almost 75% of Obama's nominees to the lower federal courts were women or minorities (Markon and Murray 2011; Goldman, Slotnick, and Schiavoni 2011).

The parties' increased focus on diversifying the federal bench can also enhance the partisan conflict surrounding female and minority nominees. Bell (2002b) finds that women and African Americans faced longer delays than white males during periods of divided government. Solowiej, Martinek, and Brunell (2005) argue that to counter the perception that the party is not attuned to the needs of minorities and women, Republicans move quickly to confirm a Republican president's nontraditional nominees, while they slow down confirmation of these groups with a Democratic president.

Furthermore, the parties utilize minority and women nominees as sympathetic figures in wider partisan fights over the confirmation process. Thus, women and minority nominees played key roles in the public relations battle over the use of filibusters against judicial nominees during the Bush administration. Among the ten appellate nominees filibustered by Democrats during the 108th Congress, four were women and/or minorities (Binder and Maltzman 2009; Scherer 2005; Steigerwalt 2010).[2] When Republicans decided to stage a "reverse filibuster," an all-night debate to highlight Democratic intransigence on judicial nominees, they chose to focus on three female appellate nominees, Priscilla Owen (Fifth Circuit), Janice Rogers Brown (D.C. Circuit), and Carolyn Kuhl (Ninth Circuit). A Republican leadership staffer confirmed that the Republicans deliberately chose these women as "sympathetic figures who would embarrass the Democrats as unfair bullies in the public eye."

Several studies indicate that gender also influences the jurisprudence of the courts. Researchers find that female judges on the lower federal courts are more sympathetic to claims of employment discrimination and more likely to oppose restrictions on the right to an abortion (Boyd, Epstein, and Martin 2010; Scherer 2005; Peresie 2005; Davis, Haire and Songer 1993; Songer, Davis, and Haire 1994; for an exception see Walker and Barrow 1985; Segal 2000). Moreover, the presence of a woman on a panel makes the male judges more likely to rule for the plaintiff in sex discrimination cases (Boyd, Epstein, and Martin 2010; Peresie 2005). With regard to the Supreme Court, scholars find that the presence of Sandra Day O'Connor and Ruth Bader Ginsburg on the court increased support among the male justices for victims' claims in sex discrimination cases, and these two justices wrote a disproportionate number of the majority opinions on women's rights cases (O'Connor and Segal 1990; Palmer 2002).

The media attention and interest group focus on the level of diversity among a president's nominees means that senators will pay attention to the symbolism of race and gender as they craft their confirmation vote strategies. The substantive and symbolic influences of gender on nomination politics requires an investigation of whether and how gender influences the decisions of senators as they fulfill their advice and consent duties in the confirmation of Supreme Court nominees.

Nomination Politics: The Electoral and Institutional Constraints

Although gender-related issues are a prominent feature of nomination battles, the electoral and institutional incentives senators face argue against a distinctive role for gender as a determinant of senators' support for Supreme Court nominees. Rational choice theorists and new institutionalists maintain that institutional structures and the electoral context constrain the ability of members to pursue their policy preferences. With regard to Supreme Court confirmations, senators operate in an environment where the fate of the nominee is central to the reputation and policy goals of the president. Presidents utilize their nominations to the court to extend their policy imprint beyond the years of their presidency, creating intense pressure on members of the president's party to support his nominees, while members of the opposing party are compelled to mount a vigorous opposition. Indeed, Lee (2008a, 2009) finds that because the president is the leader of the party, presidential initiatives are even more polarizing than other items on the congressional agenda. In deciding whether to support a nominee, senators may also consider the president's approval rating and whether he is in the last year of his presidency (Epstein et al. 2006; Shipan and Shannon 2003; Segal, Cameron, and Cover 1992; Cameron, Cover, and Segal 1990; Krutz, Fleisher, and Bond 1998).

In addition to the president, the interest groups that form the liberal and conservative bases of the two parties pay close attention to Supreme Court nominations. The landmark decisions of the Warren Court on race, religion, and the rights of criminal defendants sparked the politicization of nomination politics and mobilized liberal and conservative activists (Goldman 1997; Bell 2002a; Scherer 2005; Steigerwalt 2010). The rejection of Reagan nominee Robert Bork based on his conservative judicial philosophy rather than his qualifications was a landmark event in the polarization of nomination politics and the involvement of interest groups. The term "Borking" of a nominee entered the political lexicon, and Bork's defeat became a rallying cause for conservatives (Epstein and Segal 2005; Bell 2002a; Ogundele and Keith 1999; Goldman 1997; Maltese 1995). The acrimony reached new levels in the George W. Bush years when Democrats began filibustering appellate nominees and Republicans threatened to eliminate filibusters on judicial nominations by deploying a procedural tactic dubbed the "nuclear option" (Epstein and Segal 2005; Binder and Maltzman 2009; Steigerwalt 2010). Despite a deal to avoid filibusters of appellate nominees except in "extraordinary circumstances," Republicans deployed the filibuster against Obama nominees to the appellate courts (Wong 2011; Goldman, Slotnick, and Schiavoni 2011). While presidents and senators continue to hone messages that target activists and base voters, denouncing, for example, judicial activists who legislate from the bench, the average voter pays little attention to confirmation politics (Bell 2002a; Scherer 2005; Steigerwalt 2010).

The politicization of court decisions and the involvement of interest groups mean that senators pay close attention to a nominee's ideological views. Studies of confirmation votes note that senators balance the nominee's qualifications with their judicial philosophy. Over time, the importance of judicial philosophy has increased as the ideological distance between the senator and the nominee has become an increasingly important determinant of their vote (Primo, Binder, and Maltzman 2008; Epstein et al 2006; Shipan and Shannon 2003; Segal, Cameron, and Cover 1992; Cameron, Cover, and Segal 1990). The confirmation of Justice Alito exemplifies this trend as he was one of the most qualified judges nominated to the Supreme Court, having graduated from an elite law school and serving on an appellate court for fifteen years. Yet his highly conservative judicial philosophy resulted in a confirmation vote in which almost all Democrats opposed his nomination. Similarly, all but five Republican senators opposed the confirmation of Elena Kagan, a former dean of Harvard Law School and Obama's solicitor general, because of her liberal judicial philosophy and political ties to the Obama administration (Goldman, Slotnick, and Schiavoni 2011).

Beyond the dynamics of presidential-congressional relations, senators' votes are moved by the impact of the nomination on the composition of the court. Ruckman (1993) notes that the confirmation process is more conflictive if the nominee represents a "critical nomination" that will shift the ideological balance of the court by, for example, replacing a liberal with a conservative or creating a new ideological majority on the court. Thus, conservative icon Antonin Scalia was confirmed in 1986 by a unanimous vote because his appointment would fill the seat of a retiring conservative justice and did not threaten the balance of power on the court. One year later, in 1987, Democrats regained control of the Senate, and Robert Bork's nomination was rejected because his nomination would have shifted the jurisprudence of the court by replacing the swing vote, Lewis Powell, with a strong ideological conservative (Ogundele and Keith 1999; Goldman 1997; Maltese 1995). Other critical nominations include replacing the chief justice or nominations that threaten the loss of representation on the court for a particular social group (Ruckman 1993). The nomination of Samuel Alito combined several critical factors as his nomination represented the loss of a woman's seat on the court and the replacement of a swing vote and ideologically moderate justice with a more strongly conservative jurist.

In sum, a senator's actions on a Supreme Court nominee are highly constrained by a number of political and institutional factors. The impact of a Supreme Court nomination on the policy goals and reputation of the president makes the vote a key test of party loyalty for members of the president's party. The consideration of a critical nomination requires a different standard for scrutiny. The heightened importance of nominations to party activists has important implications for senators' ability to raise money and mobilize voters in their election campaigns.

Replacing Sandra Day O'Connor: The Ultimate Gendered Context

The battle to replace Sandra Day O'Connor on the Supreme Court placed gender considerations at the forefront of the confirmation fight. Because she was the first woman on the Supreme Court, President Bush faced extreme pressure to replace O'Connor with another woman. The media continuously asked President Bush about whether he would replace O'Connor with a woman or perhaps the first Hispanic nominee. Even First Lady Laura Bush publicly urged her husband to appoint a woman to replace O'Connor (Barbash 2005a). O'Connor herself expressed disappointment when Bush did not tap a female nominee but turned instead to D.C. Circuit Court judge John Roberts (Greenburg 2007).

The death of Chief Justice William Rehnquist reopened the debate when Bush decided to elevate Roberts to chief justice. Democratic senators were now engaged in a two-stage game in which their vote on Roberts could send a signal to President Bush that could influence his decision of whom to nominate to replace O'Connor. According to interviews with senate staff and interest group leaders and contemporary media accounts, some senators, notably minority leader Harry Reid (D-NV), believed that taking a stand against Roberts would send a warning to President Bush not to select a more controversial nominee than Roberts and would maintain the support of activists who wanted Democrats to protect hard-won legal rights from a more conservative jurisprudence. Alternatively, other Democrats believed that a vote in favor of Roberts would demonstrate the Democrats' reasonable approach to nominations, allowing them to pressure Bush to nominate a more moderate candidate to replace O'Connor. A favorable vote on Roberts could also be used as justification for opposition to a strong conservative who was "out of the mainstream" of judicial philosophy. Judiciary Committee leader Patrick Leahy (D-VT) adhered to this viewpoint (Babington and Balz 2005; Greenburg 2007). Ultimately, Roberts was confirmed by a vote of 78-22, which included support from all Republicans and half the Democratic senators.

Following Roberts's successful confirmation, the Bush administration turned to the task of filling the O'Connor seat, preferably with a conservative woman or minority who would move the ideological balance of the court to the right. However, the administration had difficulty finding a female nominee who was both in the mold of Scalia and Thomas and could be confirmed by the Senate (Greenburg 2007). Bush's decision to nominate his White House counsel Harriet Miers for the O'Connor seat set off a firestorm among conservatives who were wary of her ideological commitment to conservative jurisprudence. A public debate raged over whether opposition to Miers was based on her judicial philosophy and qualifications or sexism (Toner, Kirkpatrick, and Kornblut 2005; Greenburg 2007).

Miers was a highly respected corporate attorney in Texas and a trailblazer for women. She was the first female president of the Dallas and later Texas bar associations and the first female managing partner in a major Dallas law firm. However, her status as White House counsel and a longtime Bush ally elicited charges of cronyism (Fletcher and Babington 2005). More importantly, as a corporate lawyer, Miers had no experience in constitutional law, and therefore her judicial philosophy was unknown to anyone but the president (Stern and Perine 2005c). Conservative interest groups, media commentators, and the blogosphere immediately mobilized against Miers, fearing that she could become another Souter, a justice with a thin record who is appointed by a Republican president and then adopts a liberal jurisprudence on key conservative issues such as abortion (DeParle 2005; Greenburg 2007). To counter the criticism of conservative groups and political pundits, the Bush administration highlighted Miers's religious faith and pro-life values, and they accused detractors of elitism and sexism (Baker and Balz 2005; Cochran 2005; Stern and Perine 2005c). Responding to the anger of conservative activists, prominent Republican senators began to publicly criticize the nomination (Hurt 2005; Kiely 2005; Kirkpatrick 2005; Hook and Wallsten 2005).

Since Bush's conservative supporters were savaging Miers, Democrats and their allies did not need to spend political capital building a case against her. Instead, they denounced Republican attacks as gender discrimination and decried the hypocrisy of Republicans who claimed judicial philosophy was not a legitimate criterion for opposition to a nominee, while at the same time they were opposing Miers because they did not know her views on issues. Indeed, feminist organizations vociferously objected to what they perceived as the sexist way in which Republicans were questioning the mental abilities of an accomplished female lawyer (Stolberg 2005). Senator Barbara Mikulski (D-MD) gave several interviews and released an indignant statement decrying the

> sexism and double standard coming out of the far right. All of a sudden they're saying that a woman who was able to become the head of the Texas Bar Association isn't qualified. They're saying a woman who was one of the first to head up a major law firm with over 400 lawyers doesn't have intellectual heft.... Ms. Miers and I are not too far apart generationally. I know how hard it was to be able to get started in a career, trying to make it in law . . . And all of a sudden when you pick a woman—we know that you always have to be twice as good. (Mikulski 2005)

According to a Democratic staffer, Mikulski "never would have voted for Miers, but she felt her treatment was sexist. She says we have to stop judging women on men's standards. When Miers went to Southern Methodist it was because the other universities were not letting women in at that time. So the criticism of her qualifications was BS."

The debacle of the Miers nomination led Bush to select another male appeals court judge, Samuel Alito, to replace O'Connor. Alito was the antithesis of Miers in every way. Ivy League educated and an appellate judge with fifteen years of experience on the court, Alito had long been a favorite of conservative groups and was widely praised by the conservative legal community (Barbash and Baker 2005). Democrats immediately denounced the nomination of Alito as a capitulation to the far right. However, Democratic Senate leaders refused to endorse a filibuster because they did not want to take the focus off the Iraq War and draw public attention to a nominee they believed would ultimately be confirmed (Stern and Perine 2006b). With little chance for success, Massachusetts Democrats Ted Kennedy, the longtime liberal leader, and John Kerry, who needed to court the support of activist groups for a potential 2008 presidential run, teamed up to mount a last-minute filibuster. The filibuster attempt failed as senators voted to invoke cloture by 72-25 with no Republicans and only half of Democrats supporting a filibuster. Ultimately Alito was confirmed by a vote of 58-42, the tightest margin of victory since Clarence Thomas. Only one Republican, Lincoln Chaffee (R-RI), a moderate in a tough re-election battle, voted against Alito, and four Democrats supported his confirmation.

Beyond the symbolism of appointing the replacement for the first female Supreme Court justice, O'Connor's retirement brought substantive issues of women's rights to the center of the debate. O'Connor was a critical swing vote on issues related to abortion, affirmative action, and employment discrimination. She had written the majority opinion in *Planned Parenthood of Southeastern Pennsylvania v. Casey*, a decision that was both credited with saving *Roe v. Wade* as a precedent and denounced for allowing states to chip away at the right to an abortion. She was also a pivotal figure in the *Stenberg v. Carhart* case regarding partial birth abortion. Thus, the nomination of Samuel Alito to replace O'Connor set up a critical nomination on several fronts as it represented a loss of a seat for women and a clear shift of the court to the right with the replacement of a moderate voice on women's issues with a more clearly conservative jurist.

The first few years of the Roberts court saw a strongly conservative shift in jurisprudence on women's rights. With slim 5-4 majorities, the Roberts court issued major decisions that limited reproductive rights and made it more difficult for workers to bring claims of employment discrimination. In both cases, Justice Ruth Bader Ginsburg, the lone female justice, took the unusual step of reading her dissents from the bench as she accused the majority of being insensitive to women's rights (Perine 2007; Barnes 2007b).

Given the clear implications of these nominations for women's rights and the fact that Roberts and Alito generally vote together on these issues, how do we explain the facts that Republicans uniformly supported Roberts's confirmation and only one Republican opposed the confirmation of O'Connor replacement Samuel Alito? What led half of Democrats to support John Roberts and slightly less than half of all Democrats to reject a filibuster against Samuel Alito while almost universally opposing his confirmation?

A Theory of the Role of Gender in Judicial Confirmation Politics: Making Choices in a Gendered and Partisan Context

On the basis of the dynamics of the confirmation process, I argue that in the presence of high levels of partisan and institutional pressure, gender considerations will have little influence on a senator's confirmation vote, even in a policy context in which substantive and symbolic gender considerations loom large, particularly the status of *Roe v. Wade* and the symbolic politics of nominating women and minorities to the federal bench. Despite the prominence of gender issues in nomination politics, the status of nominations as central motivators of the electoral bases of the parties, while practically invisible to the average voter, increases the costs of alienating leaders and colleagues by voting against the party's position. This is particularly true when the senator is a member of the president's party.

Indeed, a senator receives almost no electoral or policy benefits with constituents by voting in opposition to the party's position on a nominee. As Mayhew (1974) and Arnold (1990) note, legislators are concerned with both claiming credit for good policy benefits and avoiding blame for bad policy outcomes. Thus, for a moderate Republican woman such as Olympia Snowe (ME) or Susan Collins (ME), who utilizes her pro-choice position to attract independent and Democratic voters, the link between, for example, a vote against the Partial Birth Abortion Act and support for the pro-choice position is strong for the average voter. This vote will be heavily reported by the media and utilized by supporters and opponents in electoral campaigns.

By contrast, a vote for or against a Supreme Court nominee does not send the same clear signal to voters. Because judges are one person among a panel who are deciding cases and because the legal cases they will hear and decisions they will make are abstract and in the future, even a vote against a critical nomination such as Samuel Alito, a judge who clearly would move jurisprudence on abortion in a more conservative direction than his predecessor, Sandra Day O'Connor, would not carry the same electoral payoff/punishment with constituents in comparison with a vote against the Partial Birth Abortion Act. However, voting against the Supreme Court nominee of a Republican president and in defiance of one's party leadership would incur a significant loss of political capital and good will among party colleagues in an institution that relies heavily on personal relationships and deal making for achievement of policy goals.

Moreover, votes on legislation are more easily nuanced than votes on nominees. When voting on legislation, a senator can cast votes for alternative amendments to allow him/her to both support and oppose the party while constructing a plausible explanation for constituents. Votes on nominees cannot be ameliorated by casting strategic votes on alternative proposals. Rather, a senator must vote to seat the judge on the court or defy his/her party and president and oppose the nominee, thereby raising the profile of the vote and the political stakes for the senator. Therefore, a senator will have less leeway to vote based on gender-related concerns in confirmation politics than one would have in deliberations on legislation.

In sum, partisan and ideological concerns will dominate senators' confirmation votes, while gender will have a limited impact on senators' voting behavior even when gender issues are a highly salient factor in deliberations over a nomination. Moreover, the institutional constraints of partisan pressure will weigh most heavily on senators from the president's party. Therefore, Republicans, even those pro-choice moderates who are ideologically distant from President Bush, will be inclined to support Roberts and Alito, while Democrats will be more likely to oppose the nominees and the most liberal Democrats will be among those who are most fervently opposed.

Under these conditions, the main impact of gender will be found in senators' explanations of their votes. Representation scholars note that the explanations senators offer for their positions in floor statements and press releases serve several purposes. At the constituent level, members seek to build bonds of trust with voters to demonstrate that they are representing their interests. Within the institution, senators use their vote explanations to influence the direction of current and future deliberations by signaling other senators and the White House about their policy priorities (Fenno 1978; Mansbridge 1999). While their vote will conform to the position of their party, female senators may be more likely than male party colleagues to utilize a judge's jurisprudence on women's issues to justify their stance on a nominee. For example, a female Democrat might be even more likely than a male Democrat to cite concerns about gender discrimination as the basis for her opposition to a nominee. Similarly, a Republican woman may state that she accepts a nominee's assurances that he respects a right to privacy as justification for supporting a conservative nominee. If women are more likely to highlight women's rights concerns as motivating their votes, it would provide evidence that women do bring a different perspective to policy deliberations and that women prioritize issues related to women's rights. Moreover, a greater emphasis on women's rights in their vote explanations would indicate that female senators perceive women as an important part of their constituency and electoral coalition even when they are seeking to assuage the concerns of constituents and regain the support of activists who are angered by the senator's vote.

Analyzing Senators' Positions in Supreme Court Confirmation Battles

The Roberts and Alito votes presented senators with consecutive votes on critical nominations (Ruckman 1993). The Roberts vote filled the position of chief justice with a young nominee who could influence the direction of the Supreme Court's jurisprudence for many years to come. The Alito vote would shift the ideological balance of the court by replacing a moderate conservative with a strongly conservative nominee, and the nomination would mean a loss of representation for women on the court. Given the clear consequences for women's rights, it is important to understand the factors that influenced the actions of senators as they deliberated on President Bush's nominees.

I delineate the scope of information members had available to them on Roberts and Alito's records on women's rights by examining the Judiciary Committee hearings and media accounts of the confirmation process. To gain a deeper understanding of the influences on senators' positions and the institutional and political pressures they faced, I draw on the interviews with Senate staff and an additional set of interviews with liberal and conservative interest group leaders who are active in nomination politics.[3] Using regression analysis, I evaluate the impact of gender on the confirmation vote for Chief Justice Roberts and the cloture and confirmation votes on the Alito nomination. Finally, I examine senators' floor speeches and press releases to determine the centrality of women's rights concerns to members' explanations of their votes.

Roberts' Record on Women's Rights

A nominee's qualifications and judicial philosophy dominate the debate over Supreme Court appointments. John Roberts presented senators with a highly qualified nominee who was ideologically distant from Democrats. As an appellate judge who had only been on the D.C. Circuit for two years, Roberts's credentials allowed him to compile a record that was sufficiently conservative to satisfy conservative activists, but it lacked the paper trail of jurisprudence that could galvanize liberal opponents. Evidence of Roberts's views on women's rights came largely from the briefs and memos he had written while serving in the Ronald Reagan and George H.W. Bush administrations (Stern 2005b; Greenburg 2007).

Abortion, along with the existence of a right to privacy as its underpinning, dominates debate on Supreme Court nominees and is the most prominent women's issue debated in judicial confirmations. Elements of

Roberts's record suggested he might not support abortion rights. Memos from the Reagan and Bush years questioned a right to privacy and *Roe* (Stern 2005a, 2005b). However, in his hearing, Roberts confirmed that the Constitution includes a right to privacy but remained vague about the scope of that right. He agreed that *Roe* is a precedent that has been reaffirmed. However, he did not commit to the necessity of upholding that precedent in future cases (Stern and Perine 2005a). For senators who support reproductive rights, Roberts's responses could be tailored to justify a vote for or against the nominee.

The other major women's issue surrounding the Roberts appointment concerned his views on gender discrimination and civil rights enforcement. As a lawyer in the Reagan administration, Roberts argued for a limited role for the courts and federal agencies in enforcing anti-discrimination laws. For example, he argued for a narrow interpretation of the Title IX ban on sex discrimination in the schools. Furthermore, as deputy solicitor general, Roberts argued in *Franklin v. Gwinnett County* that Title IX did not allow a tenth grade high school girl to recover damages from her school after being sexually abused by her teacher. The court unanimously ruled against this assertion. These positions raised questions about whether Roberts believes women have a constitutional protection against sex discrimination under the Fourteenth Amendment (Nather 2005).

Other memos questioned the concept of pay equity and comparable worth. For example, one memo referred to the "canard that women are discriminated against because they receive $0.59 to every $1.00 earned by men" (Floor Statement of Debbie Stabenow, Congressional Record, September 29, 2005, S10641). In a 1984 memo, Roberts criticized three Republican congresswomen, one of whom was now Senator Olympia Snowe (R-ME), for supporting comparable worth as a mechanism for achieving pay equity. Parodying a Marxist slogan, he wrote, "I honestly find it troubling that three Republican representatives are so quick to embrace such a radical redistributive concept. Their slogan may as well be 'From each according to his ability, to each according to her gender.'" In response to media coverage of this memo, Snowe cautiously stated that she hoped that twenty-one years later Roberts had an open mind on wage discrimination against women and that she would evaluate his views and record (Brune 2005; Greenburg 2007).

Roberts's positions and the sarcastic tone of many of the memos led some senators and liberal interest groups to denounce Roberts as disrespectful to women and insensitive to women's rights (Feinstein 2005b). While in the committee hearings Roberts stated that he supported equal rights for women, he refused to distance himself from either the content or the tone of his memos, instead maintaining that he was acting as an advocate reflecting the views of his client, the Reagan administration (Greenburg 2007). Thus, a senator who supports vigorous enforcement of antidiscrimination laws could find much to criticize in Roberts's record or he or she could choose to believe that memos written more than twenty years ago when Roberts was serving as a political appointee rather than a judge are not reflective of his current thinking and judicial temperament.

Alito's Record on Women's Rights

In contrast to Roberts's short paper trail, Samuel Alito's fifteen years of service as an appellate judge provided a long record of conservative jurisprudence on hot button issues ranging from abortion to executive power. As with Roberts, opponents also drew on memos that emerged from his work in the Reagan administration. The combination of this conservative record and the fact that Alito would replace O'Connor immediately made his nomination more contentious than the Roberts appointment.

Alito's most controversial writings on women's rights concerned abortion. Reagan-era memos painted Alito as strongly opposed to abortion rights and a key player in efforts to overturn or mitigate the effects of *Roe v. Wade* (Stern and Perine 2005a; Barbash 2005b). As a judge on the Third Circuit, Alito heard what later became a landmark case on abortion rights, *Planned Parenthood of Southeastern Pennsylvania v. Casey*. In this case, Alito was the only justice who sought to uphold a requirement that women seeking abortions must notify their spouse. In his dissent, Alito dismissed concerns about the potential endangerment to women and focused instead on the interests of the state and the rights of the father (Barbash and Baker 2005; Greenhouse 2005).

When the Supreme Court took up the case, O'Connor rejected Alito's argument and struck down the spousal notification provision in reasoning that emphasized the rights of women under the Constitution. In her majority opinion, she noted that the provision "does not merely make abortions a little more difficult or expensive to obtain; for many women, it will impose a substantial obstacle. We must not blind ourselves to the fact that the significant number of women who fear for their safety and the safety of their children are likely to be deterred from procuring an abortion as surely as if the Commonwealth had outlawed abortion in all cases." Furthermore, she wrote that spousal notification "embodies a view of marriage consonant with the common law status of married women, but repugnant to our present understanding of marriage and of the nature of the rights secured by the Constitution. Women do not lose their constitutionally protected liberty when they marry" (quoted in Barbash and Baker 2005). Alito's *Casey* dissent and O'Connor's ruling became a major focus of questioning in Alito's hearings and the individual meetings with senators. Many Democrats cited this decision in their floor speeches as one of the reasons why they would vote against Alito's nomination. Moreover, in his hearings, Alito refused to refer to *Roe v. Wade* as settled law. However, he did indicate his respect for precedent and the concept of stare decisis (Stern and Perine 2006a).

Beyond abortion, senators, particularly Democrats, expressed concerns about Alito's record of favoring business over workers in employment cases including gender and race discrimination cases (Associated Press 2005; CQ Staff 2005). For example, in a federalism case concerning the Family and Medical Leave Act, Alito ruled that a Pennsylvania state employee could not use the federal statute to sue a state agency for damages for allegedly violating his right to paid sick leave. However, in 2003 in a different case, O'Connor joined a 6-3 majority to rule that the Family and Medical Leave Act was an appropriate federal response to gender discrimination, because the states had a history of basing their leave policies on the stereotype that women should stay home to take care of sick family members or newborn babies (Lane 2005). Democrats also objected to a decision related to criminal procedure that involved the search of a ten-year-old girl and her mother when the warrant only allowed for the search of the woman's husband, a suspected drug dealer (Associated Press 2005; CQ Staff 2005).

Outside of his legal opinions, senators questioned Alito about his membership in the Concerned Alumni of Princeton, a group opposed to Princeton's efforts to admit more women and minorities. Alito had cited his membership in the group in his 1985 Reagan administration job application, but he claimed to have no memory of the group and said that if he joined it, he became a member to protest Princeton's decision to eliminate the ROTC from campus. At one point in the hearings, Judge Alito's wife fled in tears after Republican senator Lindsay Graham (SC) apologized to Alito's family for Democratic efforts to portray Alito as a closet bigot. The moment was replayed on the evening news, generating sympathy for the judge and portraying Democrats as overly aggressive (Stern and Perine 2006a). The battle to define Roberts and Alito's views on women's rights extended all the way to the staging of the hearings, as the White House made sure that the family and administration officials who were seated in camera range behind Alito and Roberts during the hearings were all women (Stern 2006; Manning 2006).

Clearly, senators concerned with women's rights had much to examine in Alito's record, from his views on reproductive rights to employment discrimination and his membership in a club that opposed Princeton's efforts to diversify its student body. Particularly in the area of abortion, a major focus in Supreme Court nominations, Alito's long written record on the issue would lead pro-choice senators to oppose Alito if they based their vote on judicial philosophy. Pro-choice Republicans who wanted to find reasons to support Alito would have to rely on his statements in the hearings and private meetings with senators in which he indicated his respect for precedent and stare decisis.

Predicting Senators' Votes

The Roberts and Alito votes presented senators with consecutive votes on critical nominations (Ruckman 1993). Despite their clearly conservative records on women's rights, all Republican senators including the moderate pro-choice Republicans voted to confirm John Roberts and to invoke cloture on the nomination of Samuel Alito. Only Lincoln Chaffee (R-RI), who faced a tough re-election battle in a Democratic state, voted against Alito's confirmation. Regardless of their pro-choice views, moderate Republican senators felt compelled to support their party caucus and their president's nominee. While Republicans offered uniform support, Democrats split their votes with twenty-three Democrats supporting Roberts's confirmation and twenty-two Democrats opposed. Similarly, nineteen Democrats voted to invoke cloture on Alito, while twenty-five Democrats opposed the cloture motion. However, all but four Democrats voted against Alito's confirmation. Given that Roberts and Alito generally vote together on major constitutional questions, how do we explain these patterns of support and opposition among Democrats?

To examine the impact of gender relative to the other important influences on Democratic senators' nomination votes, I conducted regression analysis. For the Roberts confirmation vote and the Alito cloture vote I utilize a logit model in which the dependent variable measures whether or not the senator voted to confirm Roberts (1 = confirm) or to invoke cloture on Alito (1 = yes for cloture). I also conducted a logit model in which I pooled the three votes. The dependent variable measures whether or not the senator voted (1 = yes) to confirm Roberts, invoke cloture on Alito, and confirm Alito. The pooled model has the benefit of expanding the number of observations, allowing for more precision in the results and decreasing the likelihood of falsely rejecting the null hypothesis that gender has no independent effect on senator's votes. The pooled model also allows me to include the Alito confirmation vote in which only four senators voted to confirm the nominee, which increases the amount of information we have about senators' voting decisions. Dummy variables for the Roberts confirmation and Alito cloture votes account for fixed effects related to these individual nominations, while the Alito confirmation vote is the comparison or "out category." Because senators in the pooled model appear in the data set multiple times, each time they cast a vote on a nominee, I employ clustered standard errors by senator to account for the fact that the votes are not independent from each other as the vote one senator casts on Roberts will be related to his/her votes on Alito.

To assess whether gender considerations impact senators' support for a nominee, I include a variable that indicates whether the senator is a woman (1 = female senator). The other independent variables measure important factors that influence senators' votes on nominations. Since judicial philosophy has become an increasingly important influence on confirmation votes, I utilize ideological distance scores developed by Cameron, Cover, and Segal (1990) and updated by Epstein et al. (2006).[4] The scores capture the ideological distance between the nominee and the senator. Since voter opinion is of primary importance to senators, I use the state vote for President Bush in 2004 as a measure of constituent ideology. Given the importance of Supreme Court nominations to the electoral bases of the parties, a dichotomous variable measuring whether the senator is up for re-election in 2006 captures the heightened need of senators who are in cycle to maintain the support of base voters and activists who raise money and mobilize votes for candidates. Finally, a variable indicating whether the senator is a member of the Judiciary Committee accounts for the fact that Judiciary Committee members play the largest role in vetting nominees and are looked to by other senators to provide information and signals of whether to support or oppose a nominee. Moreover, interest group leaders noted that the support of Judiciary Committee members was critical to gaining Democratic caucus support for a filibuster on appellate and Supreme Court nominees.

The results in tables 4.1 and 4.2 indicate that ideology is the most substantively and statistically significant predictor of senators' votes. The ideological distance between the senator and the nominee was by far the most important influence on senators' votes in the pooled model

Table 4.1 Logit Analysis of Democratic Senators' Votes on the Roberts Confirmation Vote and the Alito Cloture Vote (Standard Errors in Parentheses)

Independent Variables	Roberts Confirmation	Alito Cloture
Female Senator	−1.11	−1.08
	(.95)	(1.18)
Ideological Distance	−5.18	−12.42*
	(3.22)	(6.04)
2004 State Vote for Bush	.13[+]	.175
	(.08)	(.12)
Judiciary Committee Member	.4	−.94
	(.94)	(1.47)
Up for Reelection 2006	−.06	1.88
	(.77)	(1.18)
Constant	−3.48	−3.0
	(4.73)	(7.7)
Log Likelihood	−22.89	−13.93
Log Likelihood Ratio χ^2	16.58	32.32
Pseudo-R^2	.27	.54
N	45	44

[+]$p \leq .1.$
*$p \leq .05.$

Table 4.2 Logit Analysis of Democratic Senators' Votes on Roberts Confirmation Vote, Alito Cloture Vote, and Alito Confirmation Vote with Clustered Standard Errors by Senator (Robust Standard Errors in Parentheses)

Independent Variables	Vote
Female Senator	−1.17[+]
	(.7)
Ideological Distance	−6.28[+]
	(3.43)
2004 State Vote for Bush	.19*
	(.08)
Judiciary Committee Member	.11
	(.83)
Up for Reelection 2006	.96[+]
	(.53)
Roberts Confirmation Vote	4.02***
	(.96)
Alito Cloture Vote	3.54***
	(.93)
Constant	−10.15*
	(5.14)
Log Pseudolikelihood	−45.32
Wald χ^2	27.03
Pseudo-R^2	.47
N	134

[+]$p \leq .1.$
*$p \leq .05.$
***$p \leq .001.$

in table 4.2 and the logit model of the Alito cloture vote in table 4.1. Ideological distance borders on significance ($p = .11$) as a determinant of a senator's vote to confirm John Roberts. The reduced significance of ideology in the Roberts confirmation vote likely reflects senators' individual strategic calculations regarding how best to influence President Bush's choice of the O'Connor replacement (i.e., a vote to confirm Roberts would demonstrate Democrats' reasonable position or a vote against him would force Bush to nominate a more moderate candidate to replace O'Connor). Conversely, for the Alito cloture vote, members could more easily rely on their ideological views as Alito embodied a critical nomination that would swing the ideological balance of the court and replace the first female justice with a male nominee.

In addition to ideological distance, the state vote for Bush is also a statistically significant predictor in the pooled vote model and the Roberts confirmation vote model as Democratic senators from states with higher rates of voting for President Bush were more likely to vote for his nominees.[5] The pressures of standing for re-election in 2006 weighed most heavily on the decision to invoke cloture on Alito's nomination ($p = .11$ in a two-tailed t-test on the Alito cloture model in table 4.1) since senators feared being portrayed as obstructionists and did not want to draw attention away from issues that favored Democrats such as the Iraq War in an election year. Despite the fact that three of the Judiciary Committee Democrats, senators Russ Feingold (D-WI), Herb Kohl (D-WI), and ranking member Patrick Leahy (D-VT), voted to confirm Roberts, membership on the Judiciary Committee is not a significant predictor of voting on the nominations.

Taking into account the major influences on confirmation votes, gender does have some impact on senators' voting decisions. While gender is always a substantively negative predictor of support for the nominees, it only approaches statistical significance ($p = .09$) in a two-tailed t-test in the pooled logit model on all three votes. To gain a better understanding of the influence of gender, I developed predicted probabilities in which gender, ideological distance, and Bush's vote in the state are varied to create a prediction for the probability that, for example, a moderate Democratic woman would vote to confirm John Roberts.[6] Figure 4.1 demonstrates that across the board Democratic women are less likely to vote in favor of advancing the nominations of Roberts and Alito than are their male colleagues with similar ideological views and levels of constituent support for President Bush. However, given the baseline probabilities and the logit curve, the votes of the most liberal and the liberal two quartiles of Democratic senators are entirely predictable

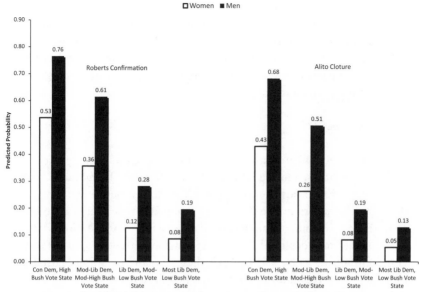

FIGURE 4.1 Predicted Probability of Voting "Yes" on Roberts Confirmation and Alito Cloture

Note: Ideological distance is varied at the 25th (conservative) and the 75th (most liberal) percentiles of the Democratic Party, as well as at the 38th percentile [= the second quartile median] (moderately liberal) and at the 63rd percentile [= the third quartile median] (liberal). The values for the Bush vote share are varied at the same percentiles, low, moderately low, moderately high, and high Bush vote state, respectively. The values for Judiciary Committee member and up for reelection are set at 0, For the Roberts vote, the nominee dummy variables are set at 1 and 0 for Roberts and Alito, respectively. For the Alito cloture vote, the nominee dummy variables are set at 0 and 1 for Roberts and Alito, respectively.

based on their ideology. Thus, there is only an 8% mean probability that the most liberal Democratic women and a 19% average probability that the most liberal Democratic men would vote to confirm Roberts, signifying that regardless of gender, the most liberal Democrats were not inclined to vote to advance President Bush's Supreme Court nominees.

The importance of gender stems from its impact on the votes of the moderately liberal and conservative two quartiles of Democratic senators. It is among these senators that confirmation votes are not entirely predictable from their ideology alone. Thus, among the moderate liberals, there is on average only a 36% probability that a female senator would vote to confirm John Roberts, while the mean probability that a male senator would confirm Roberts is 61%. Similarly, the mean probability that a moderately liberal Democratic woman would vote to invoke cloture on Samuel Alito is 26%, compared with a 51% average probability that a moderately liberal male Democrat would vote for cloture. These results demonstrate that, in a political context that is permeated with gender considerations, ideology is the main driver of senators' confirmation votes, but gender does play a role as female senators exhibit a more negative predisposition in their voting decisions and the marginal impact of gender is greatest among more ideologically conservative Democrats.

Explaining the Vote

Senators can focus on a range of constitutional issues as they consider their vote. I now examine whether female senators focus more heavily on a nominee's position on women's rights as they seek to explain their vote. Senators utilize their vote explanations to achieve multiple goals. Richard Fenno (1978) writes that legislators' explanation of their votes is key to understanding the relationship between representatives and their constituents. It is through these explanations that legislators establish their reputations with constituents and build the bonds of trust that allow them to take votes that are contrary to public opinion but reflect the legislator's view of good public policy. Senators also use their public pronouncements as opportunities for taking positions that can bolster their electoral support with specific constituencies (Fenno 1978; Mayhew 1974; Hill and Hurley 2002). Given the high profile of a Supreme Court nomination, a senator's vote and explanation of that vote is closely scrutinized by groups that provide financial and volunteer support in the next election campaign and by the media who will broadcast the senator's position to constituents and voters.

If female senators are more likely to focus on women's issues in their public explanations, it would support assertions that women prioritize women's rights concerns and they view women and potentially women's organizations as a distinct group within their election constituency (Mansbridge 1999; Williams 1998; Phillips 1995). Indeed, studies of floor debate in the House of Representatives demonstrate that women do perceive themselves as surrogates for women outside of their district, they are more likely to mention different constituencies of women in their speeches, and they are more likely to invoke their own unique perspective as women, particularly their perspective as mothers (Shogan 2001; K. Walsh 2002; Osborn and Mendez 2010; Pearson and Dancey 2010, 2011).

Within the institution, senators also utilize their vote explanations to send signals to other senators and the White House. Thus, the vote explanation is an outlet for expressing one's policy preferences even when the constraints of the institutional and political context determine the vote (Maltzman and Sigelman 1996; Hill and Hurley 2002). Moreover, senators can utilize their statements to influence the deliberative process by highlighting issues that require legislative attention. If women focus more heavily on women's interests in their statements, it would indicate that women bring a different perspective to legislative debate and place greater weight on the importance of women's issues (Mansbridge 1999; Williams 1998; Phillips 1995). Analyses of floor debates demonstrate that both Republican and Democratic women are more likely to mention women's issues in their floor speeches, particularly issues that are directly related to women as a group such as women's health and crimes against women (Shogan 2001; Walsh 2002; Osborn and Mendez 2010; Pearson and Dancey 2011).

To assess senators' justifications for their votes, I examined senators' speeches in the Congressional Record during floor debate on the Roberts and Alito nominations, the statements of Judiciary Committee members at the committee business meeting where senators vote on the nominee, and press releases of senators who did not make a statement on the floor. I noted whether a senator mentioned an issue related to women or women's rights and the nature of the issue, for example, abortion rights, gender discrimination, a desire to see more women appointed to the court, or a perception of oneself as a protector of women's rights. I also assessed the extent to which the senator discussed the issue. Thus, were women's rights mentioned as one issue among a list or did the senator devote a more extensive portion of the speech to a discussion of his or her disagreement with the nominee's record on that issue. The extent to which a senator focuses on an issue in public remarks is a good indication of the intensity he or she feels about the subject.

In the complicated dance of the confirmation process, there is a strong assumption that the president's partisans vigorously support and defend the nominee. Therefore, the majority of Republicans focused their comments on praising the nominee's qualifications and temperament and avoided discussion of judicial philosophy beyond making efforts to defend the nominee against the criticisms leveled by the opposition. Thus, the statements of Republicans focused on Roberts and Alito's impressive credentials. They also spoke of their modest temperament and the fact that these men would not be activist judges who would seek to make law from the bench, an important signal to the conservative base.

Conversely, those who oppose the nominee, in this case Democrats, must focus on issue positions to paint a picture of the nominee that demonstrates that he is out of the mainstream of judicial philosophy and will threaten important constitutional rights. Democratic senators expressed concerns about a wide range of constitutional issues including women's rights, civil rights, business-labor relations, environmental regulation, the limits of executive power, separation of church and state, and the judicial branch's respect for congressional authority.

Finally, the cross-pressured senators, generally conservative Democrats and moderate Republicans who were heavily lobbied and subjected to intense media scrutiny, focused more heavily on Senate procedure and the judges' qualifications and temperament than on issues. Those who did mention issues (for example, moderate Republicans and Democrats who voted for Roberts) reiterated their commitment to a particular constitutional right, for example, abortion rights, and then explained why the nominee's statements in the committee hearing and/or in their private meeting reassured the senator that the nominee would not threaten the future of fundamental rights, that is, the nominee respects precedent and the senator does not believe he will seek to overturn *Roe*. Thus, the statements of cross-pressured senators reflected a strategy of blame avoidance rather than credit claiming as Democrats from red states sought to avoid alienating conservative voters and moderate Republicans engaged in a political calculus that balanced loyalty to party and president with their electoral vulnerability.

Looking at the prominence of women's issues in statements across senators, table 4.3 shows that the majority of Democrats pointed to women's issues as they explained their confirmation votes. These explanations range from a brief mention of women's rights among a list of other issues to extensive discussions of the nominees' records on abortion. Only six male Democrats did not mention women's issues in their remarks on either the Alito or the Roberts nominations. Hailing from states that gave more than 50% of their votes to President Bush in 2004, these senators, including Mark Pryor (AR), Kent Conrad (ND), John D. Rockefeller (WV), Robert Byrd (WV), Tim Johnson (SD), and Ben Nelson (NE), wanted to avoid drawing attention to the nominee's views on contentious issues for fear of alienating their more conservative constituency.

While most male Democrats (75% in the debate on the Roberts nomination and 69% in the debate over Alito) cited women's issues in their explanations, Democratic women were even more likely than Democratic men to mention women's issues as a key factor in their votes. Indeed all the Democratic women referred to women or women's rights as they debated the Roberts nomination, and all of the women except Mary Landrieu (D-LA) pointed to a women's issue as a source of their opposition to Judge Alito. Finally, Democratic women were much more likely than Democratic men to mention multiple women's rights issues as they explained their votes. While only nine of the thirty-six (25%) Democratic men discussed more than one women's issue as they detailed their concerns with the Roberts nomination, six of the nine (67%) Democratic women mentioned multiple women's issues. Since Alito had a more controversial record than Roberts and he was replacing O'Connor, more Democratic men, twelve of thirty-six (33%) highlighted multiple women's issues in their remarks on the Alito nomination, while the number of Democratic women who cited multiple women's issues remained steady at 67%.

Moreover, Democratic women were the only group of senators who focused more attention on women's rights issues beyond abortion. While Democratic men and Republicans were most likely to mention abortion rights, Democratic women devoted even more attention to other women's issues, including employment discrimination, family and medical leave, sexual harassment, and Alito's membership in Concerned Alumni of Princeton. Using two sample tests of proportions (see table 4.3), I find that across both the Alito and Roberts nomination debates, Democratic women were significantly more likely to mention women's issues beyond abortion than were their male counterparts. These findings align with Osborn and Mendez's (2010) analysis of senators' participation in floor debate in the 106th Congress, in which they find that female senators are more likely to mention topics directly connected to women in their floor speeches, including women's health, crimes against women, and family leave. However, abortion was the only women's rights issue that did not exhibit gender differences in frequency of debate. The lack of gender differences in mentions of abortion reflects its position as a touchstone of partisan debate and interest group concern, making it a required subject of discussion for party members regardless of gender. Since other women's rights issues do not attract the same level of partisan attention, gender differences in the prioritization of these issues emerge. The fact that Democratic women devote more attention to women's rights issues outside of abortion supports the claim that group members bring new issues to the agenda and act as more vigorous advocates for group concerns.

Turning to Republicans, since the proponents of the nominee seek to highlight the qualifications and temperament of the nominee to delegitimize the opposition's focus on judicial philosophy, far fewer Republicans than Democrats mentioned women's issues in their explanations of support for Roberts and Alito. For example, only fifteen of the fifty male

Table 4.3 References to Women's Issues in Senators' Explanations of Their Roberts and Alito Confirmation Votes

	Roberts, % (n)			Alito, % (n)		
	Women's Issue	Abortion	Other Women's Issue	Women's Issue	Abortion	Other Women's Issue
Democratic Men (n = 36)	75 (27)	58 (21)	42 (15)	69 (25)	53 (19)	50 (18)
Democratic Women (n = 9)	100* (9)	78 (7)	88⁺ (8)	89 (8)	67 (6)	89* (8)
Difference of Proportions	p = .05	NS (p = .28)	p = .09	NS (p = .19)	NS (p = .45)	p = .03
Republican Men (n = 50)	30 (15)	22 (11)	12 (6)	36 (18)	30 (15)	22 (11)
Republican Women (n = 5)	20 (1)	20 (1)	20 (1)	60 (3)	40 (2)	20 (1)
Difference of Proportions	NS (p = .64)	NS (p = .92)	NS (p = .61)	NS (p = .29)	NS (p = .72)	NS (p = .92)

Note: Two-sample tests of proportions are used to determine whether the difference between the proportion of Democratic (Republican) men and Democratic (Republican) women speaking, for example, on a women's issue during the debate over the Robert's nomination is significant. NS = not significant.
⁺$p \leq .1$.
*$p \leq .05$.

Republicans, or 30%, mentioned a women's issue in their explanation of their vote in favor of John Roberts, and only eighteen or 36% of Republican men mentioned women's issues in their remarks on the Alito nomination. Most Republican men referring to women's issues did so to defend the nominee against Democratic criticisms on specific issues or to condemn prior decisions of activist courts, particularly on abortion. Thus, eleven of the fifteen Republican men who discussed women's issues in their remarks on the Roberts nomination and fifteen of the eighteen Republican men who mentioned women's issues as they defended the Alito nomination spoke about abortion. These references included condemning Democrats for using abortion as a litmus test for judges, highlighting the accolades of judges and prominent attorneys who were pro-choice and supported the nominations of Roberts or Alito, and denouncing specific decisions of an activist court, particularly the

Stenberg v. Carhart decision striking down partial birth abortion statutes. A smaller proportion of Republican men also countered criticism against the nominees on women's rights issues outside of abortion. For example, in the debate over the Alito nomination, several Republican men defended Alito's decisions in employment discrimination and his membership in the Concerned Alumni of Princeton.

In contrast to the gender differences found among Democrats, Republican women were no more likely than Republican men to refer to women's issues in their remarks. Unlike Republican men, the Republican women who did speak about women's issues did not make great efforts to defend the nominees against Democratic attacks about their sensitivity to women's issues. Only two of the five Republican women spoke extensively about women's issues, Susan Collins (R-ME) in her remarks on the Alito nomination and Olympia Snowe (R-ME) in defense of her vote for the Roberts nomination. Both explained why they believed the nominee would not overturn *Roe v. Wade*. While senators Kay Bailey Hutchison (R-TX) and Elizabeth Dole (R-NC) made only passing references to women's issues in their remarks on the Alito nomination, Hutchison did offer a brief explanation for Alito's actions in a sexual harassment case (Congressional Record, January 25, 2006, S62). However, none of the Republican women tried to defend Alito's membership in Concerned Alumni of Princeton or his decisions in other high-profile women's rights cases criticized by Democrats.

The silence of Republican women is all the more striking because there was a conscious effort by the Bush administration and Republican leadership in the Senate to protect the nominees from criticism that they were insensitive to women and women's rights (Stern 2006; Manning 2006). The vocal support of female senators as spokespersons for a woman's point of view would be very helpful to that goal. Indeed, senate staffers and interest group leaders noted that no one expected the moderates to publicly campaign for the nominees. They were just happy with their silence. However, several Republican staffers recalled that party leaders tried to get conservative women to play a more active role in defending the nominees but they could never get them to come to the floor and attend the press conferences. Similarly, in the debate over Harriet Miers, while Barbara Mikulski (D-MD) and feminist groups echoed the Bush administration's assertion that Miers was a victim of sexism, none of the Republican women stepped up to publicly defend her. Only fellow Texans Kay Bailey Hutchison (R-TX) and John Cornyn (R-TX) made any effort to support Miers in the media. Moreover, to date, no

Republican woman has ever served on the Judiciary Committee, despite the fact that many of the Republican women are attorneys.[7] Kay Bailey Hutchison (R-TX), Lisa Murkowski (R-AK), and Elizabeth Dole (R-NC) are all lawyers, and Kelly Ayotte (R-NH) served as her state's attorney general. Republican staff believe that the policy portfolio and fundraising potential of the Judiciary Committee is not as attractive as other committees and that the Republican women do not want to go on the Judiciary Committee because they do not want to become the female party spokesperson on abortion since such a role could jeopardize their electoral support from moderate voters. Thus, one Republican staffer said,

> [T]he establishment Republican leaders, Frist [the Republican leader (R-TN)] and Lott [former Republican leader (R-MS)] wanted [Elizabeth] Dole [R-NC] to join the Judiciary Committee, but she did not want to do it. She wanted to join committees for North Carolina: Agriculture, Banking, and Armed Services. Lott, Frist, and the other establishment leaders, they were just looking at the message of getting a pro-life woman on the committee. They want her to be the female abortion person or the gay marriage person. She did not want to be an icon for that. She has support from moderate Republican women and pro-choice Republicans that she would lose if she became a focal point for those causes. With men there is no extra symbolism to consider [in the committee assignment].

In sum, as part of their larger effort to portray Roberts and Alito as outside the mainstream of judicial philosophy, Democrats devoted more attention to the nominees' positions on women's issues than Republicans did. Among Democrats, Democratic women were more likely than were Democratic men to focus on women's issues, to discuss women's issues beyond abortion, and to mention multiple women's issues in their speeches. Given the small number of Republican women in the Senate, we cannot draw firm conclusions about their behavior. Yet Republican women did not devote more attention to women's issues in their vote explanations in comparison with Republican men. Moreover, Republican men were more likely to utilize their remarks to mount a defense of Roberts and Alito's positions on women's issues than were Republican women.

Democratic Women: A Greater Intensity of Commitment to Women's Rights

One of the major arguments for expanding the descriptive representation of women in legislatures is that it will help achieve greater substantive representation of group interests. Drawing on their shared experiences and history, women will demonstrate more of a commitment to the concerns of various groups of women, and they will bring a different perspective to deliberations that will influence the way their colleagues view issues (Mansbridge 1999; Phillips 1995; Williams 1998). Looking at the statements of Democratic women, it does appear that the nominees' positions on various women's rights issues was a more prominent concern for female senators.

Throughout the confirmation debates, the leading advocate for women was Dianne Feinstein (D-CA). As the only woman on the Judiciary Committee, Feinstein viewed herself as the protector of women and the interests of women on the committee, particularly on the issue of abortion. As she prepared for the hearings on the Roberts nomination, Feinstein explained, "As the only woman on the Judiciary Committee, I have a special responsibility to find out whatever I can about his views on women's rights"(Feinstein 2005a). Similarly, in a media interview before the hearings, she noted, "I recognize that I'm the only woman . . . I recognize that women have had to fight for everything they have gotten, every right. So I must tell you I try to look out for women's rights [in her work on the committee]" (Werner 2005).

Outlining her opposition to Roberts's confirmation when the Judiciary Committee voted to move Roberts's nomination to the floor, Feinstein focused heavily on her fears that he would not support a woman's right to choose and her concerns about his Reagan-era memos that "appeared to demonstrate a denigrating view of issues impacting women." She concluded her statement by reaffirming her role as a protector of women's rights noting, "I am the only woman on this committee. And when I started, I said that was going to be my bar, he didn't cross my bar"(Feinstein 2005b). After the committee vote, Feinstein told the press, "If there was a situation where women are dying, I'd never forgive myself" (quoted in Stern and Perine 2005b).

Similarly, Feinstein's committee and floor statements outlining her opposition to the Alito nomination focused heavily on her analysis of the nominee's position on a right to privacy and his lack of commitment to *Roe* as settled law. In the conclusion of her committee statement opposing Alito's confirmation, Feinstein asserted, "I really believe the majority of people in America believe that a woman should have certain rights of privacy, modified by the state, but a certain right to privacy. And if you know that this person is not going to respect those rights, but holds to a different theory, then you have to stand up" (Feinstein 2006). Clearly, throughout the confirmation process for both Roberts and Alito, Feinstein asserted her role as a defender of women's rights.

Outside of the Judiciary Committee, a comparison of the statements of male and female Democratic senators who represent the same state demonstrates that the Democratic women made women's issues a more central focus of their explanations. For example, Mark Pryor and Blanche Lincoln both represented the socially conservative state of Arkansas, which gave 54% of its vote to President Bush in 2004. Staffers note that abortion and gay marriage are key issues to these constituents. In his floor statement supporting the confirmation of John Roberts, Pryor focused on his participation in the Gang of 14 that sought a bipartisan compromise regarding the use of the filibuster against judicial nominees and the importance of consultation by the president when making nominations. He did not speak about issues and made only a vague reference to civil rights (Congressional Record, September 28, 2005, S10549–S10550). In announcing his vote against Judge Alito, Pryor did not make a floor statement, instead issuing a press release four days before the vote in which he stated that he cannot support Alito because of his tendency to "legislate from the bench" but that he would not support a filibuster (Pryor 2006).

By contrast, Lincoln explained both her vote in favor of John Roberts and her vote against Samuel Alito on the floor of the Senate. Announcing her support for Roberts she said she was voting for him on the basis of his qualifications and temperament. However, she remained concerned about his views on "civil rights and gender equality." She was particularly upset about Roberts's Reagan-era memos arguing for a narrow interpretation of Title IX and his refusal to distance himself from some of those memos. She also maintained that she approached her deliberations on the nomination from her point of view as a "farmer's daughter, my experience as a wife, a mother, a neighbor, to make what I believe is the right decision . . ." (Congressional Record, September 28, 2005, S10568–S10570). As in her statement on Roberts, Lincoln never mentioned abortion rights as part of her justification for voting against Samuel Alito. Again she focused on her concerns about the nominee's record on workplace discrimination and the Family and Medical Leave Act, issues that would be more reflective of her constituency than a focus on abortion and the right to privacy (Congressional Record, January 26, 2006, S167–S168).

In contrast to Lincoln and Pryor, cross-pressured Democrats representing a conservative constituency, Barbara Mikulski (D-MD) and Paul Sarbanes (D-MD) are committed liberals representing a state that gave only 43% of its votes to President Bush in 2004. Both Mikulski and Sarbanes had been re-elected multiple times to the Senate. In his statements on Roberts and Alito, Sarbanes focused his attention on the Senate's role in the confirmation process and the right to ask about judicial philosophy. His reference to women's rights was quite limited. In his floor statement on the Roberts nomination, Sarbanes included women's rights among a list of concerns about the nominee's judicial philosophy that included "voting rights, affirmative action, privacy, racial and gender equality, limitations on executive authority, and congressional power under the commerce clause" (Congressional Record, September 27, 2005, S10526). By contrast, speaking on the Roberts nomination, Mikulski went into great detail about the benefits that Title IX has provided to women and outlined her concerns about Roberts's Reagan-era memos on Title IX and the views he articulated in committee, which she felt did not demonstrate a sufficient commitment to the right to privacy and a woman's right to choose (Congressional Record, September 26, 2005, S10406–S10408).

In their explanations of their votes on the Alito nomination, Sarbanes again focused the majority of his statement on the confirmation process and Alito's position on executive power. He only briefly cited a Reagan-era memo as evidence of Alito's lack of commitment to a woman's right to choose (Congressional Record, January 26, 2006, S199–S200). Again Mikulski went into far greater depth on her concerns about Alito's commitment to women's rights. She began with a tribute to Justice O'Connor as the first woman justice who broke the glass ceiling and was a role model for women. She expressed her disappointment that President Bush did not select a woman to replace O'Connor. She voiced concerns about Alito's membership in the Concerned Alumni of Princeton, his position on employment discrimination, his record on abortion rights including his Reagan-era memos, his refusal to refer to *Roe* as settled law, and his refusal to clarify his position on spousal notification (Congressional Record, January 25, 2006, S65–S67).

While both Sarbanes and Mikulski voted against Roberts and Alito, it is clear that Mikulski felt a heightened concern for the impact of the nominees' jurisprudence on women's rights. One can see a similar pattern when examining the floor statements of Carl Levin (D-MI) and

Debbie Stabenow (D-MI). Representing the swing state of Michigan, which gave 48% of its vote to President Bush in 2004, both senators are in the second most liberal quartile of Democratic senators, with Senator Levin voting slightly more liberally than Senator Stabenow. Yet Senator Levin voted in favor of Judge Roberts, while Senator Stabenow opposed Roberts's nomination. In his floor statement, Levin focused on Roberts's qualifications and his moderate temperament. He then detailed how Roberts's answers in the hearings and in his private meeting demonstrated that he would not be an ideologue on various issues including, among others, the right to privacy because Roberts stated in his hearings that *Roe* was settled precedent entitled to respect under the principle of stare decisis (Congressional Record, September 27, 2005, S10501–S10502). By contrast, Senator Stabenow noted that while she did not have a twenty-year history of voting for Supreme Court nominees, she reflected a different experience as the first woman senator from Michigan. From that position she felt a special "responsibility to fight against discrimination and for equal rights, for the women that will come after me" (Congressional Record, September 29, 2005, S10640). Stabenow then detailed her concerns about Roberts's positions on workplace discrimination, the Family and Medical Leave Act, the pay gap, and a woman's right to privacy (Congressional Record, September 29, 2005, S10640–S10642).

Similarly, in their statements opposing the confirmation of Judge Alito, Levin as the ranking member of the Armed Services Committee deeply engaged in debates over the Iraq War, devoted the majority of his statement to his concerns about Alito's positions on executive power and did not mention women's issues (Congressional Record, January 26, 2006, S193–S195). By contrast, Stabenow framed her remarks as a senator concerned about the future of our families and children. Describing the numerous issue areas in which she believed Judge Alito's views were outside the mainstream, she went into great detail on her opposition to Alito's views on employment discrimination and his position on a woman's right to privacy, particularly his dissent in *Casey* and his position on spousal notification (Congressional Record, January 30, 2006, S269–S271).

In sum, while Democrats voted similarly on the Roberts and Alito nominations, it is clear that the women senators focused more attention on the nominees' positions on women's issues during their deliberations. By contrasting the explanations of senators who represent the same constituents, I demonstrate that women senators delved more deeply into the nominee's record on a range of women's rights concerns from abortion to employment discrimination and diversity in the membership of the court. The statements of the Democratic women demonstrate that they are bringing a different perspective that emphasizes the court's influence on women's rights to deliberations over Supreme Court nominees.

Cross-Pressured Senators: Moderate Republicans and Conservative Democrats

While the majority of senators utilize their statements and votes on judicial nominees to demonstrate their policy commitment to the activist base of their party, the moderate Republicans who represent socially liberal states that support Democratic presidential candidates and the conservative Democrats who hail from states that supported President Bush faced a more difficult task when deciding how to cast their vote and how to explain that position to their constituents. For conservative Democrats, the main concern was to avoid appearing as obstructionist liberals to culturally conservative constituencies who were being bombarded with advertisements that denounced judicial activists and the desire of liberals to ruin American culture by taking God out of the Pledge of Allegiance, sanctioning gay marriage, condoning the burning of the American flag, and supporting partial birth abortion (Becker 2005; Memmott 2005). Unnerved by the defeat of former party leader Tom Daschle (D-SD) at the hands of a Republican campaign to portray him as the chief obstructionist, these senators vigorously opposed efforts to mount a filibuster against Alito. They avoided extensive discussion of the nominees' issue positions in their statements, instead highlighting the nominees' qualifications and temperament or the proper role of the Senate in the confirmation process. Those who had joined the Gang of 14, a group of Republican and Democratic senators that struck a deal to avert the elimination of filibusters on judicial nominations, were particularly likely to highlight their role as bipartisan consensus builders.

In addition to favoring vaguely worded statements that focused on qualifications and procedure more than philosophy, many cross-pressured members delayed the announcement of their votes, and some chose to issue a brief press release rather than defend their votes on the Senate floor. Thus, the day before the confirmation vote for Samuel Alito, five Democrats from conservative states, Evan Bayh (D-IN), Byron Dorgan (D-ND), Kent Conrad (D-ND), Mary Landrieu (D-LA), and Jay Rockefeller (D-WV), and two moderate Republicans, Olympia Snowe (R-ME) and Lincoln Chafee (R-RI), were among the eleven senators C-SPAN.org listed as not yet announcing their position on the nomination (www.c-span.org/congress/alito_senate.asp accessed January 30, 2006).

For moderate Republicans, the stakes were even higher. As members of the president's party they were expected to support his nominees. The Bush administration and its conservative allies believed that early support from the moderate Republicans would demonstrate that the nominees, Roberts and Alito, were in the mainstream of legal opinion. Moreover, the support of Republican moderates would make it harder for conservative Democrats to oppose confirmation (Bolton 2005). Given the stakes, conservative groups heavily lobbied the moderate Republican senators. One conservative group leader explained, "[W]e had one-on-one meetings with the moderates where we talked about Alito's record, resolved the mischaracterizations, emphasized his impartiality and objectivity. One week before the vote we thought we had Chafee's [R-RI] vote because we had a meeting with him that went OK. We thought Snowe [R-ME] was not announcing her vote because she had to appease the NARAL (National Abortion Rights Action League) lobby or because she did not want Chafee to sit out there by himself." Ultimately, Lincoln Chaffee (R-RI) was the only Republican who opposed Samuel Alito.

While securing the endorsement of moderate Republicans was important to the president, supporting Roberts and backing Alito as a replacement for Sandra Day O'Connor could alienate the socially liberal Democrats and Independents that are key elements of the electoral coalitions that elect moderate Republican senators. Facing a conflict between their institutional and electoral interests, liberal groups heavily lobbied the moderate Republican senators. Speaking about Olympia Snowe (R-ME), one liberal group leader said that they thought they had a chance of getting Snowe to vote no on Alito replacing O'Connor because "Snowe said publicly she would not put someone on the Supreme Court that would reverse *Roe*. She gets a lot of support from pro-choice women. She does not want to have to have votes on people like Owen [an appellate nominee to the 5th Circuit that was perceived as opposing abortion rights] because it feeds the argument that she is just a rubber stamp for Bush and doing the bidding of the Republican leadership."

By contrast, supporting a Democratic president's Supreme Court nominee provides moderate Republicans with an opportunity to reinforce their pro-choice credentials and burnish the reputation for independence that attracts socially liberal voters. Thus, while Olympia Snowe (R-ME) never declared her position on Alito before the vote, she was an early and vocal supporter of Democratic president Barack Obama's nomination of Sonia Sotomayor. Thus, on the day that President Obama nominated Judge Sotomayor to the Supreme Court, it was reported that Obama's chief of staff had notified Olympia Snowe (R-ME) of the choice before the official announcement. In response, Snowe issued a positive press release in which she praised the president for "nominating a well-qualified woman, as I urged him to do during a one-on-one meeting on a variety of issues in the Oval Office earlier this month." Snowe's supportive statement came at a time when the talking points from the Republican conference were focused on emphasizing a need to reserve judgment on a nominee (Raju 2009). From the Obama administration's point of view, Snowe's statement laid the groundwork for building bipartisan support and establishing Sotomayor's credentials as a mainstream choice in the media. As for Snowe, she demonstrated her political clout and her ability to cooperate with a Democratic administration to her constituents.

Striking the right balance between a senator's electoral interests and his or her standing within the party caucus requires senators to navigate a treacherous political environment. A closer look at how the four most moderate Republicans, Arlen Specter (R-PA), Lincoln Chafee (R-RI), Olympia Snowe (R-ME), and Susan Collins (R-ME), handled the Roberts and Alito nominations illuminates the political calculations these senators make as they tried to balance their institutional roles with their electoral interests.

Re-elected in 2004 and now serving as chair of the Judiciary Committee, Arlen Specter (R-PA) played a dual role in which he was expected to shepherd Roberts and Alito to confirmation and provide cover for the other moderate Republicans to support President Bush's nominees, according to staff and interest group leaders. An early statement suggesting that President Bush should not nominate a candidate who would seek to overturn *Roe v. Wade* set off a firestorm of criticism against Specter as conservative groups launched a campaign to deny him the chairmanship of the Judiciary Committee. Republicans ultimately supported his chairmanship after extracting public promises from Specter that he would support President Bush's nominees and move them swiftly through the committee, thus limiting his independence as chairman (Perine 2004; Dewar 2004).

As the Republican Judiciary Committee chair and point man for ensuring the confirmation of John Roberts and Samuel Alito to the Supreme Court, Specter announced his support early and spoke first on the floor. His multiple floor statements went into great detail on Roberts and Alito's answers about *Roe v. Wade* and why those statements led him to believe that each nominee respects precedent and supports the principles of stare decisis and therefore was not likely to overturn *Roe* (for example, see Congressional Record, September 26, 2005, S10398–S10402, S 10403; Alito Statement, Congressional Record, January 25, 2006, S41). This detailed and public accounting helped the other moderate Republicans build their case for voting in favor of Roberts and more importantly Alito. Specter's reputation as a moderate and a supporter of women's rights and his vote against Ronald Reagan's conservative Supreme Court nominee Robert Bork lent credibility to his pronouncements on Roberts and Alito's records. Several Republican staffers highlighted the importance of Specter's support in establishing Roberts and Alito as mainstream nominees and providing cover for the other Republican moderates. According to one Republican Judiciary Committee staffer,

> Specter has turned out to be very good as chair because he shores up and gives cover to his moderate Republican colleagues and helps the nominee with the media. His support is the golden touch. It is hard to categorize the nominee as extremist if he endorses them. He voted against Bork, he [Specter] is not extremist; he is very moderate. He has the trust of the other moderate colleagues he has been working with for a long time. But he has to support the nominees now because if he went against them he would lose his chairmanship very quickly. In hearings he gives his abortion spiel where he talks about precedent and asks about superprecedents and this gives him cover with his constituents so he can say to his constituents that he asked the nominee about these things and he believed them in their answer.

While Specter's institutional position as Judiciary Committee chair forced him to take an active role in nomination politics, the actions of the other three moderate Republican senators, Susan Collins (R-ME), Olympia Snowe (R-ME), and Lincoln Chaffee (R-RI), and the tone and content of their vote explanations directly reflected the proximity of their next election and their electoral vulnerability. Of the three, Collins was in the safest position because she was not up for re-election in 2006. To help her moderate colleagues who were facing the voters, Collins, like Specter, announced her votes on Roberts and Alito early, providing political cover for Chafee and Snowe who delayed their announcements until closer to the vote. Media accounts portrayed Snowe and Chafee as more cautious and conflicted on Roberts and Alito than was Collins (Jansen 2006a, 2006b). As the vote on Alito approached, the *New York Times* noted that among Republicans, only Snowe and Chafee had expressed "serious concerns" about Alito (Kirkpatrick 2006).

The Roberts vote was the easier of the two votes because Roberts would simply replace Chief Justice Rehnquist with another conservative and many Democrats were on record supporting him. Collins, who faced the least pressure of the four, focused her statement on Roberts's qualifications and modesty as a judge and made only a passing reference to his support for precedent without directly mentioning abortion rights (Congressional Record, September 27, 2005, S10492–S10493). Since Snowe would face the voters in 2006, she felt a more immediate need to reassure her pro-choice supporters. In her floor statement, she explained her concerns about Roberts related to gender discrimination and abortion rights, and she then detailed how his answers in committee had reassured her (Congressional Record, September 26, 2005, S10408–S10410).

Also running for re-election in 2006, Chafee faced the most complicated electoral environment. Chafee first needed to survive a difficult primary against a more conservative Republican and then a tough general election against the Democratic candidate. To court pro-choice voters, Chafee won the early endorsement of NARAL, an endorsement coveted by his potential Democratic rivals. He did not want to risk losing that endorsement and the signal it sends to liberal voters (Kucinich 2005; Mulligan 2005). However, he also could not alienate the conservative voters who would decide the primary by voting against President Bush's nominees. With many Democrats supporting Roberts, Chafee kept his statement focused on Roberts's qualifications and made only a passing reference to his belief that Roberts would respect a right to privacy (Congressional Record, September 28, 2005, S10575–S10576).

Alito's conservative record on abortion and the unified opposition of Democrats increased the stakes for the Republican moderates. Given these circumstances, Republican moderates searched for the best way to support the party and avoid being blamed by their pro-choice supporters for Alito's confirmation. As a result, Susan Collins (R-ME) felt compelled to offer a more direct defense of her vote and a reaffirmation of her commitment to reproductive rights. In her floor statement, she outlined statements from Alito's hearing that convinced her that he would respect *Roe* as a precedent and she maintained that, despite statements that O'Connor, Souter, and Kennedy made in their hearings against abortion rights, the three were the critical votes upholding *Roe* when the Supreme Court decided the *Casey* case (Congressional Record, January 30, 2006, S302–S303). Conversely, while the Alito vote led Collins to try to reassure pro-choice supporters, Snowe tried to minimize attention to her vote. She delayed the announcement of her position until the day of the vote, and she did not give a floor statement, opting instead for a short press release that focused on the Senate's role in the confirmation process (Snowe 2006).

Facing the anger of pro-choice activists in his state and fearing the loss of his NARAL endorsement, Chafee delayed his decision on the Alito nomination until the day before the vote (Kucinich 2005; Cilliza 2006). As the only Republican voting against the president's Supreme Court nominee, Chafee described himself as a "pro-choice, proenvironment, pro–Bill of Rights Republican." He courted pro-choice voters by detailing in his statement why he felt Alito would threaten a woman's right to choose (Congressional Record, January 31, 2006, S342–S343). A Republican Judiciary Committee staffer highlighted the importance of electoral vulnerability in explaining the votes of the moderates, maintaining that the Republican leadership recognized Chafee's perilous electoral position and gave him more leeway to vote with his constituency since they did not need his vote to win confirmation.

> Republicans knew we did not have sixty votes for Alito, but we knew we had more than fifty. We wanted to get all the Republicans, so colleagues lobbied Snowe and Chafee, but no one will hold it [the vote] against Chafee because they know he is in a tight re-election fight in a liberal state. It was really a free vote for him because we knew Alito would win so why hurt the guy in his re-election. If the vote was 50-50 and we needed Chafee's vote, we would have gotten him to vote the right way.

In sum, the behavior of conservative Democrats and moderate Republicans during the battles to confirm John Roberts and Samuel Alito to the Supreme Court reflected a strategy of blame avoidance rather than credit claiming in which senators sought to balance their institutional roles and party loyalties with the preferences of their electoral constituencies. To avoid alienating culturally conservative voters, Democrats in red states focused their statements on process and temperament rather than issues. Meanwhile, Republican moderates engaged in a political calculus that balanced loyalty to their party and president with their electoral vulnerability by taking positions that conformed with the party while sending signals to their constituents that reaffirmed their support for reproductive rights and women's rights more broadly.

Conclusion

The politics of Supreme Court nominations is pivotal to the future of women's rights in the United States, a fact that is reinforced by the Roberts court decisions limiting abortion rights (*Gonzales v. Carhart*) and making it more difficult to bring claims of employment discrimination (*Ledbetter v. Goodyear Tire & Rubber Co.* and *Dukes v. Wal-Mart*). Clearly, senators' actions as they exercise their advice and consent duties have a direct effect on the scope of women's rights. Partisanship and ideology guide senators' confirmation votes. Thus, ideological distance from the nominee largely rules the vote decisions of opposition party senators. Still gender did influence the votes of the more cross-pressured moderate and conservative Democrats. The demands for party loyalty are particularly stringent for members of the president's party. Therefore, pro-choice Republican senators who advocate for gender equality in their legislative activity are less inclined to cast a vote against the Supreme Court nominee of a Republican president who has a record of opposition to women's rights causes.

As Douglas Arnold (1990) notes, for members of Congress, avoiding blame is often more important than being able to claim credit for policy outcomes. Because Supreme Court decisions are made long after the heat of the nomination battle and are often too complex for constituents to understand, voters will not connect court decisions they oppose to a senator's confirmation vote. While a moderate Republican woman would be attacked by abortion rights groups and lose the support of key constituents if she voted to ban partial birth abortion during the numerous times it was debated in the Senate, the Roberts court decision that upheld the partial birth abortion law will not be traced back to the senator. However, a vote against their president's nominee will immediately earn the animosity of party colleagues in an institution that relies on collegiality to achieve much of its business and could jeopardize their ability to move important initiatives in other policy arenas.

In this rigid political atmosphere, the impact of gender is more clearly reflected in senators' explanations of their votes. Through their explanations, senators seek to build trust with constituents and send signals to important electoral groups, fellow senators, and the White House. Female senators, particularly Democrats, were more likely to point to women's issues as a priority in their evaluation of the nominee, to address issues of gender equality beyond abortion, and to devote extensive portions of their statements to gender-related concerns. The centrality of women's rights to the vote explanations of Democratic women provides some evidence for the claim that women bring a distinctive perspective and set of issue priorities to deliberations over policy.

Yet the politics of Supreme Court nominations and the actions of conservative Democrats and moderate Republicans also demonstrate that policy preferences do not translate easily into legislative actions. Rather, senators' behavior is guided by significant institutional and political constraints that channel and inhibit senators' ability to pursue preferences based on gender. Gone are the days when a liberal jurist like Ruth Bader Ginsburg could be confirmed with only three dissenting votes and a conservative icon like Antonin Scalia would attract unanimous support (Epstein and Segal 2005). The evolution of judicial nominations into a key battlefield for the interests groups and activists who support the Democratic and Republican parties in elections heightens attention to a nominee's judicial philosophy. Efforts by presidents to secure their legacy by placing nominees who reflect their ideological vision on the federal courts places a premium on party loyalty. In response, senators prioritize ideology and party fealty. Thus, when President Bush nominated several very conservative women and minorities to prestigious appellate courts, Democratic women did not feel compelled to support these nominees out of a desire to see more diversity on the courts. Instead, they helped lead the fight to filibuster these appellate nominees, arguing that they would harm women's rights.[8] When President Obama nominated Sonia Sotomayor and Elena Kagan to the Supreme Court, Olympia Snowe (R-ME) and Susan Collins (R-ME) supported confirmation. Now in the Senate's minority party and without a Republican president's reputation on the line, these moderate senators could support someone who was within their comfort zone on judicial philosophy and would allow them to demonstrate their independence to their electoral coalition. By contrast, the more conservative women, senators Kay Bailey Hutchison (R-TX) and Lisa Murkowski (R-AK), noted the importance of diversity, but like the majority of their Republican colleagues, they prioritized their problems with aspects of Kagan and Sotomayor's judicial philosophy (see, for example, Hutchison and Murkowski's floor speeches opposing Sotomayor's confirmation [Congressional Record, August 5, 2009, S8840–S8842, and August 6, 2009

S8939–S8941]). In such a polarized political atmosphere, the importance of gender is drastically reduced and women pursue gender-based preferences when they make the political calculation that their actions will help achieve party goals or will not harm their relationship with party colleagues.

5

Providing for the Common Defense: Gender and National Security Politics in the Post-9/11 World

The terrorist attacks of September 11, 2001, propelled defense policy to the forefront of American politics and made national security expertise an important criterion for voters when selecting candidates for national office. The War on Terror and the country's long engagement in military actions in Iraq and Afghanistan ensure continued public attention to issues of national security. The politics of defense is debated on partisan and gendered terrain. Studies of issue ownership demonstrate that voters have long favored Republicans to handle national security (Petrocik 1996; Petrocik, Benoit, and Hansen 2003; Pope and Woon 2009; Sellers 2010). Although the magnitude of the Republican advantage declined in the 1990s and voters soured on George W. Bush's handling of the Iraq War, the public perception of the Republican Party as stronger on national defense remains (Pope and Woon 2009). At the same time, there is a voluminous literature demonstrating that voters hold gender-based stereotypes in which voters trust women candidates less on defense and foreign policy issues but favor female candidates over men on social welfare issues such as education and health (e.g., Dolan 2004; Huddy and Terkildsen 1993a). This research is joined by a public opinion literature that suggests that in comparison with men, women in the general public are more supportive of social welfare spending, less supportive of defense spending, and less likely to support war (e.g., Shapiro and Mahajan 1986; Norrander 1999, 2008; Eichenberg 2003). These assumptions about the competencies of women candidates and women more generally can influence the recruiting strategies of political parties, the calculations of potential female candidates about whether to run, and the decisions of voters on election day in a way that negatively impacts the advancement of more women to office.

Despite prevailing assumptions that women are less capable stewards of national defense, there are no studies that examine the policy activities of women officeholders on defense issues. Thus, we have no evidence to support or refute the conventional wisdom about women's propensity to engage defense issues. The Senate is an ideal place to begin examining gender differences in defense policy priorities because senators' multiple committee assignments mean that almost every senator sits on a committee with some jurisdiction over defense policy. Moreover, the strong procedural protections that allow individuals to insert themselves into policy debates provide all senators with the opportunity to weigh in on important national security concerns.

In this chapter, I analyze senators' engagement of defense policy. I examine gender differences in participation in the crafting of the annual defense authorization bill in the Democratic-controlled 107th Congress and the Republican-controlled 108th Congress (2001–2004). The authorization bill represents Congress's major statement on defense policy priorities and its response to presidential initiatives. Since issues of war and peace are among the most momentous decisions made by Congress, I also analyze senators' votes on the Iraq War resolution.

Contrary to voter stereotypes about defense policy expertise and trends in public opinion demonstrating that women are less supportive of war, there were no gender differences in support for the Iraq War resolution or the amendments offered to modify the resolution. Moreover, women and men were equally likely to offer amendments to the defense authorization bills. Focusing on the substantive content of senators' amendments, all senators were more active proponents of "soft defense initiatives" that expand benefits for military personnel and veterans rather than the "hard defense proposals" concerning weapons and war.

Yet senators are cognizant of gender stereotypes and party reputations on national security, and they utilize their policy activity strategically to counter these stereotypes. For example, both Republican and Democratic women were more active cosponsors of amendments to the defense authorization bill than were their male colleagues. Thus, these female senators engaged in position taking through cosponsorship to advertise their defense policy activism and expertise to constituents. Furthermore, Democratic women were more likely than their male partisan colleagues to cosponsor soft defense policies that provide benefits for the troops and veterans. This activism reflects the association of social welfare policies with women and the Democratic Party and allows senators to demonstrate support for our troops. Moreover, Senate staffers maintain that Democratic women must overcome the double bind of gender stereotypes and the Democratic Party's reputation for weakness on national security. Therefore, Democratic women look for opportunities to highlight their defense credentials in their legislative activity and to promote their support for the troops by appearing at military and veterans' events in their states, particularly when they are up for re-election.

Why Do Senators Work on Defense Issues?

Congressional scholars have devoted very little attention to examining the factors that motivate individual members to engage national security policy. Much of the congressional literature on defense politics focuses on the balance of power between the Congress and the president, particularly in the decision to go to war. Numerous scholars lament the increasing power of the presidency in foreign affairs, the declining influence of the congressional committees with jurisdiction over foreign policy and national security, and Congress's perceived abdication of its responsibilities in the national security arena (e.g., Deering 2005; Ornstein and Mann 2006; Fowler and Law 2008). Other scholars are less pessimistic about Congress's role, asserting that presidents pay attention to the mood of Congress and are constrained by what they anticipate Congress will accept. Moreover, congressional oversight and the power of the purse continue to be powerful mechanisms for congressional control of military action (Howell and Peevhouse 2007a, 2007b).

Research that focuses on the national security decisions of individual members generally examines roll-call voting on major weapons systems or the distributive politics of defense budget allocations. The consensus emerging from these studies indicates that ideology and constituency benefit are the major forces behind senators' decisions and level of activism on defense issues. For example, analyses of voting on major weapons systems including the B-1 bomber, the Strategic Defense Initiative, the MX missile, and the antiballistic missile point to ideology as the main driver of legislators' votes (Fleisher 1985; Wayman 1985; Lindsay 1990a, 1990b). However, subcontracting decisions on large defense projects and conflicts over base closings draw more constituent-based sentiment (Lindsay 1990a, 1990b; Mayer 1990, 1991). Institutional position, particularly committee assignments and majority party membership, are also key predictors of members' level of engagement in defense policy. For example, in their study of budget allocations, Rundquist and Carsey (2002) find a partisan distributive effect in which members of the majority party who sit on defense committees in the House and Senate receive more military procurement spending dollars in comparison with other majority party members who are not on the committee and minority party defense committee members (see also Carsey and Rundquist 1999).

Despite the emerging consensus on the factors that guide members' national security decisions, there are important limitations to our understanding of legislators' defense policy participation. First, studies of weapons procurement and allocation of defense contract dollars dominate congressional studies of defense policy making. By contrast, there are few studies that examine the predictors of decision making on nonprocurement issues such as military training or expansion of benefits for veterans and active duty personnel. Significantly, Carter (1989) finds that ideology drives support for the president's position on weapons procurement issues, while partisanship, and to a lesser extent, economic benefit, drives support for the president's position on nonprocurement issues such as funding the costs of training and maintaining the troops. Soherr-Hadwiger (1998) argues against the accepted wisdom that the largely unanimous votes for military construction appropriations bills are simply universal coalitions based on wide distribution of pork. Instead, he maintains that those without bases in their districts support these bills for ideological reasons, either reflecting their position as defense hawks or a desire to not appear soft on defense. By studying senators' engagement on what I call hard issues concerning strategic questions of weapons procurement and military readiness and soft issues regarding benefits for military personnel and veterans, I can identify the trade-offs of participation in different areas and illuminate the circumstances in which constituency interests, ideology, institutional position, or personal background factors predominate as motivators of participation.

Another problem with the congressional literature on national security is the overwhelming focus on the end stage of decision making in the form of votes or final budget allocations. This focus on outcomes inhibits our understanding of the full policy-making process and the dynamics that allow members to emerge as leaders in setting the policy agenda and designing the details of defense policy (Kingdon 2005; Hall 1996; Baumgartener and Jones 1993). It is likely that this concentration on final outcomes at the expense of process masks the influence of personal background factors such as gender or military experience and the importance of particular constituency interests on legislators' choices concerning what issues to engage in the larger defense policy arena and how much political capital to devote to specific causes.

Senators and the Political Opportunity Structure of Defense Policy Making

Senate staffers universally agree that, since 9/11, it is both an electoral and a policy imperative for senators to develop a profile on national security. In 2002, the first election since the attacks on the World Trade Center and the Pentagon, terrorism and a potential war in Iraq focused voters' attention on defense policy. Similarly, the competition between President George W. Bush and the Democratic nominee Senator John Kerry (D-MA) to demonstrate their ability to protect the country in the War on Terror and their battles over the proper conduct of the Iraq War dominated the policy debate leading up to the 2004 presidential election, forcing senators, particularly those running for re-election, to continually address security concerns regardless of their planned campaign strategies. In 2006, dissatisfaction with President George W. Bush's conduct of the Iraq War propelled Democrats to retake the majority in Congress. In 2008 the presidential candidates in the Democratic primary sparred over their past records on the Iraq War and whether senators Hillary Clinton (D-NY) and John Edwards (D-NC) regretted their votes in favor of the resolution authorizing war with Iraq. Barack Obama (D-IL) utilized his strong opposition to the war as a tool to rally liberal primary voters. The financial meltdown and long recession made the economy the dominant issue in the 2008 presidential election and the 2010 midterm elections that returned Republicans to the congressional majority. The struggling economy remained the focus of the 2012 presidential election. Still the long military engagements in Iraq and Afghanistan, the Arab Spring, a new military engagement in Libya, concerns about the nuclear programs in Iran and North Korea, the rise of China, and negotiations over how to rein in the defense budget in tough economic times ensure that national security will retain a prominent position on the congressional agenda.

The priming of security as an important frame for evaluating the competence of officeholders encourages all senators to develop a list of proposals and accomplishments on national security. The higher media profile of senators in comparison with House members means that both local and national media will seek the comments of senators on defense issues, and senators who want to develop a national reputation on security will be invited to appear on the national news and the Sunday morning talk shows (Sellers 2002, 2010). Moreover, the Senate is an incubator of presidential ambition. To demonstrate their ability to serve as commander-in-chief, senators must develop a national profile on defense issues. Thus, a Senate staffer noted that John McCain (R-AZ), the 2008 Republican nominee and a presidential candidate in 2000, "always says that every senator who is not in detox or under indictment is running for president." Indeed the Foreign Relations Committee is described as having two kinds of members, freshmen who will seek another committee assignment at the earliest opportunity and nascent presidential candidates of the past and future (Deering 2005). President Barack Obama and Vice President Joe Biden both served on the Foreign Relations Committee as well as 2004 Democratic presidential nominee John Kerry (MA). Biden and Kerry have chaired the committee. John McCain (R-AZ), the 2008 Republican nominee and a decorated Vietnam veteran, is a long-standing member of the Armed Services Committee, rising to ranking member in the 110th Congress (2007–2008). Staffers cited Hillary Clinton's (D-NY) decision to take a seat on Armed Services as evidence of her desire to build up her national security credentials in anticipation of a presidential run. Even senators who hope to be tapped as a vice-presidential nominee are concerned about having a legislative record on national security. Thus, the chief of staff to a female senator who is not active on defense policy said that the senator's staff wants her to seek a defense-related committee assignment because "if she is going to be chosen as a vice-presidential nominee in the future, she needs to be on Foreign Relations or Armed Services to have that experience."

Beyond the media, voter expectations, and presidential ambition, the policy-making process in the Senate encourages widespread participation on defense issues. First, the allocation of committees in the Senate facilitates engagement of national security. All senators receive a seat on one of the four "Super A" committees, Appropriations, Armed Services, Finance, or Foreign Relations. With the exception of Finance, each of these committees has jurisdiction over important national security concerns, giving most senators a seat at the table on defense policy (Evans

1991; Fowler and Law 2008; Deering and Smith 1997). Thus, in the 108th Congress, twenty-nine senators, more than one-fourth of the Senate, served on the Appropriations Committee. Among these senators, all but five held a seat on the Subcommittees on Defense and/or Military Construction and all but one sat on the Defense, Military Construction, and/or Homeland Security subcommittees. More than half the Senate, fifty-three members, served on either the Appropriations Committee or the Armed Services Committee, and seventy of the one hundred senators served on Appropriations, Armed Services, or Foreign Relations.[1]

Moreover, the fact that most senators serve on at least three committees means that senators can engage in multiple types of defense questions. For example, senators who serve on both the Armed Services and Veterans' Affairs committees can influence strategic decisions about the future of the military's weapons and force structure as well as the scope of benefits for active duty and retired military personnel. Thus, in the 108th Congress, five of the twenty-five members of the Armed Services Committee held seats on the Intelligence Committee, and four Armed Services members sat on the Veterans Affairs Committee. Similarly, five of the twenty-nine members of the Appropriations Committee held seats on the Intelligence Committee, and five Appropriations Committee members served on Veterans' Affairs. In addition to the multiple points of entry to influence defense policy provided by their committee assignments, the smaller size of the Senate allows senators to advance to leadership positions on security issues more quickly than their House counterparts (Evans 1991; Baker 2001; Deering and Smith 1997). Therefore, it is not unusual for freshman senators to receive defense-related subcommittee leadership positions.

Finally, as they determine the focus of their national security profile, senators are cognizant of the policy activities of their same-state colleague. Senators leverage their personal policy interests with the jurisdictions of their committee to build a policy niche. They generally do not trespass on the policy turf of their same-state counterpart unless the issue impacts the state economy. Thus a former Democratic staffer described the way Connecticut Democrats Joe Lieberman and Christopher Dodd navigate defense policy as follows:

> Dodd does Foreign Relations, and Lieberman is on Armed Services. Lieberman is interested in all elements of defense policy and is a hawk. Dodd refrains from getting involved in the nuts and bolts of military politics and leaves that to Lieberman. Defense Appropriations, procurement of the Seawolf and Virginia

subs—that is Lieberman's area. Dodd is a foreign policy big picture guy on defense issues. He will focus on things like the abuses of the detainees in the Iraq War. Dodd only gets involved in hard defense if it hits home. For example, when Lieberman works to get a contract for the Virginia sub, Dodd will be there or send a representative when it is announced. If Sikorsky loses the contract for Marine One, they both issue statements. They both have to be seen by constituents on issues where money or jobs are lost.

Clearly, senators tailor their participation on national security to their interests and strengths while navigating the legislative reputation and committee responsibilities of their same-state colleague. Defense policies that impact local economic interests will draw the attention of both senators.

Taking into account the findings of previous research on defense policy making in Congress, the primary importance of security issues since the 9/11 terrorist attacks, and the unique features of the Senate, we can begin to develop an understanding of the factors that explain the strategic decisions of senators concerning the substantive content of their defense policy profile. As one staffer put it, we want to understand what motivates a member to build his or her national security reputation on "taking care of the military and their families or on guns and bombs."

A Theory of the Impact of Gender on the
Defense Policy Activity of Senators

Given the centrality of defense issues to the national agenda and the persistence of voter stereotypes concerning women's lack of expertise in national security, it is important to discern whether there are gender differences in the level and nature of legislators' participation on national security issues. Academic research demonstrates that voters have long favored male candidates on issues of defense and foreign policy (Sanbonmatsu 2002a; Huddy and Terkildsen 1993a, 1993b; Dolan 2004; Burrell 1994; Alexander and Anderson 1993). This preference for male leadership grew after the September 11 attacks. For example, Falk and Kenski (2006) find that the proportion of the public citing defense and foreign policy as the most important problem facing the country dramatically expanded between 2000 and 2004 from 4.5% to 28% of respondents. Furthermore, individuals who prioritize national security concerns were more likely to favor a male presidential candidate even after accounting for other partisan and demographic characteristics (Kenski and Falk 2004; Falk and Kenski 2006). Similarly, Lawless (2004) finds that survey respondents favor male candidates over women to handle a military crisis, punish those responsible for the 9/11 attacks, and protect the United States from future attacks. The preference for male leadership was greatest among respondents who favored a more aggressive military policy in the War on Terror (Lawless 2004). Thus, the increased saliency of national security as a determinant of voter choice and enhanced media coverage of these issues primes negative stereotypes about women candidates in a way that could hinder women's advancement to political office if they are not able to persuasively counter these perceptions.[2] Given the preferences for male leadership on defense policy, it is not surprising that Hillary Clinton (D-NY) established herself as the candidate who was toughest on national security, criticizing Barack Obama (D-IL) as unprepared for the 3 a.m. international crisis phone call in her 2008 Democratic primary campaign (Lawrence and Rose 2010). Similarly, facing an all-male field in the contest for the 2012 Republican presidential nomination, Michele Bachmann (R-MN) continuously highlighted the importance of her seat on the House Intelligence Committee as evidence of her national security expertise (Situation Room 2011).

The stereotypes characterizing women as soft on national security and less interested in defense politics likely stem from social norms characterizing women as more compassionate and less aggressive than men. Moreover, analyses of public opinion since World War II demonstrate that women are less supportive than men of increases in military spending and deployment of troops (Shapiro and Mahajan 1986; Norrander 1999, 2008; Eichenberg 2003). Thus, it is reasonable to ask whether women in Congress are more cautious about sending troops into war once we consider their ideology, party affiliation, and constituent interests.

Taking into account the voter stereotypes that are tied to social norms about the interests and expertise of men and women and the institutional and electoral incentives and constraints faced by senators, I evaluate whether gender impacts senators' decisions to engage defense policy and the substantive content of their national security proposals. I also ask whether stereotypes about women's lack of defense policy expertise inhibit legislators' ability to gain credibility on these issues with colleagues, the media, the defense establishment, or their voting constituencies.

To answer these questions, I evaluate several hypotheses concerning the role of gender as an influence on participation in defense policy. First, I anticipate that despite gender-based stereotypes, there will be no differences in the overall sponsorship of defense-related initiatives by men and women. Instead, the institutional incentives and electoral imperatives that drive senators to be policy generalists will ensure that all senators can point to a mix of defense-related proposals they are pursuing. Thus, the large personal staffs and the breadth of senators' committee assignments that give most senators jurisdiction over some aspect of defense policy combined with the need to reassure voters that they are actively engaged in security issues will lead all senators to develop a profile on defense issues.

However, when one unpacks the substantive content of the defense proposals senators sponsor into hard initiatives relating to the training and equipping of the force and soft issues relating to benefits for military personnel and veterans, gender differences in participation may emerge. If women bring a perspective to legislating that makes them more likely to consider the needs of families, then female senators may be more active in their sponsorship of the soft defense issues that enhance the quality of life for members of the armed forces and veterans than are their male partisan colleagues. Alternatively, if negative stereotypes about women's expertise are correct, men should be more active participants than women on the hard issues of war, weapons procurement, and transformation of the strategic capabilities of the military.

Furthermore, stereotypes about women's ability to engage national security issues will have an impact beyond overall levels of participation. I hypothesize that these stereotypes circumscribe senators' efforts to establish themselves as policy experts with constituents, the media, the defense establishment, and colleagues. Prevailing negative assumptions about women's lack of expertise on defense issues will make it more difficult for women to establish their national security credentials, forcing those who choose to engage these issues to expend additional resources of political capital and staff in an effort to counter these stereotypes.

To evaluate these hypotheses about the role of gender in national security politics, I focus on defense policy activity in the Senate in the 107th (2001–2002) and 108th (2002–2003) Congresses, a period when national security was at the forefront of the congressional agenda as senators dealt with the aftermath of the 9/11 attacks, war in Afghanistan, and an impending war with Iraq. I examine senators' participation in the crafting of the FY (fiscal year) 2003 and FY 2004 defense authorization bills, which are Congress's major annual statement on defense policy. I analyze senators' votes on the Iraq War resolution and accompanying amendments to evaluate whether women are less likely to support war than are men. I utilize the interviews with Senate staff to probe senators' strategic decisions about whether to actively engage defense policy and the substantive content of their national security proposals. These interviews also shed light on how senators' defense policy activities impact their legislative profile and their reputation with constituents.

Making National Security Policy in the Senate: The Defense Authorization Bill

Although there is a large literature that laments the deference and subordination of Congress to the executive branch on matters of national security (for example, Deering 2005; Ornstein and Mann 2006; Wheeler 2004), staffers universally agree that the major congressional vehicle for influencing the direction of national security policy is the annual defense authorization bill drafted by the Armed Services Committee. While the appropriations bill provides the Pentagon with its funding, the authorization bill allows Congress to create or shape programs and weigh in on policy issues (Deering 2005). For example, during the Obama administration, Congress has used the defense authorization bill to monitor administration policy on the war in Afghanistan, debate the repeal of the "don't ask don't tell" ban on gays in the military, rein in the costs of the F-35 Joint Strike Fighter program, and prohibit the Obama administration from transferring detainees from Guantanamo Bay to prisons on U.S. soil (Oliveri 2011; Donnelly and Anderson 2010; Mulero and Donnelly 2011).[3] Clearly, through the authorization bill, senators can influence a wide range of defense policies, from military strategy and weapons development to pay raises and health insurance for the troops.

The defense authorization bill is a better vehicle for analyzing senators' engagement of national security policy than the defense appropriations bill. Observers of defense policy making in Congress note that amending activity on the defense appropriations bill is dominated by senators seeking support for constituent-oriented projects while the authorization bill is more focused on policy issues (Wheeler 2004). As one staffer put it, the defense appropriations bill is "75% pork and 25% policy, while the authorization bill is 75% policy and 25% pork." Authorizers are eager to make sure their bill passes before the appropriations bill to ensure their influence on policy is not ceded to the appropriators.[4] Thus, staffers maintain that senators who are serious about defense policy will not author stand-alone bills but will actively participate and seek to amend the authorization bill.

Given the status of the annual authorization bill as Congress's major policy statement on the conduct of defense policy, I analyzed senators' participation in the FY 2003 and FY 2004 defense authorization floor debates. In the Democratic-controlled 107th Congress, Democrats quickly passed the FY 2002 defense authorization and deferred their challenges to President Bush's policies in an effort to show solidarity after 9/11. However, the FY 2003 bill marked the return to a more partisan atmosphere as the parties utilized the bill to showcase their commitment to the troops in anticipation of the 2002 elections by touting their support for increases in military benefits and pay. Democrats attempted to bolster their party's defense credentials by offering greater benefits for military personnel and veterans, questioning President Bush's missile defense program and his plans to expand nuclear weapons research and calling for expansion of troop recruitment for the army to reduce pressure on the national guard and reserve forces as the country dealt with military actions in the War on Terror and potential war in Iraq (Towell 2002a, 2002b, 2002c). Senators also tried to alter the criteria followed by the Base Realignment and Closure Commission (BRAC) to stave off closure of home-state bases in the upcoming round of base closures, and they debated the first cancellation of a major weapons system, the Crusader Cannon, since then-Defense Secretary Cheney cancelled the navy A-12 aircraft in 1991. This program was cancelled at the request of Defense Secretary Donald Rumsfeld as part of his larger plan to transform the military to a lighter, more agile force that relies on fewer troops and more high-technology weapons and surveillance tools (Towell and McCutcheon 2002).

The FY 2004 defense authorization bill was debated in 2003, a nonelection year and the first year after Republicans regained control of the Senate. However, the parties were already beginning to position themselves for the 2004 presidential election as they competed to demonstrate their support for the troops in wartime by proposing additional increases in pay and benefits for military personnel and veterans (Sorrells 2003a, 2003b, 2003c). Since this was the first authorization bill after the start of the Iraq War, lawmakers continued to argue over the adequacy of the number of troops in the army and the impact on the guard and reserve. Senators also used the bill to question the way the Bush administration awarded contracts to rebuild Iraq. As in the FY 2003 bill, missile defense, the Bush administration's plans to expand nuclear research, and the BRAC process were all subjects of debate. In comparison with past years, the FY 2004 bill included more debate over policy issues concerning internal Pentagon operations than usual including controversies over Buy America requirements, waivers of environmental rules for military facilities, and new civilian personnel guidelines that would give the secretary of defense more control over the civilian workforce (Towell 2003; Clark 2003b, 2003c).

Understanding the Factors That Spur Activism on the Defense Authorization Bill

Clearly, both the FY 2003 and FY 2004 defense authorization bills provided senators with ample opportunities to engage a wide range of national security questions, from weapons procurement and military force structure to taking care of military families and disabled veterans. To assess the influence of gender on the strategic decisions of senators concerning which defense policy debates to engage, I coded the number and policy content of amendments senators filed to these bills, including whether the amendment concerned a hard, soft, homeland security, or constituency-related issue. Hard issues encompass the source of negative stereotypes about the interest of women in defense policy. These amendments concern weapons development such as debates over missile defense and nuclear weapons as well as questions about the structure and operation of the military such as base closures and waivers of environmental laws for military training facilities. Conversely, soft issues incorporate the more traditional social welfare concerns associated with women's presumed expertise by enhancing various benefits for military personnel in an effort to take care of military families. Soft issues include proposals such as expanding access to TRICARE (the military health insurance program), increasing survivor benefits, and enhancing pension benefits for disabled veterans. Constituency-oriented amendments relate to specific projects benefiting, for example, a military base, defense contractor, or research organization in the state.[5]

Given the jurisdiction of the authorization bill, the majority of amendments relate to hard issues of weapons procurement and force transformation, soft issues relating to benefits for military personnel, and constituency-oriented projects (see table 5.1). However, there are a small number of bills related to homeland security concerns such as funding the development of vaccines against biological weapons or providing grants to enhance state and local terrorism responsiveness.[6] Homeland security represents an emerging policy domain that is heav-

Table 5.1 107th and 108th Congresses: Sponsorship of Amendments to the Defense Authorization Bill

Bill Type	Number of Amendments	Number of Members Sponsoring
107th Congress		
Defense	163	57
Subject Categories:		
Soft	44	28
Hard	54	26
Homeland Security	12	9
Constituency	56	35
108th Congress		
Defense	107	42
Subject Categories:		
Soft	35	19
Hard	49	28
Homeland Security	2	2
Constituency	21	14

Note: Amendments are assigned to multiple subcategories if they concerned, for example, both a hard and homeland security issue.

ily influenced by constituency concerns. For example, what used to be funding for local police and firefighters is now reframed as homeland security investment in first responders. The defense authorization bill largely focuses on more traditional national security issues.[7]

In addition to amendment sponsorship, I also coded the number and policy content of the amendments senators cosponsored. Like the analysis of women's issue amendment sponsorship and cosponsorship in chapter 2, to analyze the influence of gender on the level and nature of senators' policy participation on security issues, I conduct negative binomial regression analysis. The dependent variables are a count of the number of defense-related amendments the senator sponsored/cosponsored. The analyses of cosponsorship of hard and soft defense proposals utilize an ordered logit model. The dependent variables in these models measure whether senators cosponsored 0, 1, or 2 or more hard or soft defense proposals. I utilize the ordered logit model rather than the negative binomial because the distribution of the dependent variable in these cases is bounded, with very few senators cosponsoring more than two hard or soft defense issue amendments. Negative binomial models were also tested and produce substantially the same results.

The independent variables employed in the regression analyses draw on the insights of the congressional literature on defense policy making, which highlights the importance of ideology, partisanship, committee position, and defense-related interests in the state. Studies of issue ownership indicate that the public trusts Republicans more on national security and prefers Democrats on social welfare concerns (Petrocik 1996; Petrocik, Benoit, and Hansen 2003; Pope and Woon 2009; Sellers 2010). Therefore, I pay careful attention to the implications of both party and gender that are represented by the independent variables for Republican and Democratic men and women. It is possible that differences attributed to gender could reflect the fact that more women in the Senate are Democrats and Democrats are more likely to advocate soft proposals expanding social welfare benefits for the military, while Republicans focus more attention on hard defense questions of military strategy and force structure. Indeed, a Republican defense staffer asserted that Democrats "are more comfortable on the soft issues and are less concerned about the budget implications," while a Democratic defense staffer said "throw weight, size of the navy, Joint Strike Fighter is Republican stuff. Personnel, give them a pay raise, health coverage are Democratic issues."

Since I am interested in how personal background factors enhance or inhibit a member's ability to gain credibility on an issue and forge legislative solutions, I also include a variable measuring which senators have served in the military. Commentators lament the decline of members with military experience in Congress because of their presumed expertise on defense policy and their greater connection to the needs of our troops and veterans (Cohen 2000; Feaver and Kohn 2001). If the voter stereotypes associated with gender create an additional hurdle for female senators, the credibility wielded by members who have served in the military should make it easier for these senators to emerge as leaders on national security issues.

As with the analysis of women's issues, I utilize Poole and Rosenthal's DW-NOMINATE scores to measure senators' ideology (Poole and Rosenthal 1997, 2007). While party and ideology are highly correlated, these scores allow me to capture intraparty differences in policy priorities. Additionally, research on defense voting emphasizes the importance of ideology or "hawkishness" as a predictor of member behavior on these issues (e.g., Carter 1989; Lindsay 1990a).

To assess constituency need for defense benefits and interest in defense issues, I include variables that measure the importance of defense benefits to the state economy and the presence of military forces and veterans in the state. Drawn from the census and Department of Defense publications, these variables include the state's unemployment rate, percentage of active duty military personnel in the state, the veteran population, reserve and national guard pay, total military and civil contract awards, and the total number of military installations.[8] Finally, I also include a measure of whether or not the senator is up for re-election to account for political imperatives, because senators might increase their activism on defense issues that are salient to voters in an election year.[9]

Beyond constituency interests, senators' positions within the institution affect their calculation concerning the best allocation of scarce legislative resources to meet their policy and re-election goals. I include variables measuring whether the legislator is retiring, a freshman in the first two years of his or her Senate term, and committee and party leadership positions held. While all senators can offer amendments to the authorization bill and give speeches on their defense policy positions, the 25% of senators who serve on the Armed Services Committee have the greatest knowledge of the issues in the bill because they participated in the development of the legislation in the committee and have access to staff experts on the committee and their personal staff (Evans 1991; Hall 1996; Deering and Smith 1997). Since the authorization bill provides the policy guidance for the appropriators, I also include a variable for members of the Appropriations Subcommittees on Defense and Military Construction. Other variables account for membership on committees with jurisdiction over various national security policies including membership on the Foreign Relations, Governmental Affairs, Select Intelligence, and Veterans' Affairs committees. Among committee members, the full committee chairs and ranking members have greater responsibility and greater access to information from staff and outside experts than do other senators. Therefore, I include variables that account for senators with leadership positions on the committees and subcommittees with jurisdiction over defense issues.[10]

Analyzing the Participation of Senators on the Defense Authorization Bill: Sponsorship and Cosponsorship of Defense Policy Amendments

Reflecting the widespread interest in national security policy, table 5.1 indicates that approximately half of all senators sponsored amendments to the defense authorization bill across the two congresses. Explaining the activism of senators on defense issues post- 9/11, one Republican staffer explained simply, "[W]ith defense post- 9/11 everyone has to have something." A senator's legislative agenda is "like a grocery store, if the voters want it, you have to put something on the shelf." Thus fifty-seven senators sponsored 163 amendments to the defense authorization bill in the 107th Congress, and forty-two senators sponsored 107 amendments to the authorization bill in the 108th Congress. Looking at the policy content of the amendments senators offered, in the FY 2003 authorization passed during the 107th Congress, constituency-related projects attracted the most amendments, while hard issues attracted the most amendments to the FY 2004 authorization in the 108th Congress. Across both congresses, more amendments were offered on hard issues than soft issues. However, in the Democratic-controlled 107th Congress, slightly more senators offered soft amendments than hard amendments.

Contrary to popular stereotypes, the patterns of sponsorship in table 5.2 demonstrate that, across both congresses, women and men

Table 5.2 107th and 108th Congresses: Amending the Defense Authorization Bill by Gender and Party

	Mean	Standard Deviation	Median	Sponsor, %	Minimum	Maximum
			107th Congress			
Democrats (n = 51)	1.7	2.7	1	55	0	13
Republicans (n = 49)	1.5	2.3	1	59	0	14
Democratic Men (n = 41)	1.7	2.7	1	56	0	13 Cleland (GA)
Democratic Women (n = 10)	1.7	2.5	.5	50	0	8 Landrieu (LA)
Republican Men (n = 46)	1.5	2.4	1	56.5	0	14 Warner (VA)
Republican Women (n = 3)	2.3	1.2	3	100	1	3 Collins (ME), Hutchison (TX)
			108th Congress			
Democrats (n = 49)	1	1.6	0	47	0	8
Republicans (n = 51)	1.1	1.9	0	37	0	8
Democratic Men (n = 40)	.95	1.6	0	42.5	0	8 Nelson (FL)
Democratic Women (n = 9)	1.4	1.7	1	67	0	5 Landrieu (LA)
Republican Men (n = 46)	1.1	1.95	0	37	0	8 Inhofe (OK)
Republican Women (n = 5)	1	1.4	0	40	0	3 Hutchison (TX)

of both parties sponsored equivalent numbers of amendments to the defense authorization bills. While one would expect that minority party members would offer the most amendments since these senators should have the most complaints about the bill, this pattern does not hold for the defense authorization. When the amendments are broken down by issue area (results not shown), there are few gender differences in the types of amendments that senators offered. Women, like men, offer hard amendments that largely reflect their committee responsibilities and constituent interests in defense policy. For example, in the 107th Congress, Kay Bailey Hutchison's (R-TX) amendment attempting to alter the criteria utilized in the BRAC process reflects her responsibilities as ranking member of the Appropriations Subcommittee on Military Construction and the interests of Texas, a state with numerous bases that would be subject to the commission's scrutiny for closure. Similarly, Mary Landrieu's (D-LA) amendment calling for an annual long-range plan for the construction of navy ships highlights the importance of the shipbuilding industry in her state. Confirming the importance of committee position and defense interests in the state for participation in hard defense issues, a Democratic defense staffer said, "[S]ince 9/11 committee responsibility is less of a cue for responsibility, but if you are not on Armed Services or Defense Appropriations you are not involved in the hard manpower issues. One exception is members with companies in their states will get involved in bits and pieces in whatever the companies do. Generally noncommittee member engagement is parochial on hard issues."

The one clear difference in the nature of the substantive amendments offered by men and women is that more Democratic women sponsored amendments concerning soft issues in the 108th Congress than did their male Democratic colleagues—56% of Democratic women offered soft defense amendments compared with only 18% of Democratic men. This finding provides limited support for the contention that the association of the Democratic Party and women with greater support for social welfare legislation leads Democratic women to support more benefits for military personnel and their families.

Beyond sponsorship, senators also demonstrate interest in defense issues by cosponsoring amendments to the defense authorization bill. Through cosponsorship senators can involve themselves in a wider range of defense policies, and they can build up their legislative profile for constituents. The level of commitment indicated by cosponsorship varies. In some cases cosponsors play pivotal roles in drafting an amendment and building a coalition of support. For others, the decision to cosponsor simply indicates they have been persuaded to sign on to a measure by another senator. However, all cosponsors are considered strong supporters of an amendment, and their presence is utilized to build momentum for a proposal in the effort to achieve floor consideration and passage. Moreover, the value of cosponsorship as a tool for position taking with constituents is universal (Krehbiel 1995; Wilson and Young 1997; Koger 2003). Senators can refer to amendments they have cosponsored in their efforts to build a reputation on security issues with voters. Looking at original cosponsors (those who sign on to an amendment the day it is introduced), sixty-four amendments attracted eighty-one cosponsors in the 107th Congress, and sixty-six senators cosponsored forty-seven defense-related amendments in the 108th Congress[11] (see table 5.3).

Examining bills by policy area, the soft amendments that provide or enhance benefits for military personnel and their families attract the most cosponsors, reflecting the desire of senators to bring benefits to constituents and to support the troops in wartime. As one defense staffer explained, "Since national guard and service reserves in all states have been deployed in Iraq, all members engage soft issues. It is easy for all senators to engage to help veterans and military families. It shows we support our troops and makes great press and great politics. Con-

Table 5.3 107th and 108th Congresses: Cosponsorship of Amendments to the Defense Authorization Bill

Bill Type	Number of Amendments	Number of Members Cosponsoring
107th Congress		
Defense	64	81
Subject Categories:		
Soft	19	63
Hard	26	49
Homeland Security	2	5
Constituency	17	15
108th Congress		
Defense	47	66
Subject Categories:		
Soft	12	42
Hard	26	42
Homeland Security	1	18
Constituency	8	8

stituents will ask about the benefits and local press focuses on returning soldiers and casualties." Thus, in the 107th Congress, twenty-six hard amendments attracted a total of forty-nine cosponsors, while the nineteen soft amendments attracted a total of sixty-three cosponsors (see table 5.3). The hard amendments that attracted the most cosponsors concerned issues such as missile defense, nuclear weapons, contract awards in Iraq, and the Base Realignment and Closure Commission. The soft amendments with the most cosponsors included efforts to increase survivor benefits, expand access to TRICARE (the military health insurance program), grant citizenship to deceased soldiers and their dependents, and increase benefits to disabled veterans by allowing concurrent receipt of their disability and retirement benefits.

While there were no gender differences in overall sponsorship of amendments, women are more active cosponsors of defense bills across both congresses. For example, table 5.4 indicates that in the 107th Congress, Democratic women cosponsored a mean of 3.1 defense-related amendments, compared with 1.5 amendments for Democratic men, and Republican women cosponsored a mean of 4.3 amendments, compared with 2 amendments for Republican men. Perhaps women recognize the need to shore up their defense credentials with voters, and they utilize cosponsorship of defense initiatives to boost their credibility.

The regression analyses in tables 5.5, 5.6, and 5.7 assess whether gender is an important predictor of activism on the defense authorization bill once one accounts for the major partisan, ideological, constituency, and institutional factors that are known to influence participation in national security policy making. Table 5.5 demonstrates that gender, party, and ideology exert no statistically significant influence on senators' decisions to sponsor amendments to the defense authorization bill. Instead the importance of defense benefits to the state and institutional position, particularly membership on the committee with jurisdiction over the bill, the Armed Services Committee, drive amendment sponsorship. Thus, in the 107th Congress all but three of the twenty-five members of the Armed Services Committee offered amendments to the authorization bill on the floor. The three senators who did not offer amendments were all freshmen. Senators from states with higher unemployment rates and, in the 108th Congress, senators whose states received the largest defense-related contracts were also more active participants in the amending process. Senators with military service were significantly more likely to offer amendments to the defense authorization bills than those without military experience across both congresses. The activism of these senators supports the contention that members

Table 5.4 107th and 108th Congresses: Cosponsoring Amendments to the Defense Authorization Bill by Gender and Party

	Mean	Standard Deviation	Median	Sponsor, %	Minimum	Maximum
			107th Congress			
Democrats (n = 51)	1.8	1.5	1	84	0	5
Republicans (n = 49)	2.1	1.8	2	78	0	7
Democratic Men (n = 41)	1.5	1.3	1	81	0	5 Cleland (GA), Bingaman (NM)
Democratic Women (n = 10)	3.1	1.6	3	100	1	5 Landrieu (LA), Carnahan (MO), Mikulski (MD)
Republican Men (n = 46)	2	1.8	2	76	0	7 Lott (MS)
Republican Women (n = 3)	4.3	1.2	5	100	3	5 Collins (ME), Snowe (ME)
			108th Congress			
Democrats (n = 49)	2.6	2.2	2	84	0	9
Republicans (n = 51)	.9	1.2	0	49	0	4
Democratic Men (n = 40)	2.4	2.1	2	80	0	7 Levin (MI), Bingaman (NM), Durbin (IL)
Democratic Women (n = 9)	3.6	2.6	2	100	1	9 Clinton (NY)
Republican Men (n = 46)	.74	.95	0	46	0	3 McCain (AZ), Allen (VA), Warner (VA)
Republican Women (n = 5)	2.4	1.8	3	80	0	4 Snowe (ME), Collins (ME)

with military service wield more credibility on defense issues and are more likely to emerge as leaders on national security issues.

While there are no gender differences in who sponsors amendments to the defense authorization bill, gender is an important predictor of cosponsorship. The regression analyses in table 5.6 demonstrate that Republican and Democratic women in the 107th Congress were significantly more likely to cosponsor amendments to the defense authorization bill than were their male colleagues. In the 108th Congress, with Republicans taking back control of the Senate, liberal Democrats utilized their cosponsorship activity to express their support for expand-

Table 5.5 107th and 108th Congresses: Negative Binomial Models of Sponsorship of Amendments to the Defense Authorization Bill (Standard Errors in Parentheses)

Independent Variables	107th Congress	108th Congress
Republican Women	.801	−.912
	(.715)	(1.11)
Democratic Women	−.153	−.427
	(.476)	(.588)
Republican Men	.414	−.93
	(.666)	(1.05)
Ideology	−.861	1.25
	(.76)	(1.25)
First-Term Senator	−.907[+]	−.32
	(.506)	(.554)
Retiring Senator	.54	−15.88
	(.574)	(1337)
Up for Reelection	.266	.072
	(.295)	(.381)
Military Service	.51[+]	.605[+]
	(.288)	(.363)
Total Contracts	.612	.958*
	(.479)	(.396)
Military Personnel	.131	−.343
	(.176)	(.261)
Veterans	.007	.016
	(.093)	(.118)
Reserve and Guard Pay	.732	.322
	(.416)	(.304)
Military Installations	−.971	−.806*
	(.512)	(.367)
Unemployment	.405**	.502**
	(.141)	(.177)
Armed Services	1.24***	.605
	(.375)	(.445)
Appropriations Defense and Military Construction Subcommittees	−.027	−.165
	(.305)	(.392)
Foreign Relations	−.381	−.433
	(.366)	(.471)
Governmental Affairs	−.051	−.502
	(.337)	(.448)
Select Intelligence	.197	−.604
	(.326)	(.481)
Veterans' Affairs	−.819*	−.504
	(.41)	(.48)
Defense Committee Chair	.075	.282
	(.36)	(.581)
Defense Committee Ranking Member	.061	−1.26
	(.402)	(.941)
Defense Subcommittee Chair	−.085	−.404
	(.258)	(.32)
Defense Subcommittee Ranking Member	.038	.07
	(.284)	(.323)
Same-State Senator's Defense Amendments	−.001	−.281*
	(.059)	(.133)
Constant	−2.73[+]	−2
	(1.56)	(1.98)
Dispersion Parameter	.24	.516
	(.16)	(.281)
Log Likelihood	−145.88	−118.39
Log Likelihood Ratio χ^2	55.34	43.71
Pseudo-R^2	.159	.156
N	100	100

[+]$p \leq .1$.
*$p \leq .05$.
**$p \leq .01$.
***$p \leq .001$.

Table 5.6 107th and 108th Congresses: Negative Binomial Models of Cosponsorship of Amendments to the Defense Authorization Bill (Standard Errors in Parentheses)

Independent Variables	107th Congress	108th Congress
Republican Women	.835[+]	1.04[+]
	(.45)	(.548)
Democratic Women	.911**	.205
	(.292)	(.321)
Republican Men	−.396	.133
	(.446)	(.585)
Ideology	.567	−1.66*
	(.495)	(.697)
First-Term Senator	−.399	−.061
	(.315)	(.341)
Retiring Senator	−.146	−.196
	(.439)	(.459)
Up for Reelection	.131	−.087
	(.217)	(.218)
Military Service	.286	.303
	(.194)	(.226)
Total Contracts	.17	.455*
	(.324)	(.223)
Military Personnel	−.007	−.002
	(.137)	(.129)
Veterans	−.034	−.001
	(.067)	(.07)
Reserve and Guard Pay	.009	−.019
	(.295)	(.183)
Military Installations	−.359	−.147
	(.336)	(.209)
Unemployment	.189[+]	.103
	(.097)	(.096)
Armed Services	.432[+]	.697**
	(.267)	(.263)
Appropriations Defense and Military Construction Subcommittees	−.272	−.134
	(.23)	(.242)
Foreign Relations	.194	−.153
	(.252)	(.281)
Governmental Affairs	.183	−.105
	(.231)	(.253)
Select Intelligence	.227	.378[+]
	(.219)	(.229)
Veterans' Affairs	−.165	−.19
	(.262)	(.293)
Defense Committee Chair	−.562	−.32
	(.376)	(.37)
Defense Committee Ranking Member	.457[+]	.066
	(.278)	(.269)
Defense Subcommittee Chair	.026	−.174
	(.195)	(.249)
Defense Subcommittee Ranking Member	.248	−.188
	(.186)	(.185)
Constant	.1	−.558
	(1.06)	(1.25)
Dispersion Parameter	0	.028
	(0)	(.097)
Log Likelihood	−152.92	−148.05
Log Likelihood Ratio χ^2	53.02	60.81
Pseudo-R^2	.148	.17
N	100	100

[+]$p \leq .1$.
*$p \leq .05$.
**$p \leq .01$.

Table 5.7 107th and 108th Congresses: Ordered Logit Models of Cosponsorship of Hard and Soft Defense Issues (Standard Errors in Parentheses)

Independent Variables	107th Hard	108th Hard	107th Soft	108th Soft
Republican Women		1.77	2.48	1.65
		(1.56)	(1.57)	(1.46)
Democratic Women		−.469	3.43***	1.63^
		(1.04)	(1.02)	(.839)
Republican Men		1.14	−.958	−.557
		(1.67)	(1.16)	(1.4)
Gender	3.39***	...	...	...
	(.991)			
Party	−1.85	...	...	...
	(1.22)			
Ideology	−.578	−4.64	.017	−.639
	(1.45)	(2.07)	(1.31)	(1.71)
First-Term Senator	−3.36*	.742	−1.1	.072
	(1.35)	(.897)	(.814)	(.801)
Retiring Senator	−.253	−1.2	1.21	.398
	(1.11)	(1.39)	(1.17)	(.921)
Up for Reelection	.973	.253	.607	−.16
	(.617)	(.623)	(.526)	(.559)
Military Service	.719	−.01	.414	1.1*
	(.577)	(.608)	(.489)	(.557)
Total Contracts	−.779	2.02**	2.74*	.147
	(1.21)	(.733)	(1.07)	(.59)
Military Personnel	.939*	−.294	−.705^	.273
	(.384)	(.34)	(.399)	(.355)
Veterans	.075	.235	−.065	−.01
	(.204)	(.206)	(.176)	(.201)
Reserve and Guard Pay	1.6^	−.379	−1.5^	.554
	(.866)	(.503)	(.868)	(.477)
Military Installations	−1.58	.167	.249	−.894
	(1.02)	(.553)	(.954)	(.574)
Unemployment	.037	.256	−.115	−.018
	(.288)	(.274)	(.248)	(.254)
Armed Services	4***	1.69*	.264	1.42^
	(1.11)	(.818)	(.793)	(.749)
Appropriations Defense/Defense and Military Construction Subcommittees	1.02 (.685)	.569 (.757)	−.392 (.563)	−.003 (.592)
Foreign Relations	−.196	−.525	...	...
	(.739)	(.93)		
Select Intelligence	.815	1.32^	...	...
	(.622)	(.761)		
Veterans' Affairs	...	...	−.511	−.411
			(.636)	(.696)
Defense Hard/Soft Committee Chair	−1.11	.184	−1.62	−1.82^
	(.984)	(1.28)	(1.12)	(1.12)
Defense Hard/Soft Committee Ranking Member	1.41	1.85	−1.38	−.65
	(1.38)	(2)	(1.2)	(.86)
Defense Subcommittee Chair	−2.04*	.243	1.21	−1.1^
	(.8)	(.516)	(.818)	(.674)
Defense Subcommittee Ranking Member	−.799	.435	.819	−1.35*
	(.72)	(.609)	(.588)	(.67)

Table 5.7 *(continued)*

Independent Variables	107th Hard	108th Hard	107th Soft	108th Soft
Log Likelihood	−71.56	−66.99	−81.61	−81.27
Log Likelihood Ratio χ^2	63.54	59.92	52.29	31.65
Pseudo-R^2	.308	.309	.243	.163
N	100	100	100	100

Note: I do not divide the gender variable by party in the model for cosponsorship of hard defense amendments in the 107th Congress, because all three Republican women cosponsored two hard defense bills. Therefore, the variable for Republican women is perfectly predicted. See footnote 10 for more information on the committee and subcommittee chair/ranking member variables. The ellipses indicate not utilized.
^$p \leq .11$.
*$p \leq .05$.
**$p \leq .01$.
***$p \leq .001$.

ing benefits for the troops and to protest the policies of Republican president George W. Bush. Republican women continued to cosponsor more defense-related amendments than their male colleagues. Across both congresses, committee position and constituent need for defense benefits are important predictors of which senators cosponsor amendments to the defense authorization bill. To bolster support for their amendments, sponsors recruited members of the committee with jurisdiction over the bill, the Armed Services Committee, to cosponsor their proposals. Senators with economic interest in bringing defense dollars to their states, as measured by higher rates of unemployment in the 107th Congress and total defense contracts in the 108th Congress, were also more likely to cosponsor amendments to the authorization bill.[12]

To further illuminate the influence of gender on senators' cosponsorship activity, I develop predicted probabilities to assess how many defense-related amendments senators with a given gender and party affiliation would cosponsor.[13] Thus, I vary the gender and party affiliation of the senator and set all other variables at their means. I also set ideology at the mean for each party, Republican and Democrat, and I vary committee membership by creating probabilities for senators who serve on the Armed Services Committee and those who do not have a seat on the committee with jurisdiction over the defense authorization bill. The predicted probabilities in figure 5.1 demonstrate that for example, in the 107th Congress, Republican women will cosponsor on average three more defense-related amendments than Republican men (4.3 vs. 1.2) and Democratic women will cosponsor a mean of almost two more defense-related amendments than Democratic men (2.9 vs. 1.2). This is a significant difference since senators cosponsored a mean of two amendments to the defense authorization bill in the 107th Congress.

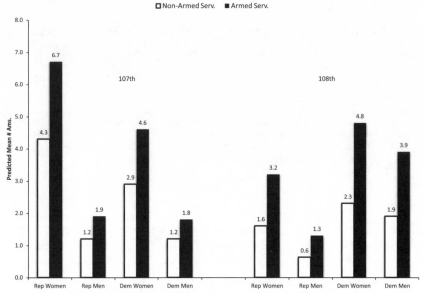

FIGURE 5.1 107th and 108th Congresses: Defense Amendment Cosponsorship

Note: DW-NOMINATE ideology scores are set at the mean for each party. Armed Services Committee membership is varied from 0 to 1, indicating a seat on the committee. All other dichotomous variables are set to the mode of 0, and continuous variables are set at their means.

Women's higher level of activism in cosponsoring defense bills partially stems from their support for soft proposals. Ordered logits in table 5.7 indicate that Democratic women across the 107th and 108th Congresses are more likely to cosponsor soft defense amendments than are Democratic men. While the coefficient for Republican women is positive across the two congresses, it borders on significance at the .11 level only in the 107th Congress. Women were also more likely to cosponsor hard amendments in the Democratic-controlled 107th Congress, but gender has no impact on cosponsorship of hard defense amendments in the 108th Congress.[14] Because I utilize ordered logit models to evaluate cosponsorship of soft defense amendments, the predicted probabilities in figures 5.2 and 5.3 indicate the mean probability that a senator would cosponsor zero, one, or two or more amendments to the defense authorization bill. Thus, in the 107th Congress, on average there is a 97% chance that a Democratic woman who is not on the Armed Services Committee will cosponsor a soft amendment, while there is a 64% probability that a Democratic man would cosponsor a soft amendment. Similarly, Republican women in the 107th Congress who are not serving on the Armed Services Committee would be 50%

☐ Non-Armed Serv. ■ Armed Serv.

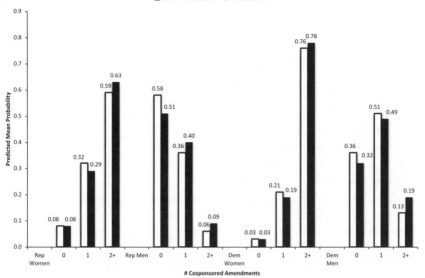

FIGURE 5.2 107th Congress: Soft Defense Amendment Cosponsorship

Note: Results indicate the mean probability that a senator will cosponsor 0, 1, or 2 or more soft defense amendments. DW-NOMINATE scores are set to the mean for each party. Armed Services Committee membership is varied from 0 to 1, indicating a seat on the committee. All other dichotomous variables are set to the mode of 0, and continuous variables are set at their means.

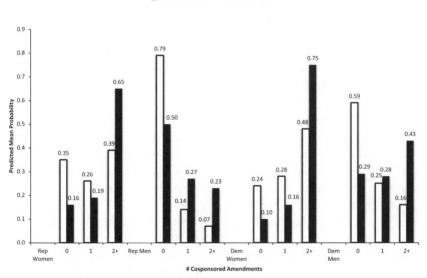

FIGURE 5.3 108th Congress: Soft Defense Amendment Cosponsorship

Note: Results indicate the mean probability that a senator will cosponsor 0, 1, or 2 or more soft defense amendments. DW-NOMINATE ideology scores are set to the mean for each party. Armed Services Committee membership is varied from 0 to 1, indicating a seat on the committee. All other dichotomous variables are set to the mode of 0, and continuous variables are set at their means.

more likely to cosponsor a soft amendment than Republican men. Thus, there is a 92% mean chance that a Republican woman would cosponsor a soft amendment compared with only a 42% mean probability that a Republican man would cosponsor a soft amendment.[15] Women are also much more likely to cosponsor two or more amendments. For example, in the 107th Congress, there is a 76% mean probability that a Democratic woman who is not on the Armed Services Committee will cosponsor two or more soft defense amendments, while on average there is only a 14% chance that a Democratic man will cosponsor two or more soft defense initiatives.

Interviews with Senate staff confirm that women are more likely to support soft defense initiatives that expand benefits for the troops and veterans, and sponsors seek out women as cosponsors because they believe women are sympathetic to these initiatives. For example, one Democratic staffer who handled defense issues for a male Democrat on the Armed Services Committee maintained,

> Women are more likely to be interested in these issues, and they are pushed into them by colleagues. Anything to do with people, humans is softer. When a senator has a bill on a personnel issue they will go to the women [on the Armed Services Committee] first for cosponsors. You can always get Collins [R-ME]. Dole [R-NC] is always interested in women. Clinton [D-NY] resisted being pushed into personnel issues except for defense health issues because of her long-standing interest in health. She wanted to talk about future combat systems. But she would always cosponsor stuff on these issues.

Similarly, another Democratic legislative assistant for defense policy said, "[W]omen are as capable on the hard issues, but the men ignore the softer issues like children and health. Because it is ignored and not as taken care of it is more obvious to the women as a need. Women have walked into a male-dominated society [in the military], and they see woefully inadequate social services."

In sum, gender has no impact on whether members sponsor amendments to the defense authorization bill. Women, like men, respond to the same electoral and institutional incentives that encourage senators to engage defense policy. Thus, all senators pay attention to the importance of defense interests to their state economies, and senators recognize the need to demonstrate national security expertise in a post-

9/11 world. The fact that women are more active cosponsors of amendments to the defense authorization bill indicates that women are more concerned about shoring up their credentials on national security with voters and stakeholder groups. Cosponsorship provides an opportunity to advertise positions on national security, an important benefit for female senators who must counter voter stereotypes portraying women as weak on defense. Women, particularly Democratic women, are more active cosponsors of soft defense policy proposals that expand benefits for military personnel and veterans. This greater activism reflects the association of the Democratic Party and women with the social welfare issues that dominate soft defense initiatives. Indeed, women are predisposed to recognize and respond to the need for more social services in the military. Policy entrepreneurs perceive women as more open to these proposals and pursue women as cosponsors as they work to build a support coalition for their soft defense initiatives.

*Authorizing War in Iraq: Are Women Less
Supportive of Using Military Force?*

While the defense authorization bill embodies Congress's annual statement on defense policy, the most monumental decision a senator faces is whether to commit the United States to war. In 2002, the Bush administration was gearing up for a potential war with Iraq, and senators had to vote on a resolution to authorize the use of military force. In this section, I analyze senators' votes on the resolution authorizing the use of force and on a series of amendments that would impose additional constraints on President Bush's ability to go to war. I find that despite public polling indicating that, in comparison with men, women are less supportive of the use of force, there were no gender differences in senators' support for war in Iraq.

It is widely believed that women are more pacifistic than men and therefore less inclined to authorize the deployment of troops. Among the general public, over time, women have been less supportive of military intervention than men in each of the military conflicts since World War II and less supportive of increased defense spending (Eichenberg 2003; Ladd 1997; Smith 1984). These issues played a particularly important role in determining the electoral gender gap in the 1980s when women were more likely than men to oppose Ronald Reagan's defense buildup and to favor a freeze on nuclear weapons development (Norrander 1999, 2008; Conover and Sapiro 1993; Shapiro and Majahan

1986). More recently, Clark and Clark (2006) argue that strong support among men and women for the War on Terror in the aftermath of the 9/11 attacks reduced the gender gap in the 2002 and 2004 elections, contributing to the Republican victory in the 2002 congressional elections and George W. Bush's re-election in 2004. Moreover, Eichenberg (2003) argues that while women are generally less supportive of war, they are more likely to support the use of force for humanitarian reasons and they are more supportive in cases in which the enemy employs violence against women as a tactic of war.

Polling in the months leading up to the Iraq War indicated that while both men and women supported President Bush's policies on Iraq, women were more hesitant to support war than men. For example, a *Los Angeles Times* poll in late January 2003 found that 49% of women compared with 65% of men supported a potential decision by President Bush "to order U.S. troops into a ground attack against Iraqi forces." (http://www.pollingreport.com/iraq18.htm). On the eve of war in March 2003, an *ABC News/Washington Post* poll indicated that 67% of men but only 51% of women supported the Bush administration policy to "disarm Iraq and remove Saddam Hussein from power, by war if necessary, working with countries that are willing to assist, even without the support of the United Nations" (http://www.pollingreport.com/iraq18 .htm). As the war dragged on and casualties mounted, support for the war declined more quickly among women. Thus, as President Bush and Democratic presidential candidate John Kerry (D-MA) debated the merits of the war, a May 2004 Quinnipiac University poll found that a majority of women were questioning the war, with 56% of men but only 44% of women agreeing that "going to war with Iraq was the right thing for the United States to do" (quoted in Dolan, Deckman, and Swers 2011). Women were also more likely to favor withdrawing troops from Iraq. Thus, in June 2006 as the Senate was debating a Democratic amendment to urge President Bush to begin redeploying troops by the end of the year, a *Washington Post/ABC News* poll indicated that 55% of women supported a deadline for withdrawing troops from Iraq, compared with only 38% of men (Balz and Morin 2006; Babington 2006).

Women's greater skepticism about the use of force over time may lead one to expect that female senators would be more opposed to granting President Bush the authority to send troops to Iraq in comparison with their male colleagues. Most famously, the first woman to serve in Congress, Jeanette Rankin (R-MT) (1917–19 and 1941–43) served for two terms, each coinciding with the beginning of one of the world wars. A pacifist, Rankin voted against war both times, casting the only no vote in the House or Senate against World War II (Kaptur 1996). More recently, immediately after the 9/11 attacks, Barbara Lee (D-CA) cast the only vote against the resolution authorizing President Bush to use "all necessary and appropriate force" to retaliate against the terrorist attacks of September 11, 2001 (Hawkings and Nutting 2003). Alternatively, in an effort to counter gender stereotypes and demonstrate they are tough on defense, female officeholders may hesitate to oppose a president's decision to use military force. To date, there are no studies that analyze gender differences in voting on national security. I analyze the determinants of senators' votes on the Iraq War resolution and a set of amendments that were designed to place limits on President Bush's ability to go to war.

The Senate voted on the Iraq War resolution on October 11, 2002, barely a month after the one-year anniversary of the 9/11 terrorist attacks and just as the 2002 election campaign season was heating up. To protect the country from future attack, President Bush promulgated a new doctrine of preemptive war in which the United States claimed the authority to launch preemptive strikes against countries that had the capability to launch attacks against the United States and that might utilize weapons of mass destruction to help terrorist groups harm the United States. The Bush administration made the case that Saddam Hussein possessed weapons of mass destruction and that he may have had ties to al-Qaeda (Daschle 2003; Wheeler 2004; Pomper 2002a).

The doctrine of preemptive war is a major departure from previous practices in which the United States would launch an attack only when faced with an imminent threat. However, politically, the debate over the Iraq War resolution was embroiled in 2002 midterm election politics. Republicans hoped to retake the Senate by capitalizing on President Bush's popularity and keeping voters focused on his strength, the War on Terror, and national security. By contrast, Democrats hoped to turn the public's attention back to the economic recession and social welfare concerns that benefit their party. At the same time, Democrats feared being labeled weak on security if they defied President Bush by questioning his plans to protect the country from terrorist attacks (Daschle 2003; Wheeler 2004). Refuting the Democratic Party's image as weak on security was particularly important to Democrats facing tough reelection battles such as southern Democrats Max Cleland (D-GA) and Mary Landrieu (D-LA) as well as potential 2004 presidential candidates including House minority leader Richard Gephardt (D-MO), Senate majority leader Tom Daschle (D-SD), Joe Lieberman (D-CT), and John Kerry (D-MA). Senators who voted against the resolution authorizing the Persian Gulf War in Iraq in 1991, such as Joe Biden (D-DE) and John Kerry (D-MA), also felt additional pressure to atone for their previous vote and support the president (Pomper 2002b; Taylor 2002; Jalonick 2002; Daschle 2003).

In this atmosphere of foreign policy danger and high electoral stakes, negotiations concerning the content of the resolution were limited to the White House and top party leaders in the House and Senate, House Speaker Dennis Hastert (D-IL), House minority leader Richard Gephardt (D-MO), Senate majority leader Tom Daschle (D-SD), and Senate minority leader Trent Lott (R-MS). Ultimately, House minority leader Richard Gephardt (D-MO), who was planning a presidential run in 2004 and did not want to look weak on defense, cut a deal with the White House that gave President Bush authority to declare war with almost no restrictions or requirements for congressional oversight (Daschle 2003; Pomper 2002d; Nather 2002b; Wheeler 2004). This resolution passed the House quickly. However, Senate leader Tom Daschle (D-SD) was not part of the deal between Gephardt and President Bush. Therefore, the Senate would vote on the Bush resolution that was introduced by Bush's strongest Democratic ally on Iraq, Joe Lieberman (D-CT); Vietnam veteran and Bush's main rival for the 2000 presidential nomination, John McCain (R-AZ); Armed Services chair John Warner (R-VA); and Evan Bayh (D-IN). The Senate would also vote on a set of amendments designed to apply various restrictions to Bush's ability to declare war.

The Bush White House was most concerned about an amendment by senior Foreign Relations Committee members Joe Biden (D-DE) and Richard Lugar (R-IN). The amendment required Bush to get a new United Nations (UN) Security Council resolution authorizing the invasion of Iraq or he must state that the threat to the United States was so great that it required unilateral action. The proposal also limited the war to eliminating the weapons of mass destruction by forcing Iraq to comply with the disarmament obligations under the Gulf War cease-fire agreement. It did not authorize regime change. Ultimately the White House convinced Lugar to drop the amendment, and it was not offered on the Senate floor (Daschle 2003; Pomper 2002c; Nather 2002a; Wheeler 2004).

An amendment by Carl Levin (D-MI), the chair of the Armed Services Committee, became the main alternative to the White House resolution. Levin's amendment required the president to gain UN authorization for war or return to Congress for a separate authorization if his efforts at the UN failed. The Durbin (D-IL) amendment challenged the preemptive war doctrine by requiring the president to demonstrate an imminent threat posed by Iraq's weapons of mass destruction rather than simply a continuing threat. The first of two amendments offered by Robert Byrd (D-WV) dealt with the balance of power between Congress and the president and reasserted the authority of Congress to declare war and the president's limited authority without congressional authorization. The second Byrd amendment sought to impose a two-year time limit for the war, subject to modification by Congress (Daschle 2003; Darlymple 2002; Martinez 2002; Wheeler 2004).[16]

Since drafting of the Iraq War resolution was largely limited to top party and committee leaders, no women were involved in the negotiation of the resolution and women did not sponsor any of the limiting amendments. Early in the process, in an effort to pressure President Bush to seek congressional authorization, Judiciary Committee members Arlen Specter (R-PA) and Dianne Feinstein (D-CA) both sponsored resolutions designed to assert congressional authority under the War Powers Act and require the Bush administration to attain a resolution before taking military action (Pomper 2002a). Mary Landrieu (D-LA), a southern Democrat with a heavy military presence in her state who faced a difficult re-election race, was one of the sixteen senators who cosponsored the White House–backed resolution. Three women, Barbara Boxer (D-CA), Barbara Mikulski (D-MD), and Debbie Stabenow (D-MI), were among the eight senators who cosponsored the Levin amendment, the major challenge to the White House–backed resolution.[17]

Once the resolution reached the floor, a senator could stake out a position against the war or in favor of a slower march toward war by voting against the war resolution, by opposing cloture on the resolution, or by voting in favor of some of the amendments that would place restrictions on Bush's ability to use force. Ultimately, the Iraq War resolution passed the Senate by an overwhelming margin of 77-23. The twenty-three senators opposing the authorization included four Democratic women, eighteen Democratic men, and one moderate Republican man, Lincoln Chafee (R-RI). However, thirty-nine senators, including thirty-seven Democrats and two Republican moderates, Lincoln Chafee (R-RI) and Arlen Specter (R-PA), expressed their hesitance about the resolution by voting to limit it in some way.

To evaluate whether gender influenced senators' votes on the Iraq War resolution or the set of amendments designed to circumscribe the president's authority, I utilize regression analysis. The first model in table 5.8 employs a logit model in which the dependent variable measures whether or not the senator voted for the Iraq War resolution. The second

Table 5.8 Logit Model of Democratic Senators Voting against the Iraq War Resolution and Negative Binomial Model of Democratic Senators Voting for Amendments to Limit the War Resolution (Standard Errors in Parentheses)

Independent Variables	Vote against War	Vote for Limiting Amendments
Democratic Women	−1.5	−.08
	(1.86)	(.348)
Ideology	−21.94**	−1.51**
	(7.87)	(.505)
Up for Reelection	−3.37*	−.471*
	(1.69)	(.235)
Military Service	−1.38	.039
	(1.07)	(.217)
Southern State	−.695	−2.04**
	(1.94)	(.74)
9/11 State (NY, NJ, CT)	−5.5+	−.901*
	(3.38)	(.391)
Military Personnel	.368	.073
	(.588)	(.1)
Veterans	−.041	−.208+
	(.441)	(.108)
Reserve and Guard Pay	−.424	−.28
	(1.19)	(.232)
Constant	.368	3.45*
	(.588)	(1.63)
Dispersion Parameter	. . .	0
		(0)
Log Likelihood	−15.39	−78.75
Log Likelihood Ratio χ^2	38.96	46.74
Pseudo-R^2	.559	.228
N	51	51

Note: The ellipses indicate not applicable.
+$p \leq .1$.
*$p \leq .05$.
**$p \leq .01$.

model in table 5.8 is a negative binomial regression in which the dependent variable is a count of the number of times a senator voted to limit the authorization for war by voting against cloture or voting for one of the four limiting amendments. The scores range from 0 (voting in favor of cloture and against all limiting amendments) to 5 (voting against cloture and for all four limiting amendments).[18] Since only one Republican voted against the war resolution and only two Republicans voted for any limiting amendments, the models analyze the voting behavior of Democrats. The independent variables draw on the congressional literature regarding legislators' voting on defense policy. A variable measuring Democratic women captures any gender effects. I also include a variable for senators with military experience, as these senators are expected to have greater credibility on issues of war. The DW-NOMINATE scores account for the ideology of senators. I expect more liberal Democrats to oppose the war and more conservative Democrats to support the use of force. I also include a variable accounting for Democrats from southern states to address the conservatism and pro-military outlook of these constituencies. The military presence in the state is accounted for by variables measuring the proportion of active duty military, the veteran population, and reserve and national guard pay. I include a measure of which Democratic senators were up for re-election in 2002, since fears about appearing weak on defense or defying a popular president would be most intense for these senators. A final variable accounts for the senators from New York, New Jersey, and Connecticut who represent the states that had the most constituents killed in the 9/11 attacks.

The models in table 5.8 demonstrate that among Democrats, women were no more likely to vote against the war or support efforts to limit the president's authority than were Democratic men. Instead, liberal ideology is the strongest predictor of opposition to the war. Senators who faced re-election in 2002 were more supportive of the war, as they felt the most pressure to demonstrate their security credentials to the electorate by supporting the president. Democrats representing the states that lost the most citizens in the 9/11 attacks on the World Trade Center, New York, New Jersey, and Connecticut, were also more supportive of the war than other Democrats, while senators from southern states and states with a higher veteran population were significantly less likely to support the proposals to limit the scope of the war.

In sum, there is no evidence at the officeholder level to support the theory that women are more hesitant to authorize the use of force than men. While over time women in the public at large have been less supportive of sending troops into battle, in the case of the Iraq War resolution, women senators did not stake out more pacifistic positions than did their male colleagues. Women generally did not play a major role in the drafting of the resolution since the gravity of the issue and the electoral incentives limited the negotiations to the White House, party leaders, and the most powerful committee players, none of whom were women. Women senators did not offer any of the major amendments to inhibit the president's authority to use force. Analysis of the vote on the war resolution and the series of votes to limit the scope of the resolution indicate that women were no less supportive of war than were their male colleagues once one accounts for other factors that impact senators' votes. Instead, liberal ideology and a desire to avoid being labeled as weak on security by those Democrats standing for re-election in 2002 were among the most significant predictors of votes for and against the war.

Engaging Defense Policy in a Partisan and Gendered Context

The analysis of senators' defense policy participation demonstrates that men and women responded to the same ideological, institutional, and constituency forces as they determined whether to offer amendments to the annual defense authorization bill and whether they should support the Iraq War resolution. However, both Republican and Democratic women were more likely to cosponsor amendments to the defense authorization bill. Thus, women may be utilizing their cosponsorship activity to create opportunities for position taking on defense issues that would counter voter stereotypes about women's lack of expertise on national security. While all senators were more likely to cosponsor soft defense amendments that provide benefits to the troops and veterans, Democratic women were particularly active sponsors and cosponsors of these proposals. Thus, Democratic women may bring a different perspective to deliberations on defense policy that prioritizes the social welfare needs of the military and veterans. In addition to the gender differences found in the empirical analysis, Republican and Democratic Senate staffers maintained that national security policy is made in both a partisan and gendered context. National security constitutes one of the core advantages of the Republican Party, while Democrats struggle to refute the perception of their party as weak on defense. Meanwhile, stereotypes about women's interest in national security mean that women must be more deliberate in their efforts to establish themselves as experts on defense matters. Democratic women face the double bind of gender stereotypes and membership in the party that is perceived as weaker on defense.

The Partisan Context of Policy Making on National Security

Senators seeking to influence defense policy work within a highly partisan context in which all staffers agree that, since Vietnam, Republicans are seen as the more credible stewards of national security and Democrats are viewed as being anxious to improve their public image on these issues. Similarly, public opinion studies of issue ownership also identify a Republican advantage on national security (Petrocik 1996; Petrocik, Benoit, and Hansen 2003; Pope and Woon 2009). Sellers (2002, 2010) finds that when one party clearly owns an issue, as is the case with Republicans on defense, the party leadership will seek opportunities to continuously highlight that message in their media relations. Thus, while President Obama deliberated over whether to authorize a surge of troops in Afghanistan and the magnitude of that surge, Republicans sought to portray Obama as weak on defense by criticizing him as indecisive for taking too long to make the decision and urging him to follow the recommendations of the generals rather than risk losing the mission (Allen 2009; Franke-Ruta 2009). Reacting to Obama's decision to set a timetable for withdrawal from Afghanistan, Republican congressional leaders and presidential candidates accused Obama of undermining national security (Lee 2011; Herb 2012). Throughout his presidency, Republicans accused Obama of "leading from behind" on foreign policy (Krauthammer 2011). These criticisms reflect a general pattern in which Democrats are portrayed as soft on defense while Republicans are the party of national security. While the killing of Osama Bin Laden and Obama's success in the Libyan conflict have blunted the effectiveness of these criticisms, the differential in the overall reputations of the parties remains. My discussions with Senate staff indicate that this extreme issue ownership creates policy skew in which the weaker party, the Democrats, is unable to unify around alternatives or check the excesses of the party that owns the issue, the Republicans.

Senate defense policy staffers assert that the perception of Democrats as weak on defense became a bigger problem for the party after the 9/11 terrorist attacks thrust national security to the forefront of American politics. Thus, one Democratic defense policy staffer said,

> Democrats are not anxious to engage on national security but they have to post-9/11. . . . 1992, 1996 defense was not an issue on the radar screen; just missile defense, and they [Democrats] left the post–Cold War entangling alliance issues to the Republicans. All the polls before 9/11 showed more than 90% of Republicans think the Republican Party is best on national security, 30% of Democrats would agree that Republicans are better at keeping us safe and many of them are liberals, which is the Democratic Party's base. 9/11 changed everything and Democrats find themselves on the wrong side of national security expertise.

Similarly, another Democratic defense policy staffer said, "It is a self-fulfilling prophecy, Democratic pollsters before the presidential election always find that Democrats are weak on defense and then Democrats do things to not look weak that makes them look weak on defense."

Democrats also face a conflict between the desire to strengthen their national security credentials with voters and a liberal Democratic base that wants to see defense budget cuts and an end to war. This conflict makes it difficult for Democrats to develop a unifying policy on the wars in Iraq and Afghanistan and on questions about the future direction of military weapons development and force structure. Thus, a Republican defense staffer criticized Democratic efforts to attack President Bush on the Iraq War in the 2004 election, saying,

> Republicans definitely have the advantage on national secu-
> rity. Democrats have not helped themselves since 9/11 and the
> [2004] presidential campaign did not help them with Kerry say-
> ing "wrong war, wrong place, wrong time" and "knowing what
> I know now I would still vote for the war." Kerry ran to the right
> of Bush on the war calling for more troops, more money for
> special operations. [On national security] Democrats can't find
> their you-know-what with both hands. Liberal Democrats have
> legitimate questions if the only way for Democrats to be cred-
> ible on defense is to run to the right of Republicans.

Indeed, the analysis of voting on the resolution to authorize war with Iraq showed that Democratic senators standing for re-election in 2002 were less likely to vote against the Iraq War. This finding suggests that these Democratic senators feared being labeled as weak on security by the opposing candidate and voters. By 2006, mounting casualties and public dissatisfaction with President Bush's handling of the Iraq War propelled Democrats back to the majority based on a message of opposition to the war. Yet, after Democrats took over Congress, rather than withdrawing troops, President Bush successfully pursued a troop surge that was later credited with turning around the war. In 2008, Barack Obama's (D-IL) strong opposition to the war helped him with liberal voters in the Democratic presidential primary against Hillary Clinton (D-NY), who refused to renounce her vote in favor of the Iraq War resolution (Lawrence and Rose 2010). However, the financial collapse and deep recession of 2008 pushed national security and other noneconomic issues off the radar.

Beyond questions of war, other staffers maintained that Democrats' concern over their national security image also affects long-term decisions on weapons development and the structure of the military. For example, since Ronald Reagan began pushing for the development of a missile defense system, Democrats have had difficulty pushing back against a program they view as ineffective and too costly. Thus, a Democratic staffer said, "[M]issile defense is the third rail for Democrats on military policy. This is where policy and politics diverge. Republicans have been brilliant in packaging the issue, and Democrats are drawn to the light and feel compelled to lick the bug killer. If there is a 1% chance of saving Chicago, is it worth spending $1 billion? Voters will say yes when compared to 0% chance." Another Democratic staffer explained that during the Clinton administration, Senate Democrats were ready to oppose missile defense,

> Senator [—] was all ready to make a full legislative push and press statements against missile defense. He made the statements, drafted the bills, and then three weeks before the vote we hear from the Clinton administration that they don't want Senate Democrats to oppose missile defense because Clinton does not want to look weak on defense. In the end only three Democrats voted against creating missile defense. Since then, Democrats have been trying to cut the funding for and undermine the missile defense program that they voted for.

Finally, speaking about defense policy in the Republican administration of George W. Bush, a Republican defense staffer asserted that Democratic disarray and internal conflicts with their base give Republicans the upper hand on charting national security policy. "Republicans have Democrats where they want them on defense. Democrats have a problem with their own constituency that wants to know why you are not against the F-22 and DDX destroyer, but Democrats are scared politically to offer amendments to eliminate stupid defense ideas so Republicans are in the driver's seat. They have freedom of action on hardware or policy with no trouble unless other Republicans have problems with their ideas."

In sum, staffers believe that Democrats are paralyzed by their reputation as soft on defense in comparison with Republicans. Consequently, Democrats find it difficult to unify around policy alternatives on defense issues. Democrats must balance the views of a liberal Democratic base seeking an end to war and defense budget cuts with the need to demonstrate competence and toughness on national security in a post-9/11 political environment. As a result, Republicans believe they have more room to push their defense policy objectives forward on issues ranging from the conduct of war to weapons development. While the gap in the value of the party labels on defense issues varies with the advent of each new Republican and Democratic presidential administration and the public's evaluation of their performance on national security issues, the overarching view of Republicans as the national security party remains.

The Gendered Context of Defense Policy Making

In addition to the partisan context, senators engaging defense issues work within a gendered context in which stereotypes about women's policy expertise create an additional hurdle for women senators seeking to gain credibility on defense issues. The women recognize this vulnerability and devote extra effort to building their reputation with voters, the media, the defense establishment, and other senators. Democratic women are the most anxious about these stereotypes because they face the dual challenge of gender stereotypes and the Democratic Party's reputation as weak on national security.

Establishing their defense credentials with voters, and more broadly, constituents, is a primary concern according to staffers for Republican and Democratic women senators. A Republican staffer stated simply, "[W]omen definitely have a higher mountain to get over with voters on military issues and with the constituent groups [military veterans, defense contractors] that pay attention in their state." To establish their expertise, women work to develop a legislative profile on defense issues and promote their policy expertise through outreach to constituents and voters. For example, one staffer pointed to the value of committee seats on defense-related committees for women senators trying to earn their bona fides with voters. "Women want to get on defense and foreign policy committees to establish their credibility on the issue. Voters don't question a man's ability on defense issues. Senior male senators with no defense experience, no one will say they are not tough. Women need these committees to show they are tough and fit to lead in that area because the women are not likely to have served in the military." Similarly, the decision of Hillary Clinton (D-NY) to seek a seat on Armed Services was often brought up as evidence of her desire to show voters she has the capability to become commander-in-chief.

The need to demonstrate toughness is even more imperative for Democratic women who face the double bind of gender and being associated with the Democratic Party's reputation as soft on defense. Thus, a Democratic staffer said, "On defense women have a hurdle and Democratic women have an extra hurdle. They have to work harder to prove themselves to voters on defense and foreign policy issues. They will offer amendments and more bills to support the troops." Another Democratic staffer maintained, "Republican women get more credibility on defense because they are men with different body parts, but they carry the Republican tide, which is stronger on defense. Hutchison [R-TX], Murray [D-WA], and Mikulski [D-MD] are all on Defense Appropriations, but Hutchison is more associated with the subject." Similarly, a Democratic staffer complained, "The Democratic Party is not good at giving cover to their members on defense issues the way the Republicans are, so the Republican women can always rely on the view of their party as good on defense to protect them with voters."

To inoculate themselves with voters, women senators also utilize their constituent events to raise their profile on defense policy. Thus, the chief of staff for a Democratic woman noted that constituent events related to defense or veterans take on heightened importance for female senators. "If a politician will normally do 10% of their public events on foreign policy then they will do more public events, 25%, to get themselves in front of those audiences more." Similarly, another Democratic chief of staff noted, "[T]hey visit the bases and all the commanders, the families of those overseas. They want to seem strong on defense. All the senators do the Memorial and Veterans Day events, but the women are concerned about it to a more extraordinary degree, it is never just another event for them. They also look for opportunities to be a leader for the active military, guard, reservists, and veterans and of course protecting their bases in the BRAC process."

Female senators, particularly Democratic women, also design their campaign strategies to demonstrate strength on national security and refute the criticism that they are weak on defense. Several staffers referred to Mary Landrieu's (D-LA) reputation as "Military Mary" on the hill. "Landrieu is very vocal on defense. She never met a shipbuilding program she did not like, which is because of the Louisiana shipbuilding industry. She has a conservative electorate and is not helped by being a woman. She needs to be more pro-military and guns than the military in that electorate. In her 2002 campaign she had camouflage 'Military Mary' bumper stickers." Conversely, staff reported that Landrieu's Democratic counterpart, John Breaux (D-LA), who retired in 2004, did not feel compelled to trumpet his national security credentials and utilized his reputation as a centrist dealmaker to move his reputation from a House member who protected home industries to a national player on health and tax issues.

Similarly, in discussions with campaign managers for senators up for re-election in 2004, all managers noted the desirability of securing endorsements from veterans' groups to enhance the candidate's image on national security. But managers for female Democratic candidates expressed more of a sense of urgency and reported working harder to get these endorsements than managers for Republican candidates (male or female) and male Democratic candidates, even those who did not support the Iraq War. Thus, a campaign manager for one Democratic woman described how the campaign did not think they would get the support of the state's main veterans' organization, so the "campaign created a veterans for [—] group. At a time of war, and she did not support the Iraq War resolution, they needed to show her concern about veterans and military quality of life as a way to separate her decision about the war from support for men and women in uniform." Eventually, outreach efforts by members of the campaign's veterans' group helped secure the endorsement of the major veterans' group, and the campaign manager expressed her feeling that this was an important victory for the campaign.

These staff accounts highlighting women senators' greater concern for developing their defense policy credentials and advertising them to constituents corroborate the regression findings concerning women's higher rates of cosponsorship of defense-related amendments and the greater attention of Democratic women to sponsorship and cosponsorship of the soft defense issues that show support for the troops and their families. Clearly, in choosing committee seats, planning constituent outreach, designing legislative proposals, and developing campaign strategies, women senators, especially Democrats, are particularly concerned with winning the trust of voters on issues of national security.

While there is strong evidence that women, particularly Democratic women, are more concerned about shoring up their reputation on national security with voters and constituent groups, within the Senate, staffers generally agreed that women who choose to engage national security do not face any additional hurdles with Senate colleagues. For example, a Democratic defense staffer said, "[C]redibility is not an issue among senators. Senators see individuals and abilities, what you intend to do in the club." Similarly, another longtime Democratic defense staffer said,

> It is harder to distinguish gender issues today. Credibility problems for women have diminished over time. Senatorial courtesy

still exists, so there will be no overt or detectable credibility problems, but over time a senator gets a reputation as being serious on an issue and knowledgeable or someone who just gets the deference due a senator and this is it. There was a woman who was on the [Armed Services] Committee who would be a voice for her state but was not interested in broader issues, and she got the deference on state issues but was not looked at as a heavyweight. Hillary Clinton [D-NY] was respected, disciplined, hardworking, and knowledgeable in national security issues. If you are good and demonstrate it, you get respect. Constituents see your voting record and if they are getting their share of the pie, but colleagues will see if you are engaged or not engaged.

Other staffers felt that a female senator may have to work harder to establish herself as an expert on defense policy, but once that reputation is built, gender has no impact. Thus, a Republican defense staffer said, "[I]nside the Senate it is not a big problem to be a woman. Women can undo the stereotypes by boning up on technical issues." Similarly, a Democratic defense staffer maintained, "[T]here is an original assumption that the military will deal with male members and staff first because there is the outside possibility they have military service. Up until you have a chance to act on an issue there is more automatic credibility to men, but things sort themselves out quickly when there is action. There are impediments for women getting into the conversation but what matters is the outcome. Gender is never the deciding factor."

Describing the process by which Kay Bailey Hutchison (R-TX) and Hillary Clinton (D-NY) developed their reputations on national security, staffers believed that these senators were cognizant of gender stereotypes as they worked to establish themselves as experts on defense policy issues. Therefore, they carefully planned their engagement on these issues and worked very hard to build their reputations. The evolution of Kay Bailey Hutchison's (R-TX) reputation as a player on defense issues was described as follows:

> It took time to develop her credentials on the military. She traveled wherever Texans were stationed. She had differences with the Clinton administration on the Balkans and wrote editorials in the *Washington Post* and *New York Times*. She hired a first-rate foreign policy chief of staff and hired a full bird colonel for her defense LA [Legislative Assistant]. She came to the table

with the interest and the ideas, and her staff helped insert her in the debates. Today she has leverage at the Pentagon and the State Department.

Similarly, Hillary Clinton was described as having successfully gained entry into the defense policy world by studying the issues and nurturing the right relationships with colleagues and important leaders at the Pentagon. Laying the groundwork for a presidential run, Clinton gave up her seat on the Budget Committee in the 108th Congress to become the first Senator from New York on Armed Services in the panel's more than fifty-year history (Cochran 2003). One committee staffer noted,

> Clinton has gone out of her way to engage on hard and soft defense issues and in defense planning at the closed-door level. She has been proactive on veterans' issues, but most of the issues she engages are hard defense. When she joined Armed Services she literally brought the other senators on both sides of the aisle coffee, and she did not say much, but if a Republican wanted a bill to be bipartisan they would go to her. Only recently has she emerged as a partisan Democrat, but Republicans on Armed Services love her because she knows what she is talking about. She makes a point of getting her photo taken with generals and name dropping the generals' names, "I am happy to see a particular general is here today." It is important for a senator to be comfortable with the flag officers and be able to talk about hard-edge issues. Hillary has the double problem of being a woman and running for president, and her husband's relationship with the military was disastrous so she has to repair that and find a new way of dealing with them.

Thus, staffers viewed gender as an additional constraint that Clinton and Hutchison had to consider as they sought to establish a reputation on military issues. However, they were able to navigate this additional barrier to emerge as experts in the eyes of colleagues and the defense establishment.

In addition to doing one's homework to master the substance of defense policy, senators who want to develop a reputation on national security must also attract media attention for their activities. Some staffers felt that the media is less likely to consider women as national security experts. Thus, in a 2005 article on women in the Senate, Debbie Stabenow (D-MI) complained, "[A]fter 9/11, it really pained me that Mary

Landrieu, who, at the time, chaired the Armed Services Subcommittee on Emerging Threats, was not interviewed on television. . . . Look at the Sunday-morning talk shows— very rarely are women acknowledged as authorities on a topic. . . ." (Victor 2005). In a study of the Sunday morning shows, I found that women senators had to achieve higher levels of seniority and committee leadership than male senators before they were invited to speak as defense policy experts (Swers 2007). Beyond lamenting the lack of women utilized as experts on defense, other staff felt the media was more likely to question the defense policy expertise of women senators in comparison with men. For example, one Republican staffer was disturbed by the initial reporting when Susan Collins (R-ME) was given responsibility for the Intelligence Overhaul bill created in response to the report of the 9/11 Commission. "In the beginning of the bill, the press coverage continually asked why she was qualified to take the lead on this bill, despite the fact that she had served on the Armed Services Committee for seven years. I suspect that a man would not have received as much scrutiny."

While their position as senators minimizes or eliminates the barriers for female senators as they seek to influence defense policy within Congress, staffers universally assert that the military and therefore defense politics are dominated by a male culture in which there are few female Senate staffers working on defense policy and few women in key positions in the military leadership or among defense lobbyists. This male-oriented culture creates barriers for those women who do work on defense politics as they seek to gain the respect of policy stakeholders in the Pentagon and defense lobbying community. One male Democratic staffer asserted that there is a hierarchy of who has credibility in the defense policy arena. "On and off the hill women have a harder time getting into defense issues regardless of recent advances in gender norms. The hierarchy is a man with military service doing defense policy, a man doing national security without serving in the military, a woman who served in the military (note a woman with military service is below a man without any), and a woman who never served in the military." Similarly, a female Democratic defense staffer recounted,

> Armed Services and defense as a whole is a boys club. There are not many women staff in the defense world. The high-ranking professional staff are always men. There are not many uniformed women who can then serve as Senate liaisons [from the Pentagon]. The lobbyists are mostly men. If you are a woman lobbyist in that industry you are expected to act like one of

the guys. There is a big stag fest, dinner in the winter in a big hotel in D.C. Anyone who is anyone in defense is there drinking whiskey, smoking cigars. It is a very masculine event. The few women who are there just have to suck it up and roll up their sleeves.

Female defense staffers felt that gender stereotypes were most likely to create problems in their relations with the stakeholder groups outside the Senate, particularly among older generation constituent groups and lobbyists. Thus, a female Democratic defense staffer said, "[I]t is the outside perception, Pentagon, industry, administration lobbyists. Among lobbyists it is a generational thing, Veterans of Foreign Wars is more sexist than the Reserves Association because those guys are younger. I get used to being called honey. Stereotypes can change with hard work and longevity and a willingness to learn. The military is about respect, and you gain respect with the military if you know how to deal with your [senator's] power." Similarly, a female Republican defense staffer recounted,

> It was a hard adaptation for Senator [—] to have a woman staffing his defense issues because he is old generation. It is hardest for old generation guys on and off the Hill. It is the biggest problem when interacting with constituents . . . In the first iteration of my business cards I did not put the PhD on, in the second iteration I did to be able to get taken seriously more quickly by constituents that don't want to talk to a woman.

The overwhelming dominance of men and masculine norms at the staff level reinforces findings about social identity and staffing in the literature on representative bureaucracy. Scholars note that passive/descriptive representatives, in this case men and current or former military personnel, are chosen to staff the defense policy arena because key constituencies from veterans groups to Pentagon officials and defense contractors see themselves in these staffers/bureaucrats and are more responsive to their leadership (Rosenthal and Bell 2003; Meier and Nicholson-Crotty 2006; Keiser et al. 2002).

Finally, the male culture that dominates the politics of defense and the slow integration of women into the ranks of the military creates conflict over the role of women in the military. In recent years, there have been several high-profile cases of sexual harassment and rape at military bases and in the military academies. There is also conflict over

the role of women in the military and whether to open specific combat positions to women (Manning 2005; Katzenstein 1998; Francke
1997).[19] Defense staffers believed that female senators are more likely to
care about these issues and to expend political capital pursuing policies
to address these concerns. Thus, a staffer for a female Democrat said,
"Senator X would never not engage on sexual harassment. For Warner
[the Republican Armed Services Committee chair] it may not be one of
his top five issues. Women senators think if we don't step in maybe no
one will and will push it down the road." Similarly, another Democratic
staffer said, "She [female senator] gets involved in women's issues as
they relate to defense policy. Rape in the military and making sure there
are strict rules and enforcement of law. Dual spouses in Iraq and taking
care of their needs." Another Democratic staffer who was working on a
bill to provide support groups and resources for women in the military
who have been raped maintained that women on the Armed Services
Committee are always more interested in these issues and more willing
to expend the political capital pushing the Pentagon to change.

> The defense establishment is always resistant to change, and this
> amendment was the kind of thing that changes things, anything
> with women is bringing change. They always say you can't im-
> pose these kinds of burdens on the Pentagon, that is always the
> excuse. We had Collins [R-ME], Dole [R-NC], all the women
> [on the Armed Services Committee], and Byrd [D-WV] is always
> supportive of amendments for women. In the House, Susan
> Davis [D-CA] is Personnel [Subcommittee] chair and very into
> women in the military. If we need someone to introduce some-
> thing in the House that has to do with women we go to her.

Given the high costs and small to nonexistent benefits of engaging
issues regarding women in the military, proponents must focus their
efforts on legislators who can be mobilized on the basis of an intensity
of feeling stemming from their experience and identification with the
affected group. Most recently, the role of women in the military sparked
a controversy over the place of women in combat in the Iraq War. In
2005, House Republican Armed Services Committee chair Duncan
Hunter (R-CA) attached an amendment to the defense authorization
that would scale back the role of army women in combat by prohibiting
women from serving in the forward support units that provide medical services, supplies, and logistical support to the front-line combat
units that women are barred from serving in. The Pentagon opposed

the proposal as the military already faced a troop shortage in Iraq resulting in extended deployments for current service members. Heather Wilson (R-NM), an air force veteran and the only female veteran in Congress, took the lead in fighting the proposal in the House (Scully 2005a, 2005b, 2005c; Plummer 2005).

To prevent the amendment from getting attached to the Senate defense authorization bill, a lobbyist for military women explained that her group was targeting members of the House and Senate Personnel subcommittees but that they also gave special attention to women legislators and legislators with military experience in their efforts to find champions for their proposals. "We sent a lot of material to Elizabeth Dole's [R-NC] office because as a woman with a seat on the relevant subcommittee she could be a key ally. We also sought out Olympia Snowe [R-ME] because she is a longtime friend to military women. When Snowe was on the Armed Services Committee in the late 1990s, she took a lead role in fighting the elimination of gender-integrated training." For Senate Armed Services Committee chair John Warner (R-VA), "this is a nickel issue, it is not a priority. If pushed on it he would probably rather not have women serving in combat positions in the military, but he is not foolish enough to want to turn back the clock, and he just does not want to have to deal with it on the authorization." Similarly, another lobbyist said that she was targeting female senators because the issue of women in the military is "a no-dollar issue so members have to have the passion for it" if they are going to be convinced to stake political capital on the issue.

Clearly, the politics of national security is fraught with gender implications. At the member level, female senators are cognizant of gender stereotypes and work to find ways to demonstrate to voters and constituent groups that they are strong on defense. Democratic women who confront these gender stereotypes and public perceptions that Democrats are less capable than Republicans on national security are particularly concerned about establishing their credibility on defense issues. While gender stereotypes have little impact on a senator's ability to become a player within the Senate on national security issues, military culture and defense politics are a male-dominated sphere with few female staffers and lobbyists and a small proportion of women serving in the military. Female staffers maintain that sex discrimination remains a problem in the world of defense politics and that women staffers have a more difficult time being taken seriously by stakeholder groups. Moreover, the continued slow integration of women in the military prompts female senators to champion causes related to military women including sexual harassment and rape of women in the services and the academies, health services for military women, and questions of women in combat. Their involvement in these causes stems from a greater personal connection to the needs of military women and a feeling that other senators and the Pentagon leadership will not give priority to these issues.

Conclusion

Despite long-standing stereotypes that women are less capable stewards of defense policy than men are, the comprehensive analysis of senators' engagement of national security issues finds few gender differences in overall participation. While women in the general public may be less inclined to support war, gender had no impact on senators' votes to authorize President George W. Bush to deploy troops in Iraq. Examining amending activity on Congress's major policy statement on national security, the defense authorization bill, women, like men, are policy generalists responding to the same institutional and electoral incentives. Thus committee position, particularly a seat on the Armed Services Committee, and the importance of defense benefits to the state were important drivers of senators' decisions to sponsor amendments to the defense authorization bill.

Still, when building their defense policy profiles, senators must navigate a partisan and gendered terrain in which Republicans are the national security party and women must work harder to establish their credibility on defense. Moreover, the male culture of the military and the minority status of women in the military and defense policy world create hurdles for women at the staff level. The problems created by gendered and partisan assumptions are particularly acute for Democratic women, who must overcome both gender stereotypes and association with the party that is considered weak on defense. Female senators strategically utilize their defense policy activities to counter these stereotypes and establish their defense policy expertise. Republican and Democratic women focus on building their credentials to signal expertise to voters, stakeholder groups, and administration officials. Women look to highlight their committee roles. Thus, Kay Bailey Hutchison (R-TX) and Hillary Clinton (D-NY) worked through the committee system to build their defense policy credentials. In the 2012 Republican primary, Michele Bachmann (R-MN) continuously cited her seat on the Intelligence Committee as evidence of her national security credentials. Similarly, both Republican and Democratic women were more active cosponsors of amendments to the defense authorization bill than their male partisan colleagues. Through their cosponsorship activity, women engage in position taking that enhances their credibility with voters and signals stakeholder groups about their commitment to defense policy issues. Additionally, Senate staff reported that women, particularly Democratic women, utilize their outreach at constituent events to build a reputation among voters and stakeholder groups in the state, including veterans organizations and defense contractors who care about defense policy.

Looking at the substantive content of the bills senators cosponsor, it is clear that women do bring a distinctive perspective to deliberations on military personnel issues. Accounting for the Democratic Party's association with social welfare policy, Democratic women were still more active cosponsors of legislation that expanded benefits for active duty troops and veterans. Staffers believe that women are more inclined to recognize inadequacies in the military's social safety net and to prioritize issues related to military families. Moreover, shared gender experiences and their unique status as ambitious women in a male-dominated institution make female senators more sympathetic to the needs and aspirations of women in the military. The future of the military as an all-volunteer force engaged in long-term conflicts related to the War on Terror means that returning troops and their families will have health and other social welfare needs that must be addressed. Moreover, the role of women in the various branches of military service will continue to evolve, enhancing the importance of having women with a seat at the policy-making table. Finally, continued military engagements will maintain national security expertise as an important leadership criterion for voters, requiring women candidates and officeholders to find ways to overcome persistent stereotypes about women's ability to legislate and exercise leadership on defense policy.

6 Gender and Policy Making in the New Senate Club

The advancement of women into the Senate coincided with the transformation of the Senate from an old boys club into both a more individualist and a more partisan institution. With their large staffs, multiple committee assignments, and procedural prerogatives, senators have vast resources to pursue their individual policy interests. Yet the demands of serving a statewide constituency and ever-increasing partisan polarization circumscribe senators' actions, as they must demonstrate loyalty to their partisan team. In this first comprehensive study of the impact of gender on the legislative activity of senators, I demonstrate that gender as a social identity exerts a meaningful influence on legislative behavior.

Gender affects the policy priorities of individual senators and the intensity of their commitment to issues. Beyond the preferences and perspectives of individuals, policy entrepreneurs recognize the association between gender and issue preferences. These entrepreneurs, ranging from fellow senators to interest group leaders, recruit women to their cause as they seek to build a support coalition for policy initiatives. Finally, perceptions of gendered expertise also interact with party reputations, creating incentives for participation and erecting barriers to leadership on specific issues. Moreover, gender is employed as a symbol in partisan warfare as Democrats

and to a lesser extent Republicans turn to their female members to deliver party messages designed to capture the women's vote or defend the
party against criticism that the party's policies will hurt women. Continued party polarization and tight electoral competition means that
women will increasingly be called on to champion their party's position
on women's issues.

The Policy Impact of Women in the Senate

Senators are policy generalists seeking to represent the wide range of
interests within their states and increasingly serving as national spokespersons for the positions of their political party. At the same time, the
power given to senators as individuals to develop a unique policy record
creates opportunities to translate their policy preferences into legislative action. The analyses of senators' legislative activity in the areas of
women's issues, defense policy, and judicial nominations demonstrate
that female senators are more active proponents of legislation related
to women, children, and families. Because of their gendered life experience, women senators are more likely to begin with a predisposition to
pay attention to the social welfare and feminist concerns that constitute
women's issues. Therefore, a significant amount of gender differences
stems from the personal experiences senators draw on and utilize to
connect with the problems of constituents. Policy entrepreneurs including fellow legislators, political activists, and interest group leaders recognize this predisposition. Scholars of interest group politics note that
groups look to recruit committed allies that will be willing to utilize the
expertise an organization provides to achieve action on the group's priorities (Hall and Deardorf 2006; Hall and Wayman 1990). The moral
authority that women wield on social welfare and women's rights issues
is particularly important in an institution that values individual expertise and a media culture that requires senators to develop coalitions that
can gain press attention in a crowded policy environment.

In addition to being sought out as champions for policy initiatives
on social welfare and women's rights concerns, women are recruited by
coalition leaders to cosponsor women's issue bills, speak about these
initiatives on the floor, and sell proposals in press conferences. These
coalition-building activities incorporate differing degrees of policy influence and messaging. Thus, when a conservative male Republican senator recruited a liberal Democratic woman to be his primary cosponsor
on a bill to prohibit the military from forcing women to wear abayas

when they leave the military base in Saudi Arabia, he sought out the Democratic woman because he assumed she would have a policy interest in the bill and he believed her participation would draw attention to the bill from colleagues and the media. While the female senator was recruited for her public messaging potential, her staff worked closely with the male senator's office on the substance and the selling of the proposal. Similarly, Kay Bailey Hutchison (R-TX) was clearly recruited to sponsor the Republican alternative amendment to the Lilly Ledbetter Fair Pay Act because Republicans needed a woman to counter the Democratic message that Republicans oppose equal pay for women. Still Hutchison's staff was brought in to work on crafting the amendment with the staff of the Health, Education, Labor, and Pensions (HELP) Committee's ranking member, Mike Enzi (R-WY). Moreover, Hutchison had to have signed off on the amendment if she was going to play such a prominent role in advocating and defending it on the Senate floor.

Still there will be occasions when women are simply "window dressing," such as when Senator Rick Santorum (R-PA) asked a Republican female senator to appear with him at a press conference promoting a bill related to Iraqi women's rights or when the Democratic leaders of the Banking Committee wanted to make sure that Debbie Stabenow (D-MI), the only female Democrat on the committee at the time, was able to attend press conferences because they did not want the camera to pan all white males. In sum, I maintain that a commitment to women's issues derived from personal experience is at the foundation of gender differences. Policy entrepreneurs seek to capitalize on women's gendered perspective and interests. As the number of women in the Senate grows, there are more opportunities to highlight these issues and build legislative coalitions for policy proposals on social welfare and feminist issues.

Bringing a Different Perspective and Intensity to Policy Deliberations

Beyond a greater commitment to the needs of women, children, and families, representation theorists have long asserted that women will bring a different perspective to legislative deliberation, one that considers women's unique life experience in all policy forums (Mansbridge 1999; Phillips 1995; Dovi 2002). Yet, we have little empirical evidence to support this claim. Instead, the vast majority of research focuses on female legislators' greater activism on women's issues, variously defined. By taking advantage of senators' ability to engage multiple policy issues, I demonstrate that women do bring their perspective as women and often as mothers to bear on policy dimensions outside of the traditional realm of women's issues. Thus, the analysis of senators' defense policy participation shows that women are more active proponents of policies that expand social welfare services for military personnel and veterans. As one Democratic staffer explained, the women are more inclined to see the need and respond to calls for expanding social services related to children and health in the military. Moreover, in the male-dominated sphere of defense policy making, women are more likely to mobilize around issues related to women in the military. From sexual harassment to the role of women in combat, staff believed that women were more likely to take up these causes and to push for a legislative solution.

The examination of senators' vote explanations during the confirmation battles over Supreme Court nominees John Roberts and Samuel Alito indicate that among the many constitutional issues a senator could prioritize in their deliberations, female senators, particularly Democrats, focused more attention on the nominee's record on women's rights. Furthermore, while abortion has become a litmus test for the two parties and their interest group allies in Supreme Court fights, the female senators delved more deeply into the nominees' records on other women's rights concerns, scrutinizing their positions on issues ranging from employment discrimination to family and medical leave.

Representation theorists also highlight the fact that group members will be the most aggressive advocates for group interests. Thus, women display an intensity of commitment that will make them fight for policy positions they believe are in women's interests (Mansbridge 1999; Phillips 1995; Dovi 2002). This tenacity will be especially important when interests are being negotiated away to achieve compromise. In the Senate, this intensity of commitment is most clearly displayed on feminist issues, particularly reproductive rights. Senators who champion reproductive rights must engage in recurring high-profile battles on the issue as Congress continuously debates incremental proposals to restrict funding and access to abortion and contraception. The issue of abortion is often a final sticking point in larger battles over appropriations bills and major policy initiatives. The long battle over partial birth abortion demonstrates the significance of the issue to female senators. While Republicans viewed the policy as a clear winner for them and Democrats wanted it to go away as fast as possible, female senators including liberal and conservative Democrats and moderate Republicans played leading roles in the negotiation of alternative amendments and the public debate on the issue. The women senators did not share one view on the policy, yet they were uniquely committed to the issue and heavily involved in the years long fight. Moreover, Senate staff reported that Democratic women were more likely to utilize the individual preroga- tives of senators to advocate for reproductive rights. Thus, Patty Mur- ray (D-WA) and Hilary Clinton (D-NY) utilized the power provided by holds to place a hold on multiple nominees to lead the FDA in order to force the Bush administration to take action on the over-the-counter sale of Plan B emergency contraception (Crowley 2006).

Similarly, in the protracted debate over President Obama's health reform plan, female senators pressed for broad coverage of preventive health services in the benefits package. When the Senate combined the bill passed by the more liberal HELP Committee with the more con- servative bill from the Finance Committee, majority leader Harry Reid (D-NV) dropped a broad package of women's preventive health ser- vices owing to cost concerns. Women played key roles in behind-the- scenes negotiations seeking to restore the benefits (Herszenhorn 2009). An amendment concerning coverage of mammograms and preventive health services sponsored by Barbara Mikulski (D-MD) and Olympia Snowe (R-ME) was the first amendment the Senate passed on the bill (Herszenhorn and Pear 2009; Murray and Montgomery 2009).[1] After months of intense deliberations, the issue of abortion almost sank the entire bill. Democratic women including Patty Murray (D-WA) and Bar- bara Boxer (D-CA) were pivotal players in the negotiations to secure the votes of pro-life Democrats who feared that the subsidies given to help low-income individuals purchase insurance could be used for plans that cover abortions (Alonso-Zaldivar 2009; Kane 2009).

Later, when the Obama administration issued rules guiding the im- plementation of contraceptive coverage, a furor erupted over the limited scope of the conscience clause that would exempt churches but not reli- gious employers like Catholic colleges and hospitals. Both conservative and liberal Catholic organizations and political figures railed against the policy (Brownstein 2012; Dionne 2012). Women in the administra- tion, including Health and Human Services secretary Kathleen Sebelius and senior White House advisor Valerie Jarrett, Democratic women in Congress, and women's groups pressured Obama to retain a limited ex- emption that would prioritize women's health. The press reported that while women in the administration advocated for the narrow exemp- tion, prominent male Catholics including Vice President Joe Biden and former chief of staff Bill Daley felt the policy was a mistake and would cost Obama support among Catholic and religious voters (Sweet 2012;

Brownstein 2012). Meanwhile, the Democratic women in the Senate held press conferences and took to the floor of the Senate to support the policy (see Congressional Record, February 7, 2012 S374–S379).

Ultimately the compromise President Obama adopted favored broad coverage for women's health by requiring the insurers to take direct responsibility for covering contraception, a position that was supported by liberal Catholic organizations and women's groups but opposed by conservative Catholic groups including the U.S. Conference of Catholic Bishops (Aizenman, Wallsten, and Tumulty 2012).[2] The debate over contraceptive coverage reaffirms the importance of women having a seat at the table when policies are negotiated. Moreover, the controversy highlights the significance of social identity and intensity of commitment to a policy. Democratic women were among the most aggressive advocates for wide contraceptive coverage as President Obama sought to find a compromise that would be acceptable to the disparate elements of the Democratic coalition.

Confronting Negative Gender Stereotypes: Women and Defense Policy

While there is a great deal of research focused on the impact of gender on legislative activity on various sets of women's issues, scholars have not examined the impact of negative stereotypes on senators' policy-making choices. The analysis of senators' engagement of defense policy indicates that on the issues that form the core of gender stereotypes, including the decision to go to war and support for weapons development, female senators respond to the same incentives that structure the activity of all senators. Therefore, the most liberal senators were among the most likely to oppose going to war with Iraq. Senators who offered amendments to the defense authorization on hard issues of weapons funding and force structure were members who served on defense-related committees and senators for whom defense interests were pivotal to the state economy.

Still senators' legislative profiles on defense policy indicate that female senators are cognizant of gender stereotypes and utilize their legislative activity to counter perceptions that women are less knowledgeable about defense policy and weaker on national security than male leaders. Both Republican and Democratic women were more active cosponsors of amendments to the defense authorization bill, indicating that women senators utilize their cosponsorship activity to take positions on national security. Through their cosponsorship of defense initiatives, female senators can demonstrate to voters their knowledge of defense policy and their support for the troops.

Furthermore, Democratic women are particularly concerned about refuting perceptions that they might be weak on defense. The Democratic women face the double bind of confronting gender stereotypes and a party reputation that portrays the Democratic Party as less capable than Republicans on handling national security. As a result, staff report that Democratic women are more vigilant about attending constituent events for the military and veterans and they work harder to secure the endorsement of these groups for their election campaigns.

Women Serving in a Male-Dominated Institution:
Gender and Institutional Norms

Looking at the overall position of women in the Senate, women continue to be drastically underrepresented in comparison with their numbers in the population. In 2012, women hold only seventeen Senate seats. Despite the fact that the Republicans gained seats in 2010 and are expected to win more races in 2012, the number of Republican women may decline in the 2012 election as both Kay Bailey Hutchison (R-TX) and Olympia Snowe (R-ME) are retiring and few Republican women are running in competitive races.[3] Furthermore, there are currently no minority women in the Senate. Carol Moseley-Braun (D-IL) who served one term, 1992–98, is the only African American woman who has ever served in the Senate. If she wins the 2012 Hawaii Senate race, Congresswoman Maize Hirono (D-HI) would be the first Asian American woman in the Senate. A Latina woman has never been elected to the Senate. This lack of diversity among women has meaningful policy implications as research on minority women in the House of Representatives and state legislatures indicates that in comparison with white women, minority women are more active advocates of legislation regarding welfare, poverty, and race (Reingold and Smith 2012; Bratton, Haynie, and Reingold 2006; Orey et al. 2006). The continued underrepresentation of women impacts the dynamics of the institution and the legislative behavior of the women who serve.

The institution of the Senate elevates the power of the individual. Thus, one Senate staffer asserted, "[T]he Senate is not male or female, it is one hundred individuals." Yet women continue to stand out as a minority in an institution where men determined the rules and norms of behavior. Scholars who study the position of minority groups in institutions note that institutions are both "raced and gendered" (Hawkesworth 2003). Therefore, the standard operating procedures and accepted practices within the Senate reflect the preferences, history, and norms of the dominant group, white men (Acker 1992; Kenney 1996; Hawkesworth 2003). The need to adapt to and negotiate these standards creates additional constraints for women as they craft a legislative profile and build a reputation with constituents. Conscious of their minority status, female senators worry about being perceived as a "woman senator," and they believe they need to work harder to ensure they are "taken seriously" by fellow senators, constituents, and power players in the administration.

Serving in an overwhelmingly male institution, staff for female senators reported that the women sometimes feel that they have to be vigilant to make sure they are taken seriously, and some expressed concern about balancing their policy portfolio to make sure they are not perceived as a "woman senator." Speaking about the fear of being left out of important discussions, a staffer to a female Democrat noted,

> Women are also disadvantaged as in any workplace where guys go out together for drinks and make deals and women are not there. There are famous stories about [male senator] and [male senator] boozing forty years ago in their heyday. [Female senator] might get invited but she does not go to sports bars. There was a story in *Politico* about [Vice President] Biden still going to the Senate gym and making connections and lobbying on policy. The women have their own gym in the Senate, so she [female senator] won't see Biden in the Senate gym.

Other staffers believed that the women want to counter stereotypes about women being lightweights or indecisive. One Democratic staffer explained, "[O]ne thing that does stem from her being a woman is that she wants no appearance of her being wishy-washy. She does not want to give any ammunition to the assumption that women are indecisive." A Republican staffer said, "Collins and Snowe want to know every detail about what happened in a hearing on a bill before they go in. They engage in hyperpreparation, the amount of paper they want. Lots of details, and they study and read and come to the hearing knowing more than others. They like the obscure details, and they fear being blindsided and having their credibility or expertise questioned." Another staffer said, "[A]ll women believe they have to work harder, especially the older women. [Female senator] made it ok to be a woman senator. She succeeded in a male model of leadership. She is criticized for being a hard boss. Women are criticized for this more than men. You hear it all the time about women because you expect women to be nice, but the senator is a CEO and has to be demanding; you don't know that many nice CEOs." Similarly, in research on the House of Representatives, Anzia and Berry (2011) found that because of perceived discrimination in the electoral process, the women who get elected to the House of Representatives must be more qualified than their male colleagues. As a result, the women in the House are more active legislators than their male counterparts, delivering more federal dollars home and sponsoring and cosponsoring more bills.

In addition to concerns about establishing their gravitas, staffers for both Democratic and Republican senators asserted that women do not want to be pigeonholed as women senators focusing on women's issues both because they want to be recognized as representing all the people in their state and because they believe that it undermines their potential power in the institution. Thus, a Democratic staffer explained the balance this way: "[W]ith younger women like Klobuchar [D-MN] and McCaskill [D-MO], Klobuchar identifies as a mother with young children, and this is often woven into her speeches and efforts, but her website will talk about the national guard." Indeed, several Democratic and Republican staffers implied that the most powerful female senators are powerful because they have built their reputations on issues that are not women's issues and some even avoid taking a high-profile role on women's issues. For example, a Democratic staffer said, "Mikulski [D-MD] usually coordinates when women go to the floor together on an issue. [Female Democratic senator] often does not go and does not want to participate. She is [one of] the most powerful woman senators, and she does not want to be identified as a woman senator with women's issues." Similarly, a Republican staffer asserted,

> To succeed in the Senate you must be able to compete on a man's level. Other women take a principled stand on women's rights and will do things a woman's way and not care. [Republican female senator] does not wake up motivated by women's issues. She fears being characterized as a woman legislator and wants to be part of the Senate club. Boxer [D-CA] does not care if she is identified with the women's movement. Feinstein [D-CA] seems to want to be a senator and not a woman's senator. In the House with younger women they are not as afraid to say here I am and I work on women's issues. You don't want to scare off

men or have them be threatened by you. You do not wave the
banner of women's rights in their face. To be accepted here you
have to have something to offer, not fight for my group. You
have to be trying to fit in and nonthreatening.

Other staff maintained that even liberal Democratic women who
are known for their work on women's issues want to make sure they
have a broader policy profile and are not defined by women's issues.
Thus, a Democratic staffer explained that a liberal Democratic woman
"chose to be on the DOD [Defense] Appropriations Subcommittee and
not LHHS [Labor, Health, and Human Services] because the DOD bill
is more powerful and controls more money and she does not only want
to be defined by soft issues. Men do not have to prove they are manly."
Similarly, another staffer for a liberal Democratic woman explained,
"*Meet the Press* and *Face the Nation* will call her most on abortion. She
tries to make herself available to talk about foreign policy so she does
not get pigeonholed as just a women and kids senator." Clearly, women
of both parties and across the ideological spectrum are concerned about
how their gender and their choice of legislative priorities will impact
their reputations as powerful players in the Senate.

*Critical Mass: The Importance of Numbers in
the Institution and within the Parties*

The level of power women wield individually and as a group is also
affected by their overall numbers within the institution and their political parties. Studying the position of women in corporations, Rosabeth
Moss Kanter (1977) found that when there are few women in an organization they are treated as token representatives of their group. In
response, these women feel pressure to conform and downplay gender
differences. The desire of women senators to avoid being perceived as
a woman senator focused on women's issues and the concerns about
proving themselves as serious legislators likely reflects an element of
the tokenism that Kanter identifies. Kanter maintains that as women
increase their representation in the organization and achieve a critical
mass (approximately 15%), they will feel more comfortable championing group interests and asserting their authority without being marginalized or stigmatized. Efforts to apply Kanter's theory to legislatures
have largely focused on whether women are more likely to advocate for
women's issue legislation as the proportion of women in the legislature

increases. The results of these studies have been mixed. Some studies of state legislatures and the House of Representatives do find that women are more likely to champion women's issue legislation as their numbers in the legislature rise (Saint-Germain 1989; Thomas 1994; MacDonald and O'Brien 2011). However, there is no clear threshold for the necessary proportion of women's representation. Others find that because legislators look to develop a unique legislative niche, women actually focus more attention on women's issues when their numbers are smaller and they can more easily stand out to command media coverage. Moreover, as women increase their representation, men will pay more attention to women's issue legislation, thus reducing the gap between male and female behavior (Bratton 2005; Crowley 2004). However, the main organizing force in the Senate is the political parties.

Looking at the impact of numbers in the Senate, it is clear that women senators recognize their minority status and make efforts to support each other within the institution. Purposeful collaboration and support among women senators dates to the 1992 election. Up to that point, there were only two women in the Senate, Barbara Mikulski (D-MD) and Nancy Landon Kassebaum (R-KS). When four new Democratic women were elected to the Senate in 1992, Barbara Mikulski (D-MD) established herself as the dean of the Democratic women, and she ran training sessions for the women on how to set up their office and hit the ground running. These training sessions continued as new women were elected and Mikulski extended her mentoring to both Republican and Democratic women (Mikulski et al. 2001). Staffers note that the Democratic women continue to collaborate and that the Democratic and Republican women support each other socially and occasionally on policy. One Democratic staffer recounted, "When the women first got there in the early 1990s, Mikulski as dean of the women started having a meeting of the Democratic women once a week. Now it is once a month, and they have bipartisan dinners. There are also meetings of the women chiefs of staff and meetings of the chiefs of staff to women senators where they talk about issues they can work on together. These are bipartisan meetings." Similarly, a former Democratic senator explained,

> Women senators mentor each other and have a lot of comity and cohesion, more than the men. Mikulski is the dean of the Democratic women and all women and she takes that position seriously. The cohesion and interrelations among the women are better than among the men. The women are a club within the club. They cover each other on committees, meaning if I am not

on a committee and I want to offer amendments or ask questions [at hearings], I have to ask someone on the committee to
do that form me. The women will do that for each other.

The periodic dinners attended by Democratic and Republican female senators received the most comment among staff and have been
reported on in the media (Mikulski et al. 2001; Victor 2005; Lovley
2011). Although there was disagreement about their frequency, with
some staff referring to monthly dinners and others claiming once every
two months or more, the dinners are for female senators only with no
staff and no leaks. The women offer each other camaraderie and support, talking about family and sometimes policy. This does not mean
there are no rivalries among the women as among all senators. For example, the chilly relations between Maine's Republican senators Olympia Snowe and Susan Collins were frequently noted by staff and have
been covered in the media (Sherill 2011). Several staffers pointed to
rivalries between other female colleagues representing the same state.
Still, legislators seeking to combat the toxic partisan environment in
Congress promote the idea of social mixing across party lines to reduce partisanship and promote civility. Recent efforts at strengthening
bipartisan ties include sitting with a member of the opposition party at
the State of the Union address and dinners among bipartisan groups of
senators (Raju 2012; Weiner 2011). The bipartisan dinners of female
senators have been cited as a model for promoting relationships across
party lines (Lovley 2011).

Beyond a civility and camaraderie that stem from social mixing,
staffers believe that the solidarity among the women stems from the
recognition that they are a minority in a male-dominated institution.
One staffer asserted, "Once they reached fourteen, the women have a
little voice. Mikulski sees herself as the dean of the women. They are
more willing to band together for the good of a cause. The women
have a sense of womanhood because they are a small group. They have
lunches and dinners and talk about home and family, but they also talk
about issues and how to make things happen in this male-dominated
institution." Similarly, another staffer commented, "[T]he women senators get along better than the caucus as a whole; they socialize and mix
and are not as partisan as the men. White men still run the place, men
are predominately in charge, and they [the women] believe it is an old
boys network and the women have to help each other." As the number
of women in the Senate increases and approaches parity, women will
no longer need to feel like a club within the club trying to protect their

position within the institution. Greater gender parity may also change institutional norms and by extension could affect senators' policy priorities and legislative strategy. Women who want to focus on social welfare and women's rights issues will feel less concerned about the impact of those decisions on their reputations as power players in the Senate. Female senators who prefer to focus on other issues will not worry that they will be singled out and stigmatized as not caring about women.

Critical Mass, Party Reputations, and Issue Ownership

While women may socialize and periodically collaborate on policy across party lines, Senate business is organized and dominated by the political parties. Women constitute a greater proportion of the Democratic than the Republican caucus. Their differential numbers and the political culture of the parties give women greater influence over policy making within the Democratic caucus. In the 112th Congress, women constitute 23% (twelve of fifty-three) of the Democratic caucus and only 11% (five of forty-seven) of the Republican caucus. By joining together, the Democratic women are able to leverage their numbers into greater institutional power and influence over policy. The women have utilized arguments based on a need for a woman's perspective to gain seats on influential committees including Appropriations and Finance. As they have accumulated seniority, Democratic women have advanced to committee chairs on several important committees. According to staff, Patty Murray (D-WA), the chair of the Democratic Senate Campaign Committee for the 2012 election, is close to Senate majority leader Harry Reid (D-NV) and perceived as a rising star in the caucus.

The Democratic women also work as a group to influence the party's position on policy, pressing for inclusion of women's interests in party proposals on issues such as health care and reproductive rights. Democratic women look for ways to leverage their numbers into influence over party messaging strategy. Working together as a group, they hold press conferences, campaign rallies, and colloquies on the Senate floor to press Democratic priorities and offer a female perspective on these initiatives that is designed to reach women voters. These events both highlight Democratic policy priorities and attract media attention to female senators' own initiatives. The influence Democratic women gain through their numbers is reinforced by the political culture and policy reputation of the Democratic Party. As a party, Democrats are more responsive to calls for diversity in their ranks as women and minorities constitute key voting blocks of the party. Therefore, Democratic leaders should be concerned about reflecting diversity at the leadership table. Moreover, women's issues are central to the party brand. Voters prefer Democrats to handle social welfare issues like health care and education, and women's groups are core activists in the Democratic Party. Because of the central role of social welfare and women's rights interests in the Democratic coalition and the power of women's organizations, Democratic women can gain authority and influence from their legislative activity on women's issues.

By contrast, Republican women are a smaller proportion of the Republican caucus. Their small numbers and disparate ideological views prevent Republican women from harnessing their gender to influence the party agenda or gain power within the party caucus. Moreover, women's issues are not central to the reputation of the Republican Party. Instead, the Republican brand focuses on messages of lower taxes, reducing regulation on business, and strengthening national security. Therefore, women cannot easily leverage their connection to women's interests and women voters into power and authority within the Republican caucus. As a result, Republican women do not band together to promote party positions or speak as a group to represent the perspective of women on particular issues. Because the political culture of the Republican Party focuses on individualism and is not responsive to identity-based policy claims, Republican women cannot gain seats at the leadership table by trumpeting the need for a woman's point of view. However, the Republican caucus does want to refute accusations that Republicans are a party of middle-aged white men. Therefore, the desire to highlight Republican women whose ideology reflects the majority of the caucus can help individual women in their leadership bids. More conservative women who have advanced to leadership positions within the caucus include Kay Bailey Hutchison (R-TX), who held the positions of vice chair and Policy Committee chair, and Elizabeth Dole (R-NC), who served as Republican Senate Campaign Committee chair in 2002.

Looking to the Future: Gender Politics in
a Polarized Political Environment

Partisanship and ideology are the dominant frames of contemporary political debate. Senators act as members of partisan teams, and the parties have well-established reputations for ownership of particular issues (Petrocik 1996; Petrocik, Benoit, and Hansen 2003; Pope and Woon 2009; Sellers 2010). The gender gap in public opinion and presumptions about the strengths and weaknesses of female candidates coexist with public perceptions about the issue expertise of the two parties. These party reputations interact with assumptions about gender to create differing sets of incentives and opportunities for Republican and Democratic women. As the parties become more polarized, these incentives and expectations harden in the public mind. The parties will demand greater loyalty to party positions, and the Republican and Democratic caucuses will increasingly call on women to champion causes that build the party's electoral coalition or refute gender-based criticism of party positions.

In the minds of voters, the Democratic Party is more strongly associated with social welfare and women's rights issues. Furthermore, women's groups and interest groups advocating for the expansion of the social safety net are key elements of the liberal base of the Democratic Party. The centrality of women's issues to the core message of the Democratic Party means that Democratic women will find a receptive audience for their proposals on issues such as health care, education, and women's rights. Thus, the perception of the Democratic Party as more competent on women's issues combines with perceptions of women as more committed to these causes to create additional incentives for Democratic women to prioritize legislation concerning social welfare and women's rights. As the parties continue to polarize, Democrats will utilize their positive reputation on women's issues to draw further contrasts with Republicans. Democratic women will get more opportunities to legislate on these issues and raise their public profile by selling party messages on social welfare and women's rights concerns.

By contrast, women's issues are not a key component of the Republican Party's agenda and reputation. In fact, proposals to expand social welfare programs contradict Republican principles of lower taxes and reduced government regulation. Women's rights issues incorporate policies such as expanded access to abortion and contraception that are strongly opposed by socially conservative base voters. Thus, Republican women cannot easily leverage their gender into policy leadership on these issues. Moreover, activism on some of the more contentious women's rights issues can alienate core partisans and colleagues resulting in diminished standing and ability to move other policy priorities. Instead, individual Republican women are called on to reach out to women voters who favor Republicans, such as white suburban married women, and to defend the party against Democratic accusations that Republican policies are harmful to women.

Continued partisan warfare over women's issues puts Republican women in an increasingly difficult position. Moderate Republican

women feel increasing pressure to sublimate their own policy preferences on women's rights and/or the preferences of their more socially
liberal constituency to demands for party loyalty on votes pitting the
parties against each other. Thus, in the fight to confirm President Bush's
Supreme Court nominees, John Roberts and Samuel Alito, Democrats
worked to portray these nominees as hostile to women's rights on issues
ranging from employment discrimination to abortion. Despite their pro-
choice voting records and reputations as strong supporters of women's
rights, moderate Maine Republicans Olympia Snowe and Susan Collins
did not criticize Roberts and Alito's records on women's rights and they
voted in favor of confirmation. In this case, the strong expectation that
senators side with their party and president in confirmation battles out-
weighed any qualms these female senators may have had based on the
nominees' positions on women's rights.

Since Republicans won control of the House and increased their
margins in the Senate in the 2010 elections, conservatives have renewed
their focus on women's issues. As Republicans offer more proposals to
eliminate funding for Planned Parenthood in the federal budget and
restrict health insurance coverage for abortion and contraception, moderate Republican women are frequently placed in the uncomfortable
position of reconciling their support for reproductive rights with expectations for party loyalty. Conservative women are also reticent to
engage in battles over women's issues. These women do not want to
become the public face of the Republican position on women's issues
because they will attract heightened media scrutiny as women acting
against women's interests. Moreover, they fear the demand to provide
the Republican Party with cover on these initiatives will lead women's
issues to dominate their legislative portfolio. This is not a desirable outcome since women's issues are not the path to power and influence in
the Republican Party in the same way that issues like lower taxes, de-
regulation, and national security are.

The firestorm over contraceptive coverage in the lead-up to the
2012 presidential election illustrates the dynamics of gender politics
in this polarized political environment. The controversy ignited when
the Obama administration issued a rule to require employers to provide insurance coverage of contraceptives without a copay as part of a
package of preventive health benefits. The rule included a very limited
conscience clause that exempted houses of worship but not religious
institutions like Catholic hospitals and universities. Republicans immediately blasted the rule as an attack on religious freedom. House
Speaker John Boehner (R-OH) went down to the floor of the House

to denounce the rule and to pledge that the House would reverse it through legislation. Senate minority leader McConnell called a press conference to rail against the violation of constitutionally protected religious freedom. The Republican presidential candidates battling through a tough primary each denounced the rule (Sanger-Katz 2012; Heavey 2012; McCarthy 2012a).

The rule split Democratic constituencies. Women's groups and women in Congress strongly supported the rule, while left-leaning Catholic groups and political figures, including, Vice President Biden and Virginia Democratic Senate candidate and former Democratic National Convention (DNC) chair Tim Kaine, opposed it (Sweet 2012; Brownstein 2012). Based on their personal commitment to the issue, Democratic women held press conferences, appeared on political talk shows, and took to the Senate floor to speak in favor of the rule and urge President Obama to maintain a strong stand on women's health. Ultimately, the Obama administration adopted a compromise position that would require the health insurance company, rather than the employer, to offer contraceptive coverage to women (Aizeman, Wallstein, and Tumulty 2012). This compromise pleased the various factions of the Democratic Party; however, Republicans and conservative religious groups remained incensed by the rule. The stage was now set for a partisan battle for the hearts and minds of voters that pitted the Democratic message of protecting women's health against the Republican frame of standing up for the constitutional principle of religious freedom and showcasing the contraception rule as another example of the unpopular health reform bill imposing government mandates.

Democratic women in the House and Senate played key roles in promoting the party message that Democrats would protect women's health and Republicans were engaged in a war on women. President Obama's re-election campaign and Democratic campaign committees for the national and state parties and individual candidates utilized the fight over contraceptive coverage in their fundraising campaigns (McCarthy 2012b; Feder 2012c). The new DNC chair, Congresswoman Debbie Wasserman-Schultz (D-FL), continuously denounced the Republican war on women, a phrase she had been using since House Republicans tried to defund Planned Parenthood in the early 2011 battles over the federal budget (Cook 2011; Kurtz 2012).

Meanwhile, in the Senate, Republican leaders successfully forced the Democratic majority leader Harry Reid (D-NV) to agree to debate minority whip Roy Blunt's (R-MO) amendment for a broad conscience exemption (Baker 2012a; Ryan 2012). Senate Democratic women issued press releases, held press conferences, wrote letters to editorial boards, appeared on political talk shows, and went to the Senate floor to defend the contraception rule and denounce Republican efforts to harm women's health (Shaheen, Boxer, and Murray 2012; Feder 2012c; McCarthy 2012c; Sanger-Katz 2012). The public message wars turned markedly in the Democrats' favor when the House Oversight and Government Reform Committee convened a hearing to highlight the contraception rule as a government mandate that infringes on religious beliefs and violates the freedom of conscience. The Republican-led committee scheduled an all-male panel of witnesses to discuss the issue, and the chairman, Darrell Issa (R-CA), refused to include testimony from Sandra Fluke, a Georgetown University law student, who Democrats invited to speak about the need for contraceptive coverage at Catholic universities. Issa maintained that Fluke was not an expert on religious freedom in the Constitution. Outraged by the all-male panel, Carolyn Maloney (D-NY) demanded to know "where are the women?" and she and Eleanor Holmes Norton (D-D.C.) walked out of the hearing (Feder 2012a).

The picture of the all-male committee testifying about women's health quickly went viral. Women's groups compared the panel to the all-male Judiciary Committee's interrogation of Anita Hill over her charges of sexual harassment against Supreme Court nominee Clarence Thomas. The picture became a call to action and a fundraising tool for women's organizations and Democratic campaign committees (Sanger-Katz 2012; Feder 2012b). The Senate Democratic Campaign Committee, led by Patty Murray (D-WA), produced a video explicitly denouncing a Republican war on women and calling for voters to elect more Democratic women to the Senate. The video then introduces each of the eleven Democratic women running for Senate in 2012 (http://www .youtube.com/watch?v=MohCoT_fHlU). Democratic minority leader Nancy Pelosi (D-CA) followed up by calling a special hearing with Fluke as the only witness (McCarthy 2012b; Milbank 2012). The Republican effort to focus on religious freedom was further undermined by the public statements of high-profile conservatives. Most notably, conservative radio host Rush Limbaugh called the Georgetown law student Sandra Fluke a slut and a prostitute.

Ultimately, the Senate voted to table the Blunt amendment on a straight party line vote, with three male Democrats favoring the amendment and one Republican, Olympia Snowe (R-ME), opposing it (Sanger-Katz 2012; Feder and Nocera 2012). Democrats used the vote to press their advantage with women and independent voters. At a press conference after the vote, Charles Schumer (D-NY), a key party strategist and confidante of majority leader Harry Reid (D-NV), opined that the tight vote "shows how high the stakes are for women. A Republican-led Senate might pass this bill. A Republican president, like Mitt Romney, would definitely sign it." Schumer warned that Republicans would lose independent voters over the issue (Aizenman and Helderman 2012). Indeed, polls showed a widening gender gap, with President Obama increasing his approval rating among women (Tumulty 2012). Recognizing they were losing the battle for public opinion, House leaders said they would slow down their efforts to bring a bill to the floor (Pear 2012b). To keep the pressure on House Republicans, the twelve Senate Democratic women sent a letter to House Speaker Boehner (R-OH) urging him to abandon efforts to undermine women's health (Baker 2012b). To continue the party message of a Republican war on women, Democrats decided to bring to the floor a bill reauthorizing the Violence Against Women Act. The twelve Democratic women marched to the floor to demand quick action on the bill and denounce Republican opposition as another in a string of actions demonstrating the threat that Republicans pose to women's rights (Weisman 2012b).

The debate over the contraception rule highlights the role of women in the current partisan political wars. Democratic women who feel a strong commitment to promoting women's health took a leadership role in defending the Obama rule. Participating in press conferences and floor debate and appearing on political news shows, these women took a stand on an issue that is important to them and raised their media profiles. They also helped the party build support with women voters and raise money for the upcoming elections in which control of the House, Senate, and presidency were at stake. The more liberal women who represent socially progressive states such as Patty Murray (D-WA), Kirsten Gillibrand (D-NY), and Barbara Boxer (D-CA) participated in the most party messaging activities, while Democratic women from more conservative states, some of whom faced tough re-election battles, such as Claire McCaskill (D-MO) and Mary Landrieu (D-LA), kept a lower profile, voting against the Blunt amendment and signing on to the letter urging Speaker Boehner to drop any plans to bring up legislation to undo the contraceptive coverage rule.

While Senate Democratic women played a leading role in their party's messaging efforts, Republican women adopted a much lower profile. Republican leaders recognized that Democrats would characterize their position as harming women, and they needed a Republican woman to deliver the message that Republicans are protecting religious freedom and not harming women. Freshman senator Kelly Ayotte (R-NH) took up this role. Along with Marco Rubio (R-FL), Ayotte was a primary co-sponsor of the Blunt amendment. She appeared with Republican leaders at the press conference denouncing the Obama rule. She made a floor statement, issued press releases, and appeared on news shows to empha-size that the contraceptive rule was an issue of religious freedom and not women's health (Ayotte 2012a, 2012b; McCormack 2012).

The other Republican women tried to keep a lower profile. Having more moderate views on reproductive rights, these women did not want to publicly oppose their party, and they did not want to be perceived as supporting a policy that Democrats were denouncing as part of a Republican war on women. Indeed, Senator Olympia Snowe (R-ME) had sponsored a contraceptive coverage bill in the 107th Congress; the bill had a hearing the day before the tragedy of 9/11 (Riskind 2012). The other Republican female senators did not appear in press confer-ences or speak in favor of the Republican position on the Senate floor. In the period leading up to the floor vote on the Blunt amendment, Sena-tor Lisa Murkowski (R-AK) was quoted in the *New York Times* ques-tioning why the Senate would be voting on this issue when there were other pressing matters, noting her constituents were more concerned about energy policy (Pear 2012a). Days before the vote, Senator Olym-pia Snowe (R-ME) announced that she would retire from the Senate because she was fed up with the partisan dysfunction. Some speculated that the contraceptive debate helped push her to the decision (Weisman 2012a). Freed from electoral pressures for partisan loyalty, Snowe was the only Republican to oppose the Blunt amendment (Haberkorn and Nocera 2012). Explaining her vote on the floor, Maine's other moderate Republican senator, Susan Collins, maintained that she felt the amend-ment was too broad but the Obama administration had not responded to her inquiries about how self-insured religious organizations would be treated. Therefore, she would support the Blunt amendment in hopes it would start a conversation (Congressional Record, March 1, 2012, S1168–S1169). In an interview with her state paper, the *Anchorage Daily News*, Lisa Murkowski said that she regretted her vote stating, "I have never had a vote I've taken where I have felt that I let down more people that believed in me." Murkowski maintained that she was trying to make a statement for religious freedom but the amendment was too broad, and to female voters at home, who she had heard from in large numbers, it looked like a vote against contraception (O'Malley 2012).

In sum, party conflicts focused on women's issues put Republican women in a difficult position. Those who agree with the party position can choose to take a high-profile role as party spokespersons delivering the message that as a woman they can testify that Republican policies are not anti-women. Taking on this role will lead to more media exposure and will garner favor with the party caucus and leadership. However, the senator also faces the scrutiny of a media frame that portrays them as women taking positions against women. Moreover, these conservative Republican women must be careful that these requests to defend the party do not overtake their legislative portfolio, limiting their ability to gain attention for other policy priorities. Republican women who take more liberal positions on women's issues must carefully walk a tightrope and try not to publicly oppose the party. When forced to take a position, these more moderate women must decide between taking votes that reflect their own ideological views and/or the views of constituents and voting with the party.

To date, the few Republican women who have advanced to the Senate hold ideological views that range from the middle to the more liberal end of the Republican caucus. While the House has seen an influx of more conservative women in recent years, strong conservatives in the mold of Michele Bachmann (R-MN) and former Alaska governor Sarah Palin have not advanced to the Senate. It is an open question whether more conservative Republican women will shy away from women's issues seeking to establish their reputation on core Republican themes of lower taxation and reduced government regulation or whether these women will champion conservative positions on women's issues offering the Republican Party a core of Republican women ready to advocate a conservative message on women's issues in opposition to the collaboration currently seen among Democratic women.

By analyzing legislative activity on a range of policies including women's issues, national security, and judicial nominations, I demonstrate that women across parties do focus more attention on policies related to women, children, and families. Female senators bring a perspective as women and mothers to deliberations on policies outside of women's issues. Women senators play a key strategic role in selling party messages and reaching out to women voters. As the parties continue to polarize and the Senate agenda is increasingly dominated by dueling party initiatives, the space for cross-party collaboration among women will narrow. Republican and Democratic women will play more prominent roles in party efforts to reach out to women voters as potential swing voting blocks that can deliver majority control to their respective parties in a period of tight electoral competition.

Notes

CHAPTER 1

1. According to the Center for the American Woman and Politics, in the 107th Congress, women held 13% (13) of the seats in the Senate and 13.6% (59) of the seats in the House of Representatives (Center for the American Woman and Politics 2011b).

2. Lisa Murkowski (R-AK) was appointed in December 2002 by her father, Senator Frank Murkowski, who had just won the Alaska governor's race. Murkowski served through the 108th Congress and won her first full term in the 2004 election. In 2010 she lost the Republican nomination but prevailed in the general election by running as a write-in candidate. Elizabeth Dole (R-NC) is the wife of former Senate Republican leader and presidential candidate Bob Dole (R-KS). Elizabeth Dole made a brief run for the 2000 Republican presidential nomination before running for the Senate in 2002. Dole served as chair of the Republican Senate Campaign Committee in the 2006 elections, when Republicans lost the House and Senate majority. She was defeated in the Democratic wave of 2008 (Center for the American Woman and Politics 2011a, 2011b).

3. When Elizabeth Dole (R-NC) lost her bid for re-election in 2008, the number of Republican women in the Senate dropped to four. The election of Kelly Ayotte (R-NH) in the 2010 elections raised the number of Republican women in the Senate back to five (Center for the American Woman and Politics 2011b).

4. As of this writing, former governor Linda Lingle is expected to win the Republican nomination in Hawaii, and Heather Wilson is favored to win the nomination in New Mexico. In Missouri, former state treasurer Sarah Steelman is one of three Republican candidates competing for the nomination. The 2010 Republican Senate nominee Linda McMahon is favored to win the Republican primary in Connecticut, but the seat is likely to stay Democratic (Hotline Staff 2012). Deb Fischer won a surprise victory in the Nebraska Republican primary (Cantanese 2012).

5. When the pay gap is divided by race, in comparison with each dollar earned by white men in median annual earnings, Asian women earned 82.3 cents, white (non-Hispanic) women earned 75 cents, African-American women earned 61.8 cents, and Hispanic women earned 52.9 cents (Drago and Williams 2010).

6. I conducted a series of interviews with Senate staff, senators, and interest group leaders. More information is provided about these interviews in the "Looking Ahead" section.

7. In the 112th Congress, Barbara Boxer (D-CA) is next in line in seniority to chair the Foreign Relations Committee. Among Super A committees, Foreign Relations has the most turnover and is the least coveted. Many have noted that the committee is populated with presidential hopefuls and freshmen who will seek another assignment at the first opportunity (Deering 2005; Fowler and Law 2008). Had she remained in the Senate, Olympia Snowe (R-ME) was next in line behind Orrin Hatch (R-UT) to lead the Finance Committee. Hatch used the threat of a moderate Snowe leading the Finance Committee in his effort to convince conservative Republicans to support him in his primary campaign (Canham 2012).

8. Some staffers cited the prestige of Mikulski's committee portfolio as the reason why she has never chaired a committee. Mikulski holds a seat on the Appropriations; Health, Education, Labor, and Pensions; and Intelligence committees, all sought-after posts among Democrats. Still, John McCain was elected in the same year as Mikulski, and he is now ranking member on Armed Services, another Super A committee.

9. Eight of the seventeen senators in the 112th Congress serve in all-female delegations. Six of the eight serve with women of the same party. The California and Washington senators Dianne Feinstein (CA), Barbara Boxer (CA), Patty Murray (WA), and Maria Cantwell (WA) are all Democrats. Two female Republicans, Olympia Snowe and Susan Collins, represent Maine. New Hampshire is the only mixed-party female delegation as Jeanne Shaheen is a Democrat and newly elected Senator Kelly Ayotte is a Republican.

10. Keith Poole and Howard Rosenthal created DW-NOMINATE scores. Applying spatial modeling techniques, the scores utilize all roll-call votes in a legislative session to place senators on an ideological scale ranging from −1 indicating most liberal to +1 indicating most conservative. The scores can be found at http://voteview.com/dwnl.htm.

11. The interviews ranged from thirty minutes to four hours. The discussions were semistructured and open-ended. Interview subjects were not told about the gender focus of the study. Instead subjects were asked about how

their senator developed his or her policy priorities and more specific questions about their involvement in policy debates such as the No Child Left Behind Act or the defense authorization bills depending on their level of responsibility for the issue. Questions about gender and the role of particular female senators in policy debates were interwoven into the general questions depending on the position of the staffer. Thus, a leadership staffer would be asked whether the party called on women senators to sell the party's message on the Partial Birth Abortion Act or in the debate over President Bush's Supreme Court nominees.

CHAPTER 2

1. All bill categorizations were reviewed and validated by two research assistants.

2. Senators sponsored 3,180 stand-alone bills excluding resolutions in the 107th Congress; 991 or 31% of these bills concerned women's issues. In the 108th Congress, Senators sponsored 3,033 bills; 969 or 32% encompassed women's issues.

3. In the 107th Congress the first-dimension DW-NOMINATE scores of the senators anchoring the most moderate end of the Republican Party were Chafee, –0.087; Specter, 0.033; Snowe, 0.039; and Collins, 0.082. In the 108th Congress, the ideology scores for these senators were Chafee –0.037; Snowe, 0.059; Specter, 0.061; and Collins, 0.088. Lincoln Chafee (R-RI) lost his bid for re-election in 2006. In 2010 he ran as an independent and won the race for governor of Rhode Island. Arlen Specter (R-PA) switched to the Democratic Party in the 111th Congress and was defeated in his Democratic primary bid for the nomination.

4. In the 107th Congress, Democratic women cosponsored an average of only three more education bills than Democratic men (18.4 vs. 14.6). Democratic women cosponsored a mean of only six more education bills than Democratic men in the 108th Congress (18.6 vs. 12.7). In the 107th Congress, Republican women cosponsored an average of eight more education bills than Republican men (16.3 vs. 7.6) and four more education bills than Republican men in the 108th Congress (8 vs. 3.6).

5. Kay Bailey Hutchison sponsored S.1573 Afghan Women and Children Relief Act of 2001, which passed into law in the 107th Congress. In the 108th Congress, Barbara Mikulski sponsored S.2519 Iraqi Women and Children's Liberation Act of 2004. Similarly, after President Obama authorized military action in Libya, Olympia Snowe (R-ME) introduced a resolution cosponsored by all of the women senators calling for respect for women's rights and the participation of women in government in North Africa and the Middle East (McDaniel 2011).

6. The most common event count model is the Poisson regression model. This model assumes that the probability of an event occurring at any given time is constant within a specified period and independent of all previous events. However, members who sponsor/cosponsor one bill on women's issues may be more likely to sponsor/cosponsor additional women's issue bills, thus violating the assumption of independence. The negative binomial model

accounts for this dependence through the dispersion parameter. A dispersion parameter of zero indicates an absence of dispersion and independence of events, while a dispersion parameter greater than zero indicates overdispersion (King 1989).

7. The DW-NOMINATE data can be accessed at http://voteview.com/index.asp.

8. Party affiliation and ideology are highly correlated, with a correlation coefficient of 0.91 in the 107th Congress and 0.93 in the 108th Congress. This high level of correlation creates problems of multicollinearity. However, the fact that the gender-party variables are often significant even after accounting for ideology indicates that the inclusion of both sets of variables allows me to capture the intraparty differences in legislative activity among liberals and conservatives within the two parties. The ideology scores are also correlated with some of the constituency variables, particularly the state vote for President Bush. Therefore, the impact of some of the constituency variables may be reduced. However, since gender is the main variable of interest, I include the ideology and multiple constituency variables to ensure that differences attributed to gender are not masking differences attributed to ideology or other constituency factors.

9. The Health, Education, Labor, and Pensions (HELP) Committee deals with numerous issues related to health care, education, welfare programs, and issues related to women in the workforce. The Finance Committee holds jurisdiction over a wide range of women's issues including health care programs like Medicare and Medicaid, welfare, Social Security, and tax issues such as child and dependent care tax credits. The Judiciary Committee deals with issues related to crimes against women and children and constitutional questions of women's rights such as abortion. The Special Committee on Aging does not have legislative authority; however, the committee investigates issues and conducts oversight on a range of areas that impact the elderly including health care and Social Security. The Veterans' Affairs Committee is responsible for social welfare programs for veterans such as health and education benefits. Subcommittees of the Appropriations Committee are as powerful as regular standing committees because each subcommittee is responsible for putting together an appropriations bill to fund the programs overseen by the authorizing committees. The Appropriations Subcommittee on Labor, Health and Human Services, and Education makes decisions regarding funding for each of the cabinet departments and federal agencies under its jurisdiction. In the 107th Congress, all committee and committee leadership variables reflect committee membership after James Jeffords (VT) became an Independent caucusing with the Democrats in May 2001.

10. The Special Aging and Veterans' Affairs committees do not have subcommittees. The leaders of the Labor, Health, and Human Services, and Education Subcommittee of the Appropriations Committee are included in the woman's committee chair and ranking member variables. Among the subcommittees on the Finance Committee, only the Subcommittee on Health Care and the Subcommittee on Social Security and Family Policy have jurisdictions related to women's issues. The individual subcommittees of the Judiciary Com-

mittee do not have jurisdiction over a substantial amount of women's issue legislation. Individual models that included the leaders of the Judiciary Committee's subcommittees on Youth Violence (107th Congress); Crime, Corrections, and Victims' Rights (108th Congress); Constitution, Federalism, and Property Rights (107th Congress); and Constitution, Civil Rights, and Property Rights (108th Congress) do not substantially change the results of the models and do not impact the significance of the gender coefficients.

11. Individual models that include variables for subcommittee membership are highly insignificant and do not substantially change the results of the models or the significance of the gender coefficients.

12. The large number of constituency variables are included to ensure that differences attributed to gender are not better explained by constituency concerns. However, high levels of correlation among constituency variables and between some of the constituency variables and ideology means the regression results cannot be interpreted as a definitive statement on the impact of any one constituency variable.

13. To generate predicted probabilities, I utilize *Clarify: Software for Interpreting and Presenting Statistical Results* (Tomz, Wittenberg, and King 2003). The program runs 1,000 simulations and allows one to vary the characteristics of senators while setting all other variables to a constant value. In this case, I varied the values of the gender-party variables and the ideological profiles of senators. All other continuous variables, such as the state presidential vote, were set at their means, and dichotomous variables such as committee membership were set at their modes. For the ideology variable, the DW-NOMINATE scores were set at the 25% and 75% quartiles within each party to represent liberal and conservative Democrats and moderate and conservative Republicans. The probabilities reported in figures 2.3, 2.4, and 2.5 reflect the mean number of women's issue bills a representative with a given gender, party, and ideological profile would sponsor/cosponsor. In the second set of probabilities in figures 2.3 and 2.4, the HELP Committee variable was varied from 0 to 1 to predict how many bills a senator assigned to this committee would sponsor in comparison with senators who do not sit on this committee with wide-ranging jurisdiction over women's issue legislation. In figure 2.6, the state vote for President Bush in 2000 was also varied at the 25% and 75% quartiles within each party.

14. It is difficult to compare the importance of committee position in the House and Senate because committee jurisdictions differ. Moreover, the relative power and role of subcommittees also varies across the House and Senate. However, committee position was a consistently important predictor of activism on sponsorship and cosponsorship of social welfare issues and the full set of women's issues in the House, while a House member's committee seat had no influence on his or her likelihood of sponsoring or cosponsoring a feminist bill. By contrast, in the Senate the relevance of committee position varied. Membership on the HELP Committee was the only consistently important predictor of bill sponsorship, and HELP members were also more likely to cosponsor women's issue and feminist bills in the 107th Congress. Unlike in the House, where committee membership had no relevance to activism on feminist

bills, membership on the HELP and Judiciary committees were both positive predictors of feminist bill sponsorship across the 107th and 108th Congresses. However, members of the Veterans' Affairs Committee and the Special Committee on Aging were significantly less likely to sponsor feminist bills. These committee trends may reflect the reputation of the HELP Committee as an attractive assignment for liberal Democrats and the status of the Judiciary Committee as a home to the liberal Democrats and conservative Republicans with strong views on social issues like abortion.

15. The smaller N (number of legislators/observations) in the Senate makes it harder to achieve statistically significant results. Yet there are many important statistically significant findings in the results, and these findings are consistent with previous research on the House of Representatives and state legislatures.

CHAPTER 3

1. Olympia Snowe (R-ME) was the only Republican who voted against the Hutchison amendment, which was the Republican alternative to the Ledbetter bill.

2. Kennedy introduced S. 1843 Fair Pay Restoration Act on July 20, 2007. Kennedy would later provide a key endorsement to Barack Obama right before Super Tuesday 2008, when twenty-four states held their primaries and caucuses (Kornblut and Murray 2008).

3. Kirsten Gillibrand (D-NY) is not included in the count of Democratic women serving across the 110th and 111th Congresses as she was sworn in after the bill passed (Center for the American Woman and Politics 2011b). Democratic women who spoke during floor debate on the bill in the 110th Congress included Barbara Mikulski (MD), Patty Murray (WA), Claire McCaskill (MO), Maria Cantwell (WA), Hillary Clinton (NY), and Debbie Stabenow (MI). Democratic women speaking on the bill in the 111th Congress included Barbara Mikulski (MD), Barbara Boxer (CA), Dianne Feinstein (CA), Blanche Lincoln (AR), Kay Hagan (NC), Amy Klobuchar (MN), and Claire McCaskill (MO). Among Democratic women, only Mary Landrieu (D-LA) and Jeanne Shaheen (D-NH) did not give floor speeches on the legislation. According to her office's press release, Shaheen attended a press conference to promote the bill while it was being considered on the floor. The press conference included Lilly Ledbetter, Marcia Greenberger (the President of the National Women's Law Center), Barbara Mikulski (MD), Patty Murray (WA), Blanche Lincoln (AR), Debbie Stabenow (MI), Amy Klobuchar (MN), and Jeanne Shaheen (NH) (http://shaheen.senate.gov/news/press/release/?id=5312db94-d995-4560-af65-faa45b0768f9).

4. Murkowski did cosponsor the Hutchison alternative.

5. The Hutchison alternative was the only Republican amendment that received an up or down vote on its merits. Republicans offered six other amendments that were killed by procedural votes to table the amendments. These amendments included efforts to limit the scope of the legislation such as Mike Enzi's (R-WY) amendment to restrict legal standing to the employee and

not include other affected parties or Arlen Specter's (R-PA) amendment to limit the application of the bill to discriminatory compensation and not other types· of discrimination such as promotion or transfers. Other amendments focused on labor relations more generally such as Jim DeMint's (R-SC) amendment to preserve the free choice of employees by making it harder for unions to organize and collect dues from workers. The procedural votes on these amendments fell largely on partisan lines (Langel 2009a, 2009c). Olympia Snowe (R-ME) supported efforts to table five of the six amendments. Susan Collins (R-ME) and Arlen Specter (R-PA) each voted to table three of the six Republican amendments. Lisa Murkowski (R-AK) voted to table the two amendments dealing with unions and labor rights more generally. The DeMint amendment against union organizing attracted the most opposition from Republicans, with seven Republicans voting to table the amendment.

6. Before voting for the Republican bill banning partial birth abortion, Blanche Lincoln (D-AR) voted for the most liberal Democratic alternative to the bill, the Feinstein amendment. She also supported the more moderate Durbin amendment. See the discussion of the Partial Birth Abortion Act below for a more detailed explanation of the Feinstein and Durbin alternatives.

7. The bill, sponsored by Sam Brownback (R-KS), was S. 1899 The Human Cloning Prohibition Act of 2001. The bill had thirty cosponsors, and Mary Landrieu (D-LA) was the only Democrat.

8. Murray and Clinton were angered by the fact that although the Food and Drug Administration (FDA) Advisory Committee had recommended allowing over-the-counter sale of emergency contraception, the FDA continued to delay making a decision on the matter. Convinced that FDA leaders were allowing politics and pro-life groups to influence their decision rather than science, Clinton and Murray put a hold on the nomination of President Bush's FDA nominee Lester Crawford. Clinton and Murray lifted their hold believing they had received a promise from the Bush administration that a decision would be made quickly. Instead, the FDA continued to delay its decision, and Clinton and Murray then placed a hold on Bush's next nominee to head the FDA, Andrew von Eschenbach. After securing a timetable for the decision, the senators lifted their hold (Schuler 2005a, 2005b; Crowley 2006). Ultimately Plan B was approved for over-the-counter use by women eighteen and older. Teenagers under eighteen would still require a prescription to purchase the drug (Stein 2006).

9. Abortion is not the only issue that sparks these conservative challenges to moderate Republican senators, and it is not necessarily the dominant issue. Indeed, Tea Party activism based on fiscal conservatism was a big part of the challenge to Arlen Specter (R-PA) in 2010. However, abortion is one among a package of issues that conservative candidates use to differentiate themselves and demonstrate that the moderate Republicans do not reflect conservative values and principles.

10. The other two Republicans who voted against the Republican budget proposal to eliminate funding for Planned Parenthood were Scott Brown (R-MA) and Mark Kirk (R-IL).

11. This particular meeting was recounted by two different Democratic staffers.

12. Four Democrats supported only the Feinstein and not the Daschle alternative. Twelve Democrats voted only for the Daschle alternative. One Catholic, liberal Democrat Patrick Leahy (D-VT), voted for the Feinstein amendment, which was the most liberal alternative, as well as the Daschle amendment and the Republican ban. Among pro-choice Republicans, John Chafee (R-RI) and Jim Jeffords (R-VT) supported only the Feinstein alternative. Olympia Snowe (R-ME) and Susan Collins (R-ME) voted for only the Daschle alternative, and Arlen Specter (R-PA) supported the Republican ban and none of the alternative amendments.

13. All of the female cosponsors of the Durbin amendment except Blanche Lincoln (D-AR), who was not elected to the Senate until the 106th Congress, were also cosponsors of the original Daschle alternative. Patty Murray (D-WA) and Ted Kennedy (D-MA), who cosponsored the Daschle alternative, did not cosponsor the Durbin alternative. Murray opposed the Durbin amendment, voting for the motion to table the Durbin alternative in both the 106th and 108th Congresses. The other eight cosponsors of the Durbin amendment in the 106th Congress included Joe Lieberman (D-CT), who also cosponsored the Daschle amendment, Robert Torricelli (D-NJ), Jeff Bingaman (D-NM), Daniel Akaka (D-HI), Bob Graham (D-FL), Paul Wellstone (D-MN), Chris Dodd (D-CT), and Chuck Robb (D-VA). Only Robb was not an original cosponsor. In the 108th Congress, the male senators cosponsoring the Durbin alternative included Joe Lieberman (D-CT), Chris Dodd (D-CT), Daniel Akaka (D-HI), Jeff Bingaman (D-NM), and Tom Harkin (D-IA).

14. The amendment is S. AMDT. 2323 to S. 1692 Partial-Birth Abortion Ban Act of 2000 on October 21, 1999.

15. Pennsylvania media coverage of Specter's position attributed his support for the ban to the large Catholic community in Pennsylvania and pressure from church leaders in the state as well as Specter's desire to reach out to conservative pro-life voters in anticipation of a difficult 1998 Republican primary. Specter himself claimed that his change of heart was based upon further study of the issue and listening to constituents, which led him to believe that the procedure constitutes infanticide and that supporting its use could erode public support for abortion rights (Daily News Wire Services 1996; Jesdanun 1996).

16. Author's analysis. In the 108th Congress, the Senate debated the Partial Birth Abortion Act three times. The Senate debated and passed the bill March 11–13, 2003. Senators then debated the motion to disagree, which allowed the bill to go to conference on September 17, 2003. Finally the Senate debated the conference report on October 21, 2003. Senators who spoke in any of these three debates were counted as speaking on the issue. I then divided senators who spoke by gender and party and took note of whether they were members of the committee of jurisdiction, the Judiciary Committee.

17. The other six Republican senators who did not cosponsor S. 3 Partial-Birth Abortion Ban Act of 2003 included moderate Republicans Susan Collins (R-ME), Lincoln Chafee (R-RI), and Olympia Snowe (R-ME), who all voted against the ban, as well as ban supporters Arlen Specter (R-PA), Ted Stevens (R-AK), and Conrad Burns (R-MT). Burns cosponsored the bill in the 106th Congress, and he spoke in favor of the legislation during the final floor debate

in the 108th Congress. Therefore, the fact that he was not a cosponsor of the bill in the 108th Congress was likely an oversight on his part or a mistake in the Congressional Record.

CHAPTER 4

1. Dixon was one of eleven Democratic Senators who voted to confirm Clarence Thomas (Overby et al. 1992).

2. During the confirmation process for Sonia Sotomayor, Republicans frequently pointed out that President Bush might have nominated Miguel Estrada as the first Hispanic to serve on the Supreme Court. However, Democrats filibustered his nomination for the D.C. Circuit and ultimately forced Estrada to withdraw from the process after seven failed cloture votes (Stern 2009).

3. The interest group leaders include five representatives of three liberal groups and three representatives from three conservative groups that were active in nomination politics during the George W. Bush presidency and the conflicts over his lower court and Supreme Court nominees.

4. The ideological distances scores developed by Epstein, Lindstadt, Segal, and Westerland utilize the Segal Cover scores that employ newspaper editorials to develop an ideological ranking of Supreme Court nominees. These scores are transformed through statistical bridging techniques to make them compatible with Poole-Rosenthal Common Space scores that place senators on a common liberal-conservative dimension. The ideological distance variable represents the squared value of the difference between the common space scores of the nominee and the senator (see Epstein et al. 2006 for further information).

5. The ideological distance scores and the presidential vote scores are highly correlated with a correlation coefficient of .6. However, the fact that state vote for Bush reaches statistical significance in two of the three models indicates that the ideological distance and presidential vote variables are picking up distinct and robust effects.

6. I utilize *Clarify: Software for Interpreting and Presenting Statistical Results* (Tomz, Wittenberg, and King 2003) to develop the predicted probabilities. The program runs 1,000 simulations and allows one to vary characteristics of the senators while setting all other variables to a constant value. I varied ideological distance by setting the distance at the 25% (conservative) and 75% (most liberal) quartiles among Democrats. For the moderate liberals, the distance variables were set at the midpoint between the 25% and 50% quartiles (38%). For liberals, the distance variables were set at the midpoint between the 50% and 75% quartiles (63%). The state vote for President Bush was set at the 25% quartile (most liberal), the midpoint between the 25% and 50% quartile (liberal), the midpoint between the 50% and 75% quartile (moderate liberal), and the 75% quartile (conservative). The dichotomous variables, Judiciary Committee member and up for re-election, were set at the mode of 0. The Roberts confirmation and Alito cloture vote dummy variables were set to 1 when predicting their specific vote and 0 otherwise.

7. Over time, the Judiciary Committee has had one of the smallest contingents of women among all Senate committees. To date, no Republican women

have served on the committee. The committee has never had more than two Democratic women, and for much of the time since 1992 Dianne Feinstein (D-CA) has been the only woman on the committee. She was joined by Carol Moseley Braun (D-IL) for one term in the 103d Congress (1993–94). Maria Cantwell (D-WA) served one term on the committee in the 107th Congress (2001–2002). Amy Klobuchar (D-MN) joined the committee in 2009.

8. Democrats ultimately filibustered ten of President Bush's conservative appellate nominees. The conflict came to a head in a showdown over the nuclear option in which the Gang of 14, seven Democratic and seven Republican senators, agreed not to support filibusters of lower court nominees except in "extraordinary circumstances" and that judicial philosophy should not be a criterion for a filibuster (Steigerwalt 2010; Binder and Maltzman 2009). In interviews with Democratic staff and liberal interest group leaders, many pointed to the important role of Democratic women in stealing the spine of male colleagues who feared filibustering female and minority appellate nominees including Priscilla Owen and Janice Rogers Brown.

CHAPTER 5

1. The 108th Congress committee assignment data come from *CQ's Politics in America 2004: The 108th Congress* (Hawkings and Nutting 2003). The analysis of senators' assignments was performed by the author.

2. In her study of women Senate candidates, Kahn notes that when "the salient issues and traits of the campaign complement a woman candidate's stereotypical strength, women will receive an advantage from stereotypes. In contrast, when the important campaign themes correspond to a woman's perceived weaknesses, people's stereotypes will hinder her bid for office" (Kahn 1996, 2). Similarly, Dolan (2004) found that between 1990 and 2000, the amount of gender-related information in the political context influenced whether voters increased their support for women candidates and expanded the gender gap in the vote for candidates, particularly in House races and among voters with low levels of political knowledge.

3. In the fight over the F-35, the Obama administration wanted to cut costs by eliminating funding for development of a second engine. Members of Congress were split between those who wanted to cut funding to combat waste in tough budget times and those who wanted to preserve the program for policy reasons or to save jobs in their home state (Oliveri 2011). The ban on gays in the military was ultimately lifted in a separate bill after Republicans threatened to filibuster the defense authorization over the issue (Hulse 2010).

4. In recent years, the Appropriations Committee has generally gained more power over policy at the expense of the authorizing committees. In the area of defense, the lack of control over funds and the rotating eight-year terms of the Intelligence Committee has reduced their influence in comparison with the appropriators who distribute the money. The Foreign Relations Committee has not passed a foreign aid authorization bill in more than twenty years, ceding authority over these programs to the Appropriations Subcommittee on Foreign Operations. The annual passage of the defense authorization

bill is viewed as the most important work of the Armed Services Committee, and its chair and ranking member give priority to achieving its annual passage on the floor (Deering 2005; Clark 2003a; and staff interviews).

5. In consultation with current and former staffers responsible for defense policy, I developed the following criteria for determining which amendments concerned constituency-related projects. These are programmatic earmarks that target a specific program and are generally funded at $10 million or less. These earmarks generally include an offset for the costs of the program being funded. For example, the Research and Development budget of the army will be increased by x amount for this program, and the Operations and Maintenance budget will be decreased by an equivalent amount. These amendments usually pass by voice vote or unanimous consent and are often offered in quick succession on the floor or as a manager's package without debate. For additional information on the role of constituent-oriented projects in defense policy development, see Wheeler (2004).

6. Most of the homeland security amendments in this analysis also touch on hard issues and are included in the analyses of hard amendment sponsorship and cosponsorship. These amendments include, for example, an amendment providing funding for the development of vaccines against bioterrorism and the creation of an undersecretary for intelligence in the Department of Defense.

7. The 107th and 108th Congresses saw a flurry of activity on homeland security issues as Congress created a new Department of Homeland Security and passed an intelligence reform bill to respond to the findings of the 9/11 Commission. In this analysis, I focus on the traditional defense policy issues that reflect the long-held presumptions about women's ability to handle national security issues. However, in another analysis of bill sponsorship of national security issues, I find that Democratic women were more active sponsors of homeland security bills in the 108th Congress but that gender had no impact on sponsorship of homeland security legislation in the 107th Congress. It appears that Democratic women who face the dual bind of gender stereotypes and association with the party that is perceived as weaker on defense utilized homeland security as an avenue for enhancing their credibility on national security with voters and constituents (Swers 2007).

8. The unemployment, military personnel, and veteran population variables are drawn from the U.S. Census Bureau's Statistical Abstract of the United States 2003, available at http://www.census.gov/prod/www/abs/statab.html. The variables measuring reserve and national guard pay and total military and civil contract awards are drawn from the "Atlas/Data Abstract" Fiscal Year 2001 (107th Congress) and 2003 (108th Congress) reports of the Department of Defense Washington Headquarters Services, Directorate for Information Operations and Reports, available at http://www.dior.whs.mil/mmid/mmid home.htm. The measures of the number of military installations in the state are taken from the Department of Defense Base Structure Reports for Fiscal Years 2001 and 2003, available at http://www.defenselink.mil/pubs/.

9. Additional models tested included variables measuring median household income, the urban population, representation of a southern state, and

representation of a small state. I also tested models that divided the defense contract and military installations variables by state population and models that interacted the re-election variable with the defense contract and committee position variables. The results are substantially the same.

10. The Defense Committee Chair and Ranking Member variables utilized in the models for sponsorship and cosponsorship of all defense amendments include the committee chairs and ranking members of the Armed Services Committee (coded 2) and the chairs and ranking members of other committees with jurisdiction over defense issues including the Appropriations, Foreign Relations, Governmental Affairs, Select Intelligence, and Veterans' Affairs committees (all coded 1). The Defense Subcommittee Chair and Ranking Member variables are coded as the subcommittee chairs and ranking members of the Armed Services Committee (coded 2) and the Appropriations Defense and Military Construction subcommittees (coded 1). The Select Intelligence and Veterans' Affairs committees do not have subcommittees. These Subcommittee Chair and Ranking Member variables are also used in the analysis of hard and soft amendment cosponsorship. Other subcommittee variables tested incorporated subcommittee leaders from Foreign Relations and Governmental Affairs that had jurisdiction over defense-related issues. The results of these models are substantially the same. In the models analyzing cosponsorship of hard defense issue amendments, the Hard Defense Committee Chair and Ranking Member variables include the chairs and ranking members of Armed Services (coded 2), Appropriations, Foreign Relations, and Select Intelligence (all coded 1) committees. The Committee Membership variable accounting for membership on the Defense and Military Construction subcommittees of the Appropriations Committee is replaced by a variable that only includes membership on the Defense Appropriations Subcommittee. In the model measuring cosponsorship of soft defense issues, the Soft Defense Committee Chair and Ranking Member variables include the leaders of Armed Services (coded 2) and Appropriations and Veterans' Affairs (both coded 1). In the model for cosponsorship of soft issue amendments in the 108th Congress the Committee Chair variable is the same as the Committee Chair variable for all defense amendments because none of the leaders of Appropriations, Armed Services, or Veterans' Affairs cosponsored a soft defense amendment making the Soft Defense Chair variable perfectly predictive. Models were also tested that included variables accounting for senators with party leadership positions as well as models that interacted the Defense Committee variable with the Re-election variable and the Total Defense Contracts variable to examine whether, for example, senators with seats on defense committees were even more likely to take action on defense issues when they were up for re-election. These variables were not statistically significant.

11. Staffers maintain that original cosponsors are those most likely to take a role in crafting an amendment or to have an interest in the amendment. Senators who add their names at a later date are generally not involved in the efforts to build a coalition for a proposal.

12. Across all types of participation, the number of military installations in the state is a consistently negative although generally statistically insignificant

predictor of participation in the defense authorization. The number of military installations is highly correlated with the variables measuring the value of defense contracts and reserve and guard pay. Therefore, the military installation variable is likely picking up installations that do not employ a large number of constituents and are not pivotal to the state economy such as arsenals and military silos.

13. I utilize *Clarify: Software for Interpreting and Presenting Statistical Results* (Tomz, Wittenberg, and King 2003) to generate predicted probabilities. The program runs 1,000 simulations and allows one to vary the characteristics of senators while setting all other variables to a constant value. I varied the values of the gender-party variables, and I set the DW-NOMINATE scores measuring ideology at the mean for each party. Membership on the Armed Services Committee was varied from 0 to 1 to determine the impact on cosponsorship of serving on the committee with jurisdiction over the defense authorization bill. All other continuous variables were set at their means, and the dichotomous variables were set at the mode. Figure 5.1 indicates the mean number of defense-related amendments a senator is predicted to cosponsor. Because I utilize ordered logit models rather than the negative binomial to analyze cosponsorship of hard and soft amendments, figure 5.2 predicts the mean probability that a senator would cosponsor zero, one, or two or more soft defense amendments.

14. Because all three Republican women cosponsored two hard defense bills, the coefficient for Republican women is perfectly predicted. Therefore, I could not divide the gender variable by party, and the model analyzing cosponsorship of hard defense amendments in the 107th Congress includes separate variables for gender and party.

15. I subtract the probability that a senator would not cosponsor a soft amendment from 1 to calculate the mean probability that a senator would cosponsor a soft amendment. Thus, there is a 3% probability that a Democratic woman who is not on the Armed Services Committee would cosponsor zero soft amendments in the 107th Congress, 100 − 3 = 97% mean chance that a Democratic woman would cosponsor a soft amendment.

16. In addition to the limiting amendments listed above, Intelligence Committee chair and 2004 presidential hopeful Bob Graham (D-FL) offered an amendment that challenged President Bush's designation of Iraq as the most severe threat to the United States. The amendment called on Bush to focus on the War on Terror by going after other terrorist groups including Hamas and Hezbollah (Pomper 2002b). I do not include the Graham amendment in the analysis of votes to limit the Iraq War because the Senate voted to table the amendment rather than voting on the merits of the proposal. There were only ten votes against tabling the amendment, and there was no clear signal about the intention of those who voted against the amendment.

17. Three senators filed amendments to the resolution that were never considered on the Senate floor. Barbara Boxer filed an amendment that would bar the deployment of both parents of minor children if the two parents are part of the active duty military, the reserves, or the national guard. This proposal to protect military families with children reflects Boxer's earlier efforts

in the First Gulf War to advocate against the deployment of mothers with young children (Francke 1997). Boxer also filed an additional amendment, the purpose of which could not be ascertained from a search of the congressional record or the press releases and statements on Boxer's website. Other senators filing amendments that were not considered on the floor included Mark Dayton (D-MN) and Arlen Specter (R-PA). The Dayton amendment addressed the power struggle between the president and Congress by reasserting the supremacy of congressional authority to declare war in an effort to derail the debate (Congressional Record 2002, S10243–10245). The Specter amendment would have offered the Biden-Lugar proposal, which would limit the war to destruction of weapons of mass destruction and not regime change and would require more international cooperation (Congressional Record 2002, S 10263–10264, S 10304–10305).

18. A senator who receives a score of 5 voted against cloture, in favor of the Levin amendment, in favor of the Durbin amendment, and in favor of the first and second Byrd amendments. The negative binomial model is used instead of a Poisson model because the observations are not independent since voting for one of the limiting proposals increases the likelihood that the senator would vote for another limiting proposal. The dispersion parameter of zero indicates that there is no overdispersion in the data. However, I use the negative binomial model rather than the Poisson for theoretical reasons.

19. For more information on the history of the integration of women in the military and the role of Congress and women members in various policy debates over women in the military, see, for example, Manning 2005; Francke 1997; Katzenstein 1998; Burelli 1998. Women in the House and Senate have played prominent roles in demanding and shaping the congressional response to military scandals related to sexual harassment and assault ranging from the navy's Tailhook convention in 1991 to accusations of abuse and harassment by drill instructors at army training bases in the mid-1990s and incidents of sexual assault at the Air Force Academy in 2003 (Manning 2005; Francke 1997; Katzenstein 1998; Burelli 1998).

CHAPTER 6

1. Interestingly, Mikulski's mammogram coverage amendment was also the center of a partisan battle over the role of the U.S. Preventive Services Task Force in creating coverage mandates for preventive health services. The committee had recently issued a controversial recommendation that regular mammograms should begin at age fifty, rather than forty. Lisa Murkowski (R-AK) offered a competing Republican amendment that would have set aside the task force's mammograms recommendations and barred the government from setting binding health guidelines based on task force recommendations (Herszenhorn and Pear 2009). Sponsored by a female senator, the Murkowski amendment was designed to send the message that Obama's health plan would harm women's health while Republicans were committed to protecting women's health from the arbitrary decisions of government bureaucrats.

2. The compromise did not resolve the problem of religious conscience exemptions for employers that self-insure.

3. At the time of this writing, Heather Wilson is the Republican candidate in New Mexico, and Deb Fischer won the Republican nomination in Nebraska over two more well-known candidates. Former Republican Governor Linda Lingle is expected to win the nomination in Hawaii and former state treasurer Sarah Steelman, is in a competitive primary in Missouri. According to *Roll Call*'s race rankings, Republicans are favored to win the Nebraska seat, while the Missouri and New Mexico races are considered toss-ups and the Hawaii race favors Democrats (http://www.rollcall.com/politics/2012_race_rating_map.html accessed July 20, 2012).

References

Acker, Joan. 1992. "Gendered Institution: From Sex Roles to Gendered Institutions." *Contemporary Sociology* 21: 565–69.

Adams, Greg D. 1997. "Abortion: Evidence of an Issue Evolution." *American Journal of Political Science* 41: 718–37.

Ainsworth, Scott H., and Thad E. Hall. 2011. *Abortion Politics in Congress: Strategic Incrementalism and Policy Change.* New York: Cambridge University Press.

Aizenman, N.C., and Rosalind S. Helderman. 2012. "Senate Rejects Exemption to Mandated Birth Control Coverage." *Washington Post*, March 2.

Aizenman, N.C., Peter Wallsten, and Karen Tumulty. 2012. "Obama Shifts Course on Birth Control Rule to Calm Catholic Leaders' Outrage." *Washington Post*, February 10.

Aldrich, John H., and David W. Rhode. 2000. "The Consequences of Party Organization in the House: The Role of the Majority and Minority Parties in Conditional Party Government." In *Polarized Politics: Congress and the President in a Partisan Era*, edited by Jon R. Bond and Richard Fleisher Washington, DC: CQ Press.

Alexander, Deborah, and Kristi Anderson. 1993. "Gender as a Factor in the Attribution of Leadership Traits." *Political Research Quarterly* 46: 527–45.

Allen, Jared. 2009. "Hoyer: Republicans Abandoned Focus on War in Afghanistan for Seven Years." *Hill*, October 20.

Allen, Mike, and Jonathan Martin. 2009. "How, Why Obama Picked Sotomayor." *Politico*, May 26.

Alonso-Zaldivar, Ricardo. 2009. "Senators Made Hundreds of Deals to Pass Health Bill." *Macomb Daily*, December 22.

Alpert, Bruce. 1996. "Spotlight's on Landrieu, Abortion Groups Disagree on Her Stance." *Times-Picayune*, November 1.

———. 2002a. "Landrieu Proud of Her Moderation but Record Sometimes Puts Her in Line of Fire." *Times-Picayune*, October 8.

———. 2002b. "Runoff Hinges on Who Prods Backers to Polls the Best; Both Falter in Quest to Win Over Key Blocs." *Times-Picayune*, December 1.

Alvarez, Lizette. 2000. "House Passes Ban on Abortion Procedure." *New York Times*, April 6.

Alvarez, Michael R., and John Brehm. 1995. "American Ambivalence towards Abortion Policy: Development of a Heteroskedastic Probit Model of Competing Values." *American Journal of Political Science* 39: 1055–89.

Anzia, Sarah F., and Christopher R. Berry. 2011. "The Jackie (and Jill) Robinson Effect: Why Do Congresswomen Outperform Congressmen?" *American Journal of Political Science* 55: 478–93.

Arnold, Douglas. 1990. *The Logic of Congressional Action*. New Haven: Yale University Press.

Associated Press. 2005. "Alito Strong Conservative on Liberal Court." *New York Times*, October 31.

———. 2012. "FACT CHECK: Romney's Eye-Popping Statistic on Job Losses by Women Raises Eyebrows, Too." *Washington Post*, April 12.

Ayotte, Kelly. 2012a. "Ayotte: Health Care Mandate Is Affront to Religious Freedom." February 7. http://www.ayotte.senate.gov/?p=video&id=423.

———. 2012b. "Ayotte: We Must Respect Conscience Rights for All Religions." February 8. http://www.ayotte.senate.gov/?p=video&id=426.

Babington, Charles. 2006. "Democrats Divided on Withdrawal of Troops." *Washington Post*, June 21, A4.

Babington, Charles, and Dan Balz. 2005. "Reid Will Oppose Roberts for Chief Justice." *Washington Post*, September 21, A3.

Baker, Paula. 1984. "The Domestication of Politics: Women and American Political Society, 1780–1920." *American Historical Review* 89: 620–47.

Baker, Peter, and Dan Balz. 2005. "Conservatives Confront Bush Aides." *Washington Post* October 6, A1.

Baker, Ross K. 2001. *House and Senate*. 3d ed. New York: W.W. Norton and Company.

Baker, Sam. 2012a. "Reid Will Allow Vote in Repeal of Administration's Birth Control Mandate." *Hill*, February 14.

———. 2012b. "Dem Women Senators Press Boehner to Nix Birth-Control Vote." *Hill*, March 8.

Balla, Steven J., and Christine L. Nemacheck. 2000. "Position Taking, Legislative Signaling, and Nonexpert Extremism: Cosponsorship of Managed Care Legislation in the 105th House of Representatives." *Congress & the Presidency* 27: 163–88.

Balz, Dan, and Richard Morin. 2006. "Nation Is Divided on Drawdown of Troops." *Washington Post*, June 27, A1.

Barbash, Fred. 2005a. "First Lady Wants a Woman Justice." *Washington Post*, July 12.

————. 2005b. "Memo: Alito Urged Government to Challenge Roe v. Wade." *Washington Post*, November 30.

Barbash, Fred, and Peter Baker. 2005. "Bush Selects Alito for Supreme Court." *Washington Post*, October 31.

Barnes, Robert. 2007a. "Over Ginsburg's Dissent, Court Limits Bias Suits." *Washington Post*, May 30.

————. 2007b. "Supreme Court Leans Conservative." *Washington Post*, June 25.

————. 2007c. "Exhibit A in Painting Court as Too Far Right." *Washington Post*, September 5 A19.

————. 2009. "Battle Lines Are Drawn on Sotomayor Nomination Ideology, Abortion and Remarks on Ethnicity Come to Fore." *Washington Post*, May 28.

Baumgartner, Frank R., and Bryan D. Jones. 1993. *Agendas and Instability in American Politics*. Chicago: University of Chicago Press.

Becker, Jo. 2005. "Television Ad War on Alito Begins." *Washington Post*, November 18, A3.

Bell, Lauren Cohen. 2002a. *Warring Factions: Interest Groups, Money and the New Politics of Senate Confirmation*. Columbus: Ohio State University Press.

————. 2002b. "Senatorial Discourtesy: The Senate's Use of Delay to Shape the Federal Judiciary." *Political Research Quarterly* 55: 589–607.

————. 2011. *Filibustering in the U.S. Senate*. Amherst, NY: Cambria.

Berry, Jeffrey, and Clyde Wilcox. 2009. *The Interest Group Society*. 5th ed. New York: Longman.

Billitteri, Thomas J. 2008. "Gender Pay Gap." *CQ Researcher* 18(11): 241–64.

Binder, Sarah A., and Forrest Maltzman. 2009. *Advice and Dissent: The Struggle to Shape the Federal Judiciary*. Washington, DC: Brookings Institution.

Binder, Sarah A., and Steven Smith. 1997. *Politics or Principle: Filibustering in the United States Senate*. Washington, DC: Brookings Institution Press.

Biskupic, Joan. 2009. "Ginsburg: Court Needs Another Woman." *USA Today*, May 5.

Blau, Francine D., and Lawrence M. Kahn. 2007. "The Gender Pay Gap." *Economists' Voice* 4(4): article 5.

Bolton, Alexander. 2005. "Liberal Groups Focus on 'Flipping' Centrists." *Hill*, September 14, 1.

————. 2009. "Critics Focus on Sotomayor Speech in La Raza Journal." *Hill*, May 27.

————. 2011a. "Reid: Rider on Planned Parenthood Won't Be Included in Budget Deal." *Hill*, March 17.

————. 2011b. "Senators Could Be Haunted in '12 by Planned Parenthood, Health Care Votes." *Hill*, April 14.

Boshart, Rod. 1996a. "Harkin Says Abortion Ads Reach 'New Low'— Lightfoot Spot Uses Attack by Retired Priest." *Gazette*, November 2.

———. 1996b. "Harkin Survives Lightfoot Challenge—Lightfoot's Late Surge Falls Short." *Gazette*, November 6.

Bottum, Jody. 2003. "Tom Daschle's Duty to be Morally Coherent A Weekly Standard Exclusive: The Senate Minority Leader is Ordered to Stop Calling Himself a Catholic." *The Daily Standard* April 17.

Box-Steffensmeier, Janet M., Suzanna DeBoef, and Tse-Min Lin. 2004. "The Dynamics of the Partisan Gender Gap." *American Political Science Review* 98: 515–28.

Boyd, Christina, Lee Epstein, and Andrew D. Martin. 2010. "Untangling the Causal Effects of Sex on Judging." *American Journal of Political Science* 54: 389–411.

Bradbury, Erin M., Ryan A. Davidson, and C. Lawrence Evans. 2008. "The Senate Whip System: An Exploration." Pp. 73–99 in *Why Not Parties? Party Effects in the United States Senate*, edited by Nathan W. Monroe, Jason M. Roberts, and David W. Rhode. Chicago: University of Chicago Press.

Bratton, Kathleen A. 2005. "Critical Mass Theory Revisited: The Behavior and Success of Token Women in State Legislatures." *Politics and Gender* 1: 97–125.

———. 2006. "The Behavior and Success of Latino Legislators: Evidence from the States." *Social Science Quarterly* 87: 1136–57

Bratton, Kathleen A., and Kerry L. Haynie. 1999. "Agenda-Setting and Legislative Success in State Legislatures: The Effects of Gender and Race." *Journal of Politics* 61: 658–79.

Bratton, Kathleen A., Kerry L. Haynie, and Beth Reingold. 2006. "Agenda Setting and African American Women in State Legislatures." *Journal of Women, Politics & Policy* 28: 71–96.

Bratton, Kathleen A., and Rorie L. Spill. 2001. "Clinton and Diversification of the Federal Judiciary." *Judicature* 84: 256–61.

Brown, Carrie Budoff, and Patrick O'Connor. 2009. "Health Plans on Collision Course." *Politico*, December 20.

Brownstein, Ronald. 2012. "Why Contraceptives Is the Latest Wedge Issue Dividing Democrats and Republicans." *National Journal*, February 17.

Brune, Tom. 2005. "Nominee Roberts in '84 Called Equal Pay for Women 'Radical.'" *Newsday*, August 16, A21.

Burden, Barry. 2007. *Personal Roots of Representation*. Princeton: Princeton University Press.

Burnham, Walter Dean. 1970. *Critical Elections and the Mainsprings of American Politics*. New York: W.W. Norton and Company.

Burrell, Barbara. 1994. *A Woman's Place Is in the House: Campaigning for Congress in the Feminist Era*. Ann Arbor: University of Michigan Press.

———. 2005. "Gender, Presidential Elections and Public Policy: Making Women's Votes Matter." *Journal of Women, Politics and Policy* 27: 31–50.

Burrelli, David F. *Women in the Armed Forces*. 1998. Congressional Research Service, September 29.

Caldeira, Gregory A., and Charles E. Smith, Jr. 1996. "Campaigning for the Supreme Court: The Dynamics of Public Opinion on the Thomas Nomination." *Journal of Politics* 58: 655–81.

Cameron Charles M., Albert D. Cover, and Jeffrey A. Segal. 1990. "Senate Voting on Supreme Court Nominees: A Neoinstitutional Model." *American Political Science Review* 84: 525–34.

Canham, Matt. 2012. "Maine Senator's Retirement a Blow to Hatch's Campaign." *Salt Lake Tribune*, February 28.

Canon, David T. 1999. *Race, Redistricting and Representation: The Unintended Consequences of Black Majority Districts*. Chicago: University of Chicago Press.

Cantanese. David. 2012. "Deb Fischer Wins Nebraska Senate Stunner." *Politico* May 15.

Carey, Mary Agnes. 1997. "Several Senators Reverse '95 Votes." *CQ Weekly*, May 24.

———. 1998a. "Abortion: Roe v. Wade's Challenge at 25: Hang on to the Votes." *CQ Weekly*, January 17.

———. 1998b. "Health: Senate Narrowly Sustains Veto of 'Partial Birth' Abortion Ban; Alternative Bill Introduced." *CQ Weekly*, September 19.

———. 2000. "Abortion Rights Supporters on Defensive Again as House Votes to Ban 'Partial Birth' Procedure." *CQ Weekly*, April 8.

Carney, Eliza Newlin. 1998. "Admirable Restraint? Or Feingold's Folly?" *National Journal*, October 17.

Caro, Robert. 2002. *The Years of Lyndon Johnson: Master of the Senate*. New York: Vintage Books.

Carmines Edward C., and James A. Stimson. 1989. *Issue Evolution: Race and the Transformation of American Politics*. Princeton: Princeton University.

Carroll, Susan. 2002. "Representing Women: Congresswomen's Perception of Their Representational Roles." Pp. 50–68 in *Women Transforming Congress*, edited by Cindy Simon Rosenthal. Norman: University of Oklahoma Press.

Carsey, Thomas M., and Barry Rundquist. 1999. "Party and Committee in Distributive Politics: Evidence from Defense Spending." *Journal of Politics* 61: 1156–69.

Carter, Ralph. 1989. "Senate Defense Budgeting, 1981–88. The Impacts of Ideology, Party, and Constituency Benefit on the Decision to Support the President." *American Politics Quarterly* 17: 332–47.

Center for the American Woman and Politics. 2009. "Fact Sheet: Women in Congress: Leadership Roles and Committee Chairs." New Brunswick: Eagleton Institute of Politics, Rutgers, The State University of New Jersey.

———. 2011a. "Fact Sheet: Women in the U.S. Senate 1922–2011." New Brunswick: Eagleton Institute of Politics, Rutgers, The State University of New Jersey.

———. 2011b. "Fact Sheet: Women in the U.S. Congress 2011." New Brunswick: Eagleton Institute of Politics, Rutgers, The State University of New Jersey.

Chaney, Carole K., R. Michael Alvarez, and Jonathan Nagler. 1998. "Explaining the Gender Gap in the U.S. Presidential Elections, 1980–1992." *Political Research Quarterly* 51: 311–40.

Chaney, Carole, and Barbara Sinclair. 1994. "Women and the 1992 House Elections." In *The Year of the Woman: Myths and Realities*, edited by Elizabeth Adel Cook, Sue Thomas, and Clyde Wilcox. Boulder: Westview Press.

Chodorow, Nancy. 1974. "Family Structure and Feminine Personality." In *Women, Culture, and Society*, edited by M.Z. Rosaldo and L. Lamphere. Stanford: Stanford University Press.

Cillizza, Chris. 2006. "R.I. Senate: Does Chafee's Future Hinge on Alito Vote?" *Washington Post*, January 26.

———. 2008. "Clinton's '3 A.M. Phone Call' Ad." *Washington Post*, February 29. http://voices.washingtonpost.com/thefix/eye-on-2008/hrcs-new-ad .html.

Clark, Cal, and Janet M. Clark. 2006. "The Gender Gap in the Early 21st Century: Volatility from Security Concerns." *Women in Politics: Outsiders or Insiders?* 4th ed. Edited by Lois Duke Whitaker. Upper Saddle River, NJ: Prentice Hall.

Clark, Collin. 2003a. "Defense Authorizers Losing Authority." *CQ Weekly*, September 26, 2374.

———. 2003b. "Defense Authorization Bill Hits Impasse in Conference over Buy America Provisions." *CQ Weekly*, October 3, 2462.

———. 2003c. "Fights over Policy Not Hardware Shape Defense Bill's Passage." *CQ Weekly*, November 14, 2853.

Cochran, John. 2003. "A Celebrity Senator Moving to the Democratic Center." *CQ Weekly*, June 20, 1524.

———. 2005. "A Troubled Nomination Implodes." *CQ Weekly*, October 28.

Cogan, Marin. 2011. "GOP Women Make Their Case." *Politico*, April 8.

Cohen, Elliot A. 2000. "Why the Gap Matters." *National Interest* 41: 38–48.

Cohen, Robert. 2003. "Protesters Rally on Both Sides of Abortion." *Star-Ledger*, January 23.

Conover, Pamela Johnston, and Virginia Sapiro. 1993. "Gender, Feminist Consciousness, and War." *American Journal of Political Science* 37: 1079–99.

Conway, M. Margaret, David W. Ahern, and Gertrude A. Steurnagel. 2005. *Women and Public Policy: A Revolution in Progress*. 3d ed. Washington, DC: CQ Press.

Cook, Dave. 2011. "To DNC's Wasserman Shultz, Republicans' Record Is 'Antiwoman'." *Christian Science Monitor*, June 8.

Cook, Elizabeth Adell, Ted G. Jelen, and Clyde Wilcox. 1992. *Between Two Absolutes: Public Opinion and the Politics of Abortion*. Boulder, CO: Westview Press.

Costain, Anne N. 1992. *Inviting Women's Rebellion*. Baltimore: Johns Hopkins University Press.

Cox, Gary W., and Matthew D. McCubbins. 1993. *Legislative Leviathan: Party Government in the House*. Berkeley: University of California Press.

———. 2005. *Setting the Agenda: Responsible Party Government in the U.S. House of Representatives*. Cambridge University Press.

CQ Staff. 2005. "Alito's Track Record." *CQ Weekly*, November 7, 2986.

Cramer Walsh, Katherine. 2002. "Resonating to Be Heard: Gendered Debate on the Floor of the House." Pp. 370–96 in *Women Transforming Congress*, edited by Cindy Simon Rosenthal. Norman: University of Oklahoma Press.

Crowley, Beth. 2006. "FDA Nominee Wins Panel; GOP Senators Threaten Block." *CQ Weekly*, September 25.

Crowley, Jocelyn Elise. 2004. "When Tokens Matter." *Legislative Studies Quarterly* 29: 109–36.

Cushman, John H. Jr. 1992. "Senators, Shaken by Thomas Debate, Get a Lesson in 'Gender Dynamics'." *New York Times*, March 6, Section 1, p. 8.

Dahl, Robert. 2003. *How Democratic Is the American Constitution?* 2d ed. New Haven: Yale University Press.

Daily News Wire Services. 1996. "Arlen Votes No On 'Infanticide'." *Philadelphia Daily News*, September 27.

Darlymple, Mary. 2002. "Byrd's Beloved Chamber Deaf to His Pleas for Delayed Vote." *CQ Weekly*, October 11, 2674.

Daschle, Tom, with Michael D'Orso. 2003. *Like No Other Time: The Two Years That Changed America*. New York: Three Rivers Press.

Davis, Sue, Susan Haire, and Donald R. Songer. 1993. "Voting Behavior and Gender on the U.S. Court of Appeals." *Judicature* 77: 129–33.

Deering, Christopher J. 2005. "Foreign Affairs and War." In *The Legislative Branch*, edited by Paul J. Quirk and Sarah A. Binder. New York: Oxford University Press.

Deering, Christopher J., and Steven S. Smith. 1997. *Committees in Congress*. 3d ed. Washington DC: CQ Press.

DeParle, Jason. 2005. "In Battle to Pick Next Justice, Right Says, Avoid a Kennedy." *New York Times*, June 27.

Dewar, Helen. 2004. "Specter Seeks, Gets Support." *Washington Post* November 17.

Diamond, Irene, and Nancy Hartsock. 1981. "Beyond Interests in Politics: A Comment on Virginia Sapiro's 'When are Interests Interesting? The Problem of Political Representation of Women'." *American Political Science Review* 75: 717–21.

Diascro, Jennifer Segal, and Rorie Spill Solberg. 2009. "George W. Bush's Legacy on the Federal Bench: Policy in the Face of Diversity." *Judicature* 92: 289–301.

Dionne Jr., E.J. 2012. "Obama's Breach of Faith over Contraceptive Ruling." *Washington Post*, January 29.

Dlouhy, Jennifer A. 2003a. "First Abortion Ban Since '73 Just a House Vote Away." *CQ Weekly*, March 15.

———. 2003b. "'Partial Birth' Abortion Ban Close to Historic Passage." *CQ Weekly*, October 4.

———. 2003c. "Cleared 'Partial Birth' Ban on Fast Track to Court." *CQ Weekly*, October 25 2633–35.

Dodson, Debra L. 2006. *The Impact of Women in Congress*. New York: Oxford University Press.

Dolan, Julie, Melissa Deckman, and Michele L. Swers. 2011. *Women and Politics: Paths to Power and Political Influence*. 2d ed. New York: Longman.

Dolan, Kathleen A. 2004. *Voting for Women: How the Public Evaluates Women Candidates*. Boulder: Westview Press.

Donnelly, John M., and Joanna Anderson. 2010. "Bill Advances 'Don't Ask' Repeal." *CQ Weekly*, May 31, 1338–39.

Dorr, Rheta Childe Dorr. 1910. *What Eight Million Women Want*. Boston: Small, Maynard & Company.

Dovi, Suzanne. 2002. "Preferable Descriptive Representatives? Will Just Any Woman, Black, or Latino Do?" *American Political Science Review* 96: 729–43.

Drago, Robert, and Claudia Williams 2010. "Fact Sheet: The Gender Wage Gap: 2009." Institute for Women's Policy Research, Washington, DC.

Eichenberg, Richard C. 2003. "Gender Differences in Public Attitudes toward the Use of Force by the United States, 1990–2003." *International Security* 28: 110–41.

Elder, Laurel. 2008. "Whither Republican Women: The Growing Partisan Gap among Women in Congress." *Forum* 6(1): Article 13.

Epstein, Lee, Rene Lindstadt, Jeffrey A. Segal, and Chad Westerland. 2006. "The Changing Dynamics of Senate Voting on Supreme Court Nominees." *Journal of Politics* 68: 296–307.

Epstein, Lee, and Jeffrey A. Segal 2005. *Advice and Consent: The Politics of Judicial Appointments*. New York: Oxford University Press.

Erikson, Robert S., Michael B. MacKuen, and James Stimson. 2002. *The Macro Polity*. New York: Cambridge University Press.

Evans, Jocelyn Jones. 2005. *Women, Partisanship, and the Congress*. New York: Palgrave MacMillan.

Evans, C. Lawrence. 1991. *Leadership in Committee: A Comparative Analysis of Leadership Behavior in the U.S. Senate*. Ann Arbor: University of Michigan.

Evans, C. Lawrence, and Daniel Lipinski. 2005. "Obstruction and Leadership in the U.S. Senate. In *Congress Reconsidered Eighth Edition*, edited by Lawrence C. Dodd and Bruce I. Oppenheimer. Washington DC: CQ Press.

Fagan, Amy. 2003. "Senate OKs Ban on Late Abortions; Bush Likely to Sign Partial-Birth Bill." *Washington Times*, March 14.

Falk, Erika, and Kate Kenski. 2006. "Issue Saliency and Gender Stereotypes: Support for Women as Presidents in Times of War and Terrorism." *Social Science Quarterly* 87: 1–18.

Feaver, Peter, and Richard Kohn. 2001. *Soldiers and Civilians*. Cambridge: MIT Press.

Feder, J. Lester. 2012a. "Female Dems Walk out of House Contraceptive Panel." *Politico*, February 16.

———. 2012b. "Dems: All-Male Hearing Will Hurt GOP." *Politico*, February 16.

———. 2012c. "Murray Hits GOP on Women's Health." *Politico*, February 17.

Feder, J. Lester, and Kate Nocera. 2012. "House Slows on Contraception." *Politico*, March 7.

Feinstein, Dianne. 2005a. "A Washington Report from U.S. Senator Dianne Feinstein." August 2005. http://feinstein.senate.gov/newsletters/latest-news letter.htm.

————. 2005b. "Statement by Senator Dianne Feinstein in Opposition to the Nomination of Judge John G. Roberts Jr. to be Chief Justice." September 22. http://feinstein.senate.gov/05releases/r-robertsvote.htm.

————. 2006. "Statement of Senator Dianne Feinstein on Judiciary Committee Vote on the Nomination of Judge Samuel Alito to Be an Associate Justice of the Supreme Court." January 24, 2006. http://feinstein.senate.gov/public/ index.cfm?FuseAction=NewsRoom.PressReleases&ContentRecord_ id=7929e34e-7e9c-9af9-7714-5ab541513677&Region_id=&Issue_id=).

Fenno, Richard F. 1978. *Home Style: House Members in Their Districts*. Boston: Little Brown and Company, Inc.

————. 1991. *Learning to Legislate: The Senate Education of Arlen Specter*. Washington, DC: CQ Press.

————. 2003. *Going Home: Black Representatives and Their Constituents*. Chicago: University of Chicago Press.

Fiorina, Morris P., with Samuel J. Abrams and Jeremy C. Pope. 2005. *Culture War? The Myth of a Polarized America*. New York: Pearson/Longman.

Fleisher, Richard. 1985. "Economic Benefit, Ideology, and Senate Voting on the B-1 Bomber." *American Politics Quarterly* 13: 200–11.

Fletcher, Michael A., and Charles Babington. 2005. "Conservatives Escalate Opposition to Miers." *Washington Post*, October 25, A2.

Flexner, Eleanor, and Ellen Fitzpatrick. 1996. *Century of Struggle: The Woman's Rights Movement in the United States*. Cambridge: Belknap Press of Harvard University Press.

Foerstel, Karen. 1999. "Social Policy: As Senate Passes "Partial-Birth" Ban, One Side Sees Victory within Reach, the Other Sees a Campaign Issue." *CQ Weekly*, October 23.

Fowler, James H. 2006a. "Connecting the Congress: A Study of Cosponsorship Networks." *Political Analysis* 14: 456–87.

————. 2006b. "Legislative Cosponsorship Networks in the U.S. House and Senate." *Social Networks* 28: 454–65.

Fowler, Linda L., and R. Brian Law. 2008. "Seen but Not Heard: Committee Visibility and Institutional Change in the Senate National Security Committees, 1947–2006." *Legislative Studies Quarterly* 33: 357–85.

Fox, Richard Logan. 1997. *Gender Dynamics in Congressional Elections*. Thousand Oaks, CA: Sage Publications, Inc.

Francke, Linda Bird. 1997. *Ground Zero: The Gender Wars in the Military*. New York: Simon and Schuster.

Franke-Ruta, Garance. 2009. "Cheney, Rove Take Lead in Prebutting Obama Afghanistan Speech." *Washington Post*, December 1.

Frankovic, Kathleen, and Joyce Gelb. 1992. "Public Opinion and the Thomas Nomination." *PS: Political Science and Politics* 25: 481–84.

Frederick, Brian. 2009. "Are Women Still More Liberal in a Polarized Era? The Conditional Nature of the Relationship between Descriptive and Substantive Representation." *Congress and the Presidency* 36: 181–202.

———. 2010. "Gender and Patterns of Roll-Call Voting in the Senate." *Congress and the Presidency* 37: 103–24.

———. 2011. "Gender Turnover and Roll Call Voting in the US Senate." *Journal of Women, Politics & Policy* 32: 193–210.

Freedman, Paul. 2003. "Partial Victory: The Power of an Unenforced Abortion Ban." *Slate*, December 9. http://www.slate.com/id/2092192/.

Fridkin, Kim L., and Patrick J. Kenney. 2009. "The Role of Gender Stereotypes in U.S. Senate Campaigns." *Politics & Gender* 5: 301–24.

Gamble, Katrina L. 2007. "Black Political Representation: An Examination of Legislative Activity within U.S. House Committees." *Legislative Studies Quarterly* 32: 421–46.

Gelb, Joyce, and Marian Lief Palley. 1996. *Women and Public Policies: Reassessing Gender Politics.* Charlottesville, VA: University Press of Virginia.

Gerrity, Jessica C., Tracy Osborn, and Jeanette Morehouse Mendez. 2007. "Women and Representation: A Different View of the District." *Politics & Gender* 3: 179–200.

Gillibrand, Kirsten. 2011. "Gillibrand, Senate Democratic Women Call on Republicans to End Continued Assault on Women's Health." April 13. http://gillibrand.senate.gov/newsroom/press/release/?id=7d6a5883-3f38-4f83-bef0-e7ed6d347b55).

Gilligan, Carol. 1982. *In a Different Voice: Psychological Theory and Women's Development.* Cambridge: Harvard University Press.

Glazer, Sarah. 2005. "Gender and Learning." *CQ Researcher* 15(19): 445–68.

Goldman, Sheldon. 1997. *Picking Federal Judges: Lower Court Selection from Roosevelt Through Reagan.* New Haven: Yale University Press.

Goldman, Sheldon, Sara Schiavoni, and Elliot Slotnick. 2009. "W. Bush's Judicial Legacy: Mission Accomplished." *Judicature* 92: 258–88.

Goldman, Sheldon, Elliot Slotnick, and Sara Schiavoni. 2011. "Obama's Judiciary at Midterm." *Judicature* 94: 262–303.

Grace, Stephanie. 1996a. "Abortion Debate Avoided in Race Despite Earlier Fireworks, Most Voters Are Centrists." *Times-Picayune*, October 6.

———. 1996b. "Final, Bitter Debate Keeps Jenkins, Landrieu on Attack They Say There Is Little to Admire in Opponent." *Times-Picayune*, November 1.

Greenblatt, Alan. 1998. "Republican Party: 'Big Tent' Advocates Look Likely to Defeat Abortion Measure." *CQ Weekly*, January 10.

Greenburg, Jan Crawford. 2007. *Supreme Conflict: The Inside Story of The Struggle for Control of the United States Supreme Court.* New York: Penguin Press.

Greenhouse, Linda. 2005. "Abortion Case from 1991 May Be Central in Confirmation." *New York Times*, November 1.

Gutmacher Institute. 2011. "State Policies in Brief: Bans on 'Partial Birth' Abortion." *Gutmacher Institute*, June 1.

Haberkorn, Jennifer, and Kate Nocera. 2012. "Contraceptive Amendment Fails." *Politico*, March 1.

Hall, Richard. 1996. *Participation in Congress*. New Haven: Yale University Press.

Hall, Richard L., and Alan V. Deardorf. 2006. "Lobbying as Legislative Subsidy." *American Political Science Review* 100: 69–84.

Hall, Richard, and Frank Wayman. 1990. "Buying Time: Moneyed Interests and the Mobilization of Bias in Congressional Committees." *American Political Science Review* 84: 797–820.

Hartmann, Susan M. 1989. *From Margin to Mainstream: American Women and Politics Since 1960*. Philadelphia: Temple University Press.

Harward, Brian M., and Kenneth W. Moffett. 2010. "The Calculus of Cosponsorship in the U.S. Senate." *Legislative Studies Quarterly* 35: 117–43.

Hawkesworth, Mary. 2003. "Congressional Enactments of Race-Gender: Toward a Theory of Raced-Gendered Institutions." *American Political Science Review* 97: 529–50.

Hawkings, David, and Brian Nutting. 2003. CQ *Politics in America 2004: The 108th Congress*. Washington, DC: Congressional Quarterly.

Hayes, Danny. 2011. "When Gender and Party Collide: Stereotyping in Candidate Trait Attribution." *Politics & Gender* 7: 133–65.

Haynie, Kerry L. 2001. *African American Legislators in the American States*. New York: Columbia University Press.

Heavey, Susan. 2012. "Obama Administration Defends Contraception Rule amid Mounting Criticism." *Reuters*, February 8.

Hegewisch, Ariane, Hannah Liepmann, Jeffrey Hayes, and Heidi Hartmann. 2010. "Separate and Not Equal? Gender Segregation in the Labor Market and the Gender Wage Gap." Institute for Women's Policy Research Washington, DC, 1–16.

Herb, Jeremy. 2012. "GOP Hammers Obama over Afghan Apology, Warns against Rapid Withdrawal." *Hill*, February 26.

Herszenhorn, David M. 2009. "Senate's Women Could Sway Health Bill." *New York Times*, November 23.

Herszenhorn, David M., and Jackie Calmes. 2009. "Abortion Was at the Heart of Wrangling." *New York Times*, November 8.

Herszenhorn, David M., and Robert Pear. 2009. "Senate Passes Women's Health Amendment." *New York Times*, December 3.

Hill, Kim Quaile, and Patricia A. Hurley. 2002. "Symbolic Speeches in the U.S. Senate and Their Representational Implications." *Journal of Politics* 64: 219–31.

Hook, Janet, and Peter Wallsten. 2005. "Right Stares Down White House, and Wins." *Loss Angeles Times*, October 28.

Hotline Staff. 2012. "The Hotline's Senate Race Rankings: Are You Better Off . . . ?" *National Journal*. January 26. http://www.nationaljournal.com/hotline/the-hotline-s-senate-race-rankings-are-you-better-off--20120126.

Howell, William G., and John C. Pevehouse. 2007a. "When Congress Stops Wars; Partisan Politics and Presidential Power." *Foreign Affairs* 86: 95.

————. 2007b. *While Dangers Gather: Congressional Checks on Presidential War Powers*. Princeton: Princeton University Press.

Huddy, Leonie, Erin Cassese, and Mary-Kate Lizotte. 2008. "Sources of Political Unity and Disunity among Women: Placing the Gender Gap in Perspective." In *Voting the Gender Gap*, edited by Lois Duke Whitaker. Urbana and Chicago: University of Illinois Press.

Huddy, Leonie, and Nayda Terkildsen. 1993a. "Gender Stereotypes and the Perception of Male and Female Candidates." *American Journal of Political Science* 37: 119–47.

————. 1993b. "The Consequences of Gender Stereotypes for Women Candidates at Different Levels and Types of Offices." *Political Research Quarterly* 46: 502–25.

Hulse, Carl. 2003a. "Senate Blocks an Amendment to Alter an Abortion Measure." *New York Times*, March 12.

————. 2003b. "Senate G.O.P. Holds Firm as Vote on Abortion Nears." *New York Times*, March 13.

————. 2008. "Republican Senators Block Pay Discrimination Measure." *New York Times*, April 24, A22.

————. 2010. "Senate Repeals Ban against Openly Gay Military Personnel." *New York Times*, December 18.

Hunt, Kasie. 2009. "Democrats Optimistic on Cutting Off Debate on Pay Bill." *National Journal Daily*, January 15.

Hurt, Charles. 2005. "Half of Senate Republicans Doubt Miers." *Washington Times*, October 10.

Idelson, Holly, and Elizabeth A. Palmer. 1995. "Vote in Late-Term Abortions Signals Attack on Roe." *CQ Weekly*, November 4.

Institute for Women's Policy Research. 2012. "Fact Sheet: The Gender Wage Gap: 2011." Institute for Women's Policy Research March.

Jalonick, Mary Clare. 2002. "Voters, Candidates Unclear about Impact of Iraq Vote." *CQ Weekly*, September 6, 2315–16.

Jansen, Bart. 2006a. "Collins to Vote in Favor of Alito." *Portland Press Herald*, January 27, A1.

————. 2006b. "Snowe, Collins Consent on Alito." *Portland Press Herald*, February 1, A1.

Jelen, Ted G., and Clyde Wilcox. 2005. "Attitudes toward Abortion in Poland and the U.S." *Politics & Gender* 1: 297–317.

Jesdanun, Anick. 1996. "Ardent Abortion-Rights Supporter Backs Ban on Partial-Birth Abortions." *Associated Press*, September 26.

Johnson, Fawn. 2007. "Senate Wants Quick Action on Pay Discrimination Measure." *Congress Daily PM*, August 9.

Kahn, Kim Fridkin. 1996. *The Political Consequences of Being a Woman*. New York: Columbia University Press.

Kane, Paul. 2009. "To Sway Nelson, a Hard-Won Compromise on Abortion Issue." *Washington Post*, December 29, A6.

Kane, Paul, Phillip Rucker, and David A. Fahrenthold. 2011. Government Shutdown Averted: Congress Agrees to Budget Deal, Stopgap Funding." *Washington Post*, April 9.

Kanter, Rosabeth Moss. 1977. "Some Effects of Proportions on Group Life: Skewed Sex Ratios and Responses to Token Women." *American Journal of Sociology* 82: 965–90.

Kanthak, Kristin, and Barbara Norrander. 2004. "The Enduring Gender Gap." In *Models of Voting in Presidential Elections: The 2000 Election*, edited by Herbert Weisberg and Clyde Wilcox. Stanford: Stanford University Press.

Kaptur, Marcy. 1996. *Women of Congress: A Twentieth Century Odyssey*. Washington, DC: Congressional Quarterly, Inc.

Katzenstein, Mary Fainsod. 1998. *Faithful and Fearless: Moving Feminist Protest Inside the Church and Military*. Princeton: Princeton University Press.

Kaufmann, Karen M. 2002. "Culture Wars, Secular Realignment, and the Gender Gap in Party Identification." *Political Behavior* 24 (September): 283–307.

Kaufmann, Karen M., and John R. Petrocik. 1999. "The Changing Politics of American Men: Understanding the Sources of the Gender Gap." *American Journal of Political Science* 43: 864–87.

Keiser, Lael R., Vicky M. Wilkins, Kenneth J. Meier, and Catherine A. Holland. 2002. "Lipstick and Logarithms: Gender, Institutional Context, and Representative Bureaucracy." *American Political Science Review* 96: 553–64.

Kellman, Laurie. 2008. "Republicans Kill Pay Disparity Bill." *Associated Press Online*, April 23.

Kenney, Sally J. 1996. "New Research on Gendered Political Institutions." *Political Research Quarterly* 49: 445–66.

Kenski Kate, and Erika Falk. 2004. "Of What Is That Glass Ceiling Made? A Study of Attitudes about Women and the Oval Office." *Women & Politics* 26: 57–80.

Kessler, Daniel, and Keith Krehbiel. 1996. "Dynamics of Cosponsorship." *American Political Science Review* 90: 555–66.

Kiely, Kathy. 2005. "GOP Senators Push for More on Miers." *USA Today*, October 26, A4.

King, David. 1997. *Turf Wars: How Congressional Committees Claim Jurisdiction*. Chicago: University of Chicago Press.

King, David C., and Richard E. Matland. 2003. "Sex and the Grand Old Party: An Experimental Investigation of the Effect of Candidate Sex on Support for a Republican Candidate." *American Politics Research* 31: 595–612.

King, Gary. 1989. "Variance Specification in Event Count Models: From Restrictive Assumptions to a Generalized Estimator." *American Journal of Political Science* 33: 762–84.

Kingdon, John W. 2005. *Agendas, Alternatives, and Public Policies*. 2d ed. New York: Longman.

Kirkpatrick. David D. 2005. "Senators in G.O.P. Voice New Doubt on Court Choice." *New York Times*, October 26.

———. 2006. "Wider Fight Is Seen as Alito Victory Appears Secured." *New York Times*, January 14.

Klatch, Rebecca E. 1987. *Women of the New Right*. Philadelphia: Temple University Press.

Kliff, Sarah. 2011a. "Lisa Murkowski Backs Planned Parenthood." *Politico*, March 14.

———. 2011b. "Scott Brown's Planned Parenthood Dodge?" *Politico*, March 24.

Koch, Jeffrey W. 1999. "Candidate Gender and Assessments of Senate Candidates." *Social Science Quarterly* 80: 84–96.

———. 2000. "Do Citizens Apply Gender Stereotypes to Infer Candidates Ideological Orientations?" *Journal of Politics* 62: 414–29.

Koger, Gregory. 2003. "Position Taking and Cosponsorship in the U.S. House." *Legislative Studies Quarterly* 28: 225–46.

———. 2010. *Filibustering: A Political History of Obstruction in the House and Senate* Chicago: University of Chicago Press.

Kornblut, Anne E., and Shailagh Murray. 2008. "Obama Ready on 'Day One' Kennedy Says." *Washington Post*, January 29.

Kraditor, Aileen S. 1981. *The Ideas of the Woman Suffrage Movement: 1890–1920*. New York: W. W. Norton & Company.

Krauthammer, Charles. 2011. "The Obama Doctrine: Leading from Behind." *Washington Post*, April 28.

Krehbiel, Keith. 1995. "Cosponsors and Wafflers from A to Z." *American Journal of Political Science* 39: 906–23.

Krutz, Glen S., Richard Fleisher, and Jon R. Bond. 1998. "From Abe Fortas to Zoe Baird: Why Some Presidential Nominations Fail in the Senate." *American Political Science Review* 92: 871–81.

Kucinich, Jackie. 2005. "After Chafee Backs Roberts, Foes Await NARAL's Response." *Hill*, September 21, 19.

Kurtz, Howard. 2012. "Rep. Debbie Wasserman Schultz, Obama's Body Guard." *Newsweek*, January 30.

Ladd, Everett Carll. 1997. "Media Framing of the Gender Gap." In *Women, Media, and Politics*, edited by Pippa Norris. New York: Oxford University Press.

Lane, Charles. 2005. "Alito Leans Right Where O'Connor Swung Left." *Washington Post*, November 1, A1.

Langel, Stephen. 2008. "Groups Target Vulnerable Republicans over Labor Legislation." *CongressNow*, August 27.

———. 2009a. "Securing Cloture Not a Certainty for Ledbetter Bill." *CongressNow*, January 14.

———. 2009b. "After Easy Cloture Vote, Senators Look Ahead to Debate over Ledbetter Bill, Alternative." *CongressNow*, January 15.

———. 2009c. "Senate Democrats Pass Ledbetter Bill, Virtually Sealing Enactment." *CongressNow*, January 22.

Lawless, Jennifer. 2004. "Women, War, and Winning Elections: Gender Stereotyping in the Post-September 11th Era." *Political Research Quarterly* 57: 479–90.

Lawrence, Regina G., and Melody Rose. 2010. *Hillary Clinton's Race for the White House: Gender Politics & the Media on the Campaign Trail*, Colorado: Lynne Rienner.

Lee, Don. 2011. "Republican Senators Criticize Afghan Pullout Plan." *Los Angeles Times*, July 4.

Lee, Frances E. 2008a. "Dividers, Not Uniters: Presidential Leadership and Senate Partisanship, 1981–2004." *Journal of Politics* 70: 914–28.

———. 2008b. "Agreeing to Disagree: Agenda Content and Senate Partisanship, 1981–2004." *Legislative Studies Quarterly* 33: 199–222.

———. 2009. *Beyond Ideology: Politics, Principles, and Partisanship in the U.S. Senate*. Chicago: University of Chicago Press.

———. 2010." Two-Party Competition and Senate Politics: The Permanent Campaign on the Floor of the U.S. Senate." Paper Presented at the Congress and History Conference, University of California, Berkeley, June 10–11.

———. 2011. "Individual and Partisan Activism on the Senate Floor." *The U.S. Senate: From Deliberation to Dysfunction*, edited by Burdett A. Loomis Washington, DC: CQ Press.

Lee, Frances E., and Bruce I. Oppenheimer. 1999. *Sizing Up the Senate: The Unequal Consequences of Equal Representation*. Chicago: University of Chicago Press.

Levitt, Steven D. 1996. "How Do Senators Vote? Disentangling the Role of Voter Preferences, Party Affiliation, and Senator Ideology." *American Economic Review* 86:425–41.

Levy, Dena, Charles Tien, and Rachelle Aved. 2002. "Do Differences Matter? Women Members of Congress and the Hyde Amendment." *Women & Politics* 23: 105–27.

Lindsay, John M. 1990a. "Parochialism, Policy, and Constituency Constraints: Congressional Voting on Strategic Weapons Systems." *American Journal of Political Science* 34: 936–60.

———. 1990b. "Congress and the Defense Budget: Parochialism or Policy?" In *Arms, Politics, and the Economy: Historical and Contemporary Perspectives*, edited by Robert Higgs. New York: Holmes and Meier.

Lips, Hilary M. 1995. "Gender-Role Socialization: Lessons in Femininity." In *Women: A Feminist Perspective*. 5th ed. Edited by Jo Freeman. Mountain View: Mayfield Publishing.

Liptak, Adam. 2009. "The Waves Minority Judges Always Make." *New York Times* May 31.

Lovley, Erika. 2011. "Senate Women's 'Civility' Pact." *Politico*, February 4.

Lynch, David. 1996. "An Exhilarated Harkin Looks Back on Senate Campaign." *The Gazette*. December 15.

MacDonald, Jason A., and Erin E. O'Brien. 2011. "Quasi-Experimental Design, Constituency, and Advancing Women's Interests: Reexamining the Influence of Gender on Substantive Representation." *Political Research Quarterly* 64: 472–86.

MacGillis, Alec. 2009. "Health-Care Bill's Abortion Deal Wins a Vote, but Few Friends; Complaints from Both Sides about Deal with Senator Nelson." *Washington Post*, December 22.

Markon, Jerry, and Shailagh Murray. 2011. "Federal Judicial Vacancies Reaching a Crisis Point." *Washington Post*, February 7.

Maltese, John Anthony. 1995. *The Selling of Supreme Court Nominees*. Baltimore: Johns Hopkins University Press.

Maltzman, Forrest, and Lee Sigelman. 1996. "The Politics of Talk: Unconstrained Floor Time in the U.S. House of Representatives." *Journal of Politics* 58: 819–30.

Manning, Jason. 2006. "Alito and 'The Women'." *Washington Post*, blog posted 12:42 P.M. January 11.

Manning, Lory. 2005. *Women in the Military: Where They Stand*. 5th ed. Women's Research and Education Institute.

Mansbridge, Jane. 1986. *Why We Lost the ERA*. Chicago: University of Chicago Press.

———. 1999. "Should Blacks Represent Blacks and Women Represent Women? A Contingent 'Yes'." *Journal of Politics* 61: 628–57.

Marcos, Cristina. 2011. "Centrist Senators Don't Want to Talk about Planned Parenthood." *Hill*, March 27.

Marcus, Ruth. 2010. "Elana Kagan: From Trailblazer to Less of a Big Deal." *Washington Post*, May 10.

Martin, Jonathan. 2009. "What Scotus Pick Says about Obama." *Politico*, May 26.

Martinez, Gebe. 2002. "Concerns Linger for Lawmakers Following Difficult Vote for War." *CQ Weekly*, October 11, 2671.

Matthews, Donald R. 1960. *U.S. Senators and Their World*. New York: Vintage Books.

Mayer, Kenneth R. 1990. "Patterns of Congressional Influence in Defense Contracting." In *Arms, Politics, and the Economy: Historical and Contemporary Perspectives*, edited by Robert Higgs. New York: Holmes and Meier.

———. 1991. *The Political Economy of Defense Contracting*. New Haven: Yale University Press.

Mayhew, David R. 1974. *Congress: The Electoral Connection*. New Haven: Yale University Press.

McCarty, Nolan, Keith T. Poole, and Howard Rosenthal. 1997. *Income Redistribution and the Realignment of American Politics*. Washington: DC: AEI Press.

———. 2006. *Polarized America: The Dance of Ideology and Unequal Riches*. Cambridge: MIT Press.

McCarthy, Meghan. 2012a. "Hill Squares Off over Contraception." *National Journal*, February 9.

———. 2012b. Democrats Gin Up Money ahead of Contraceptive Votes. *National Journal Daily*, March 1.

———. 2012c. How Contraception Became a Train Wreck for Republicans. *National Journal*, March 5.

McCormack, John. 2012. "Kelly Ayotte: Democrats Falsely Claim Women Will Lose Access to Contraception." *Weekly Standard*, February 29.

McDaniel, Heather. 2011. "Boxer, Feinstein Urge Congress to Protect Rights of Women in Middle East, North Africa." *San Francisco Chronicle*, March 28.

Meier, Kenneth, and Jill Nicholson-Crotty. 2006. "Gender, Representative

Bureaucracy, and Law Enforcement: The Case of Sexual Assault." *Public Administration Review* 66: 850–60.

Memmott, Mark. 2005. "Alito Ad Storm Waiting to Strike after the Holiday." *USA Today*, November 8.

Mezey, Susan Gluck. 2003. *Elusive Equality: Women's Rights, Public Policy and the Law*. Boulder: Lynne Reiner Publishers.

Mikulski, Barbara. 2005. "Mikulski Shocked at Sexism and Double Standard." October 7. http://mikulski.senate.gov/record.cfm?id=247071.

Mikulski, Barbara, Kay Bailey Hutchison, Dianne Feinstein, Barbara Boxer, Patty Murray, Olympia Snowe, Susan Collins, Mary Landrieu, and Blanche L. Lincoln with Catherine Whitney. 2001. *Nine and Counting: Women of the Senate*. New York: Perennial.

Milbank, Dana. 2012. "An Expert Witness for the GOP Gender Gap." *Washington Post*, February 24.

Minta, Michael D. 2009. "Legislative Oversight and the Substantive Representation of Black and Latino Interests in Congress." *Legislative Studies Quarterly* 34: 193–218.

_____. 2011. *Oversight: Representing the Interests of Blacks and Latinos in Congress* Princeton: Princeton University Press.

Mondics, Chris. 2003. "Specter Observers Sense a Shift Right—As the Republican Primary Nears, the Four-Term Senator Is Taking More Conservative Positions, Some Liberals Say." *Philadelphia Inquirer*, April 14.

Montgomery, Lori. 2008a. "White House Threatens to Veto Discrimination Bill." *Washington Post*, April 23, A4.

———. 2008b. "Senate Republicans Block Pay Disparity Measure." *Washington Post*, April 24 A4.

Mulligan, John E. 2005. "Abortion-Rights Group Endorses Chafee." *Providence Journal*, May 20.

Mulero, Eugene, and John M. Donnelly. 2011. "Battles Ahead for Defense Authorization." *CQ Weekly*, May 30, 1136–37.

Murkowski, Lisa. 2010. Address to Georgetown University Alumni Event. April 30.

Murray, Shailagh, and Lori Montgomery. 2009. "Senators Express Hope for a Health Reform Bill." *Washington Post*, December 2.

Nather, David. 2005. "Dianne Feinstein's Roberts Dilemma." *CQ Weekly*, August 1, 2087.

———. 2002a. "'One Voice' Lost in Debate over Iraq War Resolution." *CQ Weekly*, September 27, 2496.

———. 2002b. "Daschle's Grip on Majority Could Slip in Tussle over Iraq, Homeland Votes." *CQ Weekly*, October 4, 2608.

Norrander, Barbara. 1999. "Is the Gender Gap Growing." In *Reelection 1996: How Americans Voted*, edited by Herbert F. Weisberg and Janet M. Box-Steffensmeier. New York: Chatham House Publishers.

———. 2008. "The History of the Gender Gaps." In *Voting the Gender Gap*, edited by Lois Duke Whitaker. Urbana and Chicago: University of Illinois Press.

Norton, Noelle H. 1995. "Women, Its Not Enough to Be Elected: Committee

Position Makes a Difference." Pp. 115–140 in *Gender Power, Leadership, and Governance*, edited by Georgia Duerst-Lahti and Rita Mae Kelly. Ann Arbor: University of Michigan Press.

———. 1999. "Committee Influence over Controversial Policy: The Reproductive Policy Case." *Policy Studies Journal*, 27: 203–16.

———. 2002. "Transforming Congress from the Inside: Women in Committee." Pp. 316–40 in *Women Transforming Congress*, edited by Cindy Simon Rosenthal. Norman: University of Oklahoma Press.

O'Connor, Karen. 1996. *No Neutral Ground? Abortion Politics in an Age of Absolutes*. Boulder, CO: Westview Press.

O'Connor, Karen, and Jeffrey Segal. 1990. "Justice Sandra Day O'Connor and the Supreme Court's Reaction to Its First Female Member." *Women & Politics* 10: 95–103.

Ogundele, Ayo, and Linda Camp Keith. 1999. "Reexamining the Impact of the Bork Nomination to the Supreme Court." *Political Research Quarterly* 52: 403–20.

Oliveri, Frank. 2011. "Senate Bill Makes F-35 Restrictions." *CQ Weekly*, June 20, 1320.

O'Malley. Julia. 2012. "If Murkowski Is Moderate, Her Votes Should Be Too." *Anchorage Daily News*, March 5.

Orey, Byron D'Andra, Wendy Smooth, Kimberly Adams, and Kish Harris-Clark. 2006. "Race and Gender Matter: Refining Models of Legislative Policy Making in State Legislatures." *Journal of Women, Politics, and Policy* 28: 97–119.

Ornstein, Norman J., and Thomas E. Mann. 2006. "When Congress Checks Out." *Foreign Affairs* 85: 67.

Osborn, Tracy L. 2012. *How Women Represent Women: Political Parties, Gender, and Representation in State Legislatures*. New York: Oxford University Press.

Osborn, Tracy, and Jeanette Morehouse Mendez. 2010. "Speaking as Women: Women and Floor Speeches in the Senate." *Journal of Women, Politics, & Policy* 31: 1–21.

Ota, Alan K. 2004. "Senate GOP Gives Its Leader a Powerful New Tool." *CQ Weekly*, November 20, 2733. http://library.CQpress.com/CQweekly/weeklyreport108-000001430122.

Overby, L. Marvin, Beth M. Henschen, Michael Walsh, and Julie Strauss. 1992. "Courting Constituents? An Analysis of the Senate Confirmation Vote on Justice Clarence Thomas." *American Political Science Review* 86: 997–1003.

Palley, Marian Lief, and Howard A. Palley. 1992. "The Thomas Appointment: Defeats and Victories for Women." *PS: Political Science and Politics* 25: 473–77.

Palmer, Anna. 2008. "Women's Lobby Fails to Deliver." *Roll Call*, April 28.

Palmer, Barbara. 2002. "Justice Ruth Bader Ginsburg and the Supreme Court's Reaction to Its Second Female Member." *Women & Politics* 24: 1–23.

Palmer, Barbara, and Dennis Simon. 2008. *Breaking the Political Glass Ceiling: Women and Congressional Elections*. 2d ed. New York: Routledge.

Palmer, Elizabeth A. 1996. "Late-Term Procedure Bill Heads to Clinton for Expected Veto." *CQ Weekly*, March 30.

———. 2000a. "Supreme Court Hears Case That Could Affect Dozens of 'Partial Birth' Abortion Laws." *CQ Weekly*, April 29.

———. 2000b. "Supreme Court Abortion Ruling Complicates GOP Efforts to Craft 'Partial Birth' Ban." *CQ Weekly*, July 1.

Pear, Robert. 2012a. "Senate Nears Showdown on Contraception Policy." *New York Times*, February 28.

———. 2012b. "House G.O.P. Hesitates on Birth Control Fight." *New York Times*, March 16.

Pear, Robert, and David M. Herszenhorn. 2009. "Democrats Preserve Essence of Health Proposal." *New York Times*, September 26.

Pearson, Kathryn. 2008. "Party Loyalty and Discipline in the Individualistic Senate." Pp. 100–20 in *Why Not Parties? Party Effects in the United States Senate*, edited by Nathan W. Monroe, Jason M. Roberts, and David W. Rhode. Chicago: University of Chicago Press.

———. 2010. "Gendered Partisanship in the U.S. House of Representatives, 1989–2010." Presentation at the 2010 Annual Meeting of the American Political Science Association, Washington, DC.

Pearson, Kathryn, and Logan Dancey. 2010. "Elevating Women's Voices in Congress: Speech Participation in the House of Representatives." *Political Research Quarterly* 20: 1–14.

———. 2011. "Speaking for the Underrepresented in the House of Representatives: Voicing Women's Interests in a Partisan Era." *Politics & Gender* 7: 493–520.

Perine, Keith. 2004. "Specter Nears Judiciary Chair As Seniority Wins the Day." *CQ Weekly*, November 20, 2731–33. http://library.CQpress.com/CQweekly/weeklyreport108-000001430211.

———. 2007. "Supreme Court Upholds Partial Birth Abortion Ban." *CQ Weekly*, April 23, 1204.

Peresie, Jennifer L. 2005. "Female Judges Matter: Gender and Collegial Decisionmaking in the Federal Appellate Courts." *Yale Law Journal* 114: 1759–90.

Petrocik, John R. 1996. "Issue Ownership in Presidential Elections, with a 1980 Case Study." *American Journal of Political Science* 40: 825–50.

Petrocik, John R., William L. Benoit, and Glenn J. Hansen. 2003. "Issue Ownership and Presidential Campaigning." *Political Science Quarterly* 118: 599–626.

Phillips, Anne. 1991. *Engendering Democracy*. University Park: Pennsylvania State University Press.

———. 1995. *The Politics of Presence*. Oxford: Oxford University Press.

———. 1998. "Democracy and Representation: Or, Why Should It Matter Who Our Representatives Are?" In *Feminism and Politics*, edited by Anne Phillips. New York: Oxford University Press.

Pierce, Emily. 2003. "Abortion Conference Stalled; Harkin, Boxer Maneuver to Water Down GOP Priority." *Roll Call*, July 16.

Pitkin, Hanna Fenichel. 1967. *The Concept of Representation*. Berkley: University of California Press.

Plummer, Anne. 2005. "Female Soldiers in the Cross Hairs." *CQ Weekly*, June 3, 1498.

Pomper, Miles. 2002a. "Philosophical Conflicts Complicate Iraq Debate." *CQ Weekly*, August 2, 2096.

———. 2002b. "Bush Hopes to Avoid Battle with Congress over Iraq." *CQ Weekly*, August 30, 2251.

———. 2002c. "Lawmakers Pushing Back from Quick Vote on Iraq." *CQ Weekly*, September 13, 2352.

———. 2002d. "Senate Democrats in Disarray after Gephardt's Deal in Iraq." *CQ Weekly*, October 4, 2606.

Poole, Keith T., and Howard Rosenthal. 1997. *Congress: A Political-Economic History of Roll Call Voting*. New York: Oxford University Press.

———. 2007. *Ideology and Congress*. Piscataway, NJ: Transaction Publishers.

Pope, Jeremy, and Jonathan Woon. 2009. "Measuring Changes in American Party Reputations, 1939–2004." *Political Research Quarterly* 62: 653–61.

Primo, David M., Sarah A. Binder, and Forrest Maltzman. 2008. "Who Consents? Competing Pivots in Federal Judicial Selection." *American Journal of Political Science* 52: 471–89.

Pryor, Mark. 2006. "Statement by Senator Mark Pryor on Judge Alito's Confirmation to the Supreme Court." January 27. http://pryor.senate.gov/newsroom/details.cfm?id=250851.

Rae, Nicol C., and Colton C. Campbell. 2001. "Party Politics and Ideology in the Contemporary Senate." Pp. 1–18 in *The Contentious Senate: Partisanship, Ideology and the Myth of Cool Judgment*, edited by Colton C. Campbell and Nicol C. Rae. Lanham, MD: Rowmann and Littlefield Publishers, Inc.

Raju, Manu. 2009. "Senate GOP Holds Its Fire on Sotomayor." *Politico*, May 26.

———. 2012. "Senate Volunteers Promote Civility." *Politico*, February 27.

Ratcliffe, R.G. 2010. "Abortion Foes Not Relenting on Hutchison: Opposition Tied to Her Stand on Roe." *Houston Chronicle*, January 24.

Reingold, Beth. 1992. "Concepts of Representation among Female and Male State Legislators." *Legislative Studies Quarterly* 17: 509–37.

———. 2000. *Representing Women: Sex Gender, and Legislative Behavior in Arizona and California*. Chapel Hill: University of North Carolina Press.

Reingold, Beth, and Adrienne R. Smith. 2012. "Welfare Policymaking and Intersections of Race, Ethnicity, and Gender in U.S. State Legislatures." *American Journal of Political Science* 56(1): 131–47.

Reingold, Beth, and Michele L. Swers. 2011. "An Endogenous Approach to Women's Interests: When Interests Are Interesting in and of Themselves." *Politics & Gender* 7: 429–35.

Rhode, David W. 1991. *Parties and Leaders in the Postreform House*. Chicago: University of Chicago Press.

Riskind, Jonathan. 2012. "Snowe, Collins Backed 2001 Contraceptive Mandate Bill." *Portland Press Herald*, February 9.

Rocca, Michael S., and Gabriel R. Sanchez. 2008. "The Effect of Race and Ethnicity on Bill Sponsorship and Cosponsorship in Congress." *American Politics Research* 36: 130–52.

Rose, Meoldy. 2006. *Safe, Legal, and Unavailable: Abortion Politics in the United States.* Washington, DC: CQ Press.

Rosenthal, Cindy Simon. 1998. *When Women Lead: Integrative Leadership in State Legislatures.* New York: Oxford University Press.

———. 2008. "Climbing Higher: Opportunities and Obstacles within the Party System." In *Legislative Women: Getting Elected, Getting Ahead,* edited by Beth Reingold Boulder: Lynne Rienner Publishers.

Rosenthal, Cindy Simon, and Lauren Cohen Bell. 2003. "From Passive to Active Representation: The Case of Women Congressional Staff." *Journal of Public Administration Research and Theory* 13: 65–82.

Rossiter, Clinton, ed. 1961. *The Federalist Papers: Alexander Hamilton, James Madison, John Jay.* New York: Mentor Book.

Rovner, Julie. 2003a. "Murray Seeks to Amend, Change Focus of Abortion Debate." *Congress Daily,* March 11.

———. 2003b. "Abortion Debate Grinds on As Murray Amendment Defeated." *Congress Daily AM,* March 12.

———. 2003c. "'Sense of the Senate' Stalls 'Partial Birth' Abortion Conference." *Congress Daily AM,* September 5.

Ruckman, P. S., Jr. 1993. "The Supreme Court Critical Nominations, and the Senate Confirmation Process." *Journal of Politics* 55: 793–805.

Rundquist, Barry S., and Thomas M. Carsey. 2002. *Congress and Defense Spending: The Distributive Politics of Military Procurement.* Norman: University of Oklahoma Press.

Ryan, Josiah. 2012. "Reid Slaps Down Amendment to Repeal Obama's Contraceptive Rule." *Hill,* February 9.

Saint-Germain, Michelle. 1989. "Does Their Difference Make a Difference? The Impact of Women on Public Policy in the Arizona Legislature." *Social Science Quarterly* 70: 956–68.

Sanbonmatsu, Kira. 2002a. "Gender Stereotypes and Vote Choice." *American Journal of Political Science* 46(1): 20–34.

———. 2002b. *Gender Equality, Political Parties, and the Politics of Women's Place.* Ann Arbor: University of Michigan Press.

Sanbonmatsu, Kira, and Kathleen Dolan. 2009. "Do Gender Stereotypes Transcend Party?" *Political Research Quarterly* 62: 485–94.

Sanger-Katz, Margot. 2012. "Retreat!" *National Journal,* March 1.

Sapiro, Virginia. 1981. "Research Frontier Essay: When Are Interests Interesting? The Problem of Political Representation of Women." *American Political Science Review* 75: 701–16.

———. 1981–82. "If U.S. Senator Baker Were a Woman: An Experimental Study of Candidate Images." *Political Psychology* 2: 61–83.

Sarlin, Benjy. 2011. "Female Democratic Senators Accuse GOP of Using Shutdown to Hurt Women." *Talking Points Memo,* April 8. http://tpmdc.talkingpointsmemo.com/2011/04/female-democratic-senators-accuse-gop-of-using-shutdown-to-hurt-women.php.

Schaffner, Brian F. 2005. "Priming Gender: Campaigning on Women's Issues in U.S. Senate Elections." *American Journal of Political Science* 49: 803–17.

Scherer, Nancy. 2005. *Scoring Points: Politicians, Activists, and the Lower Federal Court Appointment Process*. Stanford: Stanford University Press.

Schickler, Eric. 2011. "The Senate at Mid-20th Century." In *The U.S. Senate: From Deliberation to Dysfunction*, edited by Burdett A. Loomis Washington, DC: CQ Press.

Schiller, Wendy. 1995. "Senators as Political Entrepreneurs: Using Bill Sponsorship to Shape Legislative Agendas." *American Journal of Political Science* 39: 186–203.

———. 2000. *Partners and Rivals: Representation in U.S. Senate Delegations*. Princeton: Princeton University Press.

———. 2002. "Sharing the Same Home Turf: How Senators from the Same State Compete for Geographic Electoral Support." Pp. 109–31 in *U.S. Senate Exceptionalism*, edited by Bruce Oppenheimer. Columbus: Ohio State University.

Schonhardt-Bailey, Cheryl. 2008. "The Congressional Debate on Partial-Birth Abortion: Constitutional Gravitas and Moral Passion." *British Journal of Political Science* 38: 383–410.

Schreiber, Ronnee. 2008. *Righting Feminism: Conservative Women and American Politics*. New York: Oxford University Press.

Schroedel Jean R., and Bruce Snyder. 1994. "Patty Murray: The Mom in Tennis Shoes Goes to the Senate." In *The Year of the Woman: Myths and Realities*, edited by Elizabeth Adel Cook, Sue Thomas, and Clyde Wilcox. Boulder: Westview Press.

Schuler, Kate. 2005a. "FDA Nominee Could Stall." *CQ Weekly*, April 11.

———. 2005b. "Senate Panel OKs FDA Nominee as Democrats Vow to Block Vote." *CQ Weekly*, June 20.

Schultheis, Emily. 2012. "Ayotte: Romney Can Win Women Voters." *Politico*, April 4.

Scully, Megan. 2005a. "Supporters Seek to Strike Women's Combat Role Provision." *Congress Daily AM*, May 24.

———. 2005b. "Amendments on Women in Combat, Tricare Await Panel." *Congress Daily PM*, May 24.

———. 2005c. "Rumsfeld, Hunter Working on Combat-Role Compromise." *Congress Daily AM*, May 25.

Seeyle, Katherine Q. 1997. "Senators Reject Democrats' Bill to Limit Abortion." *New York Times*, May 16.

———. 1998. "Veto Sustained on Bill to Ban Some Abortions." *New York Times*, September 19.

Segal, Jeffrey A., Charles M. Cameron, and Albert D. Cover. 1992. "A Spatial Model of Roll Call Voting: Senators, Constituents, Presidents, and Interest Groups in Supreme Court Confirmations." *American Journal of Political Science* 36: 96–121.

Segal, Jennifer. 2000. "Representative Decision Making on the Federal Bench: Clinton's District Court Appointees." *Political Research Quarterly* 53: 137–50.

Sellers, Patrick. 2002. "Winning Media Coverage in the U.S. Congress." Pp. 132–53 in *U.S. Senate Exceptionalism*, edited by Bruce Oppenheimer. Columbus: Ohio State University.

———. 2010. *Cycles of Spin: Strategic Communication in the U.S. Congress*. New York: Cambridge University Press.

Seltzer, Richard, Jody Newman, and Melissa Voorhees Leighton. 1997. *Sex as a Political Variable: Women as Candidates and Voters in American Elections*. Boulder: Lynne Rienner Publishers.

Shaheen, Jeanne, Barbara Boxer, and Patty Murray. 2012. "Why the Birth-Control Mandate Makes Sense." *Wall Street Journal*, February 7.

Shapiro, Robert, and Harpreet Mahajan. 1986. "Gender Differences in Policy Preferences: A Summary of Trends from the 1960s to the 1980s." *Public Opinion Quarterly* 50: 42–61.

Sherill, Martha. 2011. "Maine Senators May Not Like Each Other Much, but They Share Love of State, Job." *Washington Post*, May 5.

Shipan, Charles, and Megan L. Shannon. 2003. "Delaying Justice(s): A Duration Analysis of Supreme Court Confirmations." *American Journal of Political Science* 47: 654–68.

Shogan, Colleen. 2001. "Speaking Out: An Analysis of Democratic and Republican Women-Invoked Rhetoric of the 105th Congress." *Women & Politics* 23: 129–46.

Sides, John. 2006. "The Origins of Campaign Agendas." *British Journal of Political Science* 36: 407–36.

Sinclair, Barbara. 1989. *The Transformation of the U.S. Senate*. Baltimore: Johns Hopkins University Press.

———. 2001. "The Senate Leadership Dilemma: Passing Bills and Pursuing Partisan Advantage in a Nonmajoritarian Chamber." Pp. 65–89 in *The Contentious Senate: Partisanship, Ideology and the Myth of Cool Judgment*, edited by Colton C. Campbell and Nicol C. Rae. Lanham, MD: Rowmann and Littlefield Publishers, Inc.

———. 2002. "'The '60-Vote Senate': Strategies, Process and Outcomes." Pp. 241–61 in *U.S. Senate Exceptionalism*, edited by Bruce Oppenheimer. Columbus: Ohio State University.

———. 2006. *Party Wars: Polarization and the Politics of National Policy Making*. Norman: University of Oklahoma Press.

———. 2009. "The New World of US Senators." Pp. 1–22 in *Congress Reconsidered 9ᵗʰ Edition*, edited by Lawrence C. Dodd and Bruce I. Oppenheimer. Washington, DC: CQ Press.

Situation Room. 2011. "Interview with Presidential Candidate Michele Bachman." Transcript, November 17. http://www.realclearpolitics.com/articles/2011/11/17/interview_with_presidential_candidate_michele_bachmann_112123.html.

Skocpol, Theda. 1992. *Protecting Soldiers and Mothers*. Cambridge: Belknap Press of Harvard University Press.

Slajda, Rachel. 2009. "Kyl: 'I Don't Need Maternity Care.' Stabenow: 'Your Mom Probably Did.'" *Talking Points Memo*, September 25. http://tpmdc

.talkingpointsmemo.com/2009/09/kyl-i-dont-need-maternity-care-stabe now-your-mom-probably-did.php.

Smith, Ben, and Josh Kraushaar. 2009. "The Politics of Sotomayor." *Politico*, May 27.

Smith, Steven S. 1989. *Call to Order: Floor Politics in the House and Senate.* Washington, DC: Brookings Institution.

———. 2007. *Party Influence in Congress.* New York: Cambridge University Press.

———. 2010. "The Senate Syndrome." The Brookings Institution, Issues in Governance Studies 35, http://www.brookings.edu/papers/2010/06_cloture_smith.aspx.

Smith, Tom. 1984. "The Polls: Gender and Attitudes Toward Violence." *Public Opinion Quarterly* 48: 384–96.

Smolowe, Jill, Wendy Cole, Jeanne McDowell, and Elaine Shannon. 1992. "Politics the Feminist Machine." *Time*, May 4. http://www.time.com/time/magazine/article/0,9171,975430,00.html.

Smooth, Wendy. 2011. "Standing for Women? Which Women? The Substantive Representation of Women's Interests and the Research Imperative of Intersectionality." *Politics & Gender* 7: 436–41.

Snowe, Olympia. 2006. "Snowe Announces Support for Judge Samuel Alito's Nomination to the Supreme Court." February 1. http://snowe.senate.gov/public/index.cfm?FuseAction=PressRoom.PressReleases&ContentRecord_id=7E3603FE-E169-4B1B-952B-F4870CA9779A.

Soherr-Hadwiger, David. 1998. "Military Construction Policy: A Test of Competing Explanations of Universalism in Congress." *Legislative Studies Quarterly* 23: 57–78.

Solowiej, Lisa A., Wendy L. Martinek, and Thomas L. Brunell. 2005. "Partisan Politics: The Impact of Party in the Confirmation of Minority and Female Federal Court Nominees." *Party Politics* 11: 557–577.

Songer, Donald R., Sue Davis, and Susan Haire. 1994. "A Reappraisal of Diversification in the Federal Court: Gender Effects in the Court of Appeals." *Journal of Politics* 56: 425–39.

Sorrells, Neil. 2003a. "Veterans Funding Legislation Sparks Unusually Partisan Fight." *CQ Weekly*, May 23, 1281.

———. 2003b. "Democrats Play to Win Critical Veterans' Vote." *CQ Weekly*, June 21, 1518.

———. 2003c. "Democrats See Sizable Ground in Taking Up Soldiers' Cause." *CQ Weekly*, August 29, 2114.

Steigerwalt, Amy. 2010. *Battle over the Bench: Senators, Interest Groups, and Lower Court Confirmations.* Charlottesville: University of Virginia Press.

Stein, Rob. 2006. "FDA Approves Plan B's Over-the-Counter Sale: No Prescription Will Be Required for Women 18 or Older." *Washington Post*, August 25.

Steinhauer, Jennifer. 2012. "For Senate Democrats, Vote Revolves around Women." *New York Times*, April 18.

Stern, Seth. 2005a. "Politically a Supreme Nominee." *CQ Weekly*, July 25, 2040–43.

———. 2005b. "Hearings Unlikely to Pin Roberts Down." *CQ Weekly*, September 5, 2333–34.

———. 2006. "Cherchez Les Femmes." *CQ Weekly*, January 16, 159.

———. 2009. "Nominee Hardball: GOP's Turn at Bat." *CQ Weekly*, July 13, 1620–21.

Stern, Seth, and Keith Perine. 2005a. "Poised Roberts Fends Off Democrats." *CQ Weekly*, September 19, 2497–500.

———. 2005b. "Key Democrats Say They'll Back Roberts." *CQ Weekly*, September 26, 2567–68.

———. 2005c. "Defending Miers on All Sides." *CQ Weekly*, October 10, 2720–22.

———. 2006a. "Alito's Performance Seen as Solid." *CQ Weekly*, January 16, 186–89.

———. 2006b. "Alito Confirmed after Filibuster Fails." *CQ Weekly*, February 6, 340–41.

Stolberg, Sheryl Gay. 2003a. "Senate Makes a Curb on Abortion Likely." *New York Times*, September 18.

———. 2003b. "Ideas and Trends; A Bill Signed; but It's Not Picture Perfect." *New York Times*, November 9.

———. 2005. "First Lady Enters Debate over Nomination for Court." *New York Times*, October 12.

———. 2009. "Obama Signs Equal-Pay Legislation." *New York Times*, January 29.

Storing, Herbert J. 1981. *The Anti-Federalist: Writings by Opponents of the Constitution*. Chicago: University of Chicago Press.

Strolovitch, Dara Z. 2007. *Affirmative Advocacy: Race, Class, and Gender in Interest Group Politics*. Chicago: University of Chicago Press.

Sullivan, Amy. 2003. "A Time to Choose: How Democrats Started Losing the Abortion Debate." *Washington Monthly*, December.

Sundquist, James L. 1983. *Dynamics of the Party System: Alignment and Realignment of Political Parties in the United States*. Revised edition. Washington, DC: Brookings Institution.

Sweet, Lynn. 2012. "Why Obama Backed Down on Birth Control." *Chicago-Sun Times*, February 15.

Swers, Michele L. 2007. "Building a Reputation on National Security: The Impact of Stereotypes Related to Gender and Military Experience." *Legislative Studies Quarterly* 32: 559–95.

———. 2005. "Connecting Descriptive and Substantive Representation: An Analysis of Sex Differences in Cosponsorship Activity in the House of Representatives." *Legislative Studies Quarterly* 30: 407–33.

———. 2002. *The Difference Women Make: The Policy Impact of Women in Congress*. Chicago: University of Chicago Press.

Swers, Michele, and Stella Rouse. 2011. "Descriptive Representation: Understanding the Impact of Identity on Substantive Representation of Group Interests." In *Oxford Handbook of Congress*, edited by Eric Schickler and Frances Lee. New York: Oxford University Press.

Taylor, Andrew. 2002. "Though Neither Party Is Crying 'Politics', Election Year Puts War Vote on Fast Track." *CQ Weekly*, September 6, 2317.

Theirault, Sean M. 2008. *Party Polarization in Congress*. New York: Cambridge University Press.

Thomas, Martin. 1985. "Electoral Proximity and Senatorial Roll-Call Voting." *American Journal of Political Science* 29: 96–111.

Thomas, Sue. 1994. *How Women Legislate*. New York: Oxford University Press.

Tomz, Michael, Jason Wittenberg, and Gary King. 2003. *CLARIFY: Software for Interpreting and Presenting Statistical Results*. Version 2.1. Stanford University, University of Wisconsin, and Harvard University. January 5. http://gking.harvard.edu/.

Toner, Robin, David D. Kirkpatrick, and Anne E. Kornblut. 2005. "Steady Erosion in Support Undercut Nomination." *New York Times*, October 27.

Towell, Pat. 2002a. "Oversight of Anti-Missile Program Keeps Defense Conference at Odds." *CQ Weekly*, July 26, 2064.

———. 2002b. "Rumsfeld Says Troop Strength Is Sufficient to Conduct Military Operations in Iraq." *CQ Weekly*, September 20, 2466.

———. 2002c. "Defense Bill Action Could be Delayed to Avoid Pre-Election Veto of Veterans Law." *CQ Weekly*, October 4, 2611.

———. 2003. "Chambers Agree on Funding, Not Pentagon Operations." *CQ Weekly*, May 24, 1272.

Towell, Pat, and Chuck McCutcheon. 2002. "Crusader Down: First Salvo in Cancellation Wars." *CQ Weekly*, May 10, 1202–6.

Tumulty, Karen. 2012. "Recent Debate over Contraception Comes as GOP Loses Gains among Women." *Washington Post*, March 9.

United States Senate Democrats. 2008. "Senate Democratic Women Unveil the Checklist for Change." http://www.youtube.com/watch?v=tqmv9kU5KxI, August 20, 2008.

U.S. Chamber of Commerce. 2008. "How They Voted 2008—Senate." http://www.uschamber.com/issues/legislators/how-they-voted-2008-senate.

———. 2009. "How They Voted 2009—Senate." http://www.uschamber.com/issues/legislators/how-they-voted-2009-senate.

U.S. Senate Democratic Steering and Outreach Committee. 2008. "Congressional Women Rally for Fair Pay." July 17. http://democrats.senate.gov/checklistforchange/newsroom.cfm.

Victor, Kirk. 2005. "Still an Old Boys' Club." *National Journal*, March 12.

Walker, Thomas G. and Debora J. Barrow. 1985. "The Diversification of the Federal Bench: Policy and Process Ramifications." *Journal of Politics* 47: 596–617.

Walsh, Bill. 2002. "Landrieu Strives to Stay Close to Center Line; but Liberals, Conservatives Find Cause for Complaint in Her Votes." *Times-Picayune*, May 26.

Walsh, Katherine Cramer. 2002. "Enlarging Representation: Women Bringing Marginalized Perspectives to Floor Debate in the House of Representatives." In *Women Transforming Congress*, edited by Cindy Simon Rosenthal. Norman: University of Oklahoma Press.

Wawro, Gregory. 2000. *Legislative Entrepreneurship in the U.S. House of Representatives*. Ann Arbor: University of Michigan Press.

Wawro, Gregory J., and Eric Schickler. 2006. *Filibuster: Obstruction and Lawmaking in the U.S. Senate*. Princeton: Princeton University Press.

Wayman, Frank Whelon. 1985. "Arms Control and Strategic Arms Voting in the U.S. Senate: Patterns of Change, 1967–83." *Journal of Conflict Resolution* 29: 225–51.

Weiner, Rachel. 2011. "Examining the State of the Union's Bipartisan Odd Couples." *Washington Post*, January 24.

Weisman, Jonathan. 2012a. "After Many Tough Choices, the Choice to Quit." *New York Times*, February 29.

———. 2012b. "Women Figure Anew in Senate's Latest Battle." *New York Times*, March 14.

Weldon, S. Laurel. 2002. "Beyond Bodies: Institutional Sources of Representation for Women." *Journal of Politics* 64: 1153–74.

Werner, Erica. 2005. "Feinstein Gears Up for Roberts Hearing." WTOP Radio Network. July 30. http:/www.wtopnews.com/index.php?sid=548742&nid=116.

Wheeler, Winslow T. 2004. *The Wastrels of Defense: How Congress Sabotages U.S. Security*. Annapolis: Naval Institute Press.

White, William S. 1956. *Citadel: The Story of the United States Senate*. New York: Harper and Brothers.

Wilcox, Clyde. 1994. "Why Was 1992 the 'Year of the Woman?': Explaining Women's Gains in 1992." In *The Year of the Woman: Myths and Realities*, edited by Elizabeth Adel Cook, Sue Thomas, and Clyde Wilcox. Boulder: Westview Press.

Wilcox, Clyde, and Patrick Carr. 2009. "The Puzzling Case of the Abortion Attitudes of the Millenial Generation." In *Understanding Public Opinion*, edited by Clyde Wilcox and Barbara Norrander. Washington, DC: CQ Press.

Williams, Melissa. 1998. *Voice, Trust, and Memory: Marginalized Groups and the Failings of Liberal Representation*. Princeton: Princeton University Press.

Wilson, Rick K., and Cheryl D. Young. 1997. "Cosponsorship in the U.S. Congress." *Legislative Studies Quarterly* 22: 25–53.

Winter, Nicholas J.G. 2010. "Masculine Republicans and Feminine Democrats: Gender and Americans' Explicit and Implicit Images of the Political Parties." *Political Behavior* 32: 587–618.

Wolbrecht, Christina. 2000. *The Politics of Women's Rights: Parties, Positions, and Change*. Princeton: Princeton University Press.

———. 2002. "Female Legislators and the Women's Rights Agenda." Pp. 170–239 in *Women Transforming Congress*, edited by Cindy Simon Rosenthal. Norman: University of Oklahoma Press.

Wong, Scott. 2011. "GOP Filibusters Judicial Nominee." *Politico*, December 6.

Woon, Jonathan. 2009. "Issue Attention and Legislative Proposals in the U.S. Senate." *Legislative Studies Quarterly* 34: 29–54.

Index

116, 117, 235, 259n8; on war on women, 1, 248

NARAL (National Abortion Rights Action League): Barbara Boxer and, 112; partial birth abortion and, 126, 128, 129, 133; political endorsements by, 119, 175
National Association of Manufacturers, 104
National Republican Senate Campaign Committee, 76–77
national security. *See* defense issues
National Women's Law Center, 258n3
Nelson, Ben, 29–30, 162
Nelson, Bill, 197
new institutionalism, 143
No Child Left Behind, 9, 48, 50–51, 59, 74
North Korea, 185
Norton, Eleanor Holmes, 248
NOW (National Organization for Women), 133

Obama, Barack: contraceptive coverage and, 236, 247, 249; defense authorization bills under, 191; defense cuts and, 262n3; diversification of federal bench by, 141; election of 2012 and, 1–2; on empathy on the Supreme Court, 140–41; Foreign Relations Committee and, 186; gays in the military and, 262n3; health reform negotiations and, 29–30; Hillary Clinton's 3 a.m. phone call ad and, 19, 189; Iraq War and, 185, 218; judicial nominations and, 140–41, 143–44, 173; Libya and, 255n5; Lilly Ledbetter Fair Pay Act and, 100, 101–3, 105; Republican criticisms of defense policy of, 217; Ted Kennedy's endorsement of, 258n2. *See also* Obama health care reform
Obama, Michelle, 103

Obama health care reform: abortion and, 42, 109, 235; Blunt amendment and, 247, 248, 249–50; contraception and, 235–36, 246–50, 267n2; Finance Committee markup and, 33; maternity care in, 33; preventive services in, 235, 266n1; Republican women and, 28; Senate battles over, 9
O'Connor, Sandra Day: abortion and, 122–23, 148, 175–76; *Casey* case and, 148, 153–54; on Family and Medical Leave Act, 154; gender and jurisprudence and, 142; nomination of, 140; replacement of, 145–48, 169, 172; retirement of, 140; as swing vote on women's rights, 138
Osborn, Tracy L., 163
Owen, Priscilla, 142, 172, 262n8

Palley, Marian Lief, 53
Partial Birth Abortion Act: amendments and alternatives to, 125–34, 234–35, 259n6, 260nn12–13; Arlen Specter's position on, 260n15; Bill Clinton's veto of, 122; Blanche Lincoln and, 113; as campaign issue, 123–26; criminal penalties and, 60–61; Democratic refocusing efforts and, 56–57, 130; Democratic women's policy leadership and, 131–32, 133; emotion surrounding, 126; floor debate and, 131, 133, 260n16; health of the mother and, 122, 124, 127–30, 132; moderate Republican women and, 120, 121, 125, 149; passage of, 57, 122; procedure banned by, 121–22; recall votes and, 124; Republicans who did not cosponsor, 260–61n17; Republican women's reticence and, 132–34; signing of, 133; *Stenberg v. Carhart* and, 122; Supreme Court and, 122–23; women in drafting of, 134